A great book for everyone who thir
Economy, organizational managemenι aιιu μειουιιαι υειι ueveιupιιι~ιιι ~ g _ ___
a whole new level!
—**Magdalena Schäfer, Senior HR Manager, Organisational Psychologist**

Rebuild sets new standards and takes the reader into a whole new path for a better future and a paradigm shift on how the current and future investors and leaders must conduct business and behave towards their followers, collaborators and the wider stakeholder community. This book revolutionises the reader's views, assumptions and approaches for a more responsible, equitable and sustainable life as a whole. A must read, if you are sincerely interested to be the change you want to see!
—**Antonio Potenza, CEO Proodos Impact Capital**

Rebuild delivers exactly what it says on the cover: a toolkit for you to build a better world. It contains the most useful business and personal toolkit I've seen, and has radically transformed my worldview. Organisations, jobs and practically everything—we're trying to reinvent them, but are we succeeding? This book makes reinvention work; it's written as part guidebook, part theoretical overview with scientific underpinnings, and a completely relatable narrative with fascinating anecdotes. It is for anyone who wants to build solutions to our global challenges.
—**Marie-Nicole Schuster. Leadership development consultant**

The *Adaptive Way* chapter in *Rebuild* made me realise that seeking validation from others to build my business (Solve Earth) is a self-defeating trap, because no single person has the capability to understand fully what I, or any other person, is capable of. I can continue on my journey into the unknown with advice and guidance from others, but ultimately, I must rely on my own decision making and self-validation. This is an incredibly liberating and empowering insight that gives me the courage to take on the biggest challenges in sustainability and building a better future society.
—**Dr Gareth J Thompson, Founder, Solve Earth Limited**

We know now that organisations who embody natural and evolutionary design principles, not only thrive but build critical resilience and sustainability. This architecture also needs to be re-evolved and re-generated to meet the needs of today's global market dynamics and for our collective humanity so you hold in your hands a book that gives you a road map to a journey how this is best achieved and executed.
—**Robert Dellner, PHD Author, Integral Impact Investments (i3): Building and navigating a full-spectrum systems approach to investing**

Rebuild presents an integrated vision—one that transcends polarities and makes

the old divisions obsolete. This is one of many qualities shared by great visions. It is also a systemic vision that not only aims to transform our consciousness, but also the systems that forcefully perpetuate and enforce the old consciousness. It is a pragmatic vision based on available experiments, examples, and research, and doesn't require rebuilding society from scratch. And it is a radical vision, that doesn't focus on putting patches on the problem, but emerges from asking powerful ambitious questions like *how can we build an economy that harnesses all of the human capacities, like cooperation, compassion, and self-interest, to provision for all while regenerating all our capitals: financial, social, and natural?*
—**Chen Zvi. Climate activist in Extinction Rebellion; Researcher in systemic societal transformation**

I have seen this book develop over many years, and participated in online events organised by Graham after the crowdfunding campaign went live to support its development. The result, now published as 'Rebuild', is a thoughtful contribution to individual, organisational and societal development. It brings the fields of philosophy and practice together productively in the service of building a commons economy, arguing that we need stewards to manage assets for the benefit of current and future generations. Firmly rooted in a pragmatic application of social constructionist philosophy, Rebuild is a toolkit for individual and organisational development. It draws extensively on ideas developed by Otto Laske, Elinor Ostrom and members of the FairShares Association as well as the educational artefacts and papers published by the FairShares Institute at Sheffield Hallam University. At the heart of the argument is the case for FairShares Commons Companies that steward six capitals for future generations, and which enfranchise the founders, producers, workers, customers, users and investors who contribute and develop each form of capital. It is a bold vision, and a major step forward in realising an economy that supports sustainable development.
—**Professor Rory Ridley-Duff, FairShares Institute for Co-operative Social Entrepreneurship, Sheffield Hallam University**

REBUILD:
THE ECONOMY, LEADERSHIP, AND YOU

A toolkit for builders of a better world.

Graham Boyd and Jack Reardon
October 2020

Others have seen what is and asked why. I have seen what could be and asked why not.

—Pablo Picasso

Published by Evolutesix Books, London, UK.

Hardcover ISBN: 978-1-913629-02-1
Paperback ISBN: 978-1-913629-01-4
e-book ISBN: 978-1-913629-00-7

RELEASE 1.1.0 (NON-ERGODIC ADDED, CH. 6)

A CIP catalogue record will be available from the British Library.

Typeset using LATEX.
Cover design and illustrations by Nikyta Guleria
Editing by Anna Kierstan

This book is published in at least one electronic form under the standard Evolutesix Books pricing model of "donate what it is worth to you" to ensure the widest possible readership and usefulness. Donate via graham-boyd.biz

To all those brave souls

who have, over the past decades,

selflessly invested their

time, effort and money

in rising to our challenges

long before they became

the emergencies we now face.

Contents

Why this book now? We describe how we came to write this book, and why now is the best time ever to build a world that works for you. You will read about Graham's and Jack's drivers and journeys, about how our climate grief has shaped both of us, and this book, from long before we met. Read this book in any way you want to; reading it in a circle, randomly starting anywhere, or even backwards. Whatever works best for you. (It's pretty good at keeping doors open.)

PART I: ART AND PHYSICS

We are entering the next great shift. The meaning you make of the shift shapes the reality you experience, and the emergent strategies you can use. The lenses Picasso and Einstein used to create great shifts in art and physics can guide us today in developing adaptive capacity in yourself, your organisation, and your economy.

2. STORIES, LENSES AND MAPS —— 26

The stories, lenses and maps we use generate the unique reality each of us experiences. The types of questions we ask, and how we ask them, determines what we can see through the lens we use, and interpret with our meaning-making story templates. Cargo cults and scientism put us at risk of fooling ourselves. We need to harness conflict and manage boundaries to get out of the mess that we've got ourselves into. The six layers of our economy, from each individual through to the global economy as an ecosystem of ecosystems, and how to turn conflict into antifragility in each layer.

PART II: ECONOMY

3. HOW DO WE KNOW OUR ECONOMY? —— 49

An economy is a tool that provisions across multiple capitals, and so nature also has economies. But our current economy is failing us, because of the meaning-making stories that have created it. We need an economy that's fit for our current and future challenges. Yet we cannot control our economy; rather we need to facilitate generative emergence by transforming our existing approaches to freedom, stakeholders, property, money, and capitalism.

4. THE FREE COMPANY —— 78

The myths around what a company is only maintain our dysfunctional status quo. Like apartheid in South Africa, typical company incorporation forms exclude most stakeholders from governance and wealth sharing. The tragedy of the commons isn't what we imagine. Rather, done well the commons is a solution, and it's time for the FairShares Commons company or equivalent commons company to rise to our global challenges and build a better world.

5. THE ECONOMY OF THE FREE —— 103

To address our global challenges, we need an Economy of the Free, rather than our current Free Economy. Here's how we should construct it, and how it leads to regenerative capitalism built on regenerative businesses in regenerative ecosystems that are inherently circular. The stock market, boom and bust, trade, finance, sustainability, work and your life will all look much better in an Economy of the Free.

6. FIXING FLAWS IN ECONOMICS —— 129

Neoclassical economics is deeply flawed, because it is too much scientism, not enough science. We need to develop a general theory of economies that includes rational and irrational, thinking and feeling as complementary pairs. An economics that never assumes physics is irrelevant, satisfies thermodynamics, knows when a process is ergodic and when not, and works out of equilibrium. Such a general theory includes everything that works in the different, polarised approaches of today, is falsifiable, and most importantly predicts well what will happen. Like predicting the next crash. To get there we first need to understand the flaws.

PART III: YOU

7. WHO ARE YOU? —— 149

In answer to the age-old existential question: who am I, and who can I become, you are the forms of thought and meaning-making lenses that you use. As in Ubuntu, you are because of other people; optimised for your past, not for your future. Your biggest challenges are adaptive, not technical, meaning you need to change who you are to rise to them. Changing who you are begins with understanding how you deceive yourself, and why this is humanity's superpower. You can change yourself, primarily through real experiences, not analysis.

8. YOU ARE YOUR STORIES —— 167

Your meaning-making stories generate your experienced reality from a limited slice of what actually is. Your stories lie in a self-consistent category, or stage of meaning-making; they form frames of reference that you use to evaluate and judge what is happening, giving it meaning. Using the Ground Pattern you can grow bigger meaning-making stories, so that you can rise to your adaptive challenges.

9. YOU ARE YOUR THOUGHTS —— 202

Your thought forms come first, lenses you see actuality through, before your meaning-making stories even generate your experienced reality. Once you have mastered binary logical thinking you have the foundations for the 28 post-logical thought forms, or lenses, of the next stage: Process, Context, Relationship and Transformation thought forms. The more fluidity you have in these, the better you grasp actuality and can make your reality a good model of it.

10. YOU ARE YOUR NATURE —— 226

Your hard-wired nature is the basis for your thoughts and meaning-making. Increase your subtlety working with, not against your nature: your personal energy economy, needs, feelings (vs. judgements dressed up as feelings), your cognitive biases, and your relationship with money and power.

11. YOU ARE ONE —— 255

Who are you? Are you big enough? Understand why most self-help approaches don't work, or can even cause harm; and similarly for type indicators, declarations etc. Grow your subtlety in what you accept, what you rebel against, and how to be yourself with others. Expand your complexity of thought and meaning-making stages, so that you are satisfied at the end when you measure your own life.

PART IV: ORGANISATIONS

12. ORGANISATIONS ARE LIVING BEINGS —— 277

Organisations, and especially for-profit businesses, are an essential and natural part of human society; so they are best understood as living beings, living systems that have meaning-making capacity. To lead our businesses well we need to know their organisational energy economy (and our personal one). Two useful lenses to use are the four integral quadrants, yielding the management accountability hierarchy vs. the human capability hierarchy; and the four layers: intra-personal, inter-personal, intra-organisation, inter-organisation and stakeholders. The problem of purpose, and how to solve it through driver orientation.

13. YOUR ORGANISATION IS ITS PEOPLE —— 303

Starting and then growing an organisation begins and ends with the strength and purity of the people acting as source. Individual and cultural meaning-making creates the reality that everyone in the organisation experiences. Psychological safety, leading to deliberate personal development and high levels of interactivity is the foundation for a long-term thriving business. Learn dialogue patterns to harness the value of conflict in yourself and teams, to have an antifragile and successful business.

14. YOUR ORGANISATION IS ITS TASKS —— 341

The whole point of any organisation is to deliver useful results by executing tasks or turning human energy into business output. How you do this depends on meaning-making stories, matching the individual Size of Person with the Size of Role. Do this poorly at the leadership team level, and you suffer from a developmentally divided team; do it well and you'll thrive. Whether you use sociocracy, Holacracy, Agile, or anything of that ilk, they all need developmental approaches and a FairShares Commons style incorporation to work.

15. YOUR ORGANISATION IS ITS INCORPORATION —— 360

How can the incorporation both increase your company's financial performance and transform it into a regenerative business that addresses our global crises? By having all stakeholders aligned in the full range of ways of benefitting from the business and enabling it to succeed. How to do this? Reincorporate your company as a FairShares Commons: split past from future, money from governance; include all stakeholders and all capitals in governance and wealth sharing. So all benefit: investors, founders, staff, customers, suppliers, communities, and our natural environment.

16. CREATING YOUR FAIRSHARES COMMONS COMPANY —— 379

The practical chapter. You've decided you need your company to be at Level 5 in all three dimensions, and what to know what to do to incorporate a Level 5 FairShares Commons company. Here's how to get your company objects / purposes, stakeholders, dilution, voting, exits, and stewardship sorted out; along with a couple of examples. See why this is the best for investors and founders, because your founding intent and values are immortalized in the principles of stewardship, and protected by the constitution through the stewards.

17. GROWING REGENERATIVE BUSINESSES AND ECOSYSTEMS —— 401

We can get out of this mess by creating and scaling regenerative businesses and ecosystems based on Level 5 incorporations like the FairShares Commons. Businesses should be incorporated for a finite, rather than an infinite, lifetime, and they need far more power with and power to, rather than today's ineffectual power over.

PART V: TURNING TO ACTION

18. REASONS FOR HOPE —— 417

The climate emergency and other global crises are rightly cause for concern, and we are entering the last decade where humanity can do something. This is our best and last chance ever to create a regenerative economy that works for you, for our planet, and for profit. All we need to do is integrate what is currently separated.

19. TEN ACTIONS FOR YOU —— 423

If it is to be, it's up to me. No matter how small and powerless you are, you can act. Here are ten ideas, some of them within everyone's scope, around the central themes of this book, that will contribute.

ACKNOWLEDGEMENTS —— 426

PART VI: APPENDIX

BUILDING A GENERAL THEORY OF ECONOMIES —— 435

We need a general theory of economies, one that is falsifiable, predicts well the outcomes of any intervention, fully incorporates or aligns with all we know and will learn about physics, chemistry, human nature, motivations, the Cognitive Developmental Framework, and all else. In particular, an economics based on all 8 billion unique realities of our global population, and the non-ergodic nature of these realities and economics. Such an economics is then always relative to everything else. So Einstein's General Relativity may well give us good ideas on how to formulate it. This chapter suggests one way: accept that all decisions are rational in each person's local reality, then focus on how to connect one reality with another. Enter a decision spacetime.

CONTENTS

List of Tables

List of Figures

Preface

When you light a candle, you also cast a shadow.
—Ursula K. Le Guin

Why this book now?

As we finish this book in 2020, we both have more hope than when we met in 2015. Certainly more hope than Graham had when he left Procter and Gamble (P&G) in 2008 to address the root causes. We have more hope because finally enough people are standing up and taking action to deal with the climate emergency, and all other global scale crises, that all of us are now in[1]. And because we now know how to re-build our constructs of opposing elements, such as impact / regeneration or profit, into one complementary pairing: high impact *and* high profit.

> I (Graham) have had to fight for my hope, because my gut instinct, my intuition, has left me feeling hopeless over most of the past decade. At least we now have names for what many of us have experienced for over ten years: it's variously called climate grief, climate depression, or climate anxiety. I remember clearly cycling in and out of climate depression in 2016 and 2017 watching the Arctic summer ice melt. The worst was mid-September 2017. I was completely unable to put my physical and mental trauma into coherent sentences; at home all I could do was point at the data and hope my partner would understand why even getting out of bed was an achievement.

And yet Jack and I both know that there are reasons to hope. We know that, paradoxically, because of the growing climate awareness, anxiety, and action, there has never been a better time to build the regenerative economy and the businesses that we need. So we have written this how-to book to describe why we believe that, how to look at yourself and your world, and what to do if you are committed to building a world that works for yourself, for others, and for nature.

We can all transform how we come together as one human society of 8 billion unique individuals, the economy that our society constructs, how business works, and how each of us shows up in the world. Now is the best time ever to do that at a global scale, because we are so connected globally and have a greater understanding than ever before of all scales, from the individual to the planet.

There have been times, though, when the two of us have felt anger or despair, not hope. In 2015, when we started this journey together, it was only a climate crisis, with 10 to 15 years left before the effects of climate change were experienced by many. We both imagined that within a few years enough people would start taking action.

That didn't happen. Now we have a full-blown climate emergency, along with all our other interlinked social and environmental threats, and need immediate *effective* global action; and the latest signals from our climate, society, and environment prove that the change is coming even faster and bigger than the original worst-case scenarios. So we urge everyone to act, put into practice now the proven approaches in this how-to guide. The more of us that do, the more hope we have.

> The central pillar in delivering radical change without going through a full-scale collapse of global systems is our growing understanding of how each of our individual identities, the identity of each group of people, along with our norms and global institutions, are our meaning-making stories made concrete.

By going back to our meaning-making stories, and transforming them, we have more power than ever before to change, at a fundamental level, everything that is part of our society, and our impact on each other and the planet.

There is hope. There is always hope. We intend this book to light a new candle of hope in you, perhaps even many new candles. A candle because you will see in this book one way of making business an intrinsic force for good, and creating a new kind of global economy that makes our lives better both today and in the future because it provides a multi-solution to our challenges.

This will only make a difference if each of us then turns that hope into action. Hope without right action is meaningless.

Which begins and ends (as this book does) with a question both of us, and most likely you, have asked yourself before: *"Who am I, and what am I for?"*

How we came to write this book together

Graham

One of my earliest memories is each morning crawling through a hole in the hedge that separated our house from the nursery school next door. Also, apparently, on the morning before I was born, my mom walked through the gate in the fence separating the house from the hospital, through the back door and straight into the maternity ward I was born in. (My dad was the hospital pharmacist.)

Maybe this tendency to ignore artificial boundaries, to go straight from one domain into another, was embedded into me at birth.

Or maybe it's something that I grew into, growing up in apartheid South Africa and seeing how arbitrary and harmful many of the boundaries were. All my life I've wanted to understand why things are the way they are. Early on, that took me into taking apart then trying to put back together everything I could lay my hands on. I learnt that that didn't always (in fact, rather seldom) end up with all the parts fitting together and working the way they had done before.

I have always been a voracious reader of all kinds of books about how the physical world and how human beings work. The cognitive behavioural approaches in psychology were interesting, and helped me hold steady in the face of repeated bouts of depression. I recall beginning to read about climate change, and the limits to growth, in the early 80s, and thought then that this would happen only at the very end of my life.

I went to a highly competitive all boys school, Selborne. Mathematics and physics became my focus; and I was encouraged to find and compete in a sport that suited me. Rowing ended up as that sport. Later on at university I complemented rowing with hiking and climbing on Table Mountain.

This competitive edge has stayed with me ever since, a curse and a blessing. It drives me to always try harder, take on the toughest challenges I can find; and keeps me constantly judging myself as not good enough. It's still with me, only now I know that none of us can possibly be individually good enough for the challenges we are facing.

I dived ever deeper into theoretical physics, getting my PhD in Germany (Jülich and Bielefeld), and researching high-temperature particle physics in Pisa (Italy), and Tsukuba (Japan). By Tsukuba I was starting to think that it was time to do something completely new, so I accepted a job offer as R&D manager with P&G in Belgium. Four years later P&G decided that I would be a good person to lead the packaging unit in the R&D centre in Beijing, and so I moved to China.

I was also beginning to panic, looking at how fast humanity was heading towards multiple crises.

So in 2008 I left P&G. The Arctic ice data, and everything else, were unambiguous: by 2020 we would all experience physical consequences of the climate crisis. It was perfectly clear to me: now was the time for decisive, global action to address climate change. I found it hard to grasp how few of my friends, family, and colleagues had any sense of fear about the future. I found it hard to believe that most of the people I talked to expected the money they were putting into pension funds to still be worth something in their last years of retirement. I certainly didn't.

We clearly had just 15 to 25 years to take decisive regenerative action. But what would actually be regenerative action, rather than the degenerative action driven by blame and anger, rooted in powerlessness, from a meaning- akin to hoping for a different past, as Desmond Tutu puts it?

By 2008 the hard data had become crystal clear. We had entered the endgame of life in a climate suited to humans, with *at most* a mere two decades to take decisive action. Despite first being warned as far back as 1856 by Eunice Newton Foote[2] that carbon dioxide was a blanket keeping the Earth cosy enough for our comfortable life, and that increasing CO_2 adds blankets. Three years later the first oil well was drilled, and we began adding blankets.

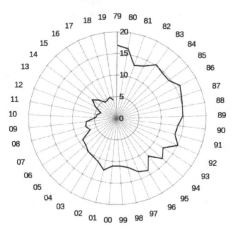

Figure 1: Plotted here is the Arctic ice volume[3] each year from 1979 to 2019 at the September minimum, after the summer melt, in $1000km^3$. As you can see, it is spiralling inexorably in, towards zero arctic ice in summer. Which will turn the mild European winters into freezing, because the Gulf stream will weaken.

The Arctic death spiral shown in Figure 1 was the clincher, and everything I have seen since then confirms that we humans consistently under-estimate how fast the climate emergency is growing. Most significantly, a few weeks before we finished final editing, a new computer simulation from Maria-Vittoria Guarino predicted complete Arctic ice melt in mid-summer[4] by 2035. A bit longer than the worst-case prediction I saw in 2009: ice-free arctic summers after 2020.

I decided then that nothing was more valuable, given my unique experiences and skills, than to commit to transforming the deep, underlying roots of the dysfunctional systems that we live in. I started by asking:

what are the anchors holding the system stable in its dysfunctionality, perpetuating the dysfunctionality of our global systems, despite decades of effort from some of the world's most insightful and committed people?

I did what any good particle physicist would do: look at the fundamental particles of our society, how they interact with each other, and then reinvent them. I needed to dive deep into economics, business design, incorporation, and operation. To do that I needed to transform who I was, and how my meaning-making stories construct the reality I experience. I did this, and continue to transform myself, thanks to the Cognitive Developmental Framework[5,6] of Otto Laske, which is woven throughout this book, and covered in Part III.

I started to get to know investors, economists, lawyers, social change leaders, developmental coaches, and all kinds of practitioners whom I had never known about before—and in some cases would never have wanted to talk to before.

I started a building-integrated photovoltaics company, and a leadership development and strategy consulting company that evolved into a learning transfer consultancy. That was when I recognised that our company must be both multistakeholder and free, if we were to stay true to our values and usage of Holacracy. This recognition and early reinvention of the company developed into the FairShares Commons described in this book. In the early 2010s I began consulting to other companies on the early stages of what is described in this book as the Adaptive Organisation model, integrating developmental interactions between people, dynamic governance, and multistakeholder incorporations.

By 2013 I had the evidence I needed: doing only Holacracy or sociocracy, or only developmental practices, or only using multi-stakeholder cooperatives or B-corps, whilst a positive step, had such huge, hidden, fragile Achilles' heels under the surface that they did far more harm than good at times.

I had now developed and proven the first version of my Adaptive Organisation approach, which integrates all three elements (legal incorporation, dynamic governance of roles and tasks, human development practices), to build antifragile organisations that have the minimum needed to deliver against our global challenges without setting people up for failure and self-blame. Anyone trying to build a business to make the world a better place with anything less than at least Level 3 (see Chapters 13 to 15) on all three axes simultaneously is, at best, gambling on improbable luck; and, at worst, can be unknowingly, naively irresponsible.

It was clear to me: we must scale fast what really works. We have squandered the luxury of time we had in the 2000s; now we must transform all business to fully regenerative by design at Level 4, better Level 5 on each of the three Adaptive Organisation axes, but especially FairShares Commons incorporation.

This provides the legal framework for a powerful approach to addressing our global challenges: multisolving[7], by Elizabeth Sawin of Climate Interactive.

Multisolving is when one single action or a few actions simultaneously solve many problems. The FairShares Commons is the most powerful way of incorporating I know of to enable companies to do this, because now multiple businesses and other entities can seamlessly collaborate in one multi-solving ecosystem, even if they are also competing. There is growing evidence that commoning the company is good business long term[8,9]. For example, in a decision in the general meeting about the company's future activities, such as supplier-sourcing strategy and guidelines, investment possibilities, etc., instead of having only the perspective of investors (whose primary need is financial return) in the decision, you have the perspectives and vote of all stakeholders across all ages.

You can identify how a single optimised action can now simultaneously deliver profit for the business and also address climate change, and urban poverty in the city a factory is based in, and food miles issues, and modern-day slavery issues in some of the supplier countries, etc. Integrate profit and impact into one single goal.

Without the FairShares Commons, any business attempting to do full-spectrum multisolving is fragile, dependent on the goodwill of the powerful investors.

I invite everyone reading this book to explore what we have written, use it, and improve it; because we can still build a better world that works, if we do a full-on job of transforming all businesses into regenerative ones.

And so, having proven to my satisfaction what works, on a fine summer's day in London I decided to hop onto the tube and drop in at the Rethinking Economics conference, organised by a visionary bunch of students who had also decided that enough was enough, to begin building allies in the daunting task of scaling the Adaptive Organisation to the global scale. And there I met ...

Jack

These days I'm teaching economics at the University of Wisconsin-Eau Claire, and see now a clear line back to my clear memories, from my early teens, of my grandfather talking to me about how we were damaging the environment, and how imperative it was to begin doing things fundamentally differently to make sure that we had a planet worth living on when *I* was a grandfather. He had founded and still ran a construction company, so he knew what he was talking about from direct experience. And he read widely, teaching himself; so I learnt to love reading, the power of the written word to drive change, and to trust my own understanding, not that of authority positions.

A few years later, once I was old enough to operate jackhammers and other construction equipment, I worked for my grandfather (and then my father) as a labourer. I still love working with my hands and building physical things that will last (even though I'm not the best with my hands), much as I have added to that enjoyment by building concepts in economics that I also hope will last. I visited some of the buildings that I helped build decades afterwards and felt pride seeing them still standing.

Across my life I've experienced setbacks, some of them leading me into dark places and depression. I've also experienced great joy in my life, especially when my two children were born. This juxtaposition of great joy and dark depressions have given me an empathy with people who are downtrodden, a commitment to do something about the pain that society's institutions sometimes impose on people. This is especially relevant for the impact that the climate emergency, and other crises will have on so many of us in the coming decades. As we write this, Covid-19 (or SARS-CoV-2) is rampaging around the world, in part because we failed to heed the warnings of SARS-CoV-1 in 2002 and MERS in 2012.

I learned from my American football coach that dark and light might be connected. One of his favourite adages was that success is defeat turned inside out. This has stayed with me, and I now realise that success and defeat are very much internal reality that I create out of my meaning-making stories.

My work in the world became clear and focused after I submitted for publication a paper pointing out a fundamental flaw in one of the central assumptions of neoclassical economics. I showed the error in the deductive logic behind the assumption that the market economy could allocate resources efficiently, without external intervention and regulation by government and labour unions. (The ecosystems of FairShares Commons companies described in this book, I believe, will prove to be able to efficiently allocate resources.)

I opened the rejection letter at my mailbox, outside in mid-winter, in freezing temperatures, and read the referee's three words of rejection: *"How dare you."*

So I sat down on a snowbank, flipped the rejection letter over, and sketched on the back the outline of the *International Journal of Pluralism and Economics Education*, which is still running under my editorship just fine. That rejection led eventually to my lecturing in economics at the University of Wisconsin-Eau Claire.

This was more than just the points in the railway track of my life putting me onto a different track; it was more like instantaneously tunnelling through an insurmountable mountain range into a different valley on a completely different track.

It was clear to me that something fundamental was dreadfully wrong with neoclassical economics and economics education. It was time for me to commit my energy, time, and focus on figuring out what was dreadfully wrong and then create something that worked.

Had more economists been speaking on the side of humanity, rather than staying within the safe walls of their neoclassical castle, we would today already have an economics that properly described a viable regenerative economy.

And so, two books on pluralist economics education, and one underway, I was invited in 2015 by Rethinking Economics to speak at their summer London conference.

Graham and Jack

"Jack, how has economic theory taken into account the latest research into the different stages of adult development, and how each stage has a different rationality when taking decisions?" Graham asked, at the end of Jack's talk.

Not having any answer to that left the two of us in a long conversation for the rest of the day, and deep into the evening over a meal in a nearby pub.

We played truant on the second day of the conference, and continued talking. The rest, you can read between here and the end of the book.

Writing it has been a journey filled with generative conflict. Each of us sees some things very differently, which has triggered heated arguments at times, but has also been enormously valuable in crafting this book. And each of us shares the common belief which has held us together in each of those arguments: a belief that economics and business has the power that we need to rise to the challenge to build a better world, if we can only break free of the old paradigms.

Each of us had been on a life path that made this book likely to be written. If we hadn't met there, we would have met sooner or later. And if the two of us hadn't written this book, one of us would have written a similar book with somebody else.

Or two different people would have written it together, and Jack and I would have wished that we had put pen to paper. It was a one in a million chance that brought us together, not fate; but given what each of us was doing, there were very many chances for us to meet.

As the much missed Terry Pratchett said, one in a million chances happen nine times out of ten. If you have a million of these one in a million chances, one of them is bound to happen.

This book is a circle

And so this book is not really ours. Everything in it was ready to be written, and just needed the sparks of conflict and connection; then the decision to put effort into it, to channel and focus what was all around us into this specific constellation of words. What is unique about this book comes out of the unique generative spark emerging as our distinct meaning-making stories ran with each other, exploring new landscapes in consciousness, society, economics and business.

We wish we could write the way Picasso painted: showing everything simultaneously. This book is a linear representation of nested circles. In writing, we had to start somewhere, but actually all starting points are as good. So read this book in any order that suits you. Some of you will want to read the macro why of Part II first, then the meso how and what of Part IV, and finally the micro of Part III; others will prefer the reverse order. A few will read the way Graham reads detective novels: first the last two pages, to find out who did it; then the first two pages, to find out if the whole plot is obvious; then sampling a few pages here and there, to find out if it's entertaining—and only if it ticks all these boxes, reading everything.

We have written this book as best possible so that each part can be read as independently as possible of the other parts. There is ample cross-referencing, so whichever chapter you are reading, wherever we use something from an earlier or a later chapter, you'll find a link to it. We hope that will make it easier to navigate.

This book took far longer to write than we originally believed. The world has changed significantly since we started. We have written and rewritten each chapter across the entire five-year period, so there is no linear timeline to events we refer to in the present, (such as the Covid-19 pandemic that emerged during the final editing).

We use "I" in this book to mean Jack or Graham speaking for themselves, as well as Jack and Graham speaking with one voice together.

So from now on "I" means Jack and Graham, or Jack, or Graham. So I (Jack and Graham together) use "you" to refer to you as one person reading this, and all of you reading this book. I use "we" primarily to refer to everybody—including me (Jack and Graham).

This book is for you

If you are anybody who wants to do something to make the world a better place, for yourself and the next generations, I have written this book for you.

I especially hope that the younger you are, the more inspiration you will get by seeing how much of today's world has been invented, and can be reinvented to address our global crises. I hope this book can help you figure out how to create your own curriculum to learn what you will need in the future, so that you minimise the time spent learning what is past its sell-by date.

I hope that this book will inspire all founders, leaders, and staff of for-profits, non-profits, impact businesses, multinationals, and NGOs; people passionate about their projects, and anybody working on anything, to understand why you are doing what you are doing, and how you can grow yourself to have a greater impact.

I believe that business, in the broadest sense, from individual freelancers to the world's largest multinationals, now have more power to resolve our global challenges than any other institution. Throughout this book I use the phrase profitable business to mean growing all capitals, not just financial profit. I see profit in all capitals and regeneration as equivalent.

I hope, if you are an investor, whether impact-flavoured or traditionally-flavoured, will find in this book what you want to invest in the ways we need to address our global challenges. You are a vital part of our journey and destination. You will find, in this book, how you can protect the integrity of your values, the difference you want to make in the world with your money, and have a 1000x bigger outcomes on all metrics (see Section **??**) through requiring your investees incorporate as FairShares Commons, and reach at least Level 3 in organisation design and human interactivity—described in full in Part IV.

I hope that climate change experts and activists, indeed experts in all disciplines (especially economics and business), civil servants and politicians, will find that our perspective on why economics and business is what it is, and what we can change to make it work for all of us, at least thought-provoking enough to trigger them into finding something even better.

Have fun reading this book. And remember, if it lights a candle for you, to keep a wary eye open for the shadow it also creates.

The cover tells the story

by Nikyta Guleria

I designed this cover to capture the essence of the book; a book embedded with ideas that were taking form long before Graham and I began working together six years ago. Excited to take on the challenge, this book was more than an omnibus of stories that gave me hope and spelled optimism. It was a medley of practical tools, researched methodologies, and voices of reason, captured in a way that left me visualizing a vibrant cohesive world. It also gave me the ability to recognize the gray inadequacies of today's world, ones that bar us from meeting large-scale change and transformation. It is this contrast between today's 'old world' and tomorrow's 'new world' that sits center stage in the cover artwork.

In order to rebuild without risking catastrophic collapse, we must simultaneously build the new and dismantle the old world, without losing the life support of the old, nor succumbing to the toxicity of the old world (denoted in gray undertones) dominating the lives that most of us still live. A world that fails almost everyone on the planet today; and prevents the next generations from thriving. A world that is slowly but surely showing its cracks.

This world's systems and structures systemically exclude, or discriminate against, people who would love to contribute to a thriving society; sometimes driving them to the fringes of society. Capturing the physically and psychologically dangerous elements rooted in our workplace practices and cultures, at best, I was able to share glimpses of what this waste of human lives, potential, and resources looks like, seen in the form of burn-out, unrest, depression, homelessness, and even loss of life.

Step by step we need to dismantle our linear use-and-dump mentality and practices (depicted through deforestation, garbage pileups, and demolitions), dismantle everything putting toxic waste into nature and our communities (oil well, factory chimneys, and fumes), and replacing them with circular, fully regenerative practices.

We live in this very fading, graying old world, that often blocks us from seeing the vibrant, regenerative world we ought all to thrive in (depicted in bright hues of blue, green and purple). This new world doesn't exist yet and we cannot know what it will look like, nor can we know all the elements we will need to build it. But we do know the regenerative, life-giving essence it must have (depicted as individual and overlapping elements moving in harmony). In order to see this new world unfold, it will need us to look through new lenses, just as Picasso and the other founders of cubism did. Look for the eyes and faces in the new world, representing the capacity we most need now: to see what others cannot yet see, to imagine possibilities others cannot yet imagine, and to build what others cannot yet build.

The book beautifully articulates a connection between the 'economy', 'leadership' and 'you', as a constant, sustainable, even regenerative motion, like the cyclic nature of waves and tides of our oceans and atmosphere or the 'waves' of seasons we see moving at a glacial speed, shaping our landscape. A constant re-generative motion that is conducive to shaping everything, connecting everything, and vital for moving energy and resources to where life needs it.

As I imagined this world together with the authors, the image in our minds was dominated by colourful waves representing building blocks that are still to be defined; hope, flow, celebrations, the visible and the hidden, opportunities and threats, emotions, adventures, successes, failures, and everything in between and neither; and much more. They represent the opportunities we have right now to ride the tide, as Brutus points at in Shakespeare's Julius Caesar:

> *There is a tide in the affairs of men*
> *Which, taken at the flood, leads on to fortune.*

In the midst of complex and chaotic legacy ways of living and operating, Graham and Jack, through their words, have managed to paint a clear and pure picture of what tomorrow could look like, by connecting the dots and highlighting the red threads that string together our conscious and unconscious worlds, clearing the path for individuals and organizations to take action and create a future befitting for humanity in the 21st century.

Part One

Art and Physics

In which we introduce the foundations of this book: your experienced reality is a consequence of how you look at the world, i.e., the lenses you look through. Cubism, relativity and quantum mechanics give us new lenses on business and economics.

CHAPTER 1

Reasons for Hope

Every valuable human being must be a radical and a rebel, for what they must aim at is to make things better than they are.

—Niels Bohr[10]

You may never know what results come from your action. But if you do nothing, there will be no result

—Mahatma Gandhi

1.1 Shift happens

Are you experiencing climate anxiety? Are you experiencing climate grief? Are you tempted to give up hope, and join the ranks of the doomists preparing for complete system collapse? Are you actively doing whatever you can to prevent even more harm, and to regenerate our environment and society?

We are at the beginning of the biggest shift that humanity has experienced in at least 75,000 years, since the eruption of the Toba volcano caused so much pollution that it triggered a rapid change in the global climate, and humankind faced near extinction. This time it may even be a more severe shift.

I am doing this chapter a few months after 2019 broke a number of records for the hottest ever, and for the biggest fires across swathes of Australia and Western USA. A year of ever more ice loss from glaciers, the Arctic and Antarctic, microparticle pollution, ocean-wide plastic pollution, modern-day slavery, in fact so much that we could fill the entire book just listing everything. And now, as we

3

do the final proofs, the virus SARS-CoV-2 is causing Covid-19 and ravaging most countries; another warning shot (after SARS-CoV-1, MERS etc.) across our bows, warning of the unbelievably bigger threats to come.

This is a Do It Yourself (DIY) book, filled with grounded reasons for hope, even if you seldom feel hopeful. By the end you will know why now is the best time ever, and exactly what you can do yourself to build a society, an economy, and businesses that are fundamentally regenerative for you, the environment, and profit. Why we all can rise to the greatest challenge humanity has faced in tens of thousands of years, and why our choices now can make this decade humanity's finest.

Or not. The choice is ours.

It starts with you, and it starts with us. It starts with how we work together, how we incorporate business, and it starts with our economy. It starts everywhere, because we are talking about a circle, not a straight line. So start where you are; put one chapter of this book into practice, and then continue round the circle.

Wherever you start, rising to the challenge of the shift happening around you demands that you shift who you are, how you think, and how you make meaning. You could start here, where you have the most control.

We are all in emergent times, which means none of us can predict the future from the present. In emergent times, at the start of a planet-wide shift, doing what worked before better is almost certain to make things worse, faster.

Doing differently at this scale requires each of us to become someone different, especially to give up hope of being certain. We need to shift our being to rise to emergent challenges. Emergence means we cannot know what will be, only what is, and what has been. It means that uncertainty reigns, and that the reality we each experience is inherently and irreducibly nebulous, (excellently described by David Chapman[11]).

Shift happens, and shift is happening. Some people have given up; but most likely you have not. You are reading this because you are concerned, and actively searching for something practical to do. You may be feeling frustration, anxiety, perhaps even depression, but you are also motivated to act and make a difference.

You might believe that a back-to-basics approach will work. Replicating what worked in the past but trying harder. However, in our emergent reality, where shift happens that you cannot control nor predict, everything is up for grabs. Solutions that once worked, work no longer. Roads that used to look smooth and clearly marked have turned into unmarked paths petering out on impassable rocky slopes.

I have written this book so that you, your organisations, and our economy can thrive in these emergent times.

I have scanned the past for similar emergent times where great shift happened to see what worked and what did not. I have also explored a number of disciplines today that will enable you and our organisations to develop the emergent capacities needed to thrive in today's emergent times.

I start by looking at what each of us can learn from art and physics. Picasso and Einstein were key players in the transformation of art and physics a century ago. The lessons they learnt in driving that transformation are of great relevance to today.

They found that dialogue, pluralism, and multiple perspectives are essential. They also recognised that the interwoven tapestry of the meaning-making stories—those which each individual uses to attribute meaning, and to thereby create their experience of reality—shaped what we could see and understand. They recognised that understanding differently, in order to act differently, required an inner shift in their identity or being, and hence in their meaning-making stories.

To understand yourself, and to understand how to develop your emergent capacities, I've added the latest in neuroscience, psychology, and the other social sciences. I've also included the latest thinking from management, leadership, and economics so that you can develop new ways of constructing organisations to thrive in these emergent times of great shift.

You are reading a book that is designed to span multiple disciplines, and spans the scales from the microscopic quantum level, through to your size, and onto the size of our global organisations and ecosystems.

In the past, most people experienced most of the time a predictable world. The world that each of us is experiencing today has fundamentally changed; it is now inherently unpredictable and emergent. This means that there is always more than one correct view, more than one correct answer. It means that you can never fully capture any view or answer by looking at the present and the past. You can only fully determine it by looking backwards from the future after the future has emerged.

When shift is happening in nebulous emergent times, the shadows the emergent future throws on the present are as powerful a force shaping the present as the past. For example, how are your hopes or fears of what may happen already determining what you do today?

So you can no longer thrive by trying to first gather as much relevant information as possible (from your present and past) to then predict what course of action is right. The outcomes, however much data you have, and however accurately you try to predict, are always filled with inherent, irreducible uncertainty.

If you only learn more skills to predict better you will still fail, because you will still be acting from within the box of your current meaning-making stories. You need to build a bigger box of stories, by developing your adaptive capacity, and the adaptive capacity of your organisation, through getting increasingly better at recognising and embracing contradiction and ambiguity.

It has now become clear that neoclassical economics is flawed. As you will see reading this book, and as Kate Raworth[12] describes in her Guardian article[13], part of what has gone wrong in classical physics is the belief that it can serve as a basis for something as nebulous and subjective as the economy of a human society. In this book, we explore how the lenses of quantum physics and relativity can help us ask different questions that can lead us to better answers.

1.2 You make meaning

A central theme of this book is that you, like all other human beings, are extremely good at seeing patterns and making meaning. Regardless of whether the pattern and meaning is actually there, purely your fantasy, or more often somewhere in between.

Being human centres on your capacity to make meaning. You and a friend may look at exactly the same sunset (right now Jack and I are looking at the sun setting behind the foothills of the Drakensberg in South Africa). You make meaning of beauty and inspiration looking at the sunset, while your friend makes meaning of air pollution. If I am there, I will also tell you that the sunset means blue light is scattered far more than red light by the micro fluctuations of density in the air.

All of these meanings have truth, if only for you in your reality.

Even though the sun setting is a complete illusion you create from the earth turning on its axis.

You make meaning by looking at your library of meaning-making templates, and choosing one of them to make meaning in that moment. Throughout this book we will constantly be pointing at how we all actively make meaning using our own personal and unique library of possible meaning-making templates.

You are the only person experiencing exactly the reality[14] and meaning you experience as you read this book. You truly are unique, and living in your own unique reality (but, of course, broad swathes of your experienced reality are very close to the unique experienced realities of many others).

Few of these stories are purely your fantasy, almost all of them have some grounding. Equally, none of these stories can ever be complete, containing all meanings that anyone alive today, in the past, or in the future, could make.

Your meaning making shapes the reality you experience out of the raw material that is actually present. Raw material like the sunset behind the mountains.

I (Graham) remember growing up as a white teenager in apartheid South Africa during the 70s. A country divided into regions according to skin colour and tribe. The inhumane apartheid clearly could not continue much longer, but how would it end? Unable to grasp the emergent nature of such a shift, everything I predicted involved revolution and collapse. I saw no reason to hope for anything else.

Lying in bed at night, outside sounds would trigger fear, keeping me awake, afraid. Fear and hopelessness were pervasive for myself and many others who wanted and needed a better South Africa, but doubted a smooth and peaceful route to it could exist.

On 11 February 1990, everything changed for good. Nelson Mandela was released from prison without nearly the violence I had feared. Unique in world history: when had the founder of the armed wing of an anti-government struggle movement been released peacefully? Even better, Mandela was already leading dialogue between groups previously unwilling to talk, laying the foundation for a truth and reconciliation process, for restorative rather than punitive justice.

Mandela, de Klerk, Tutu, and many South Africans rejected worn-out maps and lenses, and invented a new emergent strategy. Suddenly there was hope: hope that a new South Africa, that all South Africans could participate in and prosper, might emerge.

I learned three important lessons growing up in South Africa: much of the world is emergent, not predictable; fear is not the only emotional response to an impending great shift: hope is equally plausible and attainable; and, we can equip ourselves to thrive in an emergent world. When we do, radically new options emerge.

I hope this shows why it is an unhelpful, self-fulfilling prophecy to choose the doomist 'we are doomed, total systems collapse is the only possible outcome' stance: because the meaning-making you use co-creates the reality you experience. There is always potential in an emergence-filled world.

1.3 Emergent strategies

If you are focusing on generating outcomes that you cannot see, predict, or control from where you stand now, and are maximising the chance of seeing the value of the outcomes as they emerge—and making use of them just in time—you have an emergent strategy.

Choose wisely how you make meaning of what is happening now, so that you can adopt an emergent strategy that gives you the best chance of a good outcome. The late Barbara Marx Hubbard was a pioneer of making meaning of the crises and chaos of today as the birthing of a new era of humanity[15], rather than the end of civilisation. Since we will only know after we have done our best which of the two it is; and the choice of meaning we make determines what we do; choose the meaning making most likely to enable the outcome you desire.

The Theory U approach, popularised by Otto Scharmer[16] and derived from the scientific approach that led to quantum physics, is a superb way of choosing and then finding wise action. The essence is to let go of what you know, poke at things, see what happens, and then learn.

So chip away at the meaning-making stories shaping your reality so that you can better see what actually is, not what you want to see. As you've just read above, your meaning-making stories play a central role in shaping the reality that you experience—your internally shaped experience of reality is always a simplification and distortion of what actually is. You will read a lot more about this in Chapters 7 to 11, and especially in Section 10.5 on cognitive biases.

Nothing else works if you are in an emergent context, because the events streaming your way are inherently and unpredictably nebulous and complex, unfolding in new and unfamiliar ways. If your context is unpredictable and new, your strategy must be capable of generating new outcomes that you cannot predict before you start acting. Your actions, your tactics, and often even your strategy itself, can only be articulated just in time. Your choices and actions generate unpredictable and unfamiliar outcomes, which in turn generate unfamiliar and unpredictable changes in the subsequent strategy and actions.

An emergent strategy creates a prosperous future through innovation and taking ownership of creating something new. It depends on you developing your adaptive capacity, not just your skills or competencies. Taking a back-to-basics approach, insisting on doing harder or better what worked well for you in the past, will not work. This is blind faith, not grounded hope.

> Unfortunately, during the final year of writing this book, I (Jack) was going through a very emotional divorce—emotional because we still loved each other, but after a marriage of 26 years we could no longer live together.
> Initially, we tried to rekindle the vestiges of old sparks by recreating what had worked so well, so long ago: revisiting our honeymoon, and

even wearing a favorite suit of mine that my wife had bought for our rehearsal dinner.

Sadly, we realized that back-to-basics didn't work. Circumstances had changed and we had changed, so rather than going back to the past and replicating what had magically worked then, we needed to move to the present. Were we deluded by blind faith? No, not really; just an honest attempt to recreate what had once worked for us, but, alas, that magical past only existed in memory.

You can find no better example than Kodak, whose scientists developed the digital camera in 1975[17]. They built the first commercial digital camera (the Apple QuickTake) in 1994, but didn't dare let anyone know. In 2005 Kodak was the largest manufacturer of digital cameras in the world. By 2012 it was bankrupt.

What went wrong? The emergent digital photography stories were incompatible with Kodak's meaning-making story. Too many of Kodak's management and shareholders assumed that the company would prosper by sticking with the highly profitable past (emulsion-based photographic film) and were confident that they could control the pace of change. They failed to see the emergent change, and failed to follow an emergent strategy.

When you have a successful emergent strategy, you neither abandon nor emulate the past. You give up on the hope that establishing a successful path to the future means doing better what you already know. You give up hope that you can identify what is right by finding the right lens to look at your world through.

Emergent strategies require you to use multiple lenses to view reality, and to work with multiple disciplines in an integrated way. You will need to work simultaneously with contradictory beliefs, recognising that they are all needed in order to make sense of your emergent reality and so that you can have generative dialogues with others who have widely different views from yours.

An emergent strategy is 90% about the stories, only 10% about the facts. We write the stories, and so we choose the future; we can choose the future we want, as Christiana Figueres and Tom Rivett-Carnac describe in their book *The Future We Choose: Surviving the Climate Crisis*[18].

Developing the capacity to use multiple lenses was at the core of the transformation of art and physics a century ago. Whether you are more artistic, or more scientific, you can learn from the parallels in the crises you are facing today with those faced by artists and physicists back then.

1.4 Applying Picasso and Einstein
Classical

The story here begins with the Italian artist Giotto di Bondone (1276-1337), who convinced everyone (well, almost everyone) that art should have only one perspective: a human perspective. Before Giotto, European artists were expected to portray reality from God's perspective, without depth.

But for Giotto, a painting should begin and end with what you would see as a human being. To do this on a two-dimensional canvas he portrayed the depth of a three-dimensional landscape by making distant objects smaller than near objects, and parallel lines move closer together the further away they were in the landscape.

The outcome was that all lines of sight converge on your eye as a viewer of the painting, in exactly the same way they would do if you were standing at the spot where the artist had stood in the physical landscape[19].

So art became technical, based on geometry and measurable laws. Giotto shifted from God-centric to human-centric. But his goal was still to paint one, privileged, geometric-centred perspective, not the nuanced perspective of all of you and your diverse meaning-making stories.

Similarly, Isaac Newton revolutionised physics by using a new lens to see everything that happened on earth and in space. He and his peers developed the deterministic world of classical physics.

Newton convincingly demonstrated that nature's deterministic laws could be discovered by combining human reason and mathematics with the hard unambiguous data coming from observation and measurement.

His *Principia*, published in 1687, provided the foundation of the new worldview, gave hope and understanding to everyone, and led to the Industrial Revolution.

And so a new reality was born, with a can-do spirit of optimism.

Giotto and Newton used similar thinking and triggered a great shift in art and physics. The worlds of art and physics complemented each other: both were based on Euclid's geometry, and both co-evolved during the age of Enlightenment.

Soon, this new worldview dominated all aspects of life.

Towards the end of the 19th century, however, the hurried pace of technological change and a growing amount of unambiguous hard data began to challenge these concepts in physics. For example, in classical physics, describing the world as either particles or waves, the data from experiments using X-rays showed that something wasn't working[20].

Picasso and Braque

Pablo Picasso (1881-1985) and Georges Braque (1882-1963) were also dissatisfied with art's capacity to portray the emergent reality that they were seeing. So they created Cubism[1], which was seen by many as a revolution of the same size and importance as Giotto's revolution five centuries earlier[19].

Giotto expected that privileged viewers could only see what they could see from where they stood, and that an artist was expected to simply reproduce this privileged view of reality. If you wanted to see more, you needed to walk around the object, and portray this in a fixed sequence.

But this assumes that reality is exactly what you see, and no more than you see. Picasso and Braque realised that reality is far more than that. Reality is not just what you can see, it is not just what it seems, and it's filled with subjectivity, paradox, contradiction, and is inherently nebulous. So why represent this reality with a monolithic, linear, geometric perspective?

Cubism sliced and diced the representation of an object, and presented simultaneously all sides from all perspectives. No single perspective is privileged in Cubism. Picasso and Braque created a new road where no one had ever travelled, a new road that was far better at getting to where they wanted to get to: understanding the rapidly changing reality they were experiencing.

By ending the privileged one-eye point of view, Cubism paved the way for Surrealism and abstract art. And most importantly, they have given you a set of pluralistic, non-linear tools to understand yourself, your organisation, and your economy.

You can only succeed in the emergent reality you are experiencing by using multiple lenses. Throughout this book you'll read more about how a lens is a tool that you use to see more clearly something relevant by hiding the irrelevant background, and how to use multiple ones. New lenses have long driven great shifts in civilisation. For example, the invention of eyeglasses doubled the skilled craft workforce and their productivity, and led directly to the invention of the microscope and telescope[21].

For example, governments, to neutralise any perceived threat to their stability and security, start with raw data: chatter, tip-offs, sightings, wiretaps, etc. But once the data is collected, the real work of sorting it and making sense begins[22]. If only

---

[1]Cubism was penned by the conventional (and well-established) French art critic Louis Vauxcelles. Attending a 1907 exhibition in Paris, he labeled Picasso and Braque's initial exhibit a "bunch of little cubes". Incidentally, Vauxcelles had earlier attended a 1905 exhibit of painters wildly experimenting with splashy colors (directly influencing Cubism) and derisively quipped that the paintings look like "wild beasts". Fauve, the French name for a wild beast, stuck as an appellation for this important group of artists.

one lens was used for this, a lot would be missed. Multiple lenses are required, across all scales from global down to the smallest local scale, spanning police, government, psychology, economic, sociological, historical, and many more, in order to see clearly; and each lens may cause help to be seen as a threat.

Your choice of lens determines the reality you experience, as does your choice to use just one lens or multiple lenses. Your choice of lenses determines whether you can use an emergent strategy or not. You need multiple lenses, giving you multiple perspectives, none of which is privileged, to build a strategy fit for today's emergent reality.

The same emergent reality that led Picasso and Braque to use new and multiple lenses, even though they were contradictory, led Einstein to do the same in physics.

Einstein

Einstein wrestled with a number of inconsistencies in Newtonian physics, which could not explain new data.

Despite the stellar achievements of Newtonian physics in accurately describing everything from the movement of a grain of sand through the movement of apples to the movement of planets and stars, it was getting harder to make accurate calculations of anything moving very fast or anything very small. These problems led to quantum physics and relativity, which accurately describe how the world works when things are extremely small and extremely big.

Newton assumed that mass, energy, space, and time were separate and distinct; and that each could be measured without influencing the others[23]. Objects had mass, and moved against a neutral and irrelevant backdrop of space and time. An object's motion through inert space, and the time it took to move, could be predicted and depicted to any precision. Two viewers, anywhere in the universe, would see exactly the same events and sequence of events.

However, the closer physicists looked at the world, the more clear it became that it wasn't behaving this way. Einstein saw that if two of you observe the same events from widely different places, and / or you are moving at different speeds, you may well end up seeing a different sequence of events; and possibly even different events. It was clear that events were relative and subjective to the observer, rather than objective. None of your views is absolutely correct, none of them privileged.

Einstein's general theory of relativity was even more profound. Although Newton could explain how objects were attracted to each other, he could not explain why they were attracted to each other. He could not explain gravity.

Newton was troubled by his inability. Einstein was equally troubled, but fortunate to be living in a time where solid experimental data was emerging that he then used to develop his theory of general relativity. General relativity describes how massive objects (think of the Earth) distort the surrounding space; and because they distort the surrounding space, they change how objects move.

Think of putting a heavy cannonball onto the middle of a trampoline. The cannonball distorts what had been a flat surface, changing the way a light marble will then move if you put it onto the trampoline. It will automatically roll towards the heavy cannonball because the cannonball has distorted space. This is how gravity is created, where a large object such as a planet or even a black hole distorts space by its very presence. It creates the reality that it and any other object near it experiences by changing space.

Einstein realised that gravity is unlike the three other fundamental forces (the electromagnetic, weak, and strong forces); it is, in fact, not a force. Rather, it is geometry. At large scales, matter shapes spacetime (creates the geometry of spacetime), and then spacetime (geometry) tells matter how to move.

Space is even more present and active at a subatomic scale. What Newton had thought was a neutral vacuum, inert and playing no role in the movement of small particles, turns out in quantum mechanics to have such a powerful effect, e.g. it's better to think of the vacuum as the primary source of an electron's properties, rather than the electron itself having these properties in isolation.

Throughout the book, especially in Chapter 11, we will go deeper into how your meaning-making stories, and those you are embedded in, are an active, not a neutral background; colouring, shaping, or even creating the reality you experience.

You may find that Einstein's theories sound counterintuitive, or not even understandable. You, as everyone else does, experience the three spatial dimensions and time as very different. But to really understand how our world actually works, we need to abandon this simple view, and shift to thinking in terms of four dimensions; time and space are one.

When you use the lens of four dimensional spacetime, you can accurately and reliably predict what will happen, and you find that outcomes which seemed wrong using Newton's physics are perfectly normal and understandable. You can only get here if you give up on using Newton's single, paradox-free lens, and instead adopt Einstein's multiple, paradoxical lens.

Picasso and Einstein: a complementary pair

General relativity and Cubism both changed the game in the same way. Using them, you can now understand reality by making sense of the apparent contradiction between what you see and experience (reality) and what actually is (actuality). You now have ways of understanding the intrinsic ambiguity inherent in actuality.

General relativity and Cubism recognise that actuality is inherently what it is and all that it is, so any lens will distort what you experience, and give you a false and misleading picture. Yet you cannot not use your lenses.

In a nutshell, you need an appropriate combination of accurate and up-to-date lenses in order to match the reality you experience as closely as possible to actuality.

Newton simply assumed that an independent observer could measure objectively, without any distortion or influencing what was observed. Einstein realised that this fundamental assumption was not valid, that this assumption was why classical theory gave certain useless, and sometimes even harmful, predictions.

If you say that an electron is inside the box, and someone else claims that the electron is outside the box, both of you can be right.

Two people with mutually exclusive realities can both be right. These paradoxes are ubiquitous throughout life.

You have far more chance of success if you give up on only seeing opposites as mutually exclusive. You have undoubtedly learnt early in your life that something is either true or false, right or wrong. In art, quantum physics, and in life itself, sometimes two perspectives are mutually exclusive pairs, and at other times they are complementary pairs. Both are true, rather than either / or.

I believe that, to deal with the emergent reality and crises of today, complementarity must be the starting point across all the disciplines needed. Complementary pairs are used throughout this book, and described in Chapter 2.

Quantum physics is weird, but this is how our world works. Richard Feynman, widely regarded as Einstein's equal in his generation, said that if you do not find quantum physics confusing, then you do not understand it. Humans cannot understand it because we are one to two metres tall, and can only understand the world through the basic common sense and observation possible as a being that size. You cannot directly experience quantum reality.

But your mobile phone, and many of the other conveniences of modern life, all rely on relativity and quantum physics.

Nobel laureate Walter Heisenberg developed his uncertainty principle in 1927. The uncertainty principle reflects an inherent unknowability in nature that has nothing to do with our human ability to know. For example, an electron's momentum and its position are a complementary pair. The more you know about an electron's momentum, the less you can know about its position, and vice versa. This finally laid to rest the myth that a neutral observer can just look at an electron, and see all actuality without creating the reality that the observer sees. Uncertainty and subjectivity exist at the most fundamental level of nature.

Some people interpret this as saying that everything that you experience, you create; and that you have total control over what you experience. This is absolutely not what quantum mechanics or the uncertainty principle is saying. Rather, it says that when you observe an electron, your action of observing creates the final reality that you see, out of a limited range of possible outcomes.

A similar uncertainty principle is at work in art. For example, Cubism criticises much of the earlier art: the more precisely the painter has painted depth and perception from a single privileged perspective, the less freedom you as viewer have to engage with the painting and experience what you might experience looking at the actual landscape. Picasso deeply understood that the reality you experience of a work of art is co-created by the artist capturing a limited range of possibilities, and by you, the viewer, looking at the art and shaping the final reality you experience.

If you apply these uncertainty principles to the emergent world you are living in today, you can probably already see that the more detail you have in defining and executing your strategy the less you can recognise emergent possibilities for success. If you are about to start up a business, this points at (like Heisenberg's uncertainty principle) getting the right balance between putting time into detailed strategy; and time into improvising, testing minimum viable prototypes, and pivoting when new learnings come your way.

In the emergent reality you live in, at best on the border between complex and chaos, there are fundamental limits on what you can know. You seldom have any more than just enough time to react and alter course and strategy. Reacting quickly to imperfect, incomplete data that you've got because you tried something counts far more than waiting until you have the perfect analysis of complete data before acting.

Picasso and Einstein took huge risks abandoning the well-established perspectives used by their contemporaries.

They took these risks because they knew that if they didn't they would not be able to live with themselves. They knew that the reality they were experiencing required them to take them. In that sense, they may not really have seen this as risk-taking. Later in this book you will develop more clarity on how your meaning-making stories, your nature, and your capacity to use different thought forms, creates your reality, including your perception of risk and reward.

To thrive in the emergent world you live in, you need to see these meaning-making stories clearly, so that you can reframe the reality that they shape to one that is more helpful to you.

Once you can transform your meaning-making stories, you can become antifragile. You can grow your capacity to thrive, from fragile, through resilient and robust, to antifragile. Resilient simply means the capacity to survive unchanged in the face of attack, while antifragile is the capacity to transform in the face of attack, becoming more able to thrive because of the attack. (See *Antifragility*[24] for more.)

You will see in this book how to reapply the essence of the transformation a century ago in art and physics to build new types of organisations that are also anti-fragile: developmental, self-organising, and incorporated as FairShares Commons, or free companies.

You will also learn how you can use these to transform your identity, self-development, and ability to develop your emergent capacity. This will give you antifragility. I believe all this is essential for you, your organisation, and our economy to thrive.

1.5 Developing your adaptive capacity

Part III on page 149, Chapters 7 through to 11, is all about how you can develop your adaptive capacity.

You all have the potential to do this, and it is imperative if we are all going to rise to the adaptive challenges facing us. Developing your adaptive capacity is a real challenge, though, because it means accepting the inherent ambiguity, uncertainty and unpredictability in your life.

The first step is to know who you are and where you've been. Just as Einstein taught us that the properties of a particle (say an electron) are not independently owned by the particle itself, but instead depend on the entire context of the particle, including the path it has travelled, the same is true for you. Who you uniquely are depends on the path you've travelled and the meaning that you have created and attached to that path through your interactions with others.

The Ubuntu philosophy of Southern Africa captures the inherent interconnectedness of everyone and everything very well. "I am because we are", or "I am because you are", are the two common translations into English of the essence of Ubuntu. This has much in common with Picasso's art, relativity, and quantum physics.

Ubuntu recognises that none of us can become human, let alone our full selves, without the influence of everyone else around us. It reflects the full interconnectedness of everyone and everything. The meaning-making stories that define who you are today have been shaped by everybody that you and they have interacted with; and onwards down the links of interaction. This interconnectedness is at the very heart of what it is to be human.

Path dependency and interconnectedness are central to how the world works. This new perspective a century ago in physics and art now needs to be repeated in business and economics, and relearnt at an individual level by many in the West.

So who you are, and the decisions you take, depends on your entire history, your beliefs about your future, your context and the meaning that you have made of your context. The internal reality that you've constructed, and the maps you use to navigate through life.

Who you are is emergent, meaning that your identity and your path through life is created by each step you take. In Part III you can learn how to tilt the emergent probabilities in your favour, and Part IV covers how to do the same for your business.

Think back to when you were 10 years old, and who you wanted to become when you grew up. For some of you reading this, you will likely say *Yikes, I'm glad that that didn't happen*. You cannot control who you are, nor who you will become, from who you are today.

Some of you will find this lack of control a bit scary. But it has a powerful upside. Who you are, and the reality that you will experience in the future, is fluid. Even just a few minutes in the future, who you are and the reality you will experience can change within the range of options open to you.

You are emergent, and your future is emergent. Both are created by the meaning-making stories you are using to shape your reality out of the countless events and possibilities in actuality, and that you have no control over.

There is a fundamental limit to how well you can plan and steer. If you try to predict who you should become and then steer yourself there in a predictive, controlled way, you are far more likely to lose opportunities that you might later prefer.

Some of you reading this may already have experienced your midlife crisis, or the quarter-life crisis that some experience in their mid-20s to mid-30s. Any mid-something crisis has, at its root, the fact that the lenses and meaning-making stories that have worked for you before are failing you now. You have two choices: either you embrace the lesson that the world is giving you, and change the lenses and meaning-making stories that you use as maps to navigate your life, or you try to go back to your past. And, as we've said before, trying to go back to the past, trying to shrink your world to one that fits the smaller maps that you built when younger and less wise, usually fails.

I find Otto Laske's map of maps, the Constructive Developmental Framework (CDF)[5,6] especially useful. The CDF is the central foundation of our book. In Part III you will learn how to use this map to connect what is and what can be, who you are and who you can become, and to develop your adaptive capacity.

Central to this map is the developmental sequence of self-identity, i.e., the categories of meaning-making stories that adults progress through as they age, along with the forms of thought that you develop over time. The self-identity development is derived from Kegan's work on stages of adult development, and the thought forms from the Frankfurt School of philosophy.

To transform yourself, your organisation, and your economy, the better you understand where you are in this CDF map of maps, the better you can adapt yourself to who your reality is calling for you to become. Keep in mind, this is not a deterministic map. It is a map of probabilities and emergence in the face of adaptive challenges. It does not tell you exactly who you are, nor can it predict exactly who you will become. Far more, as in quantum physics, it lays out categories and descriptions of territory.

I cannot emphasise enough that there is nothing in the CDF map of maps saying that you are better or worse than somebody who is somewhere else in this map of maps. Any given stage is not better or worse than any other stage. As you will uncover later in the book, any judgement of better or worse is so dependent on context and perspective that any attempt to judge anything or anyone as inherently better or worse without stating clearly the context and your unique internal frame of reference is fundamentally flawed.

As well as Kegan's stages of adult development, the CDF framework enables you to recognise how we take in information from the outside world and put it together in your thoughts to make sense of what is happening. The more subtly you can work with multiple forms of thought, the less likely you are to bias or distort the picture you build up as your internal reality from the puzzle pieces you take in. No matter how fluid you are using all the different forms of thought, the internal reality that you construct is always an incomplete and distorted representation of what actually is.

The bigger your adaptive capacity in different forms of thought (also called sense making), the more able you are to go beyond linear logic forms of thought, and deeper into the 28 different patterns often called meta-thinking, transformational thinking, or dialectic thinking. You can read about this in detail in Chapter 9.

The third element of the CDF map of maps (Chapter 10) helps you work with your innate and unchangeable nature in a more subtle way. The aspects of your nature, like your psychological traits and needs, that you either cannot change, or at best only very slowly. Neuroscience suggests that many of these are hardwired into us, either in our DNA, or at a very early stage of our lives. Recognising these and learning how to work with them in a subtle way, harnessing the value that they bring to help you succeed when your emergent reality throws surprises, should be your focus.

For example, some of you reading this might experience periods of depression or anxiety, and you may well have wished that you could edit out everything in your genes that predisposes you to them. But by doing so you might at the same time edit out traits and strengths that you need now or will need soon. Your depression might be one side of a superb strength that you have, of feeling intuitively the gap between what could be and what is. When you turn the strength outwards, you invent a breakthrough product that solves problems people didn't even know they had, and a start-up that perhaps transforms the climate emergency. No one who is lacking this strength would ever see that product. When you turn the exact same strength inwards, and see the gap between who you are now and could be, then your feeling of the gap turns into depression.

While I (Jack) have experienced much joy in my life, I've also endured severe and debilitating depression. Without getting into the details of why, or how I have dealt with it, depression is an integral part of who I am. And, while I wouldn't wish this on anyone, it has given me a creative edge, a humility, empathy, sense of humor—yes!—and an understanding that I couldn't have obtained otherwise. It has given me the creative tools to write this book (along with three other works of non-fiction) and the lively imagination to write two novels.

Of course, I do not offer my past as a formula for creative success, only the well-worked advice that rather than delete the ostensibly harmful/negative aspects of your personality (like depression), re-edit them into positive meaning-making stories (like creative edge) to enable you to be who you can be.

Those of you who have read about Picasso and Einstein as people will know that they were not universally acclaimed as nice, comfortable people to spend time with. Words like arrogant, inconsiderate, disparaging, and many more have been used to describe some of the interpersonal behaviours of one or both of them. Both had a restlessness, a drive to ask questions and constantly explore new areas, and to know everything. This enabled them to create their radical breakthroughs in their fields, yet made the relationship others had with them fraught with issues.

Their single-minded focus, a dogged determination, and the belief that they were alive with a specific mission and purpose, that failing to fulfil that mission and purpose was the most relevant measure that their lives would be measured against, is the characteristic that enabled them to ignore the opinions of others, to keep going for decades, despite setback after setback. And today we judge that as their strength. This is the same characteristic that, in their interpersonal context, was and is judged as arrogant.

I believe this is another example of the complementarity of strengths and weaknesses. Of how the same root characteristic shows up in one situation as a strength, and in another situation as a weakness. As Peter Drucker says[25], when you hire someone with a superb strength in one area, you will always get with it an equally big weakness, so the organisation's purpose is to make the strength productive and the weakness irrelevant through shaping the context.

As you read this book, you will likely also see the value of simply accepting some of your weaknesses in order to make their complementary strengths even stronger, and partnering with somebody very different to you, so that together your different strengths are made productive and none of your different weaknesses gets in the way.

Tying it all together, Part III centres on how you construct your self-identity and the reality you experience through your meaning-making stories, which act both as lenses to see through and maps to navigate by. You, as an individual, will read about cutting-edge approaches to growing and transforming your own meaning-making capacity, so that you can rise to the challenges you are facing, and build the new kinds of organisations we need to construct a regenerative economy capable of addressing our global challenges.

1.6 Developing Adaptive Organisations

Any organisation lacking the full adaptive capacity we describe in this book will fall short of its potential. Developing Adaptive Organisations, and business ecosystems built of Adaptive Organisations, is the focus of Part IV.

An Adaptive Organisation has the capacity to:

- see clearly what is happening;

- see clearly the difference between the relevant and irrelevant;

- attach appropriate meaning to what is happening;

- act appropriately.

An Adaptive Organisation must be antifragile, i.e., not only withstanding damaging events, but transforming through them to become even more capable[24].

This can mean that characteristics your meaning-making stories have always seen as a weakness to remove can end up a strength that you require. An Adaptive Organisation has the capacity to thrive, because it uses a multiplicity of perspectives, in situations where you cannot decide until long afterwards whether a given characteristic is a strength or a weakness, or even both.

An Adaptive Organisation can evaluate how much complexity and adaptive capacity is required by each role within, while evaluating the adaptive capacity of each individual, so that the organisation's adaptive demands and supplies are matched. We need this to build a regenerative economy capable of addressing our global crises.

I will take you through the specific characteristics of Adaptive Organisations in sufficient detail in Part IV, Chapters 12 to 17, for you to begin building your own.

Part IV begins by looking at the organisation as a living being with its own meaning-making stories, composed of individuals with their own meaning-making stories interacting with each other.

Approaches like Sociocracy, Holacracy, and requisite organisation design can be ideal complements. Add developmental approaches like the Evolutesix Adaptive Way, and the organisation can harness conflict to grow each individual, team, and the organisation as a whole.

However, this is not enough to become antifragile and adaptive. The new, crucial component is the FairShares Commons legal structure. This structure enables all stakeholders, from each individual consumer through to the planet's natural environment, to engage in the company reaching its full regenerative potential across all capitals. This incorporation is vital if multiple businesses that together form a circular economy are to trust each other over the decades needed for a large circular economy to function, and to go beyond a circular economy into a fully regenerative economy across all capitals.

I will also discuss successful examples of Adaptive Organisations, especially those already using the full FairShares Commons or parts of that incorporation, such as Evolutesix, founded by one of the authors (Graham), which I believe is a successful prototype.

1.7 Society and the economy

This is the focus of Part II on Page 49, and culminates in Chapter 5, where we paint what we believe the general essence of a viable regenerative economy ought to look like. An economy we call The Economy of the Free, quite different to what we have today, which is a free economy.

Can you define an economy? You spend your life in your economy; you have an intuitive idea of what it is and how it works.

I define an economy as a tool invented by society to do the job of provisioning for us all. We need an economy in order to buy needed goods and services; and to sell, share, and even offer for free, what we can produce.

Because the economy has been created by society, it can never be independent, separate from society. And society, in turn, is dependent on our natural environment's capacity to support human life.

To understand, know, and change our economy we must choose multiple lenses and maps, i.e., meaning-making stories. You'll read more about the meaning-making story stages in Part III, and will recognise that if you grow to a later stage, and a higher meta-thinking fluidity, you can see more clearly emergent complexities and ambiguities than you once did, when you could only use the lenses available at lower stages and fluidity of thought.

Unfortunately, too many influential experts, including economists and managers, have a meaning-making centred prior to Stage 4. Many are at a stage where self-identity and expertise are synonymous, so any challenge to their discipline is interpreted as a challenge to self-identity, making it difficult or even impossible for them to deploy multiple lenses and maps. This is at the heart of much of the friction between different disciplines, and between society and the economists.

Steve Keen[26] wrote that if you could invite a late 19th century physicist, biologist, mathematician, chemist, and an economist to the 21st century, each would be bewildered, not recognising their discipline's progress—save the economists, who would pick up right where they left off.

What you will see, in the language of this book, is that Keen is pointing at the relevance to the reality that they shape of developmental stages of individuals and professional groups. Many professional groups have too many people who still derive their sense of self-identity and self-esteem from their expertise and their belonging to a community of similar experts. This is a barrier to addressing our global challenges when the expertise is well past its sell-by date. In this book, for obvious reasons, I will write about economics and business professionals, but it is equally applicable to all professions.

Many of you are reading this book precisely because you know intuitively that something is as fundamentally wrong with our economy and economics as once was wrong with flat-earth navigation theory. The fact that we have a climate emergency, and all the other injustices is, I believe, overwhelmingly conclusive evidence.

Just as physicists and artists realised a century ago that classical art and physics could never do the job, but rather a radical transcend-and-include revolution was needed, so too is it time to make a radical shift to what comes next, after neoclassical economics and current business practices.

In economics and business, practitioners continue to use single lenses, often anchored in the classical reality of the 19th century. Often without hard data to evidence that their lens is valid today, just assuming that since it once worked in one context, it will always work in today's contexts.

In Chapter 5, I paint a picture of the Economy of the Free, an economy that I believe will work for you, and all life on our planet. Then you can read how we will build one with the building blocks of the Adaptive Organisation covered in Part IV, including the Adaptive Way covered in Part III.

Using the philosophy of Ubuntu as one of a number of different lenses for economics and business, practitioners can help us find our way to get better at describing our economy.

Because it is an element of human life, business and our economy is emergent and inherently nebulous. It emerges from the highly interconnected, path-dependent, intangible essence of human life. Using this lens to look at our economy you see the rationality in those decisions that neoclassical economics considers irrational. One reason why much in economics is now failing to do the job we need lies in its failing to build off the very interconnected, path-dependent, meaning-making, story-dependent essence of what a human being is.

I believe that a crucial part of the regenerative economy we need is the inclusion of all stakeholders directly in the governance of, and sharing the wealth generated by, our business. This means that companies themselves can no longer be deemed property of the investor, but, like all human legal persons, are fully free. Which makes the crucial difference between the current free economy, and the Economy of the Free.

Inspired by the Ubuntu "I am because you are", and everything else we cover in this book, we close Part II with a concept that we hope will provoke the development of an approach to *what we can say about economies* that integrates everything valid across the full breadth of today's complementary approaches. Taking general relativity as a metaphor, I propose a geometric approach to economics, which I suggest could be named a general theory of economies.

By the end of the book, you will have read everything that should help you to make a difference to the crises we are facing. Everything that is useful for you to develop the adaptive capacity in yourself, your organisation, and your economy to rise to the adaptive challenges at your doorstep.

Keep in mind what we wrote in the preface: read the parts in whichever order best fits you and your needs.

1.8 Hope

A good example of working with emergence, that delivered far more success than I (Graham) or anyone else had any reason to hope for, was the process of transforming South Africa into an all-stakeholder democracy. Yes, much still needs to be done, and there is much to be criticised; South Africa has fallen short of the vision. Yet looking at the emergent context in the late 1980s and 1990s, the process succeeded spectacularly compared to all probable outcomes.

The Mont Fleur meetings[27], near Cape Town, were critical in developing the adaptive capacity (multiple lenses, accurate maps, dialogue, pluralism, and Stage 4 and 5 meaning-making in individuals and organisations) needed to develop a viable route to a post-apartheid South Africa. Key players from all groups, each initially following their own strategy to build a viable future, came together. Through emergent dialogue they fully grasped the consequences of each other's meaning-making stories, and the reality these stories were creating. Each group clearly understood that each strategy offered elements:

- needed in the desired future South Africa; and

- potentially sabotaging the journey to this desired new South Africa.

The dialogue shifted from 'us vs. them' to integrating the unique value of each, recognising the inherent oneness of all. Everyone actively listened with empathy, learning to use each other's lenses and meaning-making stories. the dialogue process then spread across the country, engaging people from every walk of life with much-needed empathy, based on multiple maps and lenses.

Compared to the lack of such dialogue in many of today's leaders, the maturity of the South African leaders then is obvious. Today you often see people splitting into opposing camps, unable (or unwilling) to understand the other, let alone dialogue, or even appreciate what is valuable in each other's uniqueness. If South Africa had insisted then on simplistic right versus wrong according to whichever lens the most powerful person used, a viable transition would have never occurred. The only viable transition is one that works for almost everyone, and that hears every perspective.

The South African experience suggests five key ingredients for any successful adaptive strategy fit for our emergent reality filled with adaptive challenges.

- Recognise that the inherent, irreducible contradictions in your reality are real, not an artifact of right or wrong perspectives; and so all lenses must be used simultaneously to see all contradictions.

- Realise the inherent impossibility of knowing all qualitative and quantitative aspects in advance.

- Develop emergent capacities in individuals and organisations, along with the requisite structures and processes; only then can we have emergent dialogue.

- Accept that your meaning-making stories shape or even create the reality that you experience. Learn how to change your stories to change the reality you experience.

- It's up to you to act, especially to build something new that works better than the old.

The emergent Mont Fleur dialogue succeeded in South Africa, because everyone realised that pure competition between the parties would lead to a South Africa none of them wanted; but the right mix of collaboration and competition could. Section 6.5 reproduces this in the context of business to show how our economy can have at least 1,000 times more power to reverse our headlong rush into a climate catastrophe, maybe even 1,000,000 times more, if we incorporate in a multistakeholder collaborative way, such as the FairShares Commons described in this book.

This is why I (Jack and Graham) wrote this book. There are still emergent ways of turning planet Earth around, despite the growing fatalistic despair. We just cannot see them from where we are now, using the lenses we currently have.

CHAPTER 2

Stories, lenses and maps

Reality is merely an illusion, albeit a very persistent one.
—Albert Einstein

You do not see things as they are, you see things as you are.
—Anonymous[1].

2.1 Asking questions

When my (Jack) kids were younger I told them that there was no such thing as a stupid question; that the only wrong question was the one not asked. But now I realise that there can be wrong questions, or at least harmful questions, because questions are fateful: they determine where you start, where you look, and where you end, if you end at all. In a way each question already includes its answer.

Far too many in today's world dogmatically believe that they know the right answer. That the only issue is not implementing that one answer well enough.

However, effectively addressing the challenges we face today can only be done by creating generative dialogue including multiple answers across all relevant disciplines, perspectives, and groups of people. Even more valuable than answers and

---

[1]This has been attributed to so many different people the origin is best referenced as anonymous

knowledge of historical answers to historical questions[2] is the capacity to ask generative questions.

So you can also see that, rather than being about right or wrong, questions should be more about generating new understanding, ones that neither entrench your current understanding, nor create misunderstanding.

The word 'mu' (Japanese, Korean) or 'wu' (Chinese), is often used in zen to say: *please un-ask the question because it takes you away from understanding*. You can only know a viable question when you realise that the answers point in the wrong direction.

Truly powerful questions are generative: they lead you to more answers and more questions in unexpected ways.

For example, each time Ernest Rutherford asked *where is the electron?* he got a different answer. This told him clearly that something was fundamentally wrong with classical mechanics. Eventually he began questioning the question, realising that asking *where is the electron* prevented him from seeing and understanding the true nature of an electron: it has no place.

If you have been asking questions, and none of the answers have worked, maybe you are in the same place as Rutherford. These could be questions like: how do we regulate business, or fix the banks. I believe that questions like these are taking us further away from understanding what the root causes actually are, and how to build a system that works for all of us and for our planet.

Every question assumes that some class of answers exists. For example, Rutherford's question assumed that the concept of position had meaning and that an answer existed. It's a very rare question that is both useful and assumes nothing. Even the very broad question, *how can we build an economy that works*, often assumes human society as it is now.

In the language of Chapter 9, specifically thought form C6, every question is based on some frame of reference. If the frame of reference is valid, you might get useful answers to the question, but if the entire frame of reference is invalid, then the question as a whole is invalid, and no answers to the question can have any connection with actuality—except by coincidence. Which is why I emphasize in this book the importance of uncovering the frames of reference you are using. The more fluid you are in all 28 thought forms of Chapter 9, the better and faster you

---

[2] I realise that this statement itself, is me claiming dogmatically that I know the right answer. As you read the rest of this section, maybe you will be the person who can point out to me why I am wrong, and convince me that questioning and generative dialogue are irrelevant. Which I guess then means that we are in a generative dialogue, and I'm right! We are back to complementary pairs, and two opposite statements being simultaneously true.

can see what is missing in how you are making sense of actuality.

Of course, you might also be using the wrong technique or tool to answer the question. Perhaps you are measuring the height of a wall, but the tape measure you are using is itself 10cm longer at midday at 35°C compared to early in the morning when the temperature is 15°C, giving you useless answers without your realising it.

However, this is easier to deal with. The underlying question itself is a valid question to be asking, and calibrating your tools and techniques will quickly lead you to realise that you need to use a tape measure that stays the same length at all temperatures.

Harder for all of us, and for both of us writing this book: we knew something was wrong with the economy and business design, but we cannot be sure if even the questions are helpful. For Jack and Graham, given the probably outdated and myopic, disciplined-based lenses we were each using, we both needed the other's lenses.

The questions you ask, and how / what answer you hear, are created by the lenses you use. Which means that there are always inherent limits to what you know, and can know. Just as in quantum physics.

2.2 Lenses

Because the first seven years of my (Graham's) working career was in theoretical high-temperature particle physics, I have looked at everything I've touched since then through the lenses of a particle physicist. For example, I am always asking myself how the final performance of an entire business can be improved by working on the smallest particles that make up that business and their interactions.

If you want to dive deeper into why the economy is failing, what it should be, and what's needed in our toolkit to get there, you have to know which lenses you are using and how they shape what you see. You also need to know which lenses others are using, and how they shape what they see, and you then need to make a judgement call about which lenses you could use.

By shape I mean that lenses always distort actuality, just as the Mercator projection distorts our spherical planet as it creates a flat map.

You also need to actively look for what you don't know you don't know. Which lenses don't you know exist, and so you don't know what you would see through them? Most of us only use the standard lenses of our discipline. The result is that we can fail to see clearly trends that are driving disruptive change.

Our current education paradigm focuses too much on simply transmitting the current canonical thinking in each discipline, rather than how to think for yourself, how to ask questions, how to validate your answers against actuality, and how to defend against your own cognitive biases. This leads to those whom Nassim Taleb[28] labels *Intellectual Yet Idiot* or *IYI*.

One reason why you imagine that a single lens is enough is because you trust your memories and your knowledge. But your mind changes the past you remember, and constantly reshapes what you know, because it fails to remember what actually was[29,30]. You only remember the last time you remembered. So your knowledge, and your memory of the past, constantly changes, being reconstructed by your minds. Like space interacting with an electron, your mind is far from an inert canvas remembering accurately what was; far more it creates your memory—a reshaped version of what was.

Any lens distorts when it does its job. It needs to hide some things so that you can see others more clearly. The distortion is even greater when you attempt to communicate what you see through your lens to another, who can only interpret through their own lens. So first you have to agree on a lens or lenses, before you can discuss what you see, let alone agree.

For example, when Picasso attempted to capture the essence of a horse (seen through his lenses) on a single canvas, few people were able to see what he saw as the essence of horseness. You do your best to represent the essence you see through a concrete medium, as with these concrete words on paper, knowing that different people will interpret a different form.

So there is an inherent challenge in finding lenses good enough for the actuality you are dealing with.

If you have spent time in physics and art over the past century, you will know that seeing actuality in the form of complementary pairs is the starting point of modern physics. Quantum physics depends on using a multiplicity of conflicting lenses to get a handle of complementary pairs. You see some examples in Table 2.1.

One consequence of shifting from "either / or" questions to "and" questions is that you shift to a broader view. Instead of looking for which complementary pair is right and which one is wrong, you look at the pairs as an integration of opposites.

The observer is central to creating the reality that the observer experiences. So if you are the CEO of your company, and you subscribe to the idea that an organisation is a machine, when you look at your organisation you will see a machine, and build a machine. Equally, if you look at your organisation as a complex adaptive system, you will build a complex adaptive system. All the books by a pioneer in applying these concepts to leadership and business, Margaret Wheatley, are well worth reading[31,32].

However, two more factors are important in determining the results that your

Tangible	Intangible
Observed	Observer
Particle	Wave
Entity	Interactions
Position	Momentum
Duration	Energy
Painter	Viewer
Perspective	Complementary perspective(s)

Table 2.1: Inherent, irreducible complementarity in quantum mechanics and cubism. Both columns, and the integration of each pair into a new transcending concept are equally and irreducibly real and needed in order to make sense of what is going on.

organisation actually delivers. First, you are not the only observer creating the reality of your organisation. Every person who touches your organisation is an observer, and shapes its reality across whatever scale they touch.

Second, you can only shape the reality of your business within the boundaries that your business offers you. If your business is more than just a machine, or more than just a complex adaptive system, you will end up with something that has a hidden nature that you are blind to. Your business will deliver results that you did not expect, do not see where they came from, and cannot reliably reproduce.

As you read in Chapter 1, when physicists recognised that they were seeing unexpected results, and could neither see where they had come from, nor reliably reproduce them, they realised that the fundamental paradigms of classical mechanics (nature as a machine) were simply not fit for purpose in the realm of the very small and the very large.

And so quantum physics was born.

Physicists had to abandon the simplistic notion that particles, waves, and the forces between them were in any sense independent building blocks of reality. They had to become comfortable with the inescapable fact that all particles were waves, and all waves were particles. There was no way of disentangling the two. Everything was inherently both.

This led to their realisation that thinking of particles and their interactions as two distinct things was equally flawed—instead, particles and their interactions were, in some deeper sense, one and the same thing. This extended concepts prevalent in many philosophies and religions around the world[33] to fundamental physics, bringing a new depth of useful understanding and precision to what physics can say about actuality.

In classical physics, the particle is primary, and it creates its interactions with its neighbouring particles. Quantum physics turns that on its head. In many cases it was a more helpful starting point to regard the interactions as primary, where the interactions themselves pulled the particles into existence.

As you will see in this book, you will get a far better handle on how to deliver the results your organisation expects from you, and that you are accountable for getting your organisation to deliver, by seeing both the interactions between the people in your organisation and the people in your organisation as equally foundational and independent. The interactions between people create the nature of how each person shows up, at least as much as the individuals and their nature create the interactions between them. Given the nature of the challenges we face today, we find it helpful to regard the interactions as having more power to shape the people than vice versa.

Particles	Interaction
Investor	Votes and dialogue
Staff	Dialogue, positional power, strikes
External stakeholders	Dialogue, law, money, reputation
Organisation as a machine	Organisation as a living being
Rules and policy	Culture

Table 2.2: Inherent, irreducible complementarity in business.

What would we get if we applied this thinking to your business? If the interaction has characteristics that are predefined, and that call into existence the nature of the particles that interact, what are these pairs? How does the predefined type of interaction create the very reality that the particles experience?

Investing shareholders interact in a very narrow and defined way. They typically interact within the constraints of a general meeting, often through the medium of exercising a yes / no vote. Sometimes it's done through dialogue in pairs, or small groups. More often it's done simply by listening to whoever is addressing the shareholders, one to many.

Staff interact mainly through dialogue and hierarchical layers. The patterns of hierarchical power and many the patterns of dialogue are predefined and exist independently of any individual member of staff. This is similar for all external stakeholders, as summarised in Table 2.2.

So if you look at an organisation as a classical physicist would, as if particles were primary and created the interactions, you will get surprising results, would not see where they came from, and would not know how to reliably reproduce the desired and suppress the undesired results.

One final thought on complementary pairs. All three perspectives (the duality of each components' uniqueness and difference; and their non-dual oneness) are an inherent and necessary part of how the world works. If you only had the pair's non-duality as one, you lose all the power that comes from each in their uniqueness, and if you only have each as an either / or uniqueness, you lose everything that you get with the duality.

2.3 Maps

Your maps go together with your lenses. You use a map to simplify actuality so that you can get from A to B without overwhelming yourself with irrelevant detail. Just as lenses hide and distort most of actuality, so too do maps. Choose a map that hides what is irrelevant, so that what is relevant can be seen clearly, and you can navigate well to your desired destination. Choose a map that hides or distorts what is relevant, and you will get lost.

A superb example is the map of the London tube. Early on, it showed each station in a faithful representation of its position on the surface of London. After a while, with lots of people struggling to use those maps, it became clear to Harry Beck in 1933 that knowing exactly where each tube station was, was irrelevant information. What was relevant was being able to clearly see the connectivity between lines and stations in order to figure out which combination of lines connected where you were to where you needed to be.

This map of connectivity is now standard around the world for many transport maps. Like many disruptive innovations that challenged the lenses and maps of the era, Harry's connectivity map was regarded by the authorities of the time as way too radical. But because normal people found it enormously useful, it took hold and became the global standard.

Maps that work in a predictive context fail miserably in an emergent context, because they hide the very information you need to thrive with emergence. An emergent map is like a probability field in physics, or a painting by Picasso. It tells you about all the categories of outcomes; it describes different scenarios, without attempting to pin down any details. The map itself changes depending on who is using it; it's not absolute in itself, you shape it because it's you using it, rather than somebody else.

Such emergent maps were used in South Africa to navigate the country out of apartheid. They were used at each decision to inform a judgement call. Everyone knew that no choice could ever be right, since the transition was emergent, not predictive—right could only be known long afterwards. But an emergent map is still useful, because it gives guidance on which choices open up more potential for emergence, and therefore options for thriving; and which choices shut them down.

One good example of how long it might take to know if an outcome was good or bad is illustrated by the quote from the then Chinese president Zhou Enlai. His words in 1972 *"it is too early to tell"*, when asked by the then French president Mitterand whether he thought the revolution was good or bad, are usually believed to refer to the French Revolution that started in 1789, and fit perfectly to it. However, he was referring to the student revolution of 1968, only four years previously.

You use mental maps, constructed in your past, to help you understand what you are seeing now and to make choices. No single map can be absolutely right in all contexts, at all times, everywhere; nor is there a privileged frame of reference.

Most intractable arguments in families, business, and politics happen when you fail to realise that each of you is using different maps and lenses. For example, those voting in the Brexit referendum for the UK to leave the EU thought that they had made the best decision, based on their lenses and maps; while those voting to remain thought that they were making the best decision. No discussion on whether Brexit is a wise or unwise choice can happen without first comparing maps with each other, and discussing what the maps are saying, what they are highlighting and what they are hiding, and getting to shared clarity on what is actually relevant to the binary choice of in or out.

That map check made a huge difference in the path South Africa followed into its post-apartheid future.

You can only make progress if you see clearly which maps and lenses each person is using, and then compare them, knowing that there is no privileged perspective or frame of reference. How relevant is each? What is missing? What is useful?

You cannot not use maps and lenses. The best you can do is recognise which ones you are using, and shift the dialogue, or argument, to focus on them all, not just the consequences of a specific map or lens.

The lens is a tool to generate an inner perspective that is useful. After you've looked at something through a lens, and perhaps compared it to one of your internal maps, maybe by evaluating what you are seeing as good or bad, helpful or harmful, or somewhere in between, you end up having a perspective.

Using multiple lenses and multiple maps enables you to have multiple perspectives. In today's nebulous, emergent reality, you can often only grasp what is actually happening and make wise choices if you use multiple perspectives—even if those perspectives seem to conflict or even exclude each other.

This was the big lesson that physicists and artists needed to learn a century ago: contradictory perspectives might all be needed to grasp what is actually happening. Which is why mining and refining conflict is such a vital capacity today. I (Graham) experienced this travelling through the Alps to an internal meeting, which gave me more capacity to mine and refine the conflicts we had in the meeting.

I imagine you've been told, as often as I have, to get a perspective. A year ago I was on my way to an internal Evolutesix off-site strategy meeting, and I had my suspicion that during the two-week period we would experience internal conflict. In Evolutesix we look at conflict through the lens of developmental value. We see conflict as the most valuable resource that an individual or organisation has to understand where meaning-making stories fit their context and needs.

Using the best dialogue tools available to mine and refine this conflict, we can get at the gold nuggets we need to adapt ourselves and our organisations to stay at the maximum fit between who we are and the challenges we are facing. For this to work, though, we need to have the conflict in perspective. This means that we have the most objective yardstick we can find to compare the conflict to, and decide whether the conflict is small, medium, or big.

So I decided to travel down to the meeting over a couple of days by motorbike through the Austrian Alps. I knew that spending a few days in the middle of nature, surrounded by some of Europe's highest mountains, would make sure that my frame of reference lay in mountains that stayed unchanged across generations.

I got even more perspective than I had bargained for. First, early in the morning on the first day of my journey, the front bearings of my motorbike collapsed. I managed to coax the bike to the next village, where I stopped and waited for rescue. That evening I was back in Brussels, figuring out what to do. I also realised how extremely lucky I was. The bearings could easily have gone a thousand kilometres later in the middle of an Alpine pass, steeply banked over, and under heavy braking because of a rock fall on the exit to a hairpin bend. Instead, it happened whilst I was riding slowly enjoying the scenery approaching the Luxemburg border.

The second perspective was deciding anyway to travel by car, and simply do in one day what I had planned to do over two days. A very wise decision, because the second unexpected perspective that I got was visiting a glacier in the Alps. Driving up the valley I passed a sign in the middle of verdant vegetation marking where the glacier's snout had been when the valley was first explored in the mid-1800s. I continued to drive up the valley, going up hundreds of metres and about 20km further along before I reached the current edge of the glacier. Seeing myself as incredibly lucky, looking at how the Alps in total have barely changed across hundreds of human generations, and yet how rapidly climate change is melting the Alpine ice, meant that I compared whatever conflict I was experiencing during our meeting to the frames of reference of these two perspectives. That helped me see that whatever was happening in the moment in that meeting, it was insignificant compared to our environmental crises.

2.4 Meaning-making stories

Pablo Picasso recognised the power that stories have in shaping or even creating the reality that you experience. His whole life revolved around the power of his stories, and harnessing the power of stories to make a difference in the world.

Picasso rejected using his father's name, and instead took his mother's. He realised early on that the name he had been using carried with it the story his father lived by. He rejected his father's story of not ruffling anybody's feathers, as he saw that this story had shaped his father's reality as a mediocre artist. Picasso wanted to stand out, to make a difference, and his story centred on taking risks to do so.

Throughout this book, you will gain understanding of the central role stories play.

I don't mean trivial stories, the kind of detective or fantasy story that you read for entertainment. What I mean are the deep stories that you use to work out what everything means. In the example above, Picasso's father shaped his life around a story of harm if he stood out, if he ruffled anybody's feathers. Picasso shaped his reality with a very different story: that if he failed to ruffle feathers he would fail to make a difference in the world, then he would fail to reach the pinnacle of art that was in him, and that meant he would be a failure.

Meaning-making stories, which we introduced in the last chapter, are distinct to stories. Most of your meaning-making stories are so deeply hidden that you are not even aware that they're there. You are still using them, though, to give meaning to yourself, to others, and to what you experience.

I (Graham) was out hiking alone, taking a break from writing this book, when a slippery rock took me down crossing a stream about a kilometre from Granny Dot's (where we were staying). I crashed onto my right hip, twisting it and bruising my hip muscles. Getting home was painful, and it took well over two weeks before I could even get dressed without sitting down or supporting myself, let alone continuing the long, productive walks with Jack.

One of my meaning-making stories, creating the reality I experienced, was how unlucky I was to have fallen, anger at my carelessness and sad that I could no longer go for a strenuous walk every day to clear my brain and write more creatively and effectively. When that meaning-making story was active and telling me what falling meant, I felt sad, less motivated, and was less able to write well. More than the pain of sitting brought physically.

Another meaning-making story active in me was just how lucky a person I am. Even though I'm in my mid-50s writing this book, I'm still physically fit, and I'm still able to hike long distances, compared to some of my schoolmates who have already passed away or lost some of their fitness. I could so easily have broken a leg, or done myself a permanent damage. Enormously lucky.

The third meaning-making story active in me was that this fall had come about because I had been paying too much attention to meaning-making stories around what other people might think if I didn't get back by the time I had said I would. So I was hurrying, paying less attention than I normally do, in part because I'd already stepped on this rock going the other way 90 minutes previously. This meta-story I was using to chip away at some of these older stories that have been running my life, telling me what I should do, and what it means if I fail to do so.

Meaning-making stories are quite different to stories of something. I can tell you a story, and the story I tell is all that it is at the time. Meaning-making stories are the hidden templates you use to create the reality you experience, by giving meaning to the small part of actuality you are aware of. They are deeply hidden; you are unaware of most of them. So you are subject to them, almost a victim of them, blindly accepting them as actuality because you have no idea they are creating your experienced reality.

The purpose of meaning-making stories is to generate your experienced reality out of an actuality that can have inherent meaning, or not.

Your meaning-making stories can be anywhere from a pure fiction, leading to your experienced reality being castles in the sky, or just shapes you see in the clouds, through to 100% anchored in actuality, leading to your experienced reality being identical to actuality. This book shows you the best approaches we know of to become steadily more aware of where and when the meaning-making stories creating your experienced reality have no grounding in actuality, and how to adjust them so that they become ever more grounded in it. Less fantasy and more real. Actuality always has far more potential than the reality you experience.

> I'm sitting on the edge of the tree-covered valley, with a constant stream of white butterflies fluttering from right to left across the entire 50km depth between me and the distant, hazy blue mountains.
> I think, what if my meaning-making story creating my reality tells me I'm a butterfly? Is that helpful or harmful?
> It is entirely dependent on the actuality I'm embedded in, and what I do with it. If I am on the edge of a mountain, and leap off expecting to be able to flutter across the valley to the other side, the gap between my meaning-making story and actuality will lead to a painful fall, broken bones, and possibly death.
> However, for Muhammed Ali, the meaning-making story of floating like a butterfly and stinging like a bee is grounded in actuality and leads to success.

Meaning-making stories are the central theme of this book because they shape all scales, from the global economy to the smallest aspects of your life. And so are the biggest barriers we all face in rising to the adaptive challenges in our lives. They're the biggest barrier we all face in rising to the adaptive challenges of our climate emergency and the 17 SDGs. If your stories don't have any place in them for your challenges, you cannot accept them. If your stories lack any place in them for a decision or an action, you will never make that decision, nor take that action. And if that decision or action happens to be essential for you to thrive, your story is a threat to you.

This book is about recognising your stories, and mastering the skills of enabling your stories to rewrite themselves. You cannot rewrite them directly by using thought alone; they have a life of their own, just as in a book I (Graham) love, the *Never Ending Story*[34] by Michael Ende.

But what you can do is deliberately create experiences for yourself that trigger your stories to rewrite themselves.

2.5 Reality vs. Actuality

Quantum physics is clear: when you look at an electron, what you *see* and can *say* about it is not the same as what it *is*. What you see and can say is reality; what it is, is actuality.

The reality you experience is the model of actuality you create inside your awareness. You never experience what *is*, only your inner experienced *story* about what is. There are a number of aspects of how you construct your inner model which mean that everything you experience is a distorted part of everything that actually is. The better you know your meaning-making story *about* what is, the closer you can bring your internally experienced reality to what actually *is*, by iteratively adjusting your meaning-making.

Part of the gap between your inner experienced reality, and what actually is, lies in your neurobiology. The physical lenses you use, your eyes, ears, touch, smell, and taste all amplify a small fraction of everything around you, taking in nothing of the rest. If you had the eyes of a cat, you would take in a very different slice of actuality, and even if the rest of you were the same, you would construct a very different inner reality.

For example, you are physically blind 15% of the day. (This is also a metaphor for the intangible themes of this book.) When you're driving, crossing the road, or doing anything else that may have very fast potential surprises, 15% of the time your eye is not transmitting anything into your brain. Your eye constantly jumps between focusing on one thing to focusing on another. Between every jump, your eye shuts down so that you are not permanently nauseous the way you are if you watch a flickering movie for too long. But anything that happens during those jumps you physically cannot see.

In addition, the way that your vision works is not at all like a camera. Your eye does not simply take in a constant stream of images and pass them on to the brain for processing. Your eye receives from the brain the hypothesis image that the brain expects to see based on its current model, i.e. your current inner reality. All your brain gets from the eye is the small amount of data telling it where its model differs from the data that the eye is actually receiving. So all you are getting is information that inner reality is different to external actuality.

Then, just to make things a bit worse, you are actually living in the past. Between all your different senses, including ones that may come from your intuition, it takes your brain about half a second to process all the information and update your inner reality model. So by the time that you are fully conscious of your constructed reality, it's half a second out of date.

If something happens that threatens you in less than half a second, say a very loud and unexpected noise, your subconscious brain gets you moving a few tenths of a second before you are aware that you are running. Of course, if you're on the starting blocks of a sprint, your brain has already included a starting pistol and that you will be running in its future projection of your inner reality. So everything gets smoothed out and you experience a continuously unfolding reality.

The reality you experience is an inner model, constantly updated based on the input from your senses, but this input is already distorted and biased by the previous iteration of your inner model. It's never completely unbiased, unfiltered raw data.

Be on your guard against the charismatic or glamorous playing games with your inner reality to benefit themselves. Especially anyone undermining your awareness of the power you have. For yourself, and those you care about, certainly; and because we need all of our power to rebuild a better world. Use this book, especially the chapters of Part III, to resiliently anchor your inner reality in what actually is.

The character Magrat Garlick, in *Lord and Ladies*[35] puts it well when she describes the inner reality people construct when elves (the Lords and Ladies) project their desired reality and glamour into people:

> *We'll never be as free as them, as beautiful as them, as clever as them, as light as them; we are animals ... What they take is everything ... What they give is fear.*

As Granny Weatherwax puts it in the same book, even though we are strong and they are weak, what they project makes us believe the opposite.

Your reality is completely inside you. But, you certainly do not have the freedom to experience any reality. You cannot simply make it what you wanted to be. Not even in your dreams, weird because your brain is constantly constructing an inner reality that it can believe in, but in the absence of any actual data from your senses to ground and calibrated. Even then, you can only dream based on the possibilities that your brain is equipped for, by neurobiology and your past experiences.

Before you are born, your neurophysiology is pretty much unformed potential, out of the differentiation that your genes have brought in. Then your senses and your brain begin to change based on the reality you experience, which depends on the meaning-making stories of your parents and anyone else interacting with you in your early childhood. These stories shape the patterns that you look for when you're looking at something, shaping which sounds you can hear clearly and speak clearly, and much more.

Hopefully from this you can see why this book is so focused on stories. The only reality you can ever experience is your inner story now. Your inner reality is shaped by your entire history of experienced inner reality, not just in terms of the distilled memories that you use to attribute the meaning and shape your inner reality, but also in the very neurobiological hardware that you are using. Sadly, your inner reality cannot be anything you want. You are constrained to experience an inner reality within boundaries.

So if anybody tries to criticise you and your grasp of reality, all they're really saying is that *your* grasp of *their* inner reality is weak. Well, that's cool, there's no way you ever could truly grasp anyone else's inner reality. In fact, it has become quite clear that you experience your own, unique, individual reality because the combined effect of your brain, your senses, your nervous system, your forms of thought, your meaning-making stories, your entire life path to now, expectations of the future, and much more, is as unique to you as your fingerprint is[14].

Look at the meaning of what happens in your life as a complementary pair of any inherent meaning and the meaning made by your meaning-making stories. Sometimes it's purely one, at other times purely the other, and then again a mix of both together. This brings together the two mutually exclusive worldviews[36].

Eternalism: everything that is and happens has intrinsic meaning, determined by some divine plan or cosmic inevitability.

Nihilism: nothing that is or happens has any intrinsic meaning, all meaning is created by ourselves.

Bring them together into one complementary pair named meaningness, and the mutual validity of both sets of worldviews becomes visible.

2.6 Your chimp, human and computer systems

Steve Peters in his book *The Chimp Paradox*[37] describes your mind as having three systems: chimp, human, and computer.

Chimp. Your inner chimp system always wants more, takes in a limited slice of the world, and interprets it through the reactive meaning-making stories it began learning in the first couple of years of your life. Your inner chimp then tries to take control of you through feeding your emotional stories through to your computer. It's also called your limbic brain.

Human. Your human system only begins after the age of two, when your hardware has developed enough. Your human system tries to act rationally, look at the facts, and makes meaning of them through stories you have internalised.

Computer. The computer system is your library of stories and behaviours. Both the chimp and human systems consult the library, pull out the stories and behaviours they each think is best for you, and then fight with each other to drive your behaviours.

The rest of this book is all about getting more books and behaviours into your library, your organisation's library, and our economy's library.

When we do this well, we have a huge edge over all other species in creating an environment in which each of us can thrive, because it gives us the ability to predict what will happen decades into the future, and prepare for it. It gives us the ability to prepare today for the drought that is likely to come sometime in the next 10 years.

However, prediction alone is not enough. We need to find ways of bringing all our human systems together so that we can act on our predictions. That our human activities were certain to generate climate change, and a climate emergency if we failed to change our behaviour in time, was already clear by the 1980s.

If you listen carefully to what someone is saying, you can sometimes hear the different systems showing up in and between their words. I had the privilege of sitting next to, and chatting with, a wise South African, Sheila Sisulu, former ambassador to the US, in London in 2009 at a meeting preparing perspectives for the G20. We started talking about how she was listening to the politician currently speaking, and advised me: *"Listen to the unspoken subtext. Between the words used, he's saying 'bla-bla-bla we don't understand what's happening, we don't know what to do.'"*

I listened to the subtexts, heard a very different message to the one in the words, and have never stopped listening for what is really being said.

2.7 Cargo Cults

During the Second World War, the military built airfields on a number of the South Sea Islands. Streams of aeroplanes flew in with their holds full of useful goodies, flew out again empty, and returned with more cargo. After the war ended, most of these airfields were dismantled completely. The equipment was removed, the personnel left, and the aeroplanes full of useful goodies stopped coming.

The islanders missed their share of the useful goodies. They asked themselves what they needed to do or be for the aeroplanes to come back with their holds full of them. So they repaired what was left of the airfields, or cleaned out long stretches of land to look like them. They lit fires along the airfields, built wooden huts that looked like control towers, and had someone sit in the wooden hut wearing a shaped piece of wood on either side of his head with sticks of bamboo poking out the top like a headset.

It looked to them as if they were doing everything that the military had been doing. Whilst they were doing the visible rituals, they had none of the hidden engines, and none of the underlying worldview and paradigms. They could not know that these hidden engines mattered, not the irrelevant visible rituals.

The physicist Richard Feynman used this *Cargo Cult* as a story[38,39] to show the difference between real science and scientism. In scientism people do the visible behaviours of a scientist, but without the underlying engine that makes science work. This engine is: using intuition very strongly to imagine how the world might work, and what you might be able to say about it; and then brutally doing all you can to rip your ideas and everybody else's ideas to pieces.

Ideas that survive long enough become evidence-based theories, or clarity on what we can, with confidence, say about how the world works.

Too much of what you will find in today's self-help, business studies, economics, and much more is scientism. You can read more about this in the excellent book *Overshoot*[40]. Protect yourself against the disasters that follow the fake hope cargo cults lead to. Stay sceptical. Stay empirical.

There is one very good way to tell whether what you are seeing and believing is coming purely out of an internally generated reality anchored in your biases (Section 10.5) and other meaning-making stories, or if it has a sufficient basis in how the world actually works.

This is the brutal process that scientists have developed to counteract, as best as is humanly possible, situations where our self-deception tendency might lead us to build bridges that collapse in the first strong wind. Like the bridge built across the Tacoma Narrows in Washington, where the engineers failed to take into account that the wind would play it like a guitar string until it vibrated itself to pieces.

Empiricism, or the scientific process, is far more than just collecting evidence, it is the brutal adherence to three key elements.

1. Letting go of what you believe you know to be true, so that you can follow all kinds of crazy ideas to their conclusion. Like Einstein letting go of what everyone knew to be true: gravity is a force; and then seeing where that took him.

2. Actively disconnecting your self-worth from old meaning-making stories and your biases. From being seen as right, or a need to be seen to follow the

norms. Even the most brilliant scientists struggle at times with this one, which also requires rigorous adherence to the third principle.

3. Always focus on finding evidence to prove something false, never look for evidence to prove something true. Because you never can prove something in actuality to be true. The best you can ever do is fail to find instances where you can prove it false. Everything that has risen in status from model to theory is no more than knowledge under construction, never complete (thought form P5 in Chapter 9).

If you have ever worked in fundamental science and attended a conference between practising scientists, you will have seen how extraordinarily brutal they are to each other when talking about their research. However, they are also enormously kind to each other as human beings. This is how scientists harness conflict to uncover what they can, and cannot, say about deeply hidden aspects of actuality.

Brutal, because everyone wants to prove the other's statements false. But not the other person. We need far more of the above three principles across all our disciplines, including economics. Our human survival depends on us going beyond scientism.

2.8 Harnessing, not managing, conflict

How does your meaning-making, which is created by your meaning-making stories, generate your experience of conflict? Do you then end up feeling anxious, leading you to want to reduce or escape conflict? Or do you feel excited, and want to lean deeper into the conflict?

I (Jack and Graham) developed conflict-avoiding meaning-making stories during the early part of my life, and they are still active in me. I have learnt, though, that conflict is very often simply hard data on a mismatch between my inner reality and actuality, or that someone else has different meaning-making to me, generating a different reality to mine from the same actuality.

In both cases, harnessing that conflict, mining and refining it for the valuable gold it brings on what actually is, is vital for being more effective. I (Jack and Graham) have found our conflict invaluable in creating this book, even when it has been painful in the moment.

If each of us are to rise to the adaptive challenges we are facing, we must get steadily better every day at harnessing, not managing, conflict. The essence of this book is a how-to manual of the state-of-the-art techniques to mining and refining conflict across all six layers of the hierarchy listed below. If you have room to improve in harnessing conflict for growth, this book is for you.

Each layer requires the layers below it to already be working well, in order to reach full effectiveness in a mature stage; and even more so on the change journey towards mature harnessing of conflict or tension. Here is our proposed current best approach in each of these layers:

6 Inter-ecosystem All the layers below, plus the full emergent aspects of open systems in interaction with each other;

5 Inner-ecosystem e.g., The FairShares Commons or similar applied to the whole ecosystem and all companies within it, (see Parts II and IV);

4 Inter-organisational The FairShares Commons or similar incorporation for almost all kinds of entities, except perhaps a pure trust, or a wholly owned subsidiary of a FairShares Commons;

3 Inner-organisational Extensions of sociocracy, Holacracy, and other forms of dynamic organisation design or governance (see Part IV);

2 Inter-personal Interactions between people, culture, etc. all belongs here. The Evolutesix Adaptive Way for teams, covered in Part IV, does this well;

1 Inner-personal Who I am, my inner voices and motivations, meaning-making etc. The Evolutesix Adaptive Way for individuals, in Part III, does this well.

Each successive layer encompasses the full complexity of the layers below, and adds more of its own. For example, think of yourself. At layer 1, you have all the complexity of who you are, all the different voices telling you who to be and what to do for whom. At layer 2, with just two people, you have all that for two people and your relationship. And so on up to the level 6 level, the interaction between huge ecosystems that contain thousands of people and hundreds of businesses.

But, no level is more important than any other level; and actually level 1, who you are, was shaped by the level 6 you and your ancestors have been in. So really it's also a circle ...

Effectiveness at each level depends on how well generative conflict is harnessed. The Evolutesix Adaptive Way is designed to harness conflict, to the extent that we even have a pattern called Tiggering[3], which is about deliberately creating conflict when there is too little. Of course, this is always done with mutual compassion for the other and only by invitation!

Harnessing conflict is critical in business, especially startups. 65% of startup failures are caused by conflict or tensions between the co-founders[41]. We are in the mess we're in because we humans are so poor at harnessing conflict generatively.

---

[3]I (Graham) even have a sticker of Tigger, from Winnie the Pooh, on my computer as a reminder.

Only managing or avoiding conflict limits our ability to grow and transform the thinking we have today, to get what we need to thrive tomorrow.

If we can mine and refine the critical conflicts today between different disciplines, or paradigms in each discipline, we have a chance of escaping Planck's Principle. Max Planck, a pioneer in quantum physics, wrote *A great scientific truth does not triumph by convincing its opponents and making them see the light, but rather because its opponents eventually die, and a new generation grows up familiar with it.*

2.9 Boundaries

Boundaries are very relevant to all the sections of this book. We need boundaries to have clarity on what is unique about each individual entity, from the planet's boundaries making Earth the uniquely life-supporting planet that it is, down to the cell walls defining the unique identity of each of your cells.

If your cells did not have a clear wall defining what is inside and what is outside the cell, you could not be a functional human being; instead, you would still be a large puddle of primordial soup. However, if your cell walls were 100% solid boundaries, you would be a completely inert dead statue. What makes you a thriving, living organism, is the dynamic interplay between what is inside and outside semipermeable, fuzzy boundaries, at all scales.

We need to construct boundaries in society. Each of us needs to have a self-identity that is uniquely ours. As you will read in Chapter 8, one part of us developing our self-identity is the stage where we construct it by internalising the norms and culture of the group we belong to. At the next scale up, we need to have clearly defined social groups. Social groups emerge when a number of people declare some difference to another group to be the defining characteristic separating one group from the other. This is the basis of most of our isms.

This is also the basis of how we incorporate businesses. Keep in mind that incorporation is a social construct that we have invented to define boundaries between stakeholders. The boundaries between stakeholders defined by a limited company, or a trust, or a cooperative, create different kinds of unique business identity.

Similarly, the boundaries between different disciplines like economics, leadership, and engineering, and the boundaries between different factions within disciplines, are vital for each discipline to develop the unique strength that that discipline can bring to us.

However, every boundary reaches a point where it holds us back and where it's time to recognise that the boundary is semipermeable, or even an illusion that we have constructed to simplify our lives.

Physicists recognised that this is how the world works at a quantum level when they realised that the boundary between the concept of particle and wave was one that nature recognised in some contexts, and was absent in others. That led to seeing particles and waves as complementary pairs which had both an individual uniqueness and a common oneness.

This is also behind the new FairShares Commons incorporation, which represents the common oneness across all stakeholders, whilst retaining just enough of the uniqueness that differentiates stakeholders and each company from other companies in the ecosystem.

As you read this book, keep an eye open for where boundaries in your reality are holding you, your business, and our society back.

2.10 How did we get into this mess?

Napoleon is often reputed to have said that he would rather promote somebody who was naturally lucky; and never to attribute to enemy action anything that he could explain with human incompetence.

Whilst it's only natural to want to blame and punish other people for being evil or criminal, especially the more you feel pain, anxiety, anger, or any other strong emotion, I believe that few of the people who played a role getting us into this mess were inherently bad.

Almost all were not much different to you or me, simply doing what was in front of them to do, without sufficient understanding of the long-term implications of what they were doing, or how related any single action was to everything else that was happening. Simply a collective incompetence that required inhuman superpowers to see clearly in advance.

Add the inevitable random bad luck that always happens, and you have a recipe for the mess we are in.

Getting out of this mess means avoiding repeating the same kind of collective incompetence and fragility in the face of bad luck. One foundation of such fragile sensitivity to bad luck and incompetence lies in focusing on blaming others for what they did in the past, instead of focusing on what we can do now from where we are to build a future we want to have.

Part Two

Economy

These chapters give an overview of how the economy as it is has emerged, and propose ways of reinventing the economy, and creating the one that can rebuild our capacity to thrive: the Economy of the Free. Drawing on apartheid as a metaphor you'll see why our current structuring of companies cannot deliver the economy our society needs, how the FairShares Commons addresses that issue, and how a new approach to economics can address the issues of neoclassical economics.

If you are an investor or a founder, especially if you are expressing your values and beliefs around impact, sutainability, circularity, or regeneration, you will see how to protect your companies continuing to express your intent long after later investors have come in, and even after you are no longer involved.

CHAPTER 3

How do we know our economy?

*Classic economic theory, based as it is on an inadequate
theory of human motivation, could be revolutionised by
accepting the reality of higher human needs, including the
impulse to self-actualisation and the love for the highest
values.*
—*Abraham Maslow*

*If you jump, you might fall on the wrong side of the rope.
But if you are not willing to take the risk of breaking your
neck what good is it? You don't jump at all. You have to
wake people up. To revolutionise their way of identifying
things, you've got to create images they won't accept.*
—*Pablo Picasso*[42]

The economy is not some distant philosophical entity, belonging to somebody else. It is your economy, it's with you wherever you are, awake or asleep, 24 hours a day. Your economy is Ubuntu at a global level. You shape your economy, your economy shapes you, and once you've added it all up, 7.9 billion people are shaping each other through the economy.

When you work, you contribute to production; when you buy or get given products or services, you are contributing directly or indirectly to the flow of goods and services in the economy.

Your economy is nebulous and emergent, changing every time you or anybody else does anything in it. You can understand each part in perfect detail and still have no idea of how it really works. You can only understand the economy as a whole, just as you as a living being can only be understood as a whole. No heart surgeon can ever understand you, no matter how well they understand your physical heart.

Just like in quantum physics, there are always inherently unknowable, emergent areas in the economy.

Also, just as in Picasso's art, many perspectives are needed to understand the economy, even perspectives that appear to be inconsistent with each other. (This is thought form T7 in Chapter 9.) Really understanding the economy requires a high fluidity in all 28 transformational thought forms of Chapter 9.

Your economy starts with stories, not unambiguous facts. It is something that society has invented and given meaning to by bringing the dominant stories to life. So to understand your economy, not only do you need to have fluidity in sense-making through using all 28 transformational thought forms, you need to have a thorough grasp of how individuals, communities, and societies make meaning through stories that they are aware of and unaware of (Chapters7 to 8.)

The statements by a large number of leading economists and change agents on economics and business[43,44] show clearly how our current economic reality has been shaped by a set of stories that we have believed. These stories are now so hidden in our norms of behaviour and in our institutions that we've forgotten where they came from.

Just as physicists learnt a hundred years ago that physics is the study of what we can *say*, not the study of what *is*, so I see economics as the study of what we can *say* about the economy, e.g. how valuable goods and services flow within society from where they are abundant to where they are needed, not what the economy *is*. Central to that is the word "valuable"; value is our stories shaping the reality we experience. Gold, wine, the US dollar, all have value because of the meaning that society attributes to each of them.

3.1 An economy does the job of provisioning

If you need food, housing, medical care, banking services, clean air to breathe, or clean water to drink, you judge your economy to be working when it does the job of providing you with them. Your economy is failing you if it cannot provide you with all the fundamental resources you need to at least survive.

In business, especially in disruptive innovation, you ask what the job is that needs to be done, and what tool will do the job[45]. The job you might need doing is getting an internet connection from your home office, where you work, to your living room, so you can relax in the evenings. One tool to do the job is a long ethernet cable and holes in your wall. And for many years this was the only tool to do the job, until somebody realised that you could dispense with both the holes and the cable by inventing Wi-Fi. (We use 'tool' in this book to mean any way of solving a problem or achieving an outcome.)

The economy is a tool that society has invented to do the job of provisioning.

The economy concretises society's stories, giving more value to some things and less to others. These stories are anchored in our underlying human meaning-making and biases (section 10.5), creating an inherently subjective reality.

Since our economy is a tool we have invented, it can become whatever we need it to be—within the constraints of physics, of course!

The three fundamental building blocks in an economy that we focus on in this chapter are capitals, currencies, and marketplaces.

Multiple capitals, multiple currencies

A capital is a store of anything that has value to a living entity or organisation of people. We attribute value to it because it supports a living being's capacity to thrive. A currency is anything that enables or represents anything of value when it is put to work, i.e., when it flows from where it is stored to where it is needed and put to work, thereby supporting life.

Often there is a two-way flow, of two different capitals flowing in opposite directions. The marketplace facilitates the agreement on how much of one capital flowing one way is a fair return for a different capital flowing the other way.

The multiple capitals of the Integrated Reporting Initiative are widely recognised as a minimum. These capitals are all affected, transformed, or even created or destroyed by a company's activities. Each needs one or more currencies to represent the capital when it is stored, moving from one store to another, or being transformed, created, or destroyed. Some will only have a currency of attribution, not one that can be traded or used to store value—for example, your reputation as a buyer is only a currency of attribution. The currencies will have floating exchange rates between each other, representing the relative value at that point of time in a certain context.

The six capitals, and possible associated currencies in brackets, are:

- Natural (Terra);

- Human (Time, Energy, Quality Adjusted Life Year—QALY);

- Social and Relational (Reputation, e.g. on LinkedIn or eBay, connections);

- Intellectual (Number and ranking of citations, patents);

- Manufactured (Money, WIR, embodied energy);
- Financial (Money, WIR, local money-based currencies).

A systemic cause of the problems we have today is our attempt to attribute value to all the capitals using money as the only currency, rather than the currency intrinsic to each capital.

Today financial capital is relatively plentiful; it is environmental and social capital that is scarce. In many elements of environmental capital, we are so deep in overdraft that if we don't begin paying the capital back rapidly we will exceed our capacity to even pay the interest. The climate emergency, plastic pollution of our oceans, microparticle air pollution, and many more are all symptoms of this overdraft. To pay them back, we need businesses designed to multiply all capitals, not just financial capital.

All the human capitals are also scarce. Human time, attention and creativity, and human capacity to rise to adaptive challenges are all in shorter supply then we need to be able to pay back our environmental overdraft. The same is true for everything else that is put into the company across the other capitals.

Nature is an economy

You can understand your economy by comparing it to nature's economy. Nature has run the best example of a sustainable economy that we can ever hope to see. The central capital of nature is energy[1].

The difference between a living entity and anything else lies in energy. Living entities harness energy to increase their capacity to thrive. They convert energy into specific types of work in a highly efficient way. Energy is the most important capital in all of nature, including human society and its subset, our economy.

Throughout this book we will look at nested energy economies, from your personal inner energy economy, through your organisation's energy economy, to all of nature as an energy economy. Energy is a vital capital, and fortunately it is one that is renewable for as long as the sun shines.

The associated biological currencies of storage and trade are primarily fats, carbohydrates, and proteins. These currencies are highly tradable across a broad swathe of nature because nature's economy uses common metabolic pathways and DNA. In other words, nature uses an optimum balance of diversity and simplicity in the number of global energy currencies. It does a superb job of provisioning for all life and steadily increasing the capitals that life depends on.

---

[1] This is the one aspect of nature's economy that is open. Every day, energy streams into our planet from the sun in a supply that is effectively endless compared to even nature's longest life cycles.

Energy is valued by nature in days of life. For example, the value of a cup of oil is approximately one week of your life. Think of this next time you fill up your car with petrol or diesel. The true value of each litre that you use to drive away from the filling station is one month of your life, not the money you paid[2].

Nature's interconnectedness is powered by several different kinds of markets, with the energy market being the most significant. Trades in this market range from highly collaborative, such as aphids providing honeydew to ants and the ants then taking the aphids into their nests at night for protection, to the one-way brutal extreme, such as the lion eating the buck in order possess the energy stored in the buck's fat and muscle.

The mycelium of a mushroom is very much nature's equivalent to the Visa Corporation. They transfer various nutrients from one end of the forest to the other. Each nutrient is a capital, and moves in the form of some kind of currency. No surprise that the largest and oldest living organisms on earth are the mycelia of mushrooms in the old forests.

Of course, these markets look quite different from the typical market we have invented in society. But what our markets look like is a consequence of how our stories create the reality we experience.

Nature is regenerative for all capitals except energy. Energy comes into nature's economy in a fixed daily amount, is cascaded down the value chain of nature's economy, and ejected from the planet as low-value waste heat at the end of that value chain. All other capitals grow in value through nature's efforts. Higher value soil is created from lower value rock, higher-value freshwater is purified from saltwater, nitrogen is released from rocks, etc.

Almost all forms of life on the planet use either DNA or RNA as their common language to capture their stories. DNA and RNA are very much analogous to your stories that you use to figure out who you are and what you should do for whom.

So if we want to rebuild society's economy in a way that cannot only repair the damage that our economy has caused up to now, but can also enhance the capacity of life on earth to thrive, we can do no better than to mimic nature. This means creating businesses that are as deeply interwoven as all different forms of life are in nature, because they use common DNA and RNA, because they regenerate multiple capitals, and because they use common metabolic pathways.

The central message here is that economies and marketplaces occur naturally throughout life on Earth, if you look at an economy as any mechanism where valuable capital flows, via a currency, from where it is abundant to where it is scarce.

---

[2]Our back-of-an-envelope calculation of the energy content of oil, and the average energy needed per day for a human to live.

The Western economy is failing

The recent film *I, Daniel Blake* by Ken Loach illustrates quite clearly where our Western economies are failing. Whilst it is set in the UK, it's far from only in the UK that valuable people who have bad luck are failed by our economy.

All Western economies are failing, because they are detached from the stories that create most people's realities. This is even more visible now than when we first wrote this paragraph, in how badly most countries have responded to the Covid-19 pandemic; with the USA and the UK as prime examples. The starting point to reshape the economy as a tool to do the job provisioning is to ask a couple of questions. What needs do you have that your economy is poorly meeting, or not meeting at all? What problems do you have that can't be adequately, inclusively solved?

Depending on your specific needs and what you find meaningful, you may say clean air, security, healthy food, leaving a planet that your great-grandchildren will thrive on. Whatever you say, chances are you will find many areas where your economy is failing you. You know it's failing. The climate emergency, the 60 years of harvest left in much of the soil around the world, and more, is clear evidence of how your economy is failing you.

Are you invested in property in a city like London, New York, Shanghai, Dubai, Singapore or Manila, either directly or via your pension fund?

Most of the property value in these cities depends on land that is less than 15m above sea level. The ice on Greenland alone is sufficient to raise the sea level by 6m, even if it just slides onto the sea as icebergs, rather than melting completely. The loss of glacial ice is accelerating too. Since 1980 we have lost a total equivalent to slicing a 22m thick layer off the top of each glacier[46]. We won't even begin talking about the ice that is melting and sliding into the oceans on the Antarctic continent.

Property in these cities will be worthless if we fail to act globally now. Which means any investment your pension fund has made into such properties may well be worthless before you retire, as the value in this future begins to be factored into property prices.

The old lenses we've used to look at the economy distort it, just as the Mercator projection distorts land area in such a way that very few people realise how much smaller the USA is than, say, the north-western corner of Africa. These lenses hold us back from seeing clearly the trends in society and the natural ecosystems that human life depends completely on. Because we fail to see actuality clearly, we construct a poor reality, and so too many are still failing miserably to see the imperative to act now. This book shows you how to recognise the lenses you are using, and how to construct additional ones

Introducing the precariat

Our failed economy is also visible in a new socio-economic class: the precariat. Precariat is a portmanteau word combining precarious and proletariat, covered in detail in Guy Standing's book[47]. They hold down jobs, spend as much time as is humanly possible earning money, but live a precarious existence.

The precariat lacks security in many ways. If you are spending a significant number of hours on unpaid tasks that you have to do to have a few hours paid; and the amount you are paid does not average out to a healthy wage, you are part of the precariat. If you lack a company pension fund, health insurance, unemployment protection, if you lack a voice and decision power in your work, you are part of the precariat.

Many of you reading this book are either already part of the precariat, or will become part of it at some point in your life. Even if you are not, because you have a salaried job for life, the fear that pervades the precarious existence of the precariat is spreading to everybody at work, influencing your decisions.

The emergence of this new class is a clear sign that the Western economy, including our traditional investor-centric ways of incorporating, is failing to do the job of provisioning that *we* need doing.

There are also benefits that many people enjoy in the freedoms that the brings. The precariat is not an automatic consequence of these freedoms, but rather a consequence of the economy and how we incorporate failing to adapt fast enough. FairShares Commons incorporation, which we describe in Chapter 4, and unconditional basic income (UBI), in Section 5.10 are solutions.

Provisioning all of us

The core job of an economy is provisioning, yet our economy is failing to do this job for many of us. You've just read above how nature does the job of provisioning, and the core role that markets play in nature in transferring valuable resources from stores of value (capital) to where the capital is needed and can be put to work.

We all need an economy that does the job of provisioning for all of us, even if you find that your economy as you see it is doing the job sufficiently well for you. Your future is insecure because the economy is not doing the job sufficiently well for many, and is creating the climate crisis.

This means, much as a physicist did in developing a quantum physics that worked by integrating the opposites of classical physics (like particles and waves) into one, that we need to do the same with capitals, currencies, and markets. We must integrate, transcend, and include in ways that go beyond the stories that run today's economic reality. Just as nature has multiple capitals (not just energy) with multiple currencies for each, and multiple marketplaces, your economy will only work for you and everyone else if your economy is highly profitable on an all-capitals, all-currencies, and all-markets basis.

3.2 The stories that define our economy

Your economy starts with stories, which then shape the structures and your reality as you interact with your economy. These stories do that in part because they are the lenses you use to look through. This is an emerging field in economics, called narrative economics, and the topic of a very recent book of that name by Robert Schiller[48]. At last, the lessons from psychology of individuals and business performance, that the dominant meaning-making stories shape the reality that is experienced, are entering economics.

The other important lens is whatever frame of reference you use when you evaluate something as good or bad, right or wrong, beneficial or harmful. In this section I apply to our economy what we cover in detail in Chapters 7 to 11, about how to recognise and then transform the stories that shape the meaning you make. Choose for yourself, depending on your preferred learning style, whether to read those chapters on the how and what first, and then come back here for the why; or to read first this chapter on why, and then the how and what.

(I wish we could write the way Picasso painted: showing everything simultaneously.)

Each story is like the lens you use. If you look through the lens of property, you see an economy based on property. If you look through the lens of interactivity, at an economy based on property, you may see very little interactivity. To grasp your economy, and later to change it, you must look through a wide variety of lenses.

Very much like Picasso and his realisation that art had reached the end of the road and could not generate anything new and worthwhile, so long as it only allowed one single perspective on nature. He realised (at least implicitly) that every lens biases what you see, making some aspects visible while hiding and distorting other aspects. By using multiple lenses and capturing all these perspectives on canvas, Picasso was using some of the 28 transformational thought forms of Chapter 9.

Next time you're talking with someone about what is good or bad about the economy (or anything else for that matter), remember to first be clear on which lens(es) you are each using to gather data, which internal frames of reference you are each comparing to, and which meaning-making stories you are using. (How to do this is in Chapters 8 to 11.)

Your economy's identity

Your economy has an identity, just as you have. A central meaning-making story defining the USA is the story of free individuals, free of government interference. The reality of your experience in the USA emerges from that, along with all the other stories that shape the economy into one where many lack a stable job, and the money to pay for their basic needs of food, housing, health care etc.; but conversely where the shops are filled with all kinds of innovative products.

Compare that with the meaning-making story defining the USSR, creating a reality where every individual had a job, and all their basic needs covered, but where often the shops lacked what people wanted to buy, and business innovation was at a slower pace.

Jack's story: I had the privilege of teaching in the former Soviet Union. It was a fascinating time for me, yet quite apprehensive for Soviet citizens, especially the young people, knowing that socialism was not working, and that sometime in their future (most assumed later rather than sooner) there would be a reckoning, a transition to an economic system better able to provision, a transition which was expected to be violent.

Freedom was differently defined in the USSR, emphasizing freedom from economic want, and the freedom to work; but at the expense of constantly waiting in queues, unsure what would be available on any given day, along with shoddy products and a dearth of innovation. I remember one afternoon, traveling on the road with a Soviet colleague, eagerly telling him my innovative teaching and research plans for the University, when he waved his hands laughing, "Jack, this is the Soviet Union." (A well-known adage during the Soviet era was: the taller blade of grass gets cut.)

I also had the privilege of teaching in the USSR during the tumultuous year of 1991, when the 15 Republics broke away and the USSR no longer existed; and then teaching in the various Republics for many years afterward. The frames of reference that worked in the old USSR no longer worked for the new. That was obvious to all. But those who looked at either the past, the present, or the future with the wrong lens, the wrong frame of reference, were frustrated and saw nothing but failure. But the young people understood the need for new lenses, new frames of references, which gave them hope and the ability to construct a new economic system, a process which is still ongoing. The transition from one type of economy to another is all about constructing and then learning how to use the right frames of references. The latter task is arduous and can never be underestimated. This is where listening, dialoguing, patience, and empathy all come into play.

Both these economies led to power in the hands of a few, and they benefitted. Which one is better depends on which frame of reference you compare with to decide on better or worse.

Today we are entering a new meaning-making story, and so can build a new reality. One with an economy that has the best of both worlds: high levels of entrepreneurial innovation, high regeneration of all our capitals, and security for all that your basic needs will be met because you have meaningful gainful work.

A bit like the old joke: "Capitalism is a system where man [sic] exploits man, and socialism is just the opposite." For too long we have been stuck in flatland, either following a USA story or a USSR story. Like the shift from classical physics to quantum physics, it is high time we left this either / or flatland and entered the quantum world of complementary pairs.

Complementary pairs

One reason why your economy is failing to do the jobs you need done today, so that you can thrive today and build a better future for you and the generations to come, is because neoclassical economics is much more like classical physics rather than modern quantum physics. Even the analogy to classical physics I find a stretch, because of the paucity of solid data gathered using double-blind studies with reliable control groups.

It's time for economics to become much more like relativistic quantum physics. Recognising that the vacuum, the interactivity between all the parts, the effect of the observer, and the inherently unknowable nebulous nature of much of the economy is what matters. The consequence is giving up all hope of predicting most specifics. All that you can work with is other probabilities. It means understanding what is unknowable, and the two components of complementary pairs are simultaneously both one and distinct.

As we mention in Chapter 2, physicists used to believe that physical entities were either particles or waves. Light was a wave, an electron was a particle. Waves and particles were either / or opposites. Then they learned that entities transcended such simple either / or divisions. Light was a wave and a particle, depending on which lenses you looked at it through.

Capitalism and socialism are usually regarded as distinct opposites. But what if they are actually complementary pairs? That if you look at a society through the lens of capitalism, you will see a capitalistic economy and create that as the reality that most people experience. And through that, suppress the socialism that is an inherent part of a functioning economy.

Equally, if you look at society and its economy through the lens of socialism, you will see socialism and build a socialist economic reality that suppresses the essential capitalism needed for an economy to function.

The story, and the institution that concretises it into reality, form a complementary pair. We cannot build a regenerative economy that works for all without fully understanding these both as one complementary pair and as two distinct elements.

Another complementary pair is the consumer and the investor. Perhaps it's a complementary triangle of consumer, investor, and worker. And yet every worker contributes to the economy at least through their work and their consumption of food and housing. Many also contribute to the economy as investors, through the pension contributions that they pay into a pension fund. That I wrote many, and not all, is another example of how our economy is failing to do the job of provisioning.

> I (Graham) was driving down the street in Tzaneen, South Africa, back to Granny Dot's and was pulled over by a traffic policeman at one of the regular roadblocks to check drivers' licences and roadworthiness. He introduced himself as Mike, we asked each other how we were, and then he asked for my licence. I showed him my German driver's licence, and he looked at me with a big smile and said
>
> *you're a German brother.*
>
> I valued how, despite decades of decidedly unbrotherly relationships between the peoples of South Africa, I was greeted with brother; a recognition that we are all one, regardless of the superficial differences. We started chatting, as one does sometimes in South Africa, and he asked me where I came from, what I was doing.
>
> *What do you think, brother, about business possibilities between Germany and South Africa? Take someone like*

me, working for the state. I know I'll never get rich on a state salary, but sometimes I don't even know if I will get enough money to pay for all my bills this month, let alone save up enough to send my children to university and have a comfortable retirement.

I didn't have a good answer then, and I still don't. All I could think was that this was another example of how our economy is failing to do the job that society needs it to do, provisioning for all. In particular, I thought about how it's failing to do the job of provisioning for those of you in many of the essential roles that develop each of you as individuals and all of us as a stable, functioning society.

Maximising shareholder value

We describe more of the meaning-making stories that are creating the economic reality you are experiencing today in section 4.4. But the most powerful story creating today's economic reality is the story that a company exists to maximise shareholder value[43].

This story is one of the biggest myths that's taken root in the recent past. Compare Barclays bank, or Cadbury's chocolate, today and when they were founded by Quakers based on Christian values and the balanced importance of society and the individual. How visible in their results today are their founding values?

Originally, the stories of individual shareholder benefit only and the story of a company as part of your community, to be of service to all of you, were both around. Many companies were relatively small, and deeply embedded over decades in all aspects of their community. In the 1950s, companies were seen as legal persons with a role to benefit society overall.

It was during the 1960s that the stories of conservative neoclassical economists and others began to dominate. The story of shareholder primacy, that the company existed to serve the interests of investors, that investors of financial capital were the only people taking a risk that was not adequately reflected by a market remuneration; and that investors had the right to exercise control over the company, began to create the reality that we experience today.

This story failed to see the company as it is legally defined, a non-human legal person, and instead saw it as simply a collection of assets and contracts between the owners of those assets. By believing that, a meaning-making story of property ownership going all the way back to Locke, investors and many others created the economic reality we have today. Step-by-step as the story was concretising into institutions[43,49]. Many today have lost sight of the original story as just a story, and can only see the institutions as if they were unchangeable.

Biases in economics

It is impossible to talk usefully about economics without including the biases and meaning-making stories of the economists that have shaped the neoclassical and pluralist economics used to talk about our economy.

There are two cognitive biases from section 10.5 that I believe play a significant role in shaping the economy you experience today: uncertainty avoidance bias, and authority bias.

Uncertainty avoidance bias leads almost everyone, and politicians and economists are no exception, to prefer an explanation that has no uncertainty, regardless of whether it has any validity at all. However, because your economy is first and foremost a social tool that everyone has collectively constructed, and is constantly under construction (Chapter 9, thought form P5), it always will be filled with uncertainty. Any valid economic theory describing what we can say about an economy can only be a theory of probabilities and uncertainties, just as quantum physics is.

Exacerbating this is authority bias. Those few who declare themselves to be authorities, and especially those who derive their self-identity from their authority and expertise, are themselves subject to authority bias and trigger authority bias in everyone else. In any situation where you are listening and believing what somebody says because of their position, rather than because you know and have checked the validity of what they are saying, authority bias is in action.

As you've learned from the beginning, the stories that everyone uses to make meaning, are stories that at least shape, if not completely create, the reality that you experience. These biases are nothing other than a set of deeply entrenched stories that almost all of you share. The reality of the economy that you experience is not the only possible economic reality. The reality of capitalism that you experience is not the only possible capitalist reality.

Stock markets and the myth of consumer sovereignty

One central meaning-making story in economics is that the company is an ownable good. And therefore can simply be bought and sold on the stock market, just as if you are buying and selling any commodity. However, this is in stark contrast with the other central meaning-making story in company law, which is that a company is a non-human legal person.

There is a second story, which is actually an enabling myth, that of consumer sovereignty. This myth claims that consumers are in charge of companies because they can withhold purchase. This myth prevents us from seeing clearly the real meaning-making story of investor primacy. If all companies behave similarly, shifting our purchase from one to another makes no difference.

You can read much more about the consequences of integrating these stories to write a new, powerful meaning-making story fit for a regenerative economy in Chapter 4.

3.3 Your current and future challenges

We have many current and future challenges that are going to transform society. A number carry significant risks of social upheaval and pain for many if our economy fails to adapt fast enough to do the job of provisioning for all. And it can only do this job of provisioning if we recognise and work with the rapid changes in the dominant stories that shape the reality of our society and your needs. These include:

- The imperative driven by the climate emergency to rapidly shift all our energy supply out of oil and coal, where USD 20 trillion of the economy is tied up[50].

- The dramatic narrowing of specialisation driven by the increase in total knowledge, meaning that in the near future the average knowledge worker will know less than 1% of what they need to do their job, compared to 75% in 1985.

- The emergence of renewable energy and artificial intelligence is shifting energy, transport, manufacturing, and knowledge rapidly towards zero marginal cost[51].

- The growing scarcity of freshwater around the world, both for you to drink and to irrigate the fields that grow your food. (70% of our usage of freshwater is for your food.) Especially the rapid disappearance of the glaciers providing freshwater for the Himalayan regions[3].

- The Gulfstream shutting down if the Arctic ice cap shrinks much more.

- The potential in the internet of things, big data, and global interactivity to open up completely new adaptive capacities we have never had before. Will these enable us to rise to the challenge?

[3]https://ourworldindata.org/water-use-stress

- The rise of artificial intelligence is bringing with it a social transformation significantly bigger than any other shifts, from the Industrial Revolution onwards. Today most of the economy depends on knowledge workers. In the very near future many of the skilled jobs that we have today will be automated. Over the past few months, my (Graham) administrative assistant has been Amy of x.ai. All I do is send an email asking her (an artificial intelligence system) to arrange a call with five people, then accept the invitation that she has arranged at a time that suits everybody.

- In a decade or two, many things that people are currently being paid for will be done by software or physical robots. At that point, our economy will need us all to do what cannot be automated, which is entrepreneurs creating businesses, human beings caring for human beings, and creative innovation. All this (and note that, importantly, economics is not prepared to measure this activity or even to prioritise such goals) will be especially important over the next decades as we need these to deal with the consequences of climate change and all the other problems that we've created on the planet through our economy.

As these jobs disappear, and we require human beings to put more time and effort into less predictable work; where you cannot predict at the point you start, whether what you will have produced over the next five years will be the one in 1,000 innovation that is the next Facebook, or the 999 others that needed to be done to find out that they were not the next Facebook. To ensure that all thousand can be maximally creative so that we get the one Facebook, all thousand people at least need to have their basic income taken care of so that there is no disincentive to trying.

- Greater need for rapid changes in jobs, careers, and for entrepreneurs. Society needs the economy to remove obstacles to your taking risks, being entrepreneurial and innovative. And the biggest obstacles are the ones of fear around survival, in the very first days of innovation on an entrepreneur's journey, where you have an initial idea of what might work but no evidence yet that it will.

Innovators and entrepreneurs have always had some way of having their survival needs taken care of during those early days. Once, it was a wealthy patron that took care of the artists and scientists that our society and economy is today based on. In the spring of 1696, Newton was taken care of by being made Warden of the Royal Mint. Leonardo da Vinci's patrons included the Medici, Ludovico Sforza, Cesare Borgia, and King Francis I of France.

Humanity has now reached a point where the individual can no longer be seen as the primary element of reality. And so we can no longer say that it's enough to have all entrepreneurial innovation coming from a few people supported by a few patrons.

We now need a fundamental shift of our entire society and economy to one where everybody is as entrepreneurial and innovative as possible, which means that the entrepreneurial and innovation characteristic shifts from just a few to becoming the reality of all. That also means the role of the patron shifts from a few individuals into the whole of society, i.e, the UBI.

Knowledge has become less and less a competitive edge. The competitive edge emerging today is interactivity, creativity, and what you do with that knowledge. You could call this the marriage of individual wisdom with social oneness.

Speak to anyone who understands and works with individuals and communities, and they will tell you that nothing kills off innovation, wisdom, and collaboration faster than fear. We urgently need our economy to be one where wisdom and interactivity, where individuals standing fully in their uniqueness and together in our common oneness, is the primary engine for wealth creation.

Two elements of that that we believe are essential are the unconditional basic income (UBI) and FairShares Commons businesses.

This will eliminate most of the fear that people have around artificial intelligence and augmented reality. The wealth generated by all these businesses will be fairly shared amongst all stakeholders, which includes those whose businesses and professions disappear as a consequence of the artificial intelligence revolution. Because this is done directly within the economy, rather than through government handouts, with everyone participating in governance decisions, everyone will be empowered, not disempowered.

Our needs for mastery, autonomy, and making a difference, will be the primary drivers in this economy for people finding ways of contributing value to themselves, to their peers, and through that, to the economy as a whole. (More in Chapter 10.)

3.4 The economy cannot be controlled

The economy can't be controlled, nor can it even be fully understood by anyone, not even those working on it, the business leaders, economists, and politicians. No politician, bureaucrat, or economist has any hope of ruling the economy.

You have probably heard or read many times over that you cannot solve a problem with the same thinking that created it (Einstein). In the language of this book, you cannot solve an adaptive challenge (Section 7.5) with the same Size of Person

(Chapter 11) that created it.

The adaptive challenges we are facing are bigger than any challenges any human being has ever faced before, and require a new economy to address them. These challenges have a physical size as big as the planet, time horizons of centuries, and are inherently nebulous, volatile, uncertain, complex, and ambiguous.

If you are, in any way, called to step up and do something, and whatever your role, the bigger you are, the better you will rise to the challenge. Whilst especially true for economists, leaders of all sorts, and politicians, this section applies equally to all of you reading this book.

The better you know the stories that you use to shape your reality, and the better you are at then rewriting those stories, the more likely you are to shape a future reality that addresses the challenge.

The greater your fluidity in the 28 transformational thought forms of Chapter 9 the more likely you are to be able to work with the fully nebulous, complex, or even chaotic inherent nature of the challenge.

The more subtlety you can use in rising above your unique nature and set of biases, the more likely you are to address the challenge according to its nature, rather than your own nature.

In fact, I will go so far as to say that we would not have crossed the edge into our current climate crisis, nor any of the other existential crises humanity faces over the coming century, if the people who had made political, economic, and business decisions over the past century had been bigger than the decisions they made.

You need to be big to rise to today's challenges, precisely because an economy is inherently nebulous, and cannot be controlled, nor even predicted in specifics.

Our economy, and perhaps any economy, is inherently on the edge between complex and chaos in the Cynefin framework[52,53], and quite often deeper in chaos because of misguided attempts at command and control.

The Cynefin framework is essential for anyone working on the macroeconomics of our society; without familiarity with it, you cannot deliver useful results in macroeconomics today as an economist, politician, or business leader. It summarises the different nature of, and ways of dealing with, the five different conditions.

Simple Under these conditions you can get far more data than you need to understand fully what is happening. The data changes slowly or not at all, and there are no hidden, unknown interconnections. Best practice is clearly defined and validated. So you gather data, categorise, and apply best practice.

Complicated Here you can just get the data you need in time, you can draw on experience, but a little too much is new or unknown to apply best practice. So you gather data, analyse, and apply good practice.

Complex Here there are too many variables for the data you can gather, the situation is changing too fast, and there are significant hidden inter-connections. By the time you have gathered data, the conditions have already changed so far as to render the data inadequate. Now you need to take a small action, observe what happens, and then react.

Chaos Here there is just way too much happening, way too fast. So you need to immediately act on a large scale, see what happens, and react fast and big. However, there are still underlying patterns allowing some courses of action. Our climate emergency and all else in the 17 SDGs are driving us deep into this quadrant.

Disorder This is complete disorder; there is little you can do, other than hope.

As we've said, an economy is filled with irreducible ambiguity, complexity, and is inherently nebulous. It is partly created by the meaning-making of people with power over others. Since many of these factors are hidden, or change as we look at them, with deeply hidden inter-connectedness, our economy is at best Cynefin complex, and often Cynefin chaos.

Of course, our uncertainty avoiding bias leads us to want to believe that our economy is Cynefin simple or complicated, predictable and controllable. Our authority bias then leads us to follow the advice of anyone wearing the badge of authority. Not questioning whether we are following them just because of the badge, or because what they are saying is actually valid.

3.5 Institutions

For society to function well though, we need institutions. (Institution here refers to established norms applicable to large groups of people, not organisations like the United Nations.) These give us protocols, and include biases. As you will read in Section 10.5 your biases can serve both you and society very well, and so become concretised into worldviews and institutions that make life very simple for us all, until they pass their sell-by date. They make our life efficient and simple because mostly we then only need to use linear logic and Type 1, or fast thinking (Chapter 9 and Kahneman[54]), to act.

Think of how much effort it would cost you if, every time you met a stranger, you needed to engage in an intense negotiation to work out how to greet them. In some languages and cultures, such as the Japanese, there are a large number of words to simply say hello to someone. Which word to use to avoid offending depends on which pre-existing relationship you and they slot into. Which is why, in such cultures, the institution of exchanging business cards first plays such an important role in even greeting a stranger.

Other institutions that have served us all well across thousands of years are institutions like marriage, trade, democracy, and many more. A highly functioning economy, that does the job of provisioning you need, depends on highly functioning institutions that are right for the time.

So to construct such an economy, like the Economy of the Free I describe in Chapter 5, the first step is to understand how to recognise the hidden meaning-making stories that have become concretised into our institutions, and the reality that these concretised stories are now creating. Both the individual parts and how they combine into a whole that is qualitatively and quantitatively different from the mere sum of the parts. You need to be fluid in applying the seven *process* thought forms of Chapter 9 to grasp how these institutions themselves change over time and thus build a reality that changes over time.

You then need to be fluid in the seven *relationship* thought forms to understand how pre-existing relationships may have shaped the individual parts and yourself as a part of your economy.

Finally, to fundamentally transform your economy into one that does the job you need it to do, you need fluidity in the seven *transformational* thought forms.

Institution: freedom

The institution of freedom is crucial to our modern society, and hence to our economy. It is a huge, multifaceted concept. Each of you reading this likely has a different meaning-making story attributing meaning to freedom, so each of you means something different with freedom.

We use freedom in its simplest sense: free to move within any relevant space.

So freedom of physical movement means being able to travel from A to B. It might mean walking to the shops, it might mean travelling by train to another country, or travelling to the moon.

It can also mean freedom to move within socio-economic space. The freedom to move from your birth in poverty to becoming CEO of a multinational, the freedom to move from one meaning-making story to another, the freedom to move from one religion to another.

Freedom also includes the freedom to move through your life along a path that is best suited to you, your nature, and your development potential. The freedom to grow into who you can become.

Boundaries place limits on the extent of freedom and are essential for freedom to function well. For example, if you want to walk from A to B in London, you are no longer free to move in all possible ways. The road and tube system places boundaries on your freedom, you can't simply walk in a straight line from A to all possible Bs; and it enables your freedom too. A complementary pair again.

However, these boundaries maximise the freedom that we all have to get from all possible As to all possible Bs with all variations of speed and distance, and to have buildings to live and work in, plus everything else we want our cities to provide us with. Freedom to move in human society is a negotiation across all freedoms of all stakeholders at all scales across all spaces to move within.

This ought to include, across time, to include stakeholders yet to be born. Burning fossil fuel today in your car, to have more freedom of movement today, takes the freedom to thrive in a comfortable climate from future generations.

Institution: stakeholders

Ubuntu fully recognises that each of us is who we are because of who we all are, and hence the necessity of including all stakeholders (for how this has created you, and how you can transform yourself, see Section 7.3.1).

If you are not actively and visibly including certain stakeholders, you lose most of the power you would otherwise have to consciously use the adaptive capacity that they bring, because you drive underground the role that they play in shaping the reality experienced.

We define the institution of stakeholder as an entity with an interest in the existence of another entity. These stakeholders can be human legal persons, non-human legal persons, alive today or yet to be born, or even already passed away; communities, interest groups, the natural environment; in fact, anything with a stake.

For example, imagine that you have founded a new kind of restaurant, following your intuition into the criteria gourmets and the Michelin guide will have in 10 years. You are a founder; you have bootstrapped the company's initial funding needs, so you also belong to the investor category. You will be doing a lot of the cooking in the kitchen so you belong to the employee category, and soon you will be managing the work of the staff you hire, so you belong to the executive category. You will quite likely eat in the restaurant, so you also belong to the customer category. You may find that you need to grow certain otherwise unobtainable ingredients yourself, making yourself a supplier.

When the organisation is still very small, you and a few family members and friends are co-investors and co-workers, much like an embryo with a few cells. There is no need for differentiation. Each of you shows up as your full selves, fully caring for yourselves, each other as human beings, and your business as a whole. Each shows up as a whole person integrating all the stakeholder categories they belong to and united by the common oneness of being part of one restaurant.

Stakeholders do not have hard boundaries, but flow into each other. It is time for the same kind of shift in how we talk about society, especially what the subsets of economics and business say, that came with quantum physics.

As we mentioned in previous chapters, in classical physics, a proton is clearly a solid particle, as is an electron and a neutron, and each only belongs to its own category of particles. Light is clearly a wave, only a wave, and has nothing in common with protons, electrons, neutrons. Then a hundred years ago quantum physics broke through and for a couple of decades war raged between the new quantum physicists and the old classical physicists.

Eventually this war settled down when it became clear that the classical mechanics could continue doing their mechanics with perfect accuracy in certain situations, but in other situations you needed the quantum mechanic to do her magic.

Central to this was the complete disappearance of the hard distinction in categories. Once physicists had become comfortable with the unarguable fact that light was inherently and irreducibly both wave and particle (called a photon), and that the known particles (e.g., the electron, proton, and neutron) were also inherently and irreducibly both particle and wave, physicists had to become comfortable with two inescapable consequences.

First of all, it became clear that as light moved from one place to another, whatever the photon was, it could not just be light. It was in constant flux, turning into countless pairs of particles and antiparticles, such as electrons and positrons. These had such a fleeting existence over such small dimensions that they were hidden inside Heisenberg's uncertainty. Equally, as an electron moved along, it was surrounded by a cloud of photons, and other electron-positron pairs.

In short, the hard distinction is not something that nature itself recognises. In nature the distinction is soft, fluid; everything is in constant flux shaping and even morphing into everything else. The hard distinction is something that human beings have imposed so that we can talk about nature with our limited language and concepts, to then build our houses and bridges in ways that they do what we need them to do.

The second transformational consequence of this, in how physicists realised they needed to describe nature, was the realisation that the vacuum was a fully active part of every single particle. The vacuum around an electron is a seething mass of photons that the electron pulls out of the vacuum, and the electron-positron pairs that each photon then transforms into and is recreated out of.

This led to a couple of frantic decades for physicists, because figuring out what an electron would do now requires you to include everything from here to infinity. Which naturally gave ridiculous answers, somewhat akin to each electron being as infinitely heavy as the entire universe might be. Eventually they figured out that something called renormalisation was the missing ingredient to give sensible answers out of this nebulous mix of everything.

Institution: property

The institution of property, or the story of what it means to own something, will continue to be an important building block of your economy and the future. But, I will provide what I hope is compelling evidence in which situations it is downright harmful in section 4.3 and in the subsection below.

John Locke wrote a description of one possible story of an economy, where if you performed work on public land you had the right to claim ownership of that land. This was the basis for capturing the USA from the trustees of the original "Land Trusts". Ownership of land in the USA had, before the arrival of European settlers, been regarded as held in trust for future generations and the lower orders of nature itself. Humans were here as trustees or stewards accountable for protecting the land. Typically, they regarded taking into account the needs of the next seven generations to be adequate.

Contrast this with Locke[55] describing, in a time where agriculture was the primary source of wealth generation for many, that you could only own land if you were deemed by yourself or your peers to be highly able to generate wealth. Otherwise you are excluded from freely using the land, but instead need to pay the landowners rent. And to make it worse, your right to challenge these decisions by engaging in governance was only possible if you were a landowner.

Two different lenses or stories creating incompatible realities, coupled with a power mismatch and human nature, gave us today's reality in the USA. If the original "trustees" of land in the USA had had more power to enforce their stories, i.e., their laws, what do you think might have happened? Climate emergency or no climate emergency? Instead, Locke's ownership story became the most influential globally.

This story of property, that you as an individual human legal person or as an individual non-human legal person could own, was, and still is, inconceivable in many old cultures and religions.

The reality you are experiencing today is a consequence of the stories of ownership coupled with the power to enforce them. Both direct physical force and indirect force through laws; and their associated systems of reward and punishment[56].

There are many simply different stories of ownership[56] spread out across the spectrum. No one owns it, and you are there both as a steward and a beneficiary of a commons that no one owns; it could be owned by everyone; it could be owned by a trust; it could be owned by the state; or it could be privately owned.

So everything around private property begins as a story giving meaning to something as mine, and not yours. It's a story of separation and exclusion. Over time, the stories get concretised into law. Remember, you get a lot of value by concretising stories into institutions. Everyone can run on highly efficient type 1 thinking, you have predictability, you can take much bigger risks because the risks are only within small domains. We could not function in groups bigger than about two people without these. And the meaning-making stories around property are amongst the cornerstones of any functioning society.

But they still are nothing other than commonly accepted meaning-making stories. No matter how well the story fitted the needs of your parents and grandparents, if the story does not fit your needs today, there is no reason to stay with the story. I see no way of rising to the adaptive challenge of climate change without surfacing the meaning-making stories of property, and evaluating them very carefully for effectiveness in adapting to the challenge of our climate emergency .

Institution: Money vs. currency

One meaning-making story creating the reality you are experiencing today is that money is a neutral background. Neoclassical economics sees money the way classical physics treated the vacuum, as an inert background. A growing body of research into money[57-59], versus all the other types of currencies, suggest that economics as a whole is on the edge of the same revolution quantum mechanics brought, in seeing that the vacuum was dynamically shaping particle behaviour.

So too are we beginning to see how money is far from being neutral in our economic calculations. In the near future, the indications are that economics will shift into the next phase of economic theory, one where the nature of money (regardless of the amount) is recognised as the primary shaper of business decisions and their consequences. Just as in quantum physics today, where the vacuum dresses the electrons and is responsible for the bulk of an electron's mass.

Money is created through debt, at a positive interest rate, so it's technically called positive interest bank debt. Most of our monies are positive interest bank debt, whether euro, US dollar, sterling, yen etc. It is a concretisation of the underlying meaning-making story behind money. One reason why the economy becomes unstable if the interest rate is negative is an artifact of using only one kind of currency, positive interest bank debt a.k.a. money. Even a zero interest rate is unstable, because that zero is the average. So for small periods of time, or in small geographical regions, the effective interest rate is negative, while nearby or a little later it is positive and the entire vacuum is unstable.

A myth that most people believe is that money comes from the state. In most countries, over 95% of the money supply is created directly by the banks. The work of Ann Pettifor[60] and Stephanie Kelton[61] shows how we could create an economy that does the job of provisioning for us all far better, if we took the current story of meaning making that has generated the reality of money supplied today and adopted another story that may well be far better at creating the reality we need to rise to the climate emergency.

For example, we already know that you might want to decide whether to plant pine trees or oak trees. If you do a net present value calculation using a range of different currencies; for example, any money, or a currency based on different fundamentals such as the Terra or Swiss WIR complementary currency, running since 1934 (code: CHW), your decision may be different in each case, even though you use the same economic formula.

To build an economy that does the job of provisioning for all, I believe that making the same leap physicists made a century ago to seeing the choice of currency as an active dynamic vacuum, and not a neutral inert one, is essential.

Each currency is simply the reality shaped by the different stories behind each currency. The story of money is positive interest bank debt, the story of the WIR is zero interest peer-to-peer business transactions, and the story of the Terra is representing in a human economy key elements of nature's economy. The conclusion, from a purely financial net present value calculation, is pine trees if you use money as the medium for the calculation, and oak trees if you use the Terra.

There are three excellent books to read for far more detail on how to recognise which currencies go with which capitals, and the minimally diverse set of currencies needed to build an economy that does the job of sustainably provisioning for all over multiple generations: two by Bernard Lietaer et al.[58,59] and the doctoral dissertation of Leander Bindewald[57]

I (Jack and Graham) see sufficiently strong indications of just how powerful each currency is in shaping the reality that emerges to believe that, if we had had an economy based on an appropriate number of complementary currencies (including money), very few of the business choices leading to the climate emergency of today would have been taken.

This claim has such far-reaching consequences of such power that it warrants repeating. If our economy was based on an appropriate basket of currencies, not just the single currency of money in different national flavours, and our economic theory recognised and could calculate exactly how each currency shaped the economic reality that you experience, we would never have gone down the decision tree that has created the reality of our climate emergency.

In 10 or 20 years time, you may well be looking at money the way physicists today look at the vacuum. As something so far from being a neutral, inert background, that it's hard to believe physicists could ever have imagined the vacuum was not playing an active role in shaping reality.

Jack and I sincerely hope that this will get sufficient attention so that the experiments capable of falsifying this hypothesis actually get run in the very near future. They'll probably need to be phenomenological simulations, rather than real experiments, given the challenge of finding enough other earthlike planets in a climate emergency to run even a minimally robust double-blind experiment!

Are you an entrepreneur, or leading a mature business? How might your business plan change completely if you use the same assumptions and a fundamentally different currency in your spreadsheet? How is the meaning-making story that has created the reality of money, i.e., positive interest bank debt, shaping your business reality? What does this mean about how you could better incorporate your business? Read on about the FairShares Commons incorporation, and ecosystem FairShares Commons companies, in Chapter 4.

Institution: capitalism

Adam Smith[4] wrote a story[63] describing a world that had never existed, but that he believed would be a significant step forward for humanity. A world where men and women are free to take care of their own interests and the greater good, with security because they are free of debt, injustice, (no precariat!); and where everything is coordinated and balanced by God for the greater good[64].

This story has played a very powerful role in creating the reality you experience, and especially some of the institutions that the story has concretised into.

We've lost key elements of his story in today's capitalism, and other elements have been reshaped by our other stories to a point where Adam Smith would not recognise his story. For example, as you will read in Section 3.5.4, the very money that we use to measure almost everything of value, and to facilitate the flow of any value from where it's abundant to where it is scarce, is itself a story of debt. Almost all the world's monies are different flavours of positive interest bank debt. Today's capitalism concretises the very opposite of his world without debt.

---

[4] Adam Smith (1723-1790) was a philosopher and considered by many to be the founder of economics. But Abdul Islahi makes a convincing case that the founders of economics were actually Islamic economists writing during a very fruitful period between the 8th and 11th centuries[62]. In his important book, *History of Islamic Economic Thought: Contributions of Muslim Scholars to Economic Thought and Analysis*, Islahi convincingly documents that many of Smith's ideas, and just about all the concepts found in today's economics textbooks, were first developed by Islamic scholars.

If you read both of his books, *The Theory of Moral Sentiments*[65] and the *The Wealth of Nations*[63] that he wrote 25 years later, he would far more likely recognise his capitalism in the regenerative capitalism I describe in section 5.3.

The dominant variant of capitalism today, and what most people think is all that capitalism can be, can be simply defined as: the means of production are ownable property, owned and governed by persons, both human and non-human legal persons, and either directly or indirectly via businesses, investment funds, and governments. Then problems come adding all the other meaning-making stories around this, leading to a ridiculously small percentage of people having controlling governance power.

Paul Mason's book[66] *Post-Capitalism* contains a lot of excellent content, and is well worth reading.

Much writing and talking is about what we do not want, without naming what we do want, now how to build it; and suggests that there is little of value in capitalism that we ought to retain. I believe that, just as quantum mechanics included what worked in classical mechanics, and transcended it by defining clearly the limits, and what worked beyond those limits, we can quickly develop the regenerative economy we need by recognising and retaining what is of value in capitalism, as well as defining clearly what is fundamentally false, and where the boundaries are.

Regenerative capitalism includes all capitals, all currencies, up to and including the capitals and currencies of our planet's ecosystem. (Section 5.3.)

I found, writing this section, that there was no definition of capitalism that everyone would agree with. Looking at the writings of different people over time, each of their capitalisms changed when they looked at it. Capitalism 30 years ago was different to today, and it differs from country to country. Typical of thought form P5, and any inherently emergent story.

So here is our attempt to lay out enough building blocks to span all the different stories of capitalism, and their concretisation, as you experience them today in your reality. From these you will recognise and categorise what you are likely to hear talking to neoclassical economists and reading their books. In the rest of this subsection, I will do my best to point out the story versus the concretisation, and the opening for economics to make the same jump that physics made from classical to quantum mechanics.

You can think of capitalism, as we experience it today, as an entire bookshelf of meaning-making stories fighting for supremacy. It is often very hard to recognise clearly what is a factual and actual versus a concretised story. This multiplicity of stories battling for supremacy is why defining capitalism is impossible. Whatever it was yesterday, it is something different today, and yet again different tomorrow.

Opening the door into the next stage of capitalism requires each of us to grow our capacity in the 28 thought forms so that we can recognise the difference between the specific concretisation, and the valuable essence, of each story.

Capitalism at work is extraordinarily dynamic and innovative. Capitalism is almost as dynamic and innovative as nature is. This is definitely something to retain. To rise to the adaptive challenges of our climate crisis and development goals, we need all the innovation and dynamism we can muster. But, of course, in a form that fits within nature's boundaries.

As you read above, the heart of capitalism is property. The meaning-making story that created the capitalism we experience says that the best way to maximise the value of something is for it to be owned by someone whose self-interest lies in maximising that value. This story of property says that if only you own something can the best decision be taken.

In Section 4.3 you will read compelling evidence that this is patently false in at least some situations, times, and places. In fact, you have already experienced in your reality at least one situation (you as property; I hope because you have never been another's property, but maybe because you have) where I expect it is perfectly clear to you that property law is the best way of destroying value. The doorway into a regenerative economy that will work lies in different meaning-making stories around property and freedom.

I'm not in any way saying here that we should eliminate property law in all cases, everywhere; what I am saying is that we need to look carefully for just where property law gives us the outcomes we need to deal with the adaptive challenges we face, when this freedom gives us what we need. And maybe we will recognise that we also need to invent something that integrates the two, in the same way that quantum physics integrated the concepts of particle and wave into one.

The current concretisation of that dynamism and innovation is, however, harmfully tied into property as the underpinning story of capitalism. This means that most of the innovation and dynamism are treated as property owned by a few, who charge rent to the many to access that. There are elements of property that we need to retain, elements of property to lose, and a new integration that goes beyond owning and non-owning. These are all stories, and there's nothing to stop us from integrating their essence into a completely new story of regenerative capitalism.

Zero marginal cost is one of the goals of capitalism, whether explicit or implicitly stated. As soon as we have zero marginal cost, the distinction between owning and not owning, private property and a commons, and capitalism and socialism, disappear. These complementary pairs become integrated, just as you read above about quantum physics.

Maximising profit, and a drive towards zero marginal cost, is another deemed building block of capitalism today. This has some validity, and much that we should keep, because it is a door into a future regenerative economy that does the job of provisioning for all. Maximising profit just needs to be broadened to take into account all capitals. Striving for zero marginal cost of capital growth for all capitals will lead to regeneration of all of them and a good, viable standard of living for us all, and in fact everything else that is alive.

The assumption that all individuals are naturally acquisitive, into bargaining, and oriented around their own self-interest is central to the modern concept of capitalism. But as you will see in Table 10.2 on Page 231 our top human needs are pretty much balanced across doing things for others and doing things for ourselves.

The door into creating a regenerative economy lies in recognising that all of these needs are part of what energises and motivates human beings to get stuck in, be productive, and create wealth. In a regenerative economy, each need is part of the description that economics gives and works with in an integrated way, recognising that each individual has a unique weighting for each need. In a regenerative economy, the individual who is strongly acquisitive and self-interested is as valuable as another altruistic and other-interested individual.

Capitalism is also built around power over, almost exclusively via the power of lots of money over little money. There is some balancing through politics, and a growing power from mass action to balance, but the power of big-money is still overwhelming. The power of big-money is also beginning to subvert mass action, subtly harnessing it in the interests of big-money.

There is nothing inherently wrong with power—as any physicist will tell you, power is just the ability to move something heavy. If we are going to move all the heavy things in order to tackle our climate crisis and the 17 SDGs, we are going to need power. This is the door into the regenerative economy. Instead of an either / or acceptance of power or rejection of power, instead of either accepting or rejecting monetary power, we expand the role of power to include all powers, especially from all capitals, into a power balance.

The final consequence of capitalism as concretised into our economic practices today is that the capitalist economy cannot do the job of provisioning for us all that it was invented to do. By failing to adequately provision for all, we have all the evidence we need to step away from the meaning-making story of capitalism today. This is not just the door to the regenerative economy you all need, it's a great big blooming rocket strapped to your back.

The founders of today's neoclassical economics had a very scientific orientation, and expected that future generations would do just what has happened in physics. Run experiments, gather data, and use hard data to finetune theories. Until the theory could no longer be tuned to include the data, and then to come up with fundamentally better theories. I imagine that most would be horrified at what has happened since then. I believe they would agree with my seeing economics as less the study of what an economy is, and more the study of what you can say about an economy. Just as physics is the study of what you can say about the physical world, and less the study of what the physical world actually is. They would be activists for updating economics to better capture what we can say about economies, and away from declaring what an economy is.

To build the regenerative economy, a big capitalism multiplying all capitals that humanity so desperately needs to repay natural capitals and repair the harm we have done to the life-carrying capacity of our planet and society, we must urgently go beyond simplistic either / or approaches. We need the complementary pair approach that quantum mechanics applies so well to nature. It is time to recognise that current capitalism and socialism are really in the same relationship as the complementary pairs of quantum mechanics; they are not restricted to only being a binary choice opposites. Some successful countries, like Norway, are successful precisely because they treat them as complementary pairs, integrating good capitalist business with good society to raise the standard of living for everybody.

It is time to harness the value of capitalism (even Marx and Engels[67] recognised the beneficial power that capitalism brings) for all capitals.

3.6 Conclusion

Hopefully by now you are seeing how our economy has been invented by concretising our meaning-making, and the difference between what an economy actually *is* (which is inherently unknowable actuality) and what we can *say* about it.

Central to this book is the theme of complementary pairs rather than opposites. Property and freedom are not opposites, they are a complementary pair. Stakeholding, stewardship and ownership are a complementary pair, neither identical nor opposites. Freedom and stakeholding are also a complementary pair.

CHAPTER 4

The free company

Freedom is a heavy load, a great and strange burden for the spirit to undertake. It is not easy. It is not a gift given, but a choice made, and the choice may be a hard one. The road goes upward towards the light; but the laden traveler may never reach the end of it.
—Ursula K. Le Guin

Designing institutions to force (or nudge) entirely self-interested individuals to achieve better outcomes has been the major goal posited by policy analysts for governments to accomplish for much of the past half century. Extensive empirical research leads me to argue that instead, a core goal of public policy should be to facilitate the development of institutions that bring out the best in humans.
—Elinor Ostrom at her 2009 Nobel lecture.

I (Graham) grew up in apartheid South Africa. I never felt safe, and struggled to see any path out of the morally wrong and socially unstable system to a viable future. I felt powerless to do anything, hopeless about the future, and angry at how South Africa was.

Are you angry about climate change, and other injustices in today's world, but feel powerless to change the system? Have you joined Extinction Rebellion, or the school strikes, and want to know what comes next? Do you want to build a new sys-

78

tem that works? This chapter is a call to action, and describes an essential building block for building a system that works.

Looking back at South Africa, I can now see clearly how apartheid was like a hidden force, a gravity, pulling at all South Africans. Anyone who tried to act differently was pulled back into the apartheid swamp and the binary choice of either defending or attacking apartheid, rather than creating a viable future. Apartheid began as a library of stories, and these stories then shaped the reality everyone experienced. Few recognised that the stories were only that, stories, with no deeper reality. But by believing them, all the structures and processes of apartheid were built.

In 2008 I decided to leave my career in the middle management of Procter and Gamble to focus on figuring out how to harness the power of business for the greater good. I also left because my work no longer felt safe. Not safe for me in the moment, and the consequences were certainly not safe for future generations. Even though P&G's clearly stated purpose was, and is, to improve lives, I observed that too many choices were made to improve shareholder returns at the cost of the quality of life of staff today and all of us in the future.

You will read more about the critical importance of psychological safety in section 13.4. Even without reading the definitions, what is your gut feeling? Do you feel psychologically safe at work? Do you feel psychologically safe in the society we have today? Do you trust your boss with your future? Do you trust the shareholders to vote for what will be good for you, your children, and your grandchildren, even if that diminishes their return on investment this quarter?

Greater inequality drives safety down. We can measure inequality with the Gini coefficient developed by the Italian sociologist Corrado Gini. It is often used to measure the gap between the wealthiest and the poorest within nations or regions. A Gini coefficient of 1 means total inequality, one person in the country has all the wealth, the rest have none; 0 means perfect equality, everyone has the same. The UN estimates 0.4 as the threshold for risk of social unrest, so any country with a Gini coefficient above 0.4 ought to be worried.

Economists are also seeing that the greater the Gini coefficient, the lower the economy's resilience, which limits individual wellbeing, growth and happiness. For an economy to go beyond resilient into antifragile the Gini coefficient needs to be near zero.

I propose we consider the Gini coefficient within each company[1], across all stakeholders, as an indicator of corporate viability. What is your company's Gini

---

[1] I hope that a researcher picks this up. I would love to see hard data on the Gini coefficients across all stakeholders, and compared to companies failing because they lost their social licence to operate.

coefficient? How large is the inequality between the total wealth of the C-suite and investors, and the salaried staff? How big is it across all stakeholders?

Companies are first and foremost social constructions that society has invented to do specific jobs that society needs doing. A Gini coefficient above 0.4 in your company is a cause for concern that you no longer have the social licence to operate. So the motivations for a 300x gap between the CEO and the lowest-paid member of staff are flawed, because they lead to the company losing its social licence to operate.

In fact, there is data that having a flat and public pay structure at all levels raises company performance[68]. What if you *boosted* your company's success by shrinking the remuneration gap to between 1 and 25; chances are you will.

My experiences in P&G, and hearing the very similar experiences of my friends in other companies, led me to deeply question the fundamentals: what are the structural foundations of trust, psychological safety, and fiduciary vs. moral responsibility in business? What might the hidden gravities be—gravities pulling well-intentioned people into the swamp of behaviour contrary to their values?

The stories that make meaning for us are the gravity making our world less psychologically safe by the day, despite the best intentions of so many people. Much of the polarised politics of today is us trying to feel safe again.

Keep Picasso in mind throughout this chapter. You may have looked through one lens all your life and see very clearly through it; but that does not mean you have seen clearly what actually is, and all that is, just as Picasso showed that there was far more to represent in a painting than traditional perspective painting could ever manage. Ask yourself what the lenses (i.e., stories) you are using might prevent you from seeing. What don't you even imagine might be invisible to you through the lenses you are using?

4.1 Incorporation and apartheid

The foundation of South Africa's apartheid is also hidden in the foundations of today's business, and is one root cause of the global problems we are facing. This common foundation is the legal construct restricting the power to govern, and the right to a share of the wealth generated, to only the investing shareholders, rather than to all stakeholders.

The word apartheid is built of two elements, with the basic meaning: *a context (heid) of separation (apart)*. Such a context of separation was the gravity driving the behaviours that harmed all South Africans, and a context of separation is the gravity driving the behaviours that are harming us all today.

Apartheid itself, and everything that apartheid means, grew out of a context, or set of stories and lenses that saw having a white skin as the reason for someone to have better capabilities and to deserve more. So only those who had a white skin were eligible to vote for politicians, own land, and enjoy most of the country's wealth. In reality, it's luck, not cause and effect. A century ago having white skin just meant that you came from Europe, which had just been lucky enough to be on a random upswing vs. other cultures to greater power and wealth through the Industrial Revolution.

Apartheid disenfranchised all other stakeholders, denying them any role in steering the country into the future, and denying them a share of the wealth generated from their past labour. All the emotional and physical injustices, the lives lived far short of their potential; and the protests inside and outside South Africa, were inevitable consequences of the construct of South African apartheid, combined with the inevitable human biases we all share, the stages of meaning-making we all go through, and a low fluidity in transformational thinking.

> On my most recent flight to South Africa, I (Jack) sat next to a white South African woman living in the US, who valued how much more creative she found the music of today's South Africa than the music she grew up with.

Stories, lenses, shape experienced reality and the constructs we build, including legal constructs. These legal constructs are just stories made concrete in law.

The insight that the Nüremberg trials of the Nazi leadership after WWII established was that even when a story is written into law, that law is not a justification for actions contrary to the overarching laws of humanity. This means that you can be tried and convicted for actions that were fully within the law at the time if any reasonable person ought to have recognised that those actions were against humanity's moral laws. You can think of these trials as establishing the primacy of actuality over reality (Section 2.4).

Does having more money, or financial power, mean that you are always more capable of making better choices in the annual general meeting of a multinational than any other stakeholder? Better against all frames of reference?

This is the equivalent meaning-making story in today's world to the story that having a white skin meant you took better governance decisions for society and nations. A story that emphasised one point of difference between people, hiding other sources of difference, and more importantly hiding our huge common ground. These stories are just lenses that highlight one small part of all that is, and hide the rest. Mistaking the distorted and limited view you see through one lens for the whole is deeply flawed, as Picasso spent his life illustrating.

The institution of business today comes from a meaning-making story emphasising one difference, money, and hiding both other differences and our huge common ground. This meaning-making story then shapes our reality, and turns into the legal constructs we have today. Constructs separating stakeholders from the company, allowing only the investor group the right to vote and a share of the wealth generated. (In Chapter 6 we describe in more detail how meaning-making stories shape our economy.)

We have invented this context of separation of stakeholders, this apartheid in business. We took the meaning in the stories as a given, created our reality to match these meaning-making stories, then concretised them in the laws we have written, as well as the norms, cultures and practices of business. Ewan McGaughey has shown quite clearly that company law in some countries[69] does not restrict voting to investors, and the summary of commonly believed myths about the company from a global consortium[43] that you'll read more about in Section 4.4 open even more space for change.

This separation prevents all but the investors from contributing their perspective, their insight into future risks and opportunities, to steer our companies into creating a viable future; and reserves most of the benefits for those investors, demotivating all others from investing discretionary effort, creativity etc.

We seldom make it a habit to become truly aware of our context, whether it's physical gravity or some other kind of gravity pulling at us, shaping the space in which we move (see the appendix); and we seldom recognise how this pull shapes everyone's behaviour, nor our ability to change it. I hope that throughout this book you are becoming steadily more aware of how your meaning-making stories shape the reality that you experience, and that you can begin changing it.

4.2 Excluding stakeholders causes crises

What is a business for?—a Harvard Business Review article[70] from Charles Handy—accelerated my journey, around 2009, to understanding how a context of separation is part of creating and anchoring many, if not all, of our challenges today.

I believe that climate change, likely everything threatening us with extinction, is an inevitable consequence of the apartheid-like shareholder context exacerbating our inevitable and normal mix of human biases, stages of meaning-making and fluidity of transformational thinking. Excluding most stakeholders—human and non-human—from the key decisions that create our shared reality produces a gravity pulling us deeper into the swamp of extinction.

When investors have all the decision power in a multinational, and enough take as a given that a company is for *"maximising shareholder value / Total Shareholder Return (TSR)"*, then decisions will be taken based on the worldview, emotional drives, and cognitive biases of investors.

There is nothing wrong with shareholder returns, i.e., the financial investor's return on investment. You need to keep a careful eye on paying back the money people have invested in your company, and enough to reward them for taking the risk. Generating a healthy level of wealth is an important role of business, and one of the best indicators that your strategies are good and being executed with excellence. But maximising TSR is certainly not the sole, not even a primary, objective. Paine's recent HBR article[71], looking at how Covid-19 has fundamentally changed our business context, shows how systemic inclusion of stakeholders is better for all, including investors.

Certainly I am against acquiring more money today by burning up the very natural capitals[2] we ought to be stewarding in trust for our children, and their children. Today's harmful outcomes are an unavoidable consequence of the apartheid-like business context our dominant meaning-making stories have generated.

This apartheid-like separation even creates split personalities in individuals.

Someone may be a wonderfully loving mother at home with her children, and then sit in an annual general meeting (AGM) representing the pension fund employing her, making choices that will harm her grandchildren. In the AGM everyone is inside the context of separation, deep in their roles, the stories and structures creating a narrow reality—that of the financial stakeholders, i.e., the shareholders. No other stakeholders are present, none can voice with power the needs of other stakeholder groups, and none have the power to vote.

As well as all the power, the financial investors also get all the rise in the company's capital value and all the dividends, i.e., surplus cash. Of course, many decisions that lead to how much dividend is issued and the rise in the company's capital value are made at an annual general meeting by those investors. Conflict of interest anyone?

In the general meetings of a typical company today there is no stakeholder class representing the needs of the children, grandchildren, or even the insects we all depend on for life; no class representing the needs of the staff, customers, suppliers, or any other stakeholders; and with an equitable level of voting power to balance the shareholder class. No one can say *"Sorry, that option costs our stakeholder group too much, even though it benefits your stakeholder group enormously. No."*

---

[2] I use capitals here to emphasise the multiplicity of capitals in nature; elsewhere I use capital where I choose to not emphasise the multiplicity.

Is it any wonder then, that, when faced with a choice between two or more options, all too often the negative consequences are borne by those stakeholders excluded from the decision in the AGM? The staff, customers, suppliers, or future generations?

Now imagine two centuries of decisions in millions of companies. Each one small and insignificant, but together adding up to the crises threatening humanity today. I have concluded over the past ten years that the apartheid-like separation of stakeholders is the common factor in South Africa and in business. This story of separation sets the stage for decisions that are contrary to the needs of all the non-financial stakeholders. Climate change and the need for the sustainable development goals is an outcome of this story of separation.

I have hope because I believe we can reapply in business today what worked in the transformation of apartheid South Africa before. Rewriting the stories that shape our reality will give us a better reality, and probably actuality too.

4.3 Incorporation and ownership

I (Jack) was surprised and initially worried when I learned that copies of one of my books were being downloaded and printed in Singapore without my knowledge or involvement. Looking through the lens of property and my need for money, I saw theft.

But, I wrote the book as a tool to do the job of disseminating insight into economics, from where it was abundant (in me) to where it was scarce (in economics students). Through this lens, these people were very kind souls giving me their time and effort increasing the power of my book to do the job I wanted it to do.

Given my perspective on how the economy is changing, and the need for multiple lenses to look at the economy through (not just the neoclassical lens) my initial trigger quickly turned into pleasure. This is what the rapidly emerging copyleft legal framework brings.

And I recognized that knowledge generates wealth when it multiplies through sharing.

Property law in nature gives us an interesting comparison. There are many solitary animals that can be regarded as owning their territory. If any other animal that competes with them for the same prey enters their territory, they go to war. Compare this with the story of ownership used by ants. All regard themselves as members of the colony, no ant claims individual ownership of anything. The colony is the living entity.

If we want a viable planet at 8 billion people (vs. only viable at under 1 billion) we need an economy based on all human beings, even all life on earth, as one living entity. We are now at a point where either all humans learn to thrive together, or we all experience a collapse.

The reality you are experiencing today is a consequence of the stories of ownership, coupled with the power to enforce them[56], inappropriately applied. It's time that we all brought these hidden stories into the light of day, and looked critically at them. Do they fit the dominant stories of our era? Are they shaping realities that enable you to thrive? You'll learn more about how to rewrite stories in Chapter 8.

In most countries in the world, concepts of ownership can no longer be legally applied to you as a human legal person. In law, global, and in almost every country in the world, slavery is illegal. Slavery is defined today by the ICC[72] following the original Slavery convention of 1926 as:

"Slavery" means, as defined in the Slavery Convention of 1926, the status or condition of a person over whom any or all of the powers attaching to the right of ownership are exercised, and "slave" means a person in such condition or status.

Enslavement of any human legal person is illegal in practically every country[3]. But we are still applying the concepts of property to the abstract group of human beings we call a company.

In Section 3.5 gave you compelling evidence that property law is certainly not always the best way of maximising the value of something. In almost all countries in the world, children are no longer classed as the property of their parents. Instead, a completely different meaning-making story is the basis for the institution of childhood. This meaning-making story tells us that being a child has the same basis in freedom as any other legal person, But recognises that this free person lacks in certain cases the capacity to take certain decisions. Parents, whether biological or appointed to take the function of a parent, then take the decision on behalf of the child's best interests. Not themselves.

---

[3] Despite that, we are still dealing with a global problem with human slavery. In 2016, on any given day, 40.3 million[73] people were classified as enslaved globally. The actual number may be higher today. The majority (24.9 million) were used as forced labour; 4.8 million in sex work, and the rest on farms and in factories. Forced marriage accounted for another 15.4 million. Over the previous five years a total of 89 million people had experienced modern slavery for some period of time. You have quite likely bought something partly manufactured, harvested, or built by someone enslaved.

Imagine, for a moment, that you had been born into a country where you are legally the property of your parents. The dominant meaning-making story was that by anchoring in law you as the property of your mum and dad would be the best way to maximise your value. All the rights of property law, giving them sole authority over what to do with you, including the decision to sell you to whoever they choose for whatever price they negotiate. And at that point losing any further right to have any further say in your life.

Even from a purely economic perspective, we already have compelling evidence that wealth generation, even in a capitalist economy, is maximised through your freedom. So we all see owning someone as dumb from a purely economic, wealth maximisation frame of reference, regardless of any judgements against a moral frame of reference.

In fact, the end of slavery was largely driven by the advent of cheap fossil fuel engines, and the subsequent realisation that the economy was better off if everyone was paid a salary for their work, which they then used in the economy to progressively raise their standard of living, after many decades of unsuccessful campaigning against slavery based on moral motivations anchored in the unique value of each human being as a meaning-making being. I believe the economic, 'what's in it for me' case will lead to faster, broader action than the moral case, because it is inclusive of all, and does not create divisive blame-defence games.

Since companies are in law classed as non-human legal persons, in 2010 I (Graham) began asking myself how the story of the company as property might be shaping the reality that we experience in the world today. You can read more about how to apply the concepts of freedom fully in creating a free company in the white paper that I wrote between 2010 and 2013[74]. Another recent paper supporting much of this has just been published by Common Wealth UK[8,9].

You will read in Section 13.4 my perspective that seeing an organisation as a living being, with its own meaning-making capacity, is an essential lens and frame of reference to use in grasping what your business truly is, and to guide your choices for it to be fully productive. How on earth could we ever have believed that applying the meaning-making stories of property, rather than the meaning-making stories of freedom, could be the basis for businesses, the second fundamental building block of a capitalist economy? (You are the first fundamental building block of a capitalist economy. You as a worker, consumer, and investor.)

Treating companies as property leads directly to many people to burn out at work, become disengaged, or spend more than 50% of their effort at work protecting themselves, at huge cost. At the global level, climate change and other injustices built into our economy are a consequence of too.

I came to the conclusion, the more I read about this and the more I thought about this, that applying the concepts of ownership to non-human legal persons was having significant consequences on everyone.

Think about a company where all the staff, from the CEO down to the most recent and junior recruit, decide to embark on a 20-year plan to become a net positive, regenerative business. The current company owners, perhaps a few wealthy and globally minded individuals, agree. But, five years into the plan, a couple of these owners sell, and another passes away, their children inheriting ownership.

A pension fund, private equity fund, or almost any other kind of investor buys all the shares. They have also bought the dominant governance power over the company. They have full power to rip out all regenerative decisions and replace them with decisions designed to extract the maximum possible "rent" from their property in the short term. In the worst case, they may deliberately strip out all value from the company over the following quarters, leaving a hollow shell.

None of the staff, nor any of the suppliers, customers, or cities that supported the company's success through direct and indirect services, nor even the natural ecosystems that enabled the company to generate financial wealth, had any governance power in that decision. When the company is sold, the staff are sold with it.

Of course, in principle the staff could all walk away. But in practice, some of them may have been required to sign legally binding contracts forcing them to stay. This is especially true in modern knowledge-based companies. Other staff may have had financial commitments, including families to support, and live in towns where this is the only company with the kind of work that they are qualified to do, that made it impossible for them to find any other source of work and income.

These consequences carry with them shadows of the concept of property to the human legal persons that are part of the company.

All of this is only possible because companies today are structured in a way that applies some or all of the concepts of property to non-human legal persons. And as you read in Chapter 12.3, regarding a company as a living being, with its own meaning-making capacity, makes a lot of sense and gives us a very effective way of understanding how an organisation can thrive, engage in society, and truly take accountability for the consequences of its decisions and actions. And so it seems only natural that the next stage of emancipation that has, over the past centuries, emancipated all human legal persons, is now extended to groups of humans and the non-human legal persons that they are part of.

Think of a scenario where the dominant story shaping our reality is that companies are the property of the investors providing the financial capital. Where only these investors have the right to buy or sell the company, and take decisions about the company as a whole? Now, can you see any antifragile[24] adaptive ways of structuring businesses and our economy in this scenario that avoid outcomes like our climate crisis and all the other injustices of our economy? I cannot.

So long as only the representatives of the needs of financial capital hold all the power in the company general meetings, without any equitable balance from all the other capitals, I do not see any way that individual businesses will take decisions capable of regenerating all the capitals that human life depends on. And, if the company as a whole is also not free of property law, I do not see any way of having a truly antifragile adaptive economy that would do the job of provisioning for all, regardless of how our context and global needs evolve.

Think about how stories are what we use to make meaning, and thereby shape the reality that we experience out of the actual raw material. Think about how even a very small shift in a story can be amplified down through a chain of stories, leading to truly horrendous outcomes.

Whilst it may never be provable mathematically, I believe it's plausible that most of the 40.3 million people enslaved in 2016 would be free, and living in an economy that did the job of provisioning properly for them as well, if no part of property law was applied at all to businesses anywhere in the world.

Explore these ideas for a while. I believe that we cannot address the adaptive challenges of climate change and the SDGs if we continue to apply any or all the concepts of property to our businesses.

One last thought here. Is it possible to use the stories of property to deal with some of the problems that emerge from the stories of property? Neoclassical economists claim that this will completely address all the root causes of our global crises. If the atmosphere is owned, if nature as a whole is owned, that will enable us to take care of the atmosphere and stop pollution. I doubt it.

This reminds me of physicists holding on to classical mechanics, attempting in the decades before quantum mechanics to get it to work for subatomic particles. They could get the equations to work, for a while, with a lot of effort. The equations became more and more fragile, more and more limited to special cases. The new quantum mechanics paradigm transcended and integrated all the old stories of classical mechanics, and so gave physics antifragile, simple, elegant ways of grasping what we could say about how the world works.

We have enough evidence for the usefulness of property in some domains as part of capitalism (the experiments of the USSR, Eastern Europe, China, etc. demonstrate the value). So I am not, in any way, arguing for the elimination of the meaning-making story of property, just as no physicist would ever claim that quantum mechanics argues against the use of particles. Quantum mechanics does not say physical particles are never useful, and that everything should be replaced by waves. Physicists use both particles and waves without any argument, choosing which one delivers the best results on a case-by-case basis.

The lesson from quantum physics is that property and freedom are complementary pairs, a dual story, not opposite ends of a single story. Somewhat like the truth square on Page 203, the meaning-making story of freedom is very different from that of property, not the opposite story. Not owned is very different to freedom, because not owned just means that no one has yet claimed ownership. Like particles and waves in physics are a complementary pair, not simple opposites in a binary choice. In a regenerative economy we will have figured out how to use both meaning-making stories simultaneously.

The new case that we are confronted with today is the global adaptive challenge of our climate crisis and the 17 SDGs. I don't believe that only using the stories of property and the laws they create is capable of giving us regenerative businesses and an economy that does the job of provisioning for all. For example, if property law is applied to you, i.e., you own yourself, maybe that will eliminate slavery and give you freedom. Using a story and laws of property to protect freedom, capitals, etc. seems to me to be a fragile and unworkably complicated way. Even if the owners include the next seven generations, or mountains, streams, and oceans.

The recent decision in New Zealand that Te Urewera National Park, Mount Taranaki and Whanganui River have full legal personhood, including freedom, recognises that property law, even if you are deemed to own yourself, falls short.

However, given the dominance of the stories of property in our reality today, hacking property law in defence of freedom can be a very good bridge. Until we recognise companies as living beings, as Mount Taranaki is by the Maori, and extend our stories and laws around freedom to non-human legal persons.

The Purpose Foundation's excellent work in pushing for the incorporation of companies that own themselves is a very necessary and excellent step forward. The FairShares Commons goes beyond this, yet still works in existing company law, shaped as it is by stories of property, to protect a company's commons. Wherever you can use existing stories and their laws in novel ways to build bridges to the future as it emerges, do so.

You may be thinking that this is all unachievable utopian thinking. So did most in the old slave-powered economy, as they could not see the transformation that cheap fossil-fuel powered machine labour was bringing, because they had insufficient fluidity in transformational thinking. We are now entering the era of zero marginal cost energy, not just cheap energy[51]; maybe the pattern is about to repeat itself, now at the scale of non-human legal persons.

4.4 Myths

Myths are prevalent in the worlds of business and economics. Like all other stories, these myths shape the reality that we end up experiencing. They are meaning-making stories in economics and business. In some countries they are no more than beliefs with no legal solidity, in others they have some legal concrete. So the experienced reality they create for us is more like clouds forming castles in the sky that we simply accept as given, not physical buildings we can safely thrive in. (Section 2.4 covers what I mean here.)

The original Greek Mythos referred to fantasies about the gods, used by the powerful rulers to shape individual behaviour, and society as a whole, maintaining social cohesion. These myths stated the origin of everything, and were inherently unquestionable.

It is time to question the myths around incorporation.

Perhaps the biggest myth is that the state avoids entrepreneurial innovation and risk, leaving it to private investors and businesses; actually, many of the innovations we depend on began with public sector investments, not private, as described well in Mariana Mazzucato's book *The entrepreneurial state*[75]. Just take a look at your smartphone: the key elements were all government-funded, as was the web, invented at CERN to make global physics collaborations easier, not by a company to make money through you sharing gifs of cats.

I summarise below some of the myths. You can read more about these myths across most of continental Europe, the UK nations, the US states, and almost all other jurisdictions, and find all the legal references, in the statement signed by a number of leading academics[44] and in Lynn Stout's book[49].

- Shareholders own the company and its assets. Not true.

  All that a shareholder owns is an intangible bundle of rights and obligations[76] (See Chapter 15 for details), represented by a piece of paper, or a string of zeros and ones held on some hard disk in some storage centre, that gives the shareholder various rights, for example the right to a share of any dividends the company decides to distribute. In most jurisdictions, though, the shareholder has no right to mandate a dividend payment. The company directors decide whether there is sufficient surplus to pay out a dividend, and at most the shareholders vote collectively yes or no to that dividend.

  The company, as a distinct legal person, owns its own assets, is responsible for its own liabilities; and anyone acting as if the company were theirs can be held legally liable. A company's assets are locked in, precisely so that the company can follow long-term business strategies; shareholders have no right to demand a company give them its assets.

- Directors of the company are there to serve the shareholders. Not true.

Company directors are legally bound to serve the company's needs to the best of their ability, they are not the agents of the shareholders. And because every company is a legal person (a clear legal actuality, not a fiction) distinct from any other legal persons like you or me associated with the company, including any shareholder, the company directors are not bound in any legally enforceable sense to maximise TSR. This "business judgement rule" exists in every major jurisdiction, and can, in principle, span all time horizons, from short to long.

The belief that a company exists to maximise TSR is a consequence of neo-classical economists' lobbying, and pressures from markets, some investors, potential hostile takeovers, and executive incentive schemes. If you look in the company law of England and Wales, and the company laws of different US states, you will find that the law as written is generically about the company's purpose is to achieve its stated objectives or purpose. Sadly many founders omit to define a very clear set of objects or purposes for the company, and so the neoclassical interpretation and pressures win when things come to court.

- Buying shares is the only way for a stakeholder to gain the right to vote in a general meeting, and voting rights must be tied to investment. Not true.

UK law, for example, refers to the members of the company, not the shareholders. So anyone who is entered into the register of voting members is eligible to vote[69]. One route to being entered in the register of members of a company lies in buying shares. Equally, the company may at a general meeting declare that any individual satisfying certain qualifying criteria is entered into the register of members and acquires the right to vote.

Most jurisdictions also have routes for investors to invest without acquiring voting rights, and for voting rights to be acquired with no investment, or minimal investment. If direct entry in the register of members is not possible, a company can easily place criteria on a specific class of voting shares based on all kinds of capitals invested by all kinds of stakeholders.

- The company's sole objective, and the focus of the AGM, is to maximise TSR. False.

Earlier in this chapter I wrote about this; I'll add here that this shift in meaning-making story, from the earlier ones seeing a company as very much part of the broader social fabric, has directly led to short-term thinking in companies, long-term wealth destruction for most stakeholders, the rising gap between the wealthy and the rest of society, and especially hides the non-financial risk-capitals invested by all stakeholders.

- The market plays a big role in funding company operations, and is the best judge of efficient use of resources. False.

Most of the capital that companies raise is prior to listing, not on the market after listing. The market enables those first investors to exit (so it does have a vital enabling role). We need it, like a dog needs a tail to wag; but today we are letting the tail wag the dog.

This myth became dominant in the second half of the last century, and has led to fatal flaws in our economy. Especially, it has taken us into a blind, lemming-like rush to the cliff-edge of our current degenerative economy. All direct stakeholders with commitment to the company, not the investors on the stock market lacking commitment (especially not the automatic trading algorithms holding shares for a few minutes), are the best judges of what is in the interests of the company.

Equally harmful, this myth has led to the emergence of so-called professional managers who stay with a company for such a short period of time that they are gone before the consequences of their decisions are seen,

- The company is a set of abstract contracts between owners. False.

Or, at least misleadingly incomplete. Recall, the word company itself comes from the Latin roots meaning *with bread* and is first and foremost a group of people who bond together into a community, building strong social relationships, in order to improve their capacity to thrive. The intangible social organisation that a company is, is far more important to business results than any tangible bundle of contracts. (see Chapter 12.)

- Money is neutral, and the only currency to use for all kinds of value in business. False.

Money, defined as positive interest bank debt, is one of many currencies we can define and use (See Section 3.5.4.) Each currency distorts and biases decisions if it is used inappropriately; and money is only appropriate for financial and some manufactured capital goods, not for natural or human capitals. We need to use other currencies there. Even a net present value calculation gives different decisions if you merely change the currency used from money to, say, the Terra[58].

If you believe these meaning-making stories, you will experience a reality that concretises them. If directors believe in the myth that their duty is to maximise TSR, forgetting that the legal personhood of the company puts it onto an equal footing to themselves and the investors as legal persons, then they will act exactly as if it were an absolute truth.

There are feedback loops in the power flows that lead to the same outcomes as if these myths were true. For example, if only the voting shareholders choose who is a director, and the directors need to earn their money or status through this role, and the incentives are designed to bolster these myths, then the shareholders can use this power to get their way.

These myths are so deeply woven into the meaning-making stories active in business and economics that they have become invisible. These stories form one of the invisible hands shaping the reality you experience today in your economy. Harnessing the power of business to rise to the challenges all of you reading this book (and everyone else connected with you) are facing, requires all of us to uncover these hidden stories that shape our reality, and to then pull away what is giving us these crises, keeping what is still useful in overcoming them.

The most important to keep is the meaning-making story of communities of people collaborating in a larger endeavour acquires itself the rights in law of a person, to become a non-human legal person, like you, a human legal person.

Inventing this story, and then for society to incorporate this story into the larger set of stories that shape our collective reality, has been a huge step forwards. Imagine that you were alive 400 years ago, perhaps making wagon wheels, and somebody tried to tell you that you should separate your wagon wheel business as an independent fictitious legal non-human person from yourself as the legal human person doing the artisanal work. You probably would have been completely unable to grasp how the company could possibly be an independent entity to you, and yet still fully dependent on you to speak on its behalf.

Just as quantum physics recognised that there was value in both particle and wave physics, and that the leap forward was to transcend and include in a radically new way the value of both, so too do we need to transcend and include here. As you read in the section on capital growth in a commons, a highly functioning commons takes care to grow the capital base. Maximising TSR has value and is a dumb idea, as Jack Welch said.

Integrate the complementary pairs: we need to keep the powerful capacity of business to multiply capital; *but must expand that to multiplying all capitals*. We need to keep the power of business to maximise TSR, *and expand shareholder to include all stakeholders*, from you and everyone like you, through to the planet's natural ecosystems as a stakeholder.

Then the tools of business for multiplying financial capital are put to work re-generating all other capitals. Such a regenerative economy will have high adaptive capacity, will be antifragile, and can give us what we need to address our 17 SDGs, including the climate emergency.

4.5 Steps in the right direction

There are numerous excellent initiatives underway to transform business into a force for good for all, many of which began decades ago. Yet they have changed business far too little far too late for us to have hope that we can address our global crises in time if we just continue trying harder to do what we have been doing.

An early, and vital, step in this direction has been freedom in the software world. Also called open source software, the big idea is that intellectual capital multiplies when it is shared freely. Today's Creative Commons licences, Wikipedia, Android, Linux, and much more have their roots in the realisation of people like Richard Stallman[77] of the need to legally protect freedom. This led to co-pyleft laws which protect the freedom to use (as opposed to copyright laws which restrict the freedom to use), such as the GNU public licence, and Creative Commons. Richard Stallman started the GNU project to create a completely free computer operating system in September 1983, and in 1985 he started the Free Software Foundation to protect intellectual freedom.

The Triple Bottom Line[78], Reporting3.0, the Integrated Reporting Initiative, Economy for the Common Good, Benefit Corporations, Purpose Companies, Transition Towns, b-corps and all the others are essential first steps towards the new reality we need. Equally, the trend towards developing leadership ethics, alternate ways of organising like Holacracy[79], sociocracy[80], and Deliberately Developmental Organisations[81] are essential components.

There are a whole range of excellent steps at the intersection of governance, society, non-profit and (social) enterprise, such as the associative democracy of Paul Hirst, or the work of Graham Smith and Simon Teasdale[82].

But even the most responsible leader using the most powerful of these tools can, at best, make small, local, and fragile changes. The apartheid-like context of separation in the legal constructs of our current incorporation leaves the door wide open for narrow self-interest to pull these improvements back to our current status quo, because only investors have legally mandated decision power, and only the investors have the majority benefit from those decisions; all others are separated from power and benefit.

Even though other stakeholders carry many of the costs of those decisions, sometimes for many generations into the future.

We need gentle ways of changing, gentle enough to keep society stable; but these will all get pulled back to the status quo, unless we also remove the root cause of the gravity pulling us back. Pressure is growing to use forceful change, even though it will destroy society and even more of nature, because we are not seeing clearly enough the difference between myth and actuality.

A growing number of people are now seeing this. Evolutesix (Graham) has starting up a startup creator and accelerator to grow startups using the Adaptive Organisation composed of the FairShares Commons legal framework, with self-organising, and developmental approaches (see Part IV).

South Africans dismantled their constitution, the source of their gravity shaping everyone's behaviour, in five years. There is nothing to stop us rewriting equally fast the foundations we build our companies on.

This will enable us to transform from the capitalism we have today to a fully regenerative capitalism, one that multiplies all capitals, from the entire planet's natural capital to your own self. For this to work, we need to clarify why there is no tragedy of the commons, so long as you construct it consistently.

4.6 Commons

In this book we call a common resource a commons if:

- everyone who benefits from it is also part of taking care of it;

- governance is broad, inclusive, where all relevant voices and perspectives are taken into account in a decentralised, non-hierarchical way;

- there are mechanisms to protect the commons against predation.

A commons doesn't need anything external for it to work well; everything it needs is internal (except perhaps solar energy).

Tragedy of the commons

In the original article by Garrett Hardin on the *Tragedy of the Commons*[83] the key heading was *The tragedy of freedom in the commons*; and mis-perceived open access and the commons as the same.

They are not. In a highly functioning commons, only the members of the community caring for the commons can access its benefits. This has functioned well across most of human history, because of various social norms, such as the biases you will read about in section 10.5.

Tragedy there means something inevitable, and harmful. Yet there's more than enough evidence that if all the characteristics of a well-functioning commons are in place, there is no inevitable harm. In fact, the climate emergency is evidence that you are likely to have inevitable harm when the stories of property are applied.

Hardin's intent was to show how self-interest without any boundaries to freedom would lead to a tragedy. Very true, and one of this book's central themes.

But with boundaries, with appropriate legal and social protection of the commons, protection as strong as property law and social norms are today, a commons based on reciprocal freedom and custodial obligations is a more viable approach to regulating individual self-interest in order to build an economy that does a better job of provisioning. It is a more viable approach than property is to meet the different needs of each individual across the community as a whole, and use the different capacities of each individual to protect and grow the wealth of all.

A highly functional commons

Elinor Ostrom's work on highly functioning commons[84] and the recent book by Michel Bauwens[85] describe the elements critical to an antifragile, highly functioning commons.

Highly functioning commons: governance

Perhaps the most important capacity of a highly functioning commons is self-policing.

Governing a commons for the good of all of its members, including future members as yet unborn, needs to be institutionalised. The norms of interaction, of caring for a commons, of decision-making, become part of the overarching stories that every member of the community stewarding and benefiting from the commons adopts as part of their own personal stories shaping their reality.

In a highly functioning commons everyone benefits from the surplus it generates, everyone cares for it, and everyone polices it.

There is no need for any outside regulation, because all the necessary stakeholders are already part of the shared benefit, caring, and policing.

Typically, any attempt at outside regulation weakens or even destroys the capacity of a commons to function. You can look at a commons as a superb example of how a highly functioning economy with zero external government regulation can exist. A commons can please both left and right views in politics.

Highly functional commons: external defence

For a commons to thrive over long periods of time, it needs sufficient defensive power to protect itself against invasion. Once this meant castles and knights; today this mostly means law, lawyers, and accountants. Although sometimes it still means physical power.

For a company to function as a FairShares Commons, and groups of such companies to function as a commons ecosystem, it's mostly about carefully crafting your articles of incorporation. Making sure the company is structured sufficiently clearly so it can defend itself against being enslaved.

The commons across North America functioned well for centuries, in part because of power balances across all the communities that cared for and benefitted from each regional commons. Then came large sailing ships, muskets that could kill at unprecedented distances, cannons that could demolish fortifications, and diseases new to their immune systems. The stewards of a commons had no power strong enough to defend their commons against a hostile takeover. Much as you may lack the power to defend yourself from a mugger.

They also came with stories about ownership, lenses that saw only the weakness of a commons, not the advantages; and judged it as inherently primitive and inferior. So the combination of the stories shaping the reality of the Europeans arriving in the Americas, along with their firepower, created the reality we have today.

But this is a consequence of what the lenses cannot see, not absolute evidence that the stories of property create better realities than the stories of a commons in all situations, everywhere, at any time, and for all people.

Highly functioning commons: fiduciary duty

Just as a well-functioning business has very clearly defined expectations on the executives carrying out their fiduciary duties with excellence, with various mechanisms to enforce it, so too do those people acting in executive-like roles in a highly functioning commons have clearly defined fiduciary duties. These duties apply to the full breadth of all the capitals that are part of the commons, and to all the stakeholders, whether they are alive today, yet to be born, and even those who have passed on and have become ancestral members.

In a small commons pretty much all roles are simultaneously filled by all of its members. Everybody is caring for the commons in all the ways that it can be cared for without much specialisation. This is very much the same as you'll find in many small start-ups or successful long-running small cooperatives.

As any organisation scales beyond the size of ancient family units (20 to 40 people) and then beyond the size of villages (200 to 300), new structures, hierarchies, and differentiations need to come in at each scale. Most organisations around you today use only one of the many ways of differentiating and layering. (Part IV) But scaling is seldom linear, and in organisations completely new phenomena can emerge at each scale that need to be dealt with in fundamentally different ways[86].

The traditional management accountability hierarchy is not very suitable for a larger commons, especially not a global one that is capable of rising to the challenges we face today, such as the climate crisis. However, the human capacity hierarchy, combined with a functional accountability hierarchy and consent-based ways of filling specific roles of Part IV can be used to build a commons that will work at all scales.

Highly functioning commons: capital growth

Typically a commons comes into existence because some resource, valuable to all of its members, is below some threshold of supply. So it makes sense to work together so that everybody is provided with an adequate amount, nobody has too much at the expense of somebody else having too little, and that that resource continues to be available with sufficient abundance for future generations.

A highly functioning commons explicitly takes the needs of future generations into account, and it's usually had a long enough existence to also give some idea of the kinds of natural fluctuations that it is subject to. So highly functioning commons put effort into multiplying the capital. That way, even if they have a run of bad years and the capital drops to much less than what it had been, over the long run the amount of capital in the commons will steadily grow.

This is no different to how modern businesses are designed to multiply financial capital. Any modern business can run perfectly well as a commons and continue to multiply financial capital well.

But today, we need new kinds of commons. We need new kinds of businesses, that multiply all capitals. We need all-capitals commons, where all capitals are multiplied. And we need part of a nested hierarchy of ecosystems of commons producing an economy that does the job of provisioning for all.

Highly functioning commons: benefit

There are many different ways at each scale to decide how members of a commons benefit from the wealth it generates. Typically, though, a highly functional commons will use some kind of collective decision-making process that ensures the valid needs of all members are adequately met. A process that strives to be fair to all, and that if fairness is unachievable, at a minimum is equally unfair to all.

In particular, the decision is not taken by a small stakeholder group that happens to have power for some reason disconnected from the commons and the other stakeholders.

4.7 Free FairShares Commons

Buckminster Fuller said *"You never change things by fighting the existing reality. To change something, build a new paradigm that makes the existing paradigm obsolete."* The legal construct we use today is an expression of an old reality, created by a story well past its sell-by date. This story is about the culture, beliefs and actual scarcity of money in the past. High time we used a modern story matching today's scarcity: the resource scarcity of natural capital, human innovation and attention. A story creating the reality that we need to thrive within the constraint of the interdependence of life on planet Earth.

Fully adaptive organisations based on Free companies or FairShares Commons, with at least self-governing for roles and tasks, and with developmental human practices, may well be the minimum viable solution. Let's look at what pragmatic actions you can already take for another step towards this minimum viable solution. What can you do to build a new business paradigm that addresses climate emergency and other injustices?

Central is adopting inclusive legal incorporation constructs. Those of the Purpose Stiftung (a German and Swiss foundation promoting the for-purpose company form, which is also a form preventing sale of the company), and even more so those of our FairShares Commons, are sufficiently proven and ready to be adopted by those forward-looking companies that want to show the way.

These build on proven approaches used for decades, for example by Carl Zeiss, Robert Bosch, Mondragon, etc. Even Visa, in its first decade, was able to transform the completely dysfunctional relationships between players in the emerging credit card system because it included all in a democratic, citizenship-based governance. And its first CEO, Dee Hock, is clear that this way of incorporating was the major reason why Visa was so successful.

You can build a FairShares Commons now in most countries. At least one that is good enough for now. You do not need to agitate for a change in company law. Using existing company law you can easily create distributed, equitable governance and wealth sharing, such as the FairShares Commons Incorporation does.

In a FairShares company, investors still get voting rights and a share of wealth. Anything that separates investors from power and wealth is just another kind of separation, and will likely lead to harmful consequences. Few investors are fundamentally bad, most have value to contribute, but are pulled down by the system's hidden gravity, just as everyone in South Africa was pulled down by the gravity of apartheid. For any new approach to work, investors must have just the right amount of power and reward.

In a FairShares company, staff, suppliers, customers, any relevant stakeholder group, even perhaps the city and country the company is based in, can all qualify for voting rights in the general meetings, and a share of the wealth generated. These rights are not based only on buying shares with money. Rather, these rights are earned through engagement, and the investment of all capitals: financial, human and natural.

The big idea here is the same as has underpinned our modern approach to governing countries: citizenship. In the Free company, anyone that satisfies the criteria of "a citizen of good standing" has the right to engage in governance. Few today would want to go back to the days when kings and queens used countries, along with the people in them, as their personal property; the same will be true in the future for companies. So every stakeholder group has enough power to keep the costs and benefits of decisions balanced across all stakeholders, including future generations.

You may wonder how you can run a company if so many people have a vote. No differently to today. All operating decisions are still made by the executives, not the shareholders. But big decisions, like selling the company, or shifting to renewable energy, are taken by all stakeholders in the AGM or via the board.

Experience over the centuries in cities and nations shows, without any doubt, that when all are citizens, when all have rights to freedom, and an equitable share of governance and wealth is generated, then all are most likely to prosper long term. The transformation of city and national governance from an aristocratic elite to a citizenship democracy over the past centuries in much of the world has addressed historical injustices and created much good in our lives at the citizen, city and national scales. To rise to our new challenges and build a better world we need to repeat what has worked before, now at the non-human legal person, worker, investor, etc. levels.

Of course, not all old injustices are done and dusted; there are many that we still need to address. And globalisation within today's flavour of capitalism has led to new injustices.

Just as the ending of apartheid was the essential step of this trend to freedom in South Africa, I believe we now need to take the next step in companies if we are to address social injustices like climate change.

This step brings you to freedom, the freedom to be yourself in your full strength, the freedom to develop yourself into who you can become[87], as the pragmatic foundation of an economy free of the injustices of climate change, etc. It also brings freedom to the companies that are the building blocks of our economy.

When everything participates in governance and wealth sharing, including cities, nations and the natural environment, then it's a small step to see the company as a common good over multiple generations. Which requires freedom for the company itself.

Free of ownership, free to develop to its full potential as an element of society. Compare with nations and cities today; they work better because they can no longer be sold by a king to another king. Yet we still have structures allowing the shareholders of a company to sell the company.

Freedom also means the company is free to die when it is too old, or no longer has a niche in the social ecosystem. Which means that healthy evolution can work in the business ecosystems, not the harmful culling you see today.

Some ask me *"does freedom mean eliminating regulation of business?"*

Certainly not; what freedom does is shift most regulation from the slow, uninformed, indirect, external, macro regulation of today to fast, informed, direct, internal, micro regulation.

Once all stakeholders (from investors, staff, etc. to entire regions) affected by a general meeting decision are in the general meeting with power, there is far less need for the slow, clumsy regulation of state bodies. All benefit from immediate, internal micro regulation.

Ending apartheid in South Africa could only really begin once all South Africans were free and included in governance. (South Africa still has a long way to go in addressing all injustices inherited from apartheid. Governance power is still not yet well distributed, and the share of wealth even less so.)

We only begin ending the global injustices of today's capitalism once all of a company's stakeholders are included in governance and wealth sharing; and the legal person we call a company is as free as the natural persons you and I are.

Even if all companies were FairShares Commons tomorrow we would have a long way to go before the unjust consequences of our current economic and political choices are addressed. But we'd be going a lot faster than we can now, and humanity needs us to go way faster than we are now.

The FairShares Commons will enable us to rise to the global challenges we are all facing, because such a free company gives us the power to stand on the shoulders of giants, instead of reinventing the wheel[77].

4.8 Legal and economic foundations

I (Graham) realised around 2010 that the barrier I was hitting trying to making Holacracy work well in my startup lay in both the human and the incorporation dimensions shown later in the book in Figure 12.2 on Page 295. I realised we needed a way beyond the paradigm of ownership, and looked at legal research I discovered empty voting (the separation of voting power from financial risk), vote trading, hidden ownership, and how these could turn competitive stock markets into collaborative stock markets. This showed I was on the right track; all that was needed was to take these practices all the way, and structure them to enable us to create ecosystems of regenerative commons companies.

You get empty voting where an investor has voting power without the matching financial risk; for example, the investor buys both voting shares in a company and derivatives protecting them against any loss if the share price drops; or even paying out more than they invested. This means that first asset stripping, and then destroying the company, can be in the investor's financial interests. It usually at least opens up significant potential risks and costs for all stakeholders, leading to calls for regulation[88].

Equally it can lead to more efficient corporate governance[89], along with greater and broader shareholder democracy[90]. A lot of attention is paid to executive values and their decisions; but investor / shareholder values and decisions, and how effective they are, are equally important[91]. After all, the AGM vote is used by investors to decide on board membership, executive pay, mergers and acquisitions, etc. Which leads to both the consent decision making process and the inclusion of diverse categories of stakeholders in the FairShares Commons, as a way of improving the decisions of shareholders.

The conflict between Telus, a Canadian company, and Mason Capital, a US hedge fund, described by Ringe[92] is worth reading. Ringe describes well how the decoupling of voting power from financial risk distorts the traditional incentives. Whilst most cases so far have benefited investors at the cost of other stakeholders, a few changes as described in this book turn the same decoupling into a new way of building regenerative ecosystems.

How eliminating information asymmetry (the FairShares Commons does this) to empty voting and hidden ownership creates a new kind of economy, where social welfare and better market outcomes emerge, has been described by Barry et al.[93]. Julie Battilana et al. give evidence that hybrid organisations perform better[94].

Iwai has described how, much as in quantum physics, all perspectives on what a company is have validity[95], and can be integrated as complementary pairs.

CHAPTER 5

The Economy of the Free

It is good to have an end to journey toward, but it is the journey that matters in the end.
—*Ursula K Le Guin*

Let your vision be world-embracing rather than confined to your own self.
—*Baha'u'llah*

You bring a new reality into your world by first writing a new story. You begin writing a new story by imagining what might be. Leaping into an unknown potential, painting broad swathes of imaginary colour. Then growing your reality into this aspiration.

This chapter tells a story of what can be, and in part already exists. A story to replace the stories today's business 'truths' concretised. This new story already partly exists, in companies like Bridgewater[96], one of the world's largest hedge funds with USD160 billion assets under management in 2017, which has consistently used some of the elements of this new story. The founder and CEO, Ray Dalio, is quite clear that this is the reason for their phenomenal success.

Highly successful businesses like CCA, Zappos, Robert Bosch, Carl Zeiss, Mondragon, John Lewis, Interface, IKEA, Patagonia, Whole Foods, Visa up to 2007, and many more, have proven over decades each of this story's individual building blocks. There is no question that each building block has given them a competitive edge, especially in a crisis.

The important question is: how much more powerful do these building blocks become when you use them all together, and enough companies using all the building blocks form an ecosystem? Look at everything that Paul Polman accomplished during his decade as CEO of Unilever. The huge strides that the company took during those 10 years are testimony to just what can be done with the largest multinationals. And yet, the gap between how far Unilever did change and both the demands of today's crises and Paul Polman's beliefs is still much too big.

How much more could he have done if even one prototype ecosystem of the Economy of the Free existed, providing hard compelling data of the benefits to each stakeholder within their set of needs and dominant stories?

As you read this chapter, use it to light up your imagination. Imagine what an Economy of the Free can bring to you. Write your story of your Economy of the Free, and then do everything you can to grow your reality into that aspiration. I believe that together we can build the reality painted in this chapter. We just need to harness your uniquenesses, all of you reading this book, together.

You can also take encouragement from many countries; e.g., Germany, where individuals across the spectrum from politics, bureaucrats, business, and civil society are all taking initial steps to transform the entire foundations in the direction that I am pointing out in this book, for example via the Purpose Foundation's lobbying, consulting, and investment activities.

If something doesn't make sense to you yet, you may need more fluidity in one or more of the forms of thought described in Chapter 9. Without sufficient fluidity in them, I (Jack and Graham) could not have broken through the limits of the classical lenses of business and economics, nor seen the necessity of multiple perspectives to make sense of what is happening, nor could we have begun the transformational journey of bringing multiple systems into a new balance.

5.1 Overcoming obstacles

There are obstacles we need to overcome to build the Economy of the Free, a regenerative economy quite different to the free economy we have today (where precious little is free). Some key obstacles are listed below, and this book shows some actions you can take to overcome them.

Every system generates certain kinds of benefits for some or all. Any change in the system will either change those benefits, or at least trigger fears that they will change. And so the very powerful cognitive bias of loss aversion will fight back.

Whilst you may not believe these obstacles can ever be overcome, I believe they can, because I have been here before. Recall the story of South Africa in Section 1.8, describing how the Mont Fleur process overcame obstacles I (Graham) had believed insurmountable as a child. It worked because it used everything described in the rest of this book.

By applying everything in this book to yourself and your work, especially if you are a leader of any nature, you will be able to take the first steps needed to overcome the obstacles and build an Economy of the Free. And the best way to overcome any obstacle is to transform it into a supportive ally.

Power Those in positions of power benefit from today's economy, and some will be loath to lose their benefits. Benefits like power, control, money etc. They have the power to slow down transforming our economy to an Economy of the Free. In South Africa those in power (military, police, business and political leaders) were transformed into allies by creating a path to a new South Africa that was better for them than the counter-coup they could have staged to retain Apartheid.

Meaning-making stories Making the Economy of the Free the new reality requires enough of us to use the appropriate meaning-making stories. Historically transforming the meaning-making stories of large numbers of individuals has happened over at least a generation. But we do not have the time left to wait for death's role here. Fortunately, we now know how to change meaning-making stories, and describe how in this book, in Chapters 7 to 9.

Economists, lawyers, etc. People in key positions of power concretising meaning-making stories into institutions are powerful allies in change, provided they are willing to, and supported in, changing their own meaning-making stories. Because this changes their self-identity, it is akin to a little death. Who I am now, that I am likely proud of, needs to die so that the next me can live. We know how to do this, and this book gives the recipe: raise awareness of who you can be, and provide support to ease self-transformation using powerful transformation tools.

Economics discipline The authors of *Econocracy* clearly describe the disconnection between the contents of most of the economics discipline (including all the institutions), and what we need society and its economy to actually be for us to have a thriving future deep into future generations. This is not due to ignorance, because we have a good enough idea of where to go, and which steps to take first. Such as those described in this book, which is intended to catalyse action across the board.

Money Our current mono-crop currency system (i.e., money as the only currency) is an obstacle, because money cannot represent all capitals in flow in the undistorted, bias-free way needed. Couple this with the number of powerful people and institutions in the financial space and this is a barrier.

Government Local and national governments will no longer need to do much of what they currently do, in terms of regulation, taxation, etc., and so some incumbents will want to maintain the status quo. The good news is that government will become a direct stakeholder in the Economy of the Free. So there is a more desirable future, and a path to it, for government.

Company owners Loss aversion is such a powerful driver of human behaviour that we even avoid large gains if we fear the small loss needed to achieve the gain. Losing the illusion of control to gain a wealthier life overall for yourself, future generations, and the rest of society will be a big shift for many owners of today's companies. Again, this book gives powerful tools to do so, and South Africa's Mont Fleur process shows how it can work.

System inertia Overcoming the system inertia will take an Aikido-like feint. Following the advice of Buckminster Fuller, we need to build a new system rapidly, and once that is far enough, the old system will rapidly transfer resources into the new. Do not try to overcome the inertia of the old system; it will do that job by itself once a big enough prototype of the new one is visibly working better. This will also address all the above barriers.

Human capacity to imagine Our capacity to imagine what can be, how to get there, and who we can become, is far bigger than most of us realise. We just need to use it fully by developing ourselves, as described in this book, and especially our capacity for uncertainty. The work of R3.0, mentioned below, and their templates for a transition to a regenerative economy, are a superb resource of what works.

Human capacity for uncertainty This is the crux. The journey to a new economy and society that works for all people and for a better world is filled with uncertainty. It is deeply Cynefin complex, or even chaotic (see the list on P66). The bigger you develop your capacity for uncertainty, the better you can see and work with your cognitive biases, and the better you can put everything into practice to build the new system we need now.

Our current global system cannot continue unchanged; there is an inexorable current moving us towards a new system. What that will be depends on the path we take.

Ohm's law in physics states:

$$I = \frac{V}{R}.$$
$$(5.1)$$

The current flowing (I) equals the force pushing (V) divided by the resistance (R). Relevant, at least as a partial metaphor, to where we are now. Partial, because Ohm's law is linear, but we are dealing with a highly complex nonlinear open system. In the worst case, pushing for change may even maintain our dysfunctional system, not change it.

The speed of change we need, i.e., the current, will continue to increase as we head deeper into all our crises. I see two main scenarios.

Either we manage to reduce the resistance at least as fast as the current increases. Then the same, or less force is needed to drive the change. This way we are most likely to preserve all the wealth we need to build the new economy. (By wealth I mean all different kinds of capital and access to those capitals by all stakeholders.)

Or the resistance stays as it is, perhaps even increases. Then the amount of force will continue to grow. The more force is needed to drive the current we need, the more we will destroy the wealth needed to build the new economy.

5.2 Your economy, your job to change it

One story that creates your experience of the economy is that we lack the power to change it. And so, to change how the economy works, *we* somehow need to convince *them*, whoever they may be, to change themselves and the economy.

None of you needs to buy into that story. It's your economy, you can change it, it is your job to change it. Now let's dive into how you, as one individual, can take action to change it. And we must change it; even though many are enjoying a life that would have seemed like an unachievable, fantastic utopia to anyone alive a few centuries ago.

The first step is simply to recognise the extent to which the stories that we buy into take away or direct our power to act. Begin with the big shift Einstein and Picasso brought in, rather there is no single privileged perspective and there are multiple perspectives that have value. Of course, they did not say that every perspective has equal value—both clearly recognised that some perspectives give you more value than others and that some opinions are simply nonsense.

Darwin recognised that evolution[1] proceeds incrementally. There are no revolutions driven from within. The only point where nature experiences the reality of a revolution is when a major crisis catapults an ecosystem into revolution, say a rapid change in temperature triggered by some natural calamity blanketing the at-

---

[1]Another myth is that evolution is about competition between; survival of the strongest. Actually Darwin recognised that evolution is about the best fit to the conditions, which often is collaboration within groups and species. Evolution often works more on groups, less on individuals[97].

mosphere and either trapping heat in or preventing heat getting in. Such as massive volcanic eruptions, or planet-wide burning of carbon in engines.

You are a participant in our economy because you are reading this book. You may have bought the book, you may have funded the book in advance through our crowdfunding campaign, or you may have invested in the FairShares Commons publishing company that published this book. However you've done it, you're participating in the economy.

As you saw in the section on Ubuntu 7.3.1, simply participating in the economy shapes the reality that you experience, and the different realities that others experience. Your stories, your capacity for transformational thinking, and your biases shape how you participate in the economy, and thereby your experience. Begin rewriting those stories today and you will begin experiencing a different reality tomorrow.

More than anything else today, we need to grow our wisdom to choose which stories shape our reality and which stories we refuse to allow to shape it. The wiser the choices you make today, the more likely your reality tomorrow will be a reality you thrive in, and a reality you feel hope in.

But your capacity for wisdom disappears quickly in the face of fear and many other strong emotions. We are hard-wired to do this, as you will see in the sections on biases 10.5. You will see how your unique combination of biases and stories shrinks the wisdom of your choices when you are in the grip of certain strong emotions, and amplifies the wisdom of your choices when in the grip of other emotions.

Disruptive innovation for our economy

Creating the Economy of the Free described in this chapter is a large scale example of disruptive innovation. Read the book of Clayton Christensen, *The Innovator's DNA: Mastering the Five Skills of Disruptive Innovators*[45] to get more adept at applying the five skills of disruptive innovation to all aspects of your economy.

The essence of disruptive innovation begins with owning and rewriting the stories that shape the current reality. What could be more disruptive than taking the final logical step and freeing from ownership all legal persons, not just human legal persons like yourself? What could be more disruptive than reframing capitalism to include all capitals and demanding that our businesses regenerate all capitals, not just financial capital? What could be more disruptive than reframing markets to facilitate the flow of all capitals from where they are abundant to where they are needed, fully valuing each capital for what it is, not for how much money the current exchange rate between capitals allocates to it, an exchange rate that we humans have invented?

Every economy goes through periods of disruption driven by changes in context. And one of the biggest changes in context we need to respond to, at the extremes of the adaptive capacity we have in an Economy of the Free, is climate emergency and the 17 SDGs.

Another change in context that we will harness in an Economy of the Free to grow our adaptive capacity and respond to climate change is artificial intelligence. This is the next big great shift in technology, after the shifts that we have had over the past few centuries beginning with the Industrial Revolution.

At the moment, the dominant story around artificial intelligence is one of fear. In the Economy of the Free, the dominant story around artificial intelligence is one of hope. Because the foundations of artificial intelligence are all commons, rather than owned by a very small number of human and non-human legal persons. So the wealth that artificial intelligence generates across all capitals is shared by all, not just the few rent-seeking owners.

Nested living ecosystems

The nested living ecosystems[98] in an Economy of the Free all have boundaries, but the boundaries keep shifting and moving in different contexts for different people every time you look at them. You don't fall uniquely inside or outside an ecosystem. You may be deep in, strongly bridge between many, or be mostly outside; and this keeps changing.

You also can't pin down exactly what your role is and how it contributes to any of the nested living ecosystems. The big difference between any living ecosystem and the same number of elements disconnected from each other but next to each other is intuitively clear to you. You appreciate and feel comfortable with the fact that you cannot reduce any living ecosystem to the sum of its parts. The very essence of life is an emergent phenomenon that happens through the interrelatedness and interactivity of all the parts.

To do this you need Thought Form P5 from Chapter 9 to remind yourself that the ecosystem is constantly under construction, as is your knowledge of the ecosystem. This is an example of why the self-development section of this book is an essential part. Until someone has fluidity in all the thought forms needed to see something clearly, ecosystems remain too fuzzy or even hidden to work with them.

You experience daily how power is active throughout ecosystems, at all scales, and all types of power. Remember how power was once more limited to political power and money power, and in the hands of the few? An Economy of the Free is the effective, desirable end of the growing trend today, where every single capital exercises power, every single stakeholder group exercises power, in each nested layer of this ecosystem of ecosystems. This diverse spread of all powers exercised by many leads to the natural checks and balances that keep an Economy of the Free at maximum adaptive capacity and regenerative capacity. Unleashing power *to* is far more satisfying for you than the old economy's power *over*[99].

And this wide diversity of power to, in the hands of all, is enabled by the strong bonding within each ecosystem, from the local to the global. Everyone knows that they are contributing their uniqueness as an accepted and valid member of one small local micro ecosystem, one medium-sized regional ecosystem, and one global ecosystem of businesses. The full value of power in uniqueness and the full value of oneness as part of all, is enabled by the strong bonding within each ecosystem of your daily experience.

Adam Kahane's book, *Power and Love*[99] describes well the balance needed in yourself, your organisation, and your ecosystems between power to do; and love, which refers to everything that bonds us together in our oneness. Power enables your individual uniqueness to flourish at each scale, and love enables all to stand together in the strength of your common oneness at each scale.

These ecosystems have much in common with the beehives. The beehive is the primary living entity, not the individual bee. Each bee is an autonomous self-governing member of the hive; it decides for itself what to do, when, and how; with input from what all the other bees are communicating. And each bee is doing that within predefined functions that support the hive as a whole.

The hive has far greater adaptive capacity than any individual bee. The hive as a whole reacts more and faster to evolutionary drivers. If the temperature goes outside the range of an individual bee, the air conditioning bees become more active keeping the hive cool or warm. If some kind of predator comes close to the hive, the bees will attack even though each bee that stings dies in the process. Very much like you do not hesitate to sacrifice a few skin cells to pick up something rough.

Occasionally a FairShares Commons business in one of your ecosystems recognises that it is time to die. Maybe it merges with another, or because it has run its course. This is an enormous relief because zombie companies are no longer being kept alive artificially, draining financial, human, and environmental capital. Instead, companies voluntarily die gracefully when the conditions and need (a.k.a. the driver) that called that company into existence disappear, or change enough that the company no longer fits a niche. Then all the capitals and resources in it are immediately put to use elsewhere in the ecosystem, rather than wasted. This is why a FairShares Commons ecosystem is inherently better for all stakeholders. (Apart from the few only interested in taking at the cost of others, because now they cannot easily take.)

Occasionally, the smaller-scale ecosystems die in some way, because they no longer fill a niche, or perhaps they have grown too old to hold together and hold up all the power flowing through them. Again, this is a welcome and natural part of a thriving, living set of nested ecosystems.

Autopoiesis is a recognised and maximised capacity of all ecosystems at all scales. As in nature, every entity at each scale has its own natural lifespan and life cycle, from birth through growth and maturity onto old age and eventual death. This is welcomed as a fundamental source of adaptive capacity in the system.

Sex is the other essential adaptive capacity in ecosystems of living entities and between ecosystems of living entities. The necessity of exchanging, mixing and matching DNA in multiple combinations, maximises the adaptive capacity. Whilst every single company and ecosystem has a clear boundary, it also has a thriving exchange with other similar companies and ecosystems. This thriving exchange of DNA leads to offspring companies that have something new, and every time there is some big change or shift, one of these new companies and new ecosystems turns out to have exactly the new, unpredictable, and unplayable combination of DNA needed to thrive.

So FairShares companies and ecosystems die a natural death, with all their accumulated capitals shifting to those new companies and ecosystems being born because they now best fit the new challenges. This mix of random exchanges of DNA, and the high interactivity within and between ecosystems of all sizes and up and down the nested hierarchy of ecosystems, becomes a core part of living a satisfying, thriving life in businesses that are good for you to work in; in an economy that does the job of provisioning; and on a planet whose living ecosystem supports life better each year. The common ground between ecology, economy, and ecosystems is visibly harnessed, rather than relegated to dictionary entries on the origin of words.

There are no more environmental externalities because it's clear that the global business ecosystem fits into and is supported by the global natural ecosystem.

In many situations in your old economy, you really need to trust another human being to be able to work effectively with them, especially if they were part of another organisation. Often the best you could do was to set up some kind of contract based on what you do to each other if something went wrong. In an Economy of the Free, trust is now first and foremost trust in the structures, processes, and norms of how to interact with each other in an ecosystem and between ecosystems. Trust is externalised.

The biggest reason to trust lies in knowing that every time there is some breakdown or conflict, you have exactly the right tools to use that conflict to adapt and improve yourself and your ecosystem.

In physics, free energy is the fraction of the total energy that is available to nature to use. In the Economy of the Free, your free energy will be the highest it can be. You will have more energy to put to work doing the things that you enjoy, for yourself, for your friends and family, and for your colleagues. The free energy of each ecosystem at each scale is as high as possible. Very little is wasted in unproductive friction, what we call Job 2 in Part III.

Imagine how much more your life is now.

5.3 Regenerative capitalism

I firmly believe that capitalism is an essential, powerful tool that we cannot do without in rising to the adaptive challenges of our climate emergency and the 17 SDGs. But, to paraphrase Star Trek, it's not capitalism as we know it today, Jim.

We need regenerative capitalism, a big capitalism that multiplies all capitals; unlike our current small capitalism.

- Regenerative capitalism treats all capitals equitably.

- Regenerative capitalism has at least one currency for each capital. A naturally right currency, where the currency reflects the value attributed to the capital in unbiased flow. (As you will read below, in my usage of the word, what you may think of as different national currencies are all one currency: positive interest bank debt.)

- Regenerative capitalism delivers appreciation, growth of each capital in its own natural units. Regenerative capitalism harnesses the power of business, now to multiply all capitals, including natural capitals, not just money.

- Regenerative capitalism gives governance power to each capital, proportional to the overall meaning of that capital to the ecosystem. Regenerative capitalism recognises the roles of a multiplicity of stakeholders representing all the capitals as members of corporations. Each capital relevant to the corporation is part of the governance steering it into the future, and shares in the wealth generated by the corporation—the wealth generated in the capital that you represent, and an appropriate share of the wealth generated in the other capitals because of the role played by the capital you represent.

- Regenerative capitalism treats ecosystems as primary and is built up of a nested hierarchy of ecosystems stretching from your global ecosystems all the way down to you and your family.

Taken together, these facets of regenerative capitalism give you the foundation you need to build the antifragile reality we need for all to thrive[100], one going beyond a circular economy, beyond sustainability, to a regenerative economy.

This is a missing ingredient for green (or blue) economy[2], an economy for the common good[103] (an innovative business scorecard looking at a much broader range of indicators than typical business scorecards), and the triple bottom line (people, profit, and planet as equally important measures of business success, not just profit); integral impact investing[104] (integrating multiple different elements according to Wilber's[105] or Lessem's approach), and much more.

I'll expand here on what I wrote about property and freedom as complementary pairs. Clearly the concept of property is something that we need, in order to construct a viable economy, as is the concept of freedom.

At some point between you as a free-living being where it's clearly harmful to apply any concepts of property, through to the equipment you use, where the concept of property is beneficial, there's some transition zone. Maybe similar to quantum physics, a transition zone where both concepts are simultaneously valid for everything in that zone. (Even if something is owned by a group of people, as in the sharing economy, the concept of property is still being applied. For a commons to function, the concept of property is essential.)

So to build a regenerative economy, we need to figure out what best belongs in the meaning-making story of freedom only, what best belongs into the meaning-making story of property only, and what we may need to invent that integrates both as a complementary pair.

For example, take a forest. In economics today almost all forests are part of the concept of property. They may be owned by an individual, a corporation, the state, or they are not owned and therefore open to being claimed as property by anyone ready and willing to do work on the forest. Equally, the atmosphere, or the Arctic and Antarctic can fall into the concept of property, even if no one has yet claimed ownership; or into that of freedom; or into something new reflecting them as complementary pairs.

I believe that the regenerative economy we need to address our climate crisis is based on applying the meaning-making story of freedom to all large scale ecosystems, certainly all those at a planetary scale, at least down to corporations as non-human beings, and yourself as a human being. If we use anything of property at all, it will be to enable freedom (i.e., the full complementary pairing), certainly not in opposition to freedom.

---

[2] The blue economy concept is both used to refer purely to marine life[101], and inclusively by Gunter Pauli for the whole planet[102].

In a regenerative economy, where the atmosphere is as free as you are, and where your role becomes one analogous to a parent—speaking on behalf of something that is free but unable to speak itself.

The Economy of the Free is a fully regenerative economy across all capitals; the ones that we have invented that the consumer society values, and the ones that have always been part of nature because life itself values them. All the companies manufacturing any product are part of small and large circles in a circular economy. Every single product at the end of its life cycle is the raw material for something else.

The small and large circles function because the companies are all FairShares Commons companies. So all have an appropriate benefit from the wealth generated by each company in the circles as the product moves around the circular economy. Now, every company in the circle has the incentive to do what is right and regenerative for the whole across the long-term, and that is in the interests of society as a whole across seven generations.

The triple bottom line is a no-brainer because all categories of stakeholders are engaged in the decisions taken at the general meeting level. The company stewards that are legally required to veto any decision that might lead to a loss of freedom, and any decision that is benefiting the present at the expense of future generations, are naturally maintaining a triple bottom line. In fact, this triple bottom line is in the deepest spirit of John Elkington's 1994 proposal[78].

There is almost no need for regulation or legislation because the interests of all stakeholders including future generations are fully represented within each FairShares Commons company and within the ecosystems of companies at all scales. Instead of externalising the power to meet these needs to the institution of government, the power to ensure these needs are met is internalised within each company and their ecosystems. The distinction between you as a citizen, you as a consumer, you as a voter, and you as a worker and manager still exists, but you now wear all those hats within the business ecosystems you are part of.

I (Graham) am an advocate for R3.0[3]. It is developing everything needed to redesign our economy to build resilience in our social and ecological systems and regeneration beyond the baseline of social and ecological sustainability thresholds to thrivability. It has an excellent set of templates, complementing everything in this book, and our Evolutesix materials, on how to create a regenerative economy and build a better world.

I strongly recommend you join R3.0. It has nine blueprints available:

1. Reporting

---

[3] https://www.r3-0.org/

2. Accounting

3. Data

4. New business models

5. Transformation journey

6. Sustainable finance

7. Value cycles

8. Governments, multilaterals and foundations

9. Educational transformation.

For any of these approaches to work, we must build them on the freedom needed for accountability. Only the free can take accountability for the consequences of their actions. Only a free company, a commons of joint capacity inclusive of all stakeholders, can ever be the building blocks of a regenerative and circular economy.

A free economy only works well when it is an Economy of the Free.

5.4 Escaping gravity

The stories that create the reality you experience are like gravity. They are always pulling you in one direction. In the Economy of the Free, many stories have been rewritten, and you have escaped the reality of the old ones. More importantly, you are now using gravity in support of your freedom.

If you have ever tried juggling, you know that you need gravity in order to juggle. If you are in deep outer space, with almost no gravity, and you throw a ball up, it is not going to fall down. Here are a few examples of how you are escaping the old gravity and juggling with the new gravity.

The government's new role

A government's reality is as much shaped by the stories of what government means as anything else. In the new Economy of the Free, the role of government has changed fundamentally, because the story is now one of maintaining the integrity of freedoms fundamental to the Economy of the Free. From your individual freedom, through the freedom of your organisations, to the freedom of humanity as a whole to thrive.

The government is now there to maintain the overall functioning of society and our business ecosystems of the largest scale, much as you see city municipalities doing today at the city level. Almost all regulation, almost all roles of government, is now happening within the ecosystems.

For example, the needs of towns, cities, regions, and nations to have enough money to build and maintain services are now primarily met by a share of the surplus wealth generated and realising their share of capital gain.

Instead of elected government officials, and civil servants, engaging in battle on your behalf with multinationals headquartered in a different country, if you are one of the stakeholders you are directly part of these companies' general meetings and ecosystems. As a customer, as a supplier, or as a member of some other stakeholder group, you attend the general meetings and have the power directly yourself to protect your interests in a way that balances out with the needs of other stakeholder groups to protect their interests. With the seven-generation requirement, there is very little need for regulation to protect the environment long-term.

The proponents of both light and heavy government intervention end up getting what they want.

The climate emergency is now being dealt with using the full power that we have. Decades of failure by national governments to come to a global agreement on climate change and what to do about it have turned into direct agreement at all scales up to the global ecosystem because each scale representatives of that scale are coming into agreement with their neighbours.

In the Economy of the Free, governments of nations, as well as regional governments and representatives of blocs of multiple nations all have a role to play, the roles that all the other stakeholder groups and ecosystems play. Governments represent the uniqueness of one country, in balance with the different agents across all the scales of the Economy of the Free, representing the oneness and the uniqueness of each layer within the ecosystem of ecosystems.

Lobbyists still exist, but the role they play no longer has the disproportionate power that money currently buys. There's the full diversity of engagement in lobbying, dialogue and decisions at all scales of the hierarchy of ecosystems.

The economy's new stories

The central story now in the Economy of the Free is that it is illegal, ineffective, and morally wrong to apply any part of property law to any individual, any incorporated business, or any ecosystem of businesses at any scale from the smallest through to the global business ecosystem.

Different capitals may or may not be owned within that, but only to the extent that owning the capital does not prevent the freedom of any legal person, whether human or nonhuman, nor ecosystems of legal persons.

You know that your economy is inherently complex, sometimes on the edge of chaos, in the sense of Dave Snowden's Cynefin[52,53] diagram. So you no longer try to gather lots of data in order to analyse it and identify good practice. Instead, you know that the economy in detail is emergent, which means acting, monitoring, and reacting.

The story of your economy is now one of moving, changing, and adapting faster than the drivers of the economy are changing, rather than attempting to predict or control the economy.

Economists' new role

Economists now are more like sports psychologists. They develop the capacity of ecosystems at all scales to react quickly to what's happening, and grow their adaptive capacity, but it's the ecosystem itself that does the reaction and balancing.

The work of economists no longer has an anchor in the few owning property or capital and renting it to the many. The new story of economists, just as the new story of government, revolves around freedom, and multiple capitals, and the access to those capitals for all. The central role of economists is understanding freedom and the flow of capital, from where it is abundant to where it is needed or being unnecessarily constrained.

The central story of economists is now about provisioning at all scales of the ecosystem, across all capitals and currencies.

In some ways, the economist is now much closer to the story and work of a gardener or farmer. Now that businesses are legally full living beings free from any application of property law, and stewarded as any other voiceless living being would be, the role of economists is to create the conditions for these living beings to thrive. And to study the consequences of different types, numbers, and densities of businesses, in one ecosystem; the flows of capitals within ecosystems and between ecosystems, and what enables those capitals to flow.

Most importantly, the economist's role is constantly experimenting, as evolution does in nature, with small variations in how the Economy of the Free is structured and its processes. And then keeping what works better, and leaving what works less well. Providing the feedback loop that nature uses in evolution to maximise the adaptive capacity of its living ecosystems.

The central story of economists is maximising the adaptive capacity of living business ecosystems, keeping them on the edge between complexity and chaos in the Cynefin diagram, at the sweet spot for maximum speed and adaptive capacity in response to the changes of context that drive evolution.

Explore, experiment, improv

You learn how your meaning-making stories shape the reality you experience, and how to use exploration, experimentation, and improv to generate new experiences that your stories can use to rewrite themselves in chapter 8. Everything that you read about there, along with your capacity for transformational thinking from chapter 9 is what you and all the players across all stakeholder groups and ecosystems have used to dismantle the old stories and craft the stories that underpinned the Economy of the Free's reality.

Since we're talking about a Cynefin complex economy and journey towards your Economy of the Free, improv is essential. You got to the Economy of the Free by going out there and using improv to do things that differed from your old story. By just going out and doing, and seeing what happened, and then reacting, step-by-step you gained the experiences you and everyone else needed to craft the new stories that shaped the new reality.

Experts, including economists, are now highly skilled in improv and experimentation, and it is a core component of their training.

5.5 The stock market looks like

If every company was a FairShares Commons, and part of an ecosystem of them, which itself was embedded in successively larger ecosystems, our stock market would function in an inclusive way, doing the job we need it to do. It would ensure that the economy as a whole has the capacity to (re)generate wealth in all capitals.

The stock market today, as you read in Section 3.2, is created by stories, e.g., that it is better to own 100% of a small pie than a slice of a large pie. Even if your slice of a large pie has more pie in total than your owning all of a small pie. So the reality we experience on the stock market is a competition between investors for the largest percentage of the company, regardless of the impact on the company, its stakeholders, and on society at large. Protect the long-term values integrity of your impact investment by incorporating as a FairShares Commons.

The unbundling of governance, information, and wealth-sharing rights and obligations in Free and FairShares Commons companies shifts the stock market from pure competition to an optimum mix of competition and collaboration.

Steering the company into the future through your governance rights and obligations is distinct from any share of the wealth generated through past activities of the company. (Past and future are no longer hard-wired together in the bundling of rights in the share.) This means that the interaction between the people engaged in buying and selling the new kinds of shares that represent all kinds of capitals in the stock market automatically leads to an alignment of each person's selfish needs, the company's needs as a whole, and the needs of society as a whole. You can read more in the article by Jordan Barry et. al[106].

In one fell swoop, this meets the needs of everyone calling for market freedom and a minimum of government regulation; and everyone in favour of the high levels of regulation found in the highly socialist countries because the stock market delivers the objectives of both extremes in one.

By now, you might have recognised how this is the application of exactly the thinking that transformed classical physics into quantum physics. The recognition that there actually was no contradiction between particles and waves; rather, what really worked was their integration into complementary pairs. By seeing competition and collaboration through the lenses of the transformational thinking patterns of Chapter 9 we get to a libertarian capitalist stock-market that also meets the objectives of Marx!

So, unbundling the rights of shares brings a representative breadth of all stakeholders into governance and the company's welfare; and extending the legal personhood of a non-human to the full extent of the legal personhood of a human includes the right to freedom from ownership and the right to self-determination. And these both shift the entire paradigms of the stock market from our current classical paradigm to a new one.

Then what happens when we add in an ecosystem of markets spanning the full breadth of all capitals and all currencies?

We end up with the central pillar that we need in a regenerative economy; a mechanism for all capitals to grow. And this, because we all behave as ourselves, with our human spread of needs, interests, and biases. Not because some higher power (whether that is regulation and policing, religion and social coercion, or inner values) has forced us to act contrary to our stories or nature.

And this means that every capital grows in its own currency, i.e., units of value, not necessarily as measured in money.

Of course, because this is a stock market that spans all capitals, and because the stories and dynamics are based on extending freedom to all on the market, both the humans and companies as living beings, the stock market will grow everything in a way that balances from system to system. Each pie will grow to the point where all the pies are at their biggest, and not beyond that. Nothing will grow at the long-term cost of something else, just as in nature if the apex predator grows too large, it will very soon be cut back to a sustainable level.

As you have read so far in this book, it makes a lot of sense to regard a company as a living being. The natural consequence of this perspective closes the last gap between human and non-human legal persons, namely the removal of any element of property law applied to any legal person. As you have read, that opens up exactly what we need for companies to engage with full responsibility and accountability in society, including on the stock market.

5.6 Boom and bust looks like

The cycles of boom and bust that are part of the reality we experience are created by the stories that run us. Physics is full of examples similar to boom and bust that we can learn from. For example, start with a bunch of magnets all pointing in the same way. Then start up a magnetic field pointing in the opposite way and slowly increase it. At some point all the magnets will flip to the opposite direction.

In physics, these flips from one state to a very different state are very well understood. One characteristic of systems that flip from one state to another is that each element (e.g., a single magnet) only has a very small number of choices (point north or south), and there is very little diversity in the system (we're all the same kind of magnet). As soon as you increase the number of options that each individual has, and especially if you increase the diversity, you no longer get extreme flips.

The booms and busts that we have are a consequence of an economic system that emerges from our dominant stories of ownership, separation of investors from all other stakeholders, separation of the next quarter from the next seven generations, and everything that you have read in this book up to now.

The cycles in an economy of free people and companies will have quite different dynamics driving them. Boom and bust will still happen, but the antifragile nature of an Economy of the Free makes them flatter and further apart.

What you will have is what you find in nature. Within a certain sub-ecosystem, for example between the fish and the algae of a pond, if something happens that drastically reduces the number of fish eating the algae, (a heron arrives and eats them all, except the 10 babies that have just hatched) the pond may get covered by algae. Sooner or later those 10 baby fish will grow up, feed on the plentiful supply of algae, have many babies, eat up all the algae, and then begin dying off because they don't have enough food.

Boom and bust, but only that pond. All the other ponds across the world will be fine. And even that pond would have been fine if it had multiple different types of fish, multiple different types of food for the fish; in other words, a sufficiently complete ecosystem. Learning from nature as a whole, biomimicry, is now a clear part of the expertise the new generation of economics students know they need.

So you will have in the smallest ecosystems boom and bust cycles, but these will usually be harmless for the global economy.

You can see how this plays out looking at the Spanish cooperative Mondragon. It began in 1943 as a technical college founded in the Basque region of Spain by a priest and was incorporated in 1956 when he selected for graduates to build a cooperative fully in line with his humanitarian Catholic teachings. 257 companies, 74,117 employees in 2014, and whilst individual companies shut down or needed to reduce their workforce to survive during the 2008 global financial meltdown, all staff were retained and supported within the ecosystem.

Not one person was added to Spain's unemployment statistics. Compared to the average company in Spain, which collapsed, or if the company survived, shed employees and failed to hire recent graduates at such a rate that the unemployment level rose from 8% in 2007 to 20% by 2010 and peaked at 27% in 2013.

An Economy of the Free globally will be like Mondragon, scaled up and on steroids. Individual companies will be able to start, grow, and scale as rapidly as fruit flies or as slowly as a sequoia. But the ecosystem as a whole will stay well-balanced because the huge diversity and interactivity across all stakeholders and engagement of all stakeholders generates antifragility.

Even more powerfully, all scales of the economy are naturally regenerative ecosystems of companies. From small ecosystems to large, you'll have the appropriate elements from banking, manufacturing, IT, artificial intelligence, upcycling, etc. This diversity of businesses with mutual independence and interdependence is again exactly how nature creates antifragility.

You cannot ask for a better moat protecting your retirement from the consequences of our global boom and bust cycles.

You probably know people who lost their job because their company went bankrupt, or was close to bankruptcy during Covid-19, or further back in 2008. You may know people who lost their house. These people suffer the consequences of the boom and bust cycles that exist because of the dominant stories that shape the reality we experience. If you are the kind of person that solves these problems at their root cause, think of starting up a FairShares Commons company today, linked together in ecosystems with other FairShares Commons companies, and your children at least, and possibly you, will never experience that again.

5.7 Trade

Trade today is partially free. Currently 80% of our trade is between multinationals within their supply chains. This trade freedom is primarily in the interests of the multinationals and the global finance industry based on money.

In an Economy of the Free, trade will have the maximum freedom at all scales of the economy, from trade between individuals, through trade within and between local and regional business ecosystems, and onto global trade within the global business ecosystem.

The maximum freedom in trade is another application of the complementary pairs found in quantum mechanics. The freedom of each individual to be fully their unique selves and have all their unique needs met, and the freedom of all of us in our oneness as humanity to be fully ourselves together, form a complementary pair. The maximum freedom in trade will be at the sweet spot integrating those complementary pairs.

Increasing your freedom at some point begins decreasing our freedom. Vice versa, at some point increasing a community's freedom takes away freedom from individuals. You and the Economy of the Free will be at the sweet spot of this complementary pair of freedoms, but this sweet spot keeps moving, and has fuzzy edges, because it depends on everyone's inner realities.

Today, the dominant trading units are multinationals. In an Economy of the Free there will not be any dominant trading unit. Trade will happen at all scales.

In this sense, trade will be local, within the smallest of business ecosystems, and conducted through the currencies within that ecosystem. Trade will be between ecosystems of the same scale, from neighbouring ecosystems through to those halfway around the world. Trade will be up and down the hierarchy of ecosystems of ecosystems. All using the complementary currencies they find most useful to represent the full spectrum of capitals being traded.

Trade today is largely managed for you in an opaque way, by the interests and power structures of your politicians, finance industry, and multinationals. You don't have much potential to engage in governing it yourself.

In an Economy of the Free, trade is not managed for you by any higher power; it is fully emergent. Fully emergent trade, unlike managed trade, is self-organising, self-governing, and self-managing. It is autopoietic, i.e., having full capacity to create, reproduce, and shut down any aspect of itself. Creative destruction[107], upgraded to the Economy of the Free. This will result in trade automatically leading to antifragility of the global economy, because it will be the scaled-up version of each of you and your businesses' adaptive capacity.

In an Economy of the Free, there will be rules of trade. Unlike today, where the rules of trade are defined by a few individuals in positions of power, the rules of trade will emerge from the self-governing processes within and between ecosystems. In full adaptive capacity, any tensions or conflicts will be harnessed for what they are: information on what is not working, and how to adjust the rules, structures, and process of trade so that it works in the maximum interests of all and freedom of all at all scales.

There will still be power hierarchies, from you and your power through to global organisations that use their power to meet their needs.

The big difference versus today, though, is that there will be power hierarchies at all scales, of all types, that lead to an emergent dynamic equilibrium because of the wide diversity of different powerful stakeholders with different types of power. Just as in nature, the lion has the power to meet its needs, and the virus has the power to meet its needs. The virus can bring down the lion, just as much as the lion can bring down the springbok.

Nature as a whole thrives because power balance gives it the adaptive capacity that it needs.

In an Economy of the Free, trade will be local, where local best serves the interests of all; it will be regional and multiregional, where regional trade best serves the interests of all; and it will be the global business ecosystem, where global trade best serves the interests of all. Deciding on those interests and how to best serve them will be done within and between ecosystems by the stakeholders representing the interests.

You will be an intrinsic part of that decision process, representing your interests.

This will neither be self-reliant at a local or national level, nor will it be dependent on other regions or nations in the kind of polarity you see today. Rather, it will be inter-reliant and interdependent in the same way that our natural ecosystems are. Just the same as life on the planet is one interdependent and inter-reliant hierarchy of interacting scales of ecosystems, all the way down to every single living organism.

5.8 Finance looks like

In this section we are expanding the underlying story of what finance and the finance sector means. In the Economy of the Free, the finance sector includes all the capitals and their associated currencies that play a role in the economy doing its job of provisioning.

Today, large amounts of your pension fund are invested by your asset managers in businesses and assets that have no value, or are even harmful, in regenerating a planet that you will want to retire in. In an Economy of the Free, all the capitals that you put aside to make use of when you retire, or are ill, are put to work towards regeneration.

Instead of your pension being invested in mining coal for fuel, or oil for fuel (despite every € invested in extraction from the ground requiring multiple euros to extract the carbon back out of the atmosphere), your pension will only be invested in businesses that are regenerative. After all, what good does it do you to put lots of money into a pension fund, only for the underlying asset base to have no value in the world that you are going to retire into?

Finance operates at all scales and in all currencies (not just in positive interest bank debt monies) in an Economy of the Free.

So if you need any kind of capital to start up a business that is at a small scale within your local ecosystem, you will have sources of those capitals available. This will not be free, without any strings attached; in fact, your peers in the ecosystem may well demand even more scrutiny and engagement with your plans than today before you get the resources you need.

But these will be free people and free businesses that are part of your ecosystem. They will get to know you, and your track record, and develop a deep understanding of what you plan to do with the capitals that they invest with you. They will deeply understand how you will regenerate the capitals many times over if you are successful in your endeavours.

The finance sector is broad across all capitals, regenerative across all capitals, and in service of that regeneration. Not as we see it today, where capital is of service to the finance sector. Leaders have a full understanding of the nature of money, and the currencies of other capitals, along with great capacity for the post-logical thinking and systemic complexity[108] of Part III.

Money is no longer the primary basis of full power in the economy.

There are still some individuals who, through luck or their natural talents, have large quantities of money. But this does not turn them into a plutocracy with power over those in need of that capital, because all capitals are on an equal footing. So you have a large diversity of capitals and a large number of people who are wealthy in at least one of those capitals.

5.9 Sustainability looks like

In an economy where you are a free living being, and your company is too; where companies are stewarded with the next seven generations in mind, all stakeholders in the ecosystem are involved in governance and share in the wealth generation, and all capitals are valued for what they contribute to life; sustainability, regeneration and circularity will inevitably emerge fast without extra effort or cost. So whatever happens in one generation, it increases the viability of future generations.

In an Economy of the Free, there are few regulations, e.g., telling you to use the train instead of flying. Instead, you have the freedom to use your wealth across all capitals in whatever way seems best in your reality, including being part of one whole. Just as in nature, acting in what you judge best in your reality will mostly lead to bottom up, emergent outcomes best for the ecosystem as a whole, because the inherent nature of a FairShares Commons aligns your best interests with the best interests of your organisation and society.

This Economy of the Free satisfies the description of sustainability created by the Brundtland Commission:

> development that meets the needs of the present without compromising the ability of future generations to meet their own needs. [...] meeting essential needs requires not only a new era of economic growth for nations in which the majority are poor, but an assurance that those poor get their fair share of the resources required to sustain that growth. Such equity would be aided by political systems that secure effective citizen participation in decision-making, and by greater democracy, in international decision-making[109].

Clearly an Economy of the Free composed of ecosystems of FairShares Commons companies satisfies all of this. We are all poor in one or more of life's capitals, whether it's time, energy, or money. In the FairShares company, all invest the capitals they are rich in, and benefit from the wealth generated in capitals they are poor in. Because all stakeholders engage in the company's long-term direction via the general meetings, everyone is involved in decision-making.

Many distinctions between people disappear in individual companies and the economy as a whole. All show up wearing their respective stakeholder hats and engage in stewarding the company wisely into the future. Everyone involved in a FairShares Commons company is also engaged in global governance, because FairShares Commons companies naturally form into ecosystems, and ecosystems of ecosystems, that will eventually touch everyone.

5.10 Work and reward

An Economy of the Free is not purely joyful nor fully fair. It will be unfair, but the unfairness is shared by all. There will be change, and disruptions to work. There will continue to be great shifts in the types of work needed and available, and times when you must reskill yourself.

But in an Economy of the Free, the ecosystems of free FairShares Commons companies support that reskilling. Companies will neither keep themselves nor specific jobs alive purely to avoid the evolutionary pressures of changing work context and disruptive innovation. Instead, you have an unconditional basic income (UBI) and the same access to developing yourself that you may have enjoyed through free schooling. In a Economy of the Free this is now lifelong, recognising the lifelong need for development.

While writing this book the Swiss held a referendum on universal basic income (UBI), which sadly failed to pass, with only 23% of voters backing it. The proposal was to give every adult legally resident in Switzerland an income of 2,500 Swiss francs (USD 2,554) per month. But UBI will come.

An objection you may have to UBI is that it will remove incentives for people to work. There is some truth to this, but it hides other truths. The past century and a half in the industrial era, and going even further back than that, has shown the value of the right incentives and rewards for work. There is equally strong evidence that reward *dis*-incentivises work.

How can that be possible, a lot of people will be thinking now? How can paying somebody to do work, be both an incentive and a disincentive? It depends crucially on aligning why somebody is motivated to work (the meaning they make of work and themselves), and the work itself.

In today's economy, the dominant story is that work means suffering in order to earn money to consume what brings you joy.

In the Economy of the Free, work brings you the financial income that you can use to meet your needs. And work also brings you many other capitals, enabling you to meet many other needs. In particular, it becomes part of your self-development. Instead of your work being restricted to what will earn you enough money to survive, it is an inherent part of your freedom to develop into who you can become. And for your businesses to develop into who they can become.

Bringing in a basic income for all citizens is, for society and the economy, changing the background that you are embedded in. Following the principle of Ubuntu, it will lead to a fundamental change of self-identity, of our fears and hopes.

Everyone has at least some entrepreneurial, creative aspects, and some level of commitment to working on something that you find truly valuable.

Your motivation is not just money. What motivates you also includes things like the sheer joy of mastery, self-respect, the respect of your peers, the motivation of seeing the end of something that you have created being used by others, the autonomy of being able to decide for yourself, and own what you do with your own time and energy. Maybe for you, having a very clear purpose to make a difference in the world.

> When I (Jack) was younger I worked in construction. Years later I passed a building that I had helped to build and took pride in contributing to creating something of quality that was still standing, that still fulfilled its purpose.

All these will be equally possible in an Economy of the Free because people and businesses are free to make the most of themselves. Adapting the quote from Abraham Maslow (Chapter 3), in an Economy of the Free, if you are a poet, you are free to be your best poetic self; if you are gifted at multiplying capitals, you are free to multiply capitals; if you are creative, you are maximally free to create. Regardless of whether you are an individual or an organisation.

Your work and purpose are aligned. Your work will centre around everything that is of value to you, from developing yourself, through developing and caring for others, to anything else. The story of your work is now the story of your meaning in life, not the story of consumption, nor the story of survival. Your work is now one of the places where you are your best self, and the best possible playground to develop yourself into who you can become.

This is not a life of simple bliss, free of stress. Instead, you actively seek out stress because that is just what you need at work to give you the direction and energy you need to grow yourself.

5.11 Your life looks like

In an Economy of the Free, your life will be very different to what it can be in today's economy. Given that none of us have ever lived in a global Economy of the Free, it's impossible to describe precisely all the highs and lows you'll experience in your life; but some are clear!

The joy you have collaborating in a team that simply clicks, that delivers meaningful results fast and efficiently, will be there more frequently and reliably than today. Equally, the extreme tension that you feel when you are in conflict with people who see the world differently to you will remain, perhaps even more strongly than today. The big difference is that you know this is an essential part of the self-governance that gives you the freedom you enjoy.

You will revel in this freedom to be your best self, and the freedom of the Fair-Shares Commons companies you are part of to be their best selves. You will spend time enjoying the benefits of all the wealth you and your FairShares Commons companies generate across all the capitals, enabling a better life through less economic growth[110].

The shift that appeals the most to me is that in an Economy of the Free I will read headlines that talk about the regeneration of our climate. I will read headlines about the polar ice caps regaining their ice cover, ocean currents regaining their power to balance temperatures between equator and poles. I will no longer read headlines about how the high summer temperatures have yet again broken the ice melt records shown in Figure 1.

In Section 3.1.3 I described the precariat. In the Economy of the Free the precariat cannot exist, because the economy does the job of provisioning for all. It is the Collabonomics that Klaus-Michael Christensen introduced me to. You may still be working in the gig economy; you may not know from one day to the next whether you will be in paid work or not. You will not have any doubts, though, about your capacity to feed, clothe and house yourself, because the UBI[111] takes care of your basic needs.

An Economy of the Free naturally includes the elements of the economics of happiness[112]. The success in applying the happiness economy's principles across multiple scales, from business through to nations like Bhutan, demonstrates that it has value, and will emerge as part of an Economy of the Free.

If you are any kind of investor, but especially if your focus is impact, circularity, regeneration, or sustainability, and expressing yourself, your legacy and values through your investments, the FairShares Commons and Economy of the Free gives you the most powerful tool I know of to do just that, to make your money matter.

This is the kind of integration of a paradox that generates all disruptive innovation; here, by reducing your direct immediate control you get better protection over the long term of your intent and values. Because, as you will read in Chapter 16, later investors cannot easily capture the company, suppress your intent, to extract money for themselves.

CHAPTER 6

Fixing flaws in economics

*Science makes people reach selflessly for truth and
objectivity; it teaches people to accept reality, with wonder
and admiration, not to mention the deep awe and joy that
the natural order of things brings to the true scientist.*

—*Lise Meitner*

This final chapter of the economics part exposes the significant weaknesses in neoclassical economics and is written primarily for those of you really interested in economics, or in why we have taken such poor decisions over the past few decades. Neoclassical economic thinking, and its effects, are all around us, creating the life you are living, preventing the better life we could all be living.

At the end of the book is an appendix for anyone wanting to dive deeper into a potential future alternative to current economic thinking, a speculative provocation pointing at a new concept of economics to navigate through our current turbulent time and build a better world.

6.1 Why didn't you see this coming?

...asked the Queen at the London School of Economics in 2008 to a group of the most senior economists in the UK. The 2008 crash, and how little has been improved since then[113], is just one piece out of a wide range of evidence that neoclassical economics fails to accurately and reliably describe much of what actually happens in our economy. You can find much more in the excellent books *Rethinking Capitalism*[114] and the *Global Minotaur*[115].

No wonder economists are the kind of experts everyone is losing trust in[116]. Compare how economists[26] and physicists develop their theories. Physicists always follow actuality (Section 1.4.4) where it leads them, turning hypotheses into evidence-based, validated theories, as in the quote from Lise Meitner above. And when something that they believed was a theory fails to predict, then it's evidence that it is no longer a theory, but at best an approximation, a phenomenological model, or, like believing the sun orbits the Earth, pure fantasy.

Were neoclassical economics sufficiently robust and validated for a physicist to class it as a theory, every neoclassical economist would have predicted, by 2000, and with unambiguous clarity, that a crash was coming within the decade. That they didn't is sufficient evidence that neoclassical economics falls short of the scientific criteria to become a theory.

Neoclassical economics is failing us, and whilst heterodox economics gives us a lot of value, we need even better. We urgently need a general theory of economies that describes precisely what is happening now, and predicts reliably what will happen tomorrow. Including the impact on tomorrow of that prediction.

Getting there requires the characteristics of physicists like Einstein: an openness to changing their mind, extreme stubbornness, and the humility to let go of both self-identity and beliefs in the face of data.

To catalyse a very different way of talking about what an economy is, I will use different metaphors, primarily Einstein's general relativity. A metaphor is a lens explicitly chosen to hide everything that is different, so that you can begin by focusing on everything useful that is similar. Once you reach the limit of similarity, the metaphor breaks down. So clearly a metaphor is only to be taken seriously, like any other lens, against a frame of reference of usefulness.

As you read this chapter, please keep in mind the impossibility of capturing a metaphor in words. My words are no more than labels for concepts. You may use the same word to label a different concept, and different words to label the same concept. Please read into the concepts beyond the words.

Many jokes in physics start with the way physicists use impossible extremes to begin thinking. So if they are trying to understand the movement of a herd of cows being chased by a dog across a field, they will begin by saying:

let's assume we have infinitely many 500kg spheres and one 20kg sphere.

They know that there are not infinitely many in the herd, that cows have legs and a body that is far from a sphere, but it's a good starting point to separate out what is complete rubbish from everything that might be true.

Most importantly, a viable economic theory will describe everything from one individual's personal economy all the way through to the global economy. Below are some key elements that need to be well described in any general theory.

6.2 Decisions: rational or irrational?

Value is in the eye of the beholder.

The old saying, beauty is in the eye of the beholder, applies equally to all kinds of value, and all kinds of decisions. It paraphrases an essence of this book: your reality, your meaning-making is uniquely yours.

So what I see as rational, in my reality, you might see as irrational in yours. But your seeing my decision as irrational certainly does not make it an irrational decision in itself, it may only be *not your rational*.

As you can see in Figure 6.1, the opposite of rational is not rational, and the opposite of irrational is not irrational. Sometimes this collapses from a two-dimensional shape into just a straight line, and not rational is identical to irrational, but not always.

Figure 6.1: Irrational is not always the opposite of rational.

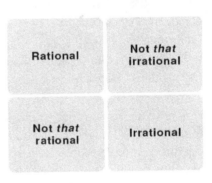

Evaluating a decision as rational requires two components, not just one.

1. The logic, or naked thinking process and outcome.

2. The frame of reference used to evaluate the options processed by the naked thinking process.

So say something about what is rational if both the thinking process and the frame of reference are included in our theory. Then you might find that all decisions are rational; and those you evaluate as irrational are simply using a different meaning-making frame of reference, and / or a different thinking process?

Thinking and feeling: a complementary pair

This also makes it clear how to include feelings and emotions into the rational decision process. If you are scared of the dark, regardless of whether or not there is a physical threat hiding in the darkness, it is rational to avoid dark spaces, even if only to reduce your experience of the fear itself. Most of us have some set of dark spaces we avoid, at least non-physical spaces of ignorance and belief.

Neurobiology has shown that any human decision is a combination of thought and feeling. A decision is the feeling you have when one of the options you are choosing between fits into the frame of reference you're using to evaluate the options against; or in the language of Chapter 9, it's the feeling you have when your sense-making works. A decision is primarily a process of feeling, rather than one of thinking.

You may believe that thinking is thinking, feeling is feeling, and ne'er the twain shall meet. But if I am taking a decision, I'm never just doing pure thinking without any other influence. How I feel at the time will be powerfully shaping how and what I'm thinking. If I'm feeling excited and confident, running fast from one decision to another, as somebody is on a trading floor, I will take a very different decision to the one I might take if I'm feeling deeply depressed because I've just heard bad news. Like the company I invested all of my client's money in yesterday having just declared bankruptcy.

So I propose that we consider thinking and feeling to be a complementary pair in the decision process, not opposites. Just like particles and waves in quantum physics.

Then for me to understand your rationality leading you to take a very different decision to the one that I might take, I must work with both your thinking and your feelings during your decision as an inseparable complementary pair.

All decisions are rational

None of us ever feels the force of gravity. If you are sitting in a chair reading this book right now, take a moment to check what your body is feeling. I doubt you'll say, *I feel gravity as a force throughout my body pulling me down*. Most likely you will say, *I feel the chair pushing up*.

Einstein's general relativity (building on Section 1.4) describes everything we attribute to gravity in a way that aligns with your felt experience. General relativity came about because Einstein asked himself whether there was any way that he could tell the difference between sitting on a chair in an elevator that was accelerating at $9.8m/s^2$ (the Earth's gravitational acceleration) or sitting on a chair in an elevator stationary on the Earth's surface.

He concluded that not being able to tell the difference was not due to his personal inability, but because there was actually no difference, there was no such thing as the force of gravity. It was a metaphor, useful in certain situations, like when we use the words sunrise and sunset even though we know it's the Earth turning, not the sun rising and setting.

I propose that in a general theory of economies, the one reliable constant is that all decisions are rational, against whichever internal reality and frame of reference the entity taking the decision was using in the moment.

After all, at the exact moment each of us takes a decision, we judge that decision to be the best and most rational decision we can take according to the frame of reference we have available to us, the context we are in, including our feelings, the meaning we are making, and the options available to us. Our experienced reality of decisions is that they are rational in the moment at that point. Somewhat the same as we never experience the Earth pulling us down, rather we feel the chair pushing up.

Any judgement of a decision as irrational is someone else judging the decision, from their inner meaning-making, their thinking-feeling processes, at another point in space, and moment in time. Or it's ourselves, some time later, when we are in a different context or emotional state, perhaps using different thinking-feeling processes and / or different meaning-making.

Einstein developed relativity by taking seriously the experimental data pointing at the crazy idea (in classical physics) that there was a universal speed limit: nothing could accelerate beyond the speed of light.

We propose that every decision taken by every person is perfectly rational; and that neoclassical economics fails in part because it assumes that there is only one reality. Rather, what will build a fully viable general theory of economies is taking every decision as perfectly rational within the decision-maker's reality, according to their frame of reference, in the moment.

This fits our experience of taking decisions. How often do you deliberately, and in full awareness of what you are doing, choose irrationally? Very seldom. Even the phrase *cut off their nose to spite their face* is rational in the moment, when spiting the face is more important than the costs.

This is also comparable to how Einstein developed his general theory of relativity by realising that what we experience sitting in a chair is the actuality, not an artefact of our subjective experience.

A final thought here, in preparation for the rest of the book: imagine how different your relationships with your colleagues, friends and family might become if you assumed that every action they took was fully rational; but within a different reality to yours? And so you then focused on exploring what their reality is, within which their action is rational? All of a sudden most of the emotional triggers disappear and are replaced by curiosity and exploration.

6.3 Thermodynamic economics

As a physicist (Graham), and having begun my university studies with physics (Jack), I find it inconceivable that the three laws of thermodynamics[1] are not satisfied by all of economic thinking.

I find it unfathomable that research into the thermodynamics of economies, (see Steve Keen[117]), has only recently begun.

No one has ever found anything anywhere in the universe that fails to satisfy the three laws of thermodynamics.

How on earth could anyone have imagined that anything in economics, a subset of human society in the benign physics of our planet, could be a valid description of how an economy actually works while failing to satisfy them?

If it did, physicists would be overjoyed at having thermodynamics, a theory that has withstood all attempts to falsify it for centuries, finally having its flaws exposed!

Thermodynamics is so well tested because energy is one of the foundations of our universe and hence of our economy. Without available energy[2], there would be no life and no economy. Regardless of which theory of value you subscribe to, be it a utility theory, labour theory, or any other theory, you have no value without free energy.

You need energy to move physical objects from A to B, or to transform them from A into B. You need energy in your brain to make meaning of what is happening, to choose between A and B, and take a decision. Everything that economics is about begins with free energy and the laws of thermodynamics.

A valid theory of economies, i.e., a general theory, must fully reflect thermodynamics.

---

[1] (1) Energy is conserved in the universe, it can neither be created nor destroyed; (2) Total entropy (disorder) increases; and (3) Entropy approaches a constant at absolute zero, typically zero.
[2] Or what a physicist calls free energy, which is quite distinct from the absolute amount of energy in a system. Free energy is the amount of energy available to do work, i.e., to move something, and is in essence the temperature difference between the highest available temperature that energy can start from, and the lowest available temperature that it can degrade to. Some scientism is based on a confusion between free energy and absolute energy.

6.4 Ergodicity

Closely related to thermodynamics is ergodicity. Many business and investment failures occur because our economy, each business, and your life, is not ergodic, yet most of economics assumes unquestioningly that everything is ergodic. Ergodicity is when the average of a *sequence* of decisions is the same as the average of the same decisions taken independently. Ergodicity means that there is no difference between the average of a thousand people taking a gamble once each, and one person taking that gamble a thousand times in succession. Economics assumes that, if you take a good gamble in sequence for long enough, you will hit the same end outcome as the average of many people taking the gamble once each. False.

The field of ergodic economics has recently emerged because a group of physicists (our physical world is often non-ergodic) showed how seldom ergodicity is valid in our economy[118-120]. As a physicist I (Graham) find it baffling that such a foundational assumption was not thoroughly tested decades ago.

For example[120], let's say you have $1,000. I offer you a gamble that if the coin you toss lands heads, I'll give you 50% more; and if it lands tales, you give me 40%. If a thousand people repeat this once, on average each person will be $50, or 5%, better off. So neoclassical economists would say that the rational decision is to accept the gamble.

However, if you repeat this gamble long enough in succession, you will end up with nothing. Which is not rational, despite neoclassical economics deeming it rational, and then covering up using the wrong statistics by claiming you are irrational! This is big for you, since the investment decisions of your pension fund are an equally non-ergodic sequence of bets over time.

This is a very simple but realistic model. In business: every time a business sells a product or service both sides are taking just this gamble. If I deliver to you, and then you don't pay, I've lost my cost of delivery (e.g., 40%), but if you do pay I've gained my costs and profit margin (e.g., 50%). Business leaders and investors assuming ergodicity are more likely to go bust unless they collaborate (Section 6.5.)

Just one of many examples where the rational decision in our economy is to refuse the gamble. Much of economics incorrectly assumes ergodicity, i.e., that the gamble is positive over a long enough sequence. Actually longer will make it worse! Because the sequence does matter, on average you have a cumulative 5.1% *loss* rate. In fact, to get the expected +5% cumulative from naive statistics you need over four times better odds: +83.8% growth vs. 40% loss per coin toss!

To understand any individual's decision, even your own, you have to integrate every influencing event along that individual's or your life path, which may well go back a number of generations. It's not for nothing that many ancient customs take

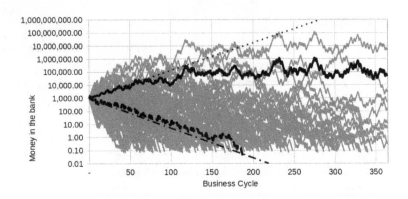

Figure 6.2: Looking at a portfolio of 100 companies (or people), each starting with $1000, each taking the 50% gain or 40% loss per coin toss 365 times in succession. If you drop below 0.01 you go bankrupt (92% here). Only a few are tremendously lucky, and only early on, making fabulous amounts of money; the average (thick black line) is dominated by them. Rising dotted black line: the expected growth from independent statistics; falling black dot-dash line: realistic statistics. Thick black dashed line: the median (middle company). Data: authors.

into account seven generations. Think: *I am my life* path *and the meaning-making stories that I have internalised because of that life path.* This means you are a process across time, not just you as you are now. (Read more in Section 11.2.)

This is also why so many 'uneducated' people are actually far better educated in how life works than graduates in all the other professions that have studied standard probability (those who Nassim Taleb[28] refers to as IYI—Intellectual Yet Idiot). Your life is *one* sequence of events, not just many events. What can happen next usually does depend on what happened before. In an extreme case, you can only win a huge amount if none of your previous bets has killed you.

Be very careful of ergodicity in all of your life decisions, and be careful of economists when they look at life through their economic lens; it may hide all non-ergodic aspects, and so be harmful to use. Business outcomes are strongly determined by luck[121] (the single company surpassing a million in Figure 6.2) in a non-ergodic economy. The figure looks a lot like VC funds today, suggesting that their delivering a return to their limited partners is a strategy based on luck, and only might work in our non-ergodic world if they are big and exit early. So how ought you, as an investor, invest differently, given that you are investing in a non-ergodic economy? Collaborative ecosystem investing; read our blogs, e.g.[122] and the next section!

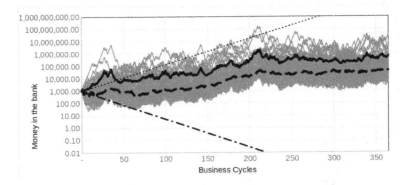

Figure 6.3: The same simulation as Figure 6.2, except between each gamble the companies collaborate; winners put 1% of their growth into a pot which is then evenly shared out to all 100 companies. So the winners only lose around 0.5%; just half a percent nett transforms the whole dynamic to one where all deliver as good or better returns to their investors than the unicorn in Figure 6.2. (Data: authors.)

One consequence of this is that no description of economies assuming ergodicity can be called a theory; it is only an approximation, because most processes are at best near-ergodic over short time spans.

We need a general theory of economies that includes all ergodic and non-ergodic aspects of our economy. Simulating such a theory accurately requires a full path-integral approach over each life and a large enough number of people to accurately represent the entire population. Predicting the global economy next year will require something like a Markov Chain simulation of perhaps half a billion simulated people and their predecessors, taken through a lifetime path-integral, with the full variety of life influences.

6.5 Competition and collaboration

So what might increase our success chances in a world filled with random good and bad fortune? A mix of collaboration and competition, that's what! Figure 6.3 shows what happens when we add just a little collaboration to the pure competition simulation of Figure 6.2, in the form of profit sharing from those companies that were lucky and made a profit.

This shows clearly the flaw in the neoclassical economics belief that perfect competition is desirable as the ideal way of distributing resources. It's not whenever non-ergodic fortune is involved. Economics then, to patch this flawed assumption, sees collaboration as a consequence of human values, irrationality, or perhaps some other utility emerging from efficiency gains due to specialisation.

If you look around you today, this is far from true. Figures 6.2 and 6.3 are pure maths; no values, ethics, leadership competence, nothing but numbers. The paths going down, not up as naive statistics hopes, is a mathematical consequence of non-ergodicity. And your life is non-ergodic!

The difference between Figures 6.2 and 6.3 is also pure maths; no values, ethics, leadership competence, nothing else. Just mathematical sharing of winnings after each gamble changes the dynamics of the whole game. If you have perfect collaboration[123], where after each round all the winnings are shared equally amongst all companies you get to the naive average.

The message is simple: if good and bad outcomes hit us unpredictably and unavoidably, we will all do better if we all share our winnings enough.

The two factors improving our odds are how much of the winnings are shared, and the size of the collaborating ecosystem of companies: the bigger the better, where the improvement grows with the square root of the number of companies.

What this shows is that businesses, and your investment in business, is best positioned to deliver results if they are in the kind of collaborative-competitive ecosystems that this book shows how to build, e.g. using the FairShares Commons incorporation to deliver the ecosystem-wide trust and sharing rules. If you want better financial returns, better impact, to deliver regenerative economy returns, whatever you want: invest in whole ecosystems of companies all incorporated to share gains with each other, not in portfolios of independent companies. (For investors: this is a little-known flaw in Modern Portfolio Theory[122].)

This is also why large companies, like Procter and Gamble, tend to have much more stable growth long-term. P&G, with 22 billion dollar brands and many more smaller ones is itself a collaborative-competitive ecosystem of businesses. When Ariel/Tide goes down, Pantene may go up; because they share the gains and losses, the company as a whole can better capitalise on good fortune despite bad fortune. Investors in P&G are investing in an ecosystem.

This is pure maths, with many more implications; for example, that the Unconditional Basic Income (UBI) will yield a better national economy than, and that collaborative-competitive cultures have an edge whenever the world becomes highly nebulous and unpredictable.

I expand on this in a blog[122] and the sequel to this book. Many of the fudge factors[118] in economics are, at least in part, an artifact of the false assumption of ergodicity being patched through equally flawed utility functions, behavioural explanations, rational vs. irrational judgements, etc.

Why haven't we seen this a long time ago, you may be wondering! Simple: very few of us are good enough, for the ever-more random, nebulous, unpredictable world we live in, at seeing the lines and connections between the dots. Ergodicity appears true if all you see are the dots. But like a child's join the dots drawing, in your life, and all our businesses, it's the lines joining the dots that make all the difference. The same set of dots connected by different lines makes a completely different image—or life. Your life *path* matters, not the collection of events in no specific order.

I wrote this book to enable you to get better at seeing the connections present; and seeing which connections you ought to create to live a better life, or make your investments more successful: master the relationship and transformation thought forms of Chapter 9.

Any really valid theory of economies must work across the full range of non-ergodicities, from perfect competition through to all opposites of perfect competition, from complete independence to complete alignment.

Clearly the extreme points of 0% or 100% perfect competition only occur for fleeting moments, much like the pendulum of a grandfather clock is only stationary for a fleeting moment at the top left and top right of its swing. Our economy is in constant dynamic motion across the space defined by the complementary pair of competition and collaboration, just as Darwin saw in nature. Thriving in the face of good and bad fortune requires collaboration to counter the negative consequences of non-ergodic life.

One issue in economics today is that competition and collaboration are seen as mutually exclusive opposites, rather than as one inseparable complementary pair, where our non-ergodic economy always has, and always needs, a mixture of both to maximise our chances.

> You can see this in how Graham and Jack have worked with each other on this book. It is the outcome of competition and collaboration as one single complementary pair. If you'd been a fly on the wall watching us right now as we discussed writing this chapter (and neither of us had swatted you), you would have seen that there was competition between the concepts each of us saw, and collaboration in each of us giving the other what we had to give. The difference in how each of us saw these concepts comes from our different histories, our different knowledge and our different perspectives on the world. The collaborative conflict enabled us to produce a far better book that either of us

could have written.

So even just between the two of us, and within the narrow space of writing this book, we have an economy based on the complementary pair of collaboration and competition. And a general theory of economies needs to accurately describe exactly what the two of us experienced as we moved half-formed thoughts and concepts through a forming process into the final fully-formed words on the page, by doing work on the thoughts and concepts. By taking decisions, making choices, using our own decision spacetime to tell us how to move and work on the resources of our thoughts and concepts, to finally produce the paragraph you are now reading.

6.6 Non-equilibrium: great shifts in culture, energy, communication

Neoclassical economics only works in an equilibrium economy[124]; and yet I doubt whether the global economy ever has been in equilibrium long enough to validly assume equilibrium. The closest we get are locally approximate equilibria over short times and small regions. Most of the time the economy is not in equilibrium.

A general theory of economies must work regardless of whether the economy is in a deep equilibrium or out of equilibrium.

It must work even in times of great change, such as for our current cultural and technical transformation, from a meaning making of burning fossil fuels to make life convenient into one where burning fossil fuels is life-threatening.

A useful general theory of economies must also be able to tell the difference between bubbles[125] and the emergence of new paradigms of value. A bubble is where the price and / or supply increases as demand increases, but the meaning-making stories are fantasy, with little grounding in actuality. By new paradigms of value, I mean that a business concept that previously had no or negligible value becomes, over time, a business concept with high value in actuality.

Both are about as far from equilibrium as you can get, yet have quite different outcomes that the theory must predict from the early signals.

To be useful, such a general theory of economies must describe the entire progression, from the first individual who comes up with something that later turns into either a bubble or a new value paradigm, through to the end state of either the bubble collapsing or the new value paradigm establishing itself.

6.7 Value is relative

Neoclassical economists approach to value, pricing, and rent is a root cause of much of today's mess[126]. It, and using GDP as a measure, is flawed. Activities can add to GDP even though they destroy total wealth; for example, an oil spill can add to GDP, even though it killed vast swathes of our life-support systems on the planet.

Two approaches in economics to value are that it is either 1) intrinsic, or 2) based on the value of the labour that went into making it. Both are sometimes just patching the false assumption of ergodicity (Sections 6.4, 6.5.)

> "What is this book's value?" we asked each other whilst writing this chapter.
> We concluded that it is neither in the book nor in the labour, and yet it is in the book and in the labour, and in both together. Paradox and complementary pairing strike again. The value depends on your frame of reference and how you use the book; whether you read it, light a fire with it, or as rubbish for recycling.
> The value changes over time, as each reader gets deeper and deeper into converting the book into insights and actions that are valuable to them (perhaps uniquely to them). The value is clearly not only in the labour of, and financial costs to Jack and myself in, creating the book's concepts, nor only in crafting the words, although that is certainly an important contributor to the value that some readers perceive in it.
> The value clearly lies in your individual meaning-making, and in how larger groups of people collectively make meaning and thereby create value and an appropriate pricing for this book. It might be a brilliant book that never gets sufficiently well known to sell widely, or it may be abysmal and filled with rubbish but just happens to catch a meme and goes viral. The value is neither in the book's utility, nor its labour, and yet both are essential parts of creating the value for you.

In a general theory of economies, *value is always in the eye of the beholder*. Value is always attributed by the beholder, according to their meaning-making frame of reference, including their emotional state, at some point in time, and including their beliefs about any relevant intrinsic, utility, labour, etc. value. So a general theory of economies must give us a mechanism to take all value drivers[66] and bring them all together into the final value that's used to take a decision.

As Jack and his co-authors wrote in their pluralist economics textbook[127], the

meaning and origin of value in economics has always been one of the most contentious areas in economics.

A general theory of economies must provide a framework to bring them all
together in a way where each complements the other, and where it becomes clear in
each situation which value driver plays which role; if one is dominant, so it's a good
enough local approximation to calculate as if it is the only driver of value; or if all
are significant, so you cannot make your life easier by using a local approximation;
and how to then include them all to represent the value used to take a decision.

I believe that the underlying reason why we have not yet such a general theory of
economies lies in the human dimension described in Part III. Too few economists
have developed the fluidity in the 28 thought forms, and the requisite meaning-
making stage of development, to be easily able to take distance from their own beliefs, to hold opposing concepts as simultaneously true, and coordinate multiple
open systems.

6.8 Externalities and conflict

An externality is one of the trickier aspects of economics, so in case you've not
yet encountered the concept, here's a quick example. You've gone shopping, and
choose to save a bit of money by buying fruit reduced to 50%. That night you and
your partner have an upset stomach, get no sleep, and both of you lose a day's income the following day. Your health costs were an externality in your decision to
buy the lower-cost fruit because you excluded those costs and risks from your economic decision.

Often people think externalities are only negative, but they can also be positive. Examples of both positive and negative externalities, well-known in business
theory and neoclassical economics, are the exclusion of essential elements of our
natural and social environment: the costs created by air pollution damaging our
health (negative); or the benefits to society of investing in education (positive), are
usually excluded—labelled as "external to the theory", even though everyone recognises that these "externalities" are central to the system working in the first place!
Heavy investment in education is a big driver of positive externalities in social, economic, and business success a couple of decades later.

We're facing the global crises of today because neoclassical economics mistakenly
believes you can exclude core elements of the whole system.

On any finite world, in any closed system, there cannot in actuality be any externalities, and any compartmentalising approach yielding externalities fails the first
test for becoming a useful theory. And so in a general theory of economies there are

no externalities: all elements and their impacts across the whole are included.

Take our climate emergency, for example. By treating our atmosphere's insulating carbon dioxide blanket as an externality, our economic decisions fail to take into account the steady "thickening" of the blanket caused by putting carbon dioxide back into the atmosphere after nature so carefully removed it to create a viable habitat for human life. So the planet is getting warmer, and will keep on warming until the increased driving force from a higher temperature forces more energy out through the "thicker" blanket, re-establishing thermodynamic equilibrium.

We've got into this mess in part because economics has tried to simplify itself by neglecting thermodynamics and making invalid assumptions of ergodicity, externalities, etc. There would be far less risk of the kind of climate emergency we are now in, had we had a general theory of economies 50 years ago. High time we develop one in with scientific rigour rather than the scientism in much of today's neoclassical economics.

Another deep cause of our mess lies in how economics includes (or doesn't) conflict and how economists approach conflict between practitioners. The general theory of economies picks up on a theme running through this book: the beneficial, generative role of conflict and tension. The conflict between different stakeholders in a business, such as the conflict between labour and management, is necessary for its structural integrity and adds value.

Conflict shapes choices in a marketplace, is essential, and has potential downsides. The conflict between buyer and seller generates the structural integrity of a market. But, a buyer who is small, perhaps only 10 years old, physically quite weak, and with a set of meaning-making stories that are harmony-seeking, negotiating a price with a large, powerfully built, middle-aged seller with psychopathic tendencies will yield a different outcome to the same two people, but swapping the role of buyer and seller.

To truly capture a theory of value that reflects society and any economy, it's vitally important that we know if value is ergodic or not, and if not always use a path integral across each individual's life segment. Price and value are usually far from ergodic because conflict is not ergodic. What you value depends on your history, the path your life has travelled along.

Neoclassical economics sweeps under the rug[128] the inherent value of conflict, and the consequences for each person's inner, unique, rational theory of value. So, neglecting how humans thrive, a zero-conflict equilibrium economy becomes the ideal to strive for.

This is mistakenly treating an extreme simplification, which may or may not be useful to get a rough idea of how an economy works, as if it is the ideal actuality[129] to aim for. Early neoclassical economists made simplifying approximations in order to be able to calculate anything, as we all lacked computers, non-ergodic statistics, and today's theories of adult development and meaning making.

Tension and conflict (at all six levels in Section 2.8, Page 43) are two of the most intractable aspects of human nature and the social sciences, and quite obviously two of the most challenging elements to include in any general theory of economies. They are also essential for life, including any economy, to function: tension and conflict are just an expression of some difference, and differences are the precursor of all the value flows that make an economy.

6.9 The role of freedom and property

There has long been an imprecise grasp of the central role of freedom and property in an economy. In a general theory of economies we must have a formulation to precisely grasp the consequences of freedom and property in an economy.

And well done if you have already recognised that we wrote role, singular, as we see freedom and property as a complementary pair, not as opposites! Freedom we define as the freedom to be yourself, including the freedom to take your own decisions according to your reality. This includes the possibility that your self is nebulous, changing, or even porous. Property we define as having the sole decision authority over something. As with any complementary pair, property and freedom are related to each other.

Freedom and property each label an entire library of contested stories of what each is, or even ought to be. For example, freedom in the US is primarily taken to be the freedom of the individual to choose and strive, seldom taking into account the impact of the individual's current environment, and past life path, on the possibility of that choice and that striving leading anywhere.

On the other hand, freedom in China is more anchored in the freedom of the community to remain harmoniously together as a community, which leads to less freedom of individual choice and speech.

Any general theory of economies must represent all kinds of freedoms across the full range from 0% to 100% and predict the characteristics of an economy as freedom slowly moves from one point to another.

More or less freedom is not necessarily better, for all definitions of better. A young child's preference for a large bowl of sweet chocolate ice cream, instead of a bowl of Brussels sprouts coated in a light flavouring of butter and nutmeg, is one that, most of the time, is not better for the child's development into a healthy adult. It may well be better for the parent to rest by having a peaceful child; though the sugar rush may make it a suboptimal choice an hour later.

Equally, more or less ownership is not necessarily better.

Each amount of freedom, and each amount of ownership, has an impact. What is important is that anything less than 100% freedom to take the decision your own reality declares rational will lead to internal stress in the moment. That stress will then have a recursive, iterative effect on the meaning making you actually use to take your next decisions[3]. Non-ergodic again; the connections across time in your life-path cannot be neglected.

For example, think of the slaves who were once property and were then declared to no longer be property. This step from being 100% property to 0% property was not the same as having complete freedom to move. Because of their entire life path, they were not free to move in socio-economic space in the same way that somebody who had never been a slave was. Elements of these hidden, systemic losses of full freedom can remain in many individual's experienced reality for generations.

We are all becoming more aware of these hidden, systemic consequences of life path over generations, as seen in the rise of Black Lives Matter, and many other movements aimed at addressing deeply embedded systemic unfairness.

Because freedom and property are complementary pairs, and each changes as you move from the scale of individual through families, small communities, regional communities, nation states, and on to the entire planet, there are boundaries on freedom and property within any specific layer imposed by the layers above and below. All this is part of a general theory of economies.

6.10 The need for free companies

The free company (e.g., the FairShares Commons) has a competitive edge in many economies because the freedom enables the company to take the best possible decision and be held fully accountable for the outcome; and naturally form collaborative-competitive ecosystems to optimise all thriving by optimising the lines connecting them.

If a company is not free, but is subject to forces (anything that can force a company to take a specific choice), or even property, somewhat like an individual being a slave, then they will make a forced choice, and be exposed to the full impact of bad luck in non-ergodic processes.

---

[3] Autocorrect in the Google Docs that I'm typing this in, is constantly suggesting that I correct my usage of "take a decision" to the more US usage "make a decision". I have chosen to keep with the more English usage, take a decision, because it reflects the way that a decision is a choice between two or more options, and all you can do is take one option and leave the others. The making comes later, after you have taken the decision, when you turn the decision into action and results.

Sometimes such a forced choice may well be the best one. For example, a company may have a decision-making board lacking the long-term perspective needed to make a wise decision, like an immature child choosing to eat chocolate ice cream instead of Brussels sprouts. Then the force of a regulation may be needed.

Or it may be a harmful one, such as where a company is forced to sacrifice the long-term interests of society and the environment by investors ignorant of ergodicity forcing higher short-term returns.

And as soon as the stresses imposed on a business, by non-ergodic misfortune and the gap between its natural and forced decision, is bigger than the strength of the business's structures to hold everything together, it will collapse or explode.

I suspect that research will show that a number of business failures are due to this. Nokia immediately springs to mind as an example.

In a free company, such as the FairShares Commons described in this book, the business has a much wider range of information included in its decision processes because every stakeholder has a voice and vote in the general meetings. Also, because the business is free to choose according to its own path, and is not constrained by the opinions and needs of the most powerful investors, it has far more room to take decisions that keep the business optimised for all, and within a viable level of stress.

So I see the FairShares Commons, or similar free incorporation approaches, as a necessary building block, in combination with other elements, for constructing a healthily thriving economy that does the job of provisioning for all.

Only a free company, like the FairShares Commons, can always take a locally rational, natural decision and therefore be held accountable for the consequences. Failing that, the company will take a non-rational, forced decision; forced by whoever has a disproportionate amount of power over the non-free company, most likely harming the company, the environment, and many stakeholders.

And how often do those with high levels of power force a company to take a decision that is rational for them—the investor, or founder, or head of the family—but is not rational for the company and ends up killing it?

You can read our current thoughts, that we hope will provide a useful catalyst for developing a general theory, in the appendix at the end of the book.

I believe that the economy as a whole can thrive best if each company is free to take the decision according to its natural path, which by definition includes all stakeholders' perspectives, including future stakeholders that may need to bear the consequences of decisions. That replaces almost all regulation, in an even better way, as the right choice is informed by all affected by it. This requires everything described in this book about developing ourselves and organisations.

Part Three

You

We humans are the alpha and omega of society, its economy, and our organisations. These chapters introduce you to how your meaning-making stories create your self-identity, and the unique reality you experience. They are the lenses you use to look at everything through. Your fluidity in the 28 thought forms of transformational thinking determine your capacity to grasp a nebulous, VUCA world, and what you can do to harness tension in your life to become who you can be, and achieve what you want to achieve, in all arenas of your life, by growing your identity, and bringing your unique reality closer to actuality. All this happens on the foundations, and within the boundaries, of your fixed nature. And it is all nebulous, unknowable.

CHAPTER 7

Who are you?

The unreflected life is not worth living
—Socrates (at his trial for corrupting Greek youth.)

A musician must make music, an artist must paint, a poet
must write, if he is to be ultimately at peace with himself.
—Abraham Maslow

Who am I? is the question that follows us throughout our life.

When I (Graham) was very young, I wasn't even aware of that question. I just lived life as it came, moving through each day, much like an old-fashioned cinema reel moving through the projector. Of course, my life was the typical emotional rollercoaster of any young child. But I wasn't aware of much beyond my immediate impulses.

I was in balance, the same balance that a pendulum has. I had my ups and downs, but I was constantly moving back to my centre, regardless of whether I was up or down. I certainly wasn't spending long periods of time down caused by buying into my judgements of myself and my environment.

Around the age of six or seven, at primary school, I lost that balance. The pendulum started getting rusted by my judgments about myself. I lost my early childhood capacity to simply let the cinema reel of my life flow without judgement.

More often than not I judged myself as not good enough. Not strong enough, not sporty enough, or too clever. Growing up in South Africa, the cultural expectations made it more important to be good at sport rather than classwork. I began shifting my awareness and actions from my impulses in the moment to my needs, which were more stable over time. I began unconsciously constructing myself so that I could better get my needs met.

Striving to get to a point where I could judge myself as good enough, and to get my balance back permanently. For a long time, I thought that balance was a fixed point, that if I got there properly I would always be balanced.

For a long time I strived to become someone who was good enough, and through that to reach a permanent balance. What made that impossible was that my internal reference frame telling me that who I needed to be, to be good enough, depended on other people. This was something I had absorbed by listening to the norms and expectations of the people and society around me, but these norms were neither self-consistent nor were they consistent with all my facets.

The result was that I always felt off-balance in a negative way. There was always some part of me that I judged inadequate, that I needed to fix before I would be good enough, and therefore happy.

Over time, I realised that balance is not a fixed destination to reach and then stay at; rather, it's like a pendulum. My objective now is not to reach this stage of resilience where I am never knocked off balance; it is rather to reach a stage of antifragility, where every time I get knocked off balance I am able to get back into balance fast and, more importantly, use the experience to increase my capacity to get back into balance.

I was also growing up within the broader social context of the final decades of apartheid South Africa. The older I got, the more aware I grew of how wrong the world I lived in was not only morally wrong, but simply not viable long term. Apartheid could never build a stable society served by a healthy economy. I grew up in a context of fear and anxiety because I knew that apartheid had to end within the next decade or two, and could not see any reason to hope that it would end without extreme pain and turmoil.

And yet who I am today, much of what I am proud of, could only have happened because of how my past has shaped me. One example: the motto of the Eastern Cape school I attended, Selborne, is "Palma Virtuti" (the reward is to the brave), which has occasionally helped me keep going on the path that led to this book. Especially knowing that bravery is not about feeling no fear, it is about doing what needs to be done when filled with fear and doubt.

This background context was like being in a turbulent river, with the current constantly pulling my balance downwards, towards self-doubt, fear, and anxiety.

I described in the first chapter how those experiences are now part of my antifragility. I'm living now in the context of climate change, resource depletion, and all the other signs that the way we are living today is simply not viable for the long term. I look around me, and I see many people who feel anxious about their future. The younger you are, the more anxious you are likely to feel, and the more fatalistic or nihilistic you may be, because you don't see any reason to hope that you will be able to thrive long into old age.

There is hope. There is always hope.

This and the following chapter offer our suggestions for you to develop your personal capacity for antifragility, so that you can harness everything that is stressing you to grow your own personal power. By growing your own power, and your capacity to collaborate with a diverse spectrum of other people, you will be better able to do what is needed to address today's challenges. And by acting together, we will create our path out of the mess we are in now, to a viable way of living and a better world where we can all thrive.

To grow your personal power, the first step is to pull apart the question "who am I?" By doing this you will become better at recognising clearly who you are and who you have been so that you can create the experiences you need in order to grow into who you can become. The "you" that has the personal capacity for antifragility to thrive and take the needed action.

7.1 Sense then meaning making

The most actionable way I've found to look at the question *"Who am I?"* is as the integration of three elements.

1. Your genes, their epigenetic expressions, and brain structures shaped in early childhood (hardware and firmware) fix your fundamental uniqueness, your natural strengths and weaknesses.

2. You assembling raw input into complete puzzles that make sense, with the puzzle pieces coming in from all your senses, and including feelings.

3. You then giving meaning to the assembled puzzle through your meaning-making stories.

These three are the foundations of the Constructive Developmental Framework (CDF), described comprehensively by Otto Laske in two volumes[5,6]. The CDF is the basis in this book for you to get to know who you are, and how you can grow into your potential of who you could become by getting ever more fluid in the thinking you can use, by growing your stories, and by becoming more subtle in how you work with and within the boundaries formed by your fixed nature.

If you know yourself through each of these three lenses, and how they have changed over your lifetime, you will know who you are, who you might become, and most importantly, what to do to become your best future self. Figure 7.1 represents the three elements of stories, thought forms, and genes.

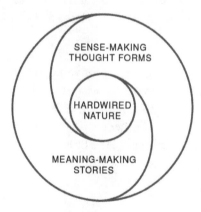

Figure 7.1: The three elements that create our experienced reality and drive our behaviour. Most of these three elements are hidden from us; we are subject to them. The more ability we have to shift them into objects we see clearly, the bigger our adaptive capacity to change ourselves.

I have borrowed Figure 7.1 from Dao/Tao philosophy. It captures, in one simple diagram, how every element of you is interwoven. It makes clear how separating the CDF into three constituent elements is at times a helpful simplification, but it also hides how everything is interwoven. It shows that there are elements you can name and know about and elements that are unknowable and unnameable.

Each of the three elements in the Figure 7.1 plays a distinct role in your experienced reality. They each act in sequence; however, like the way particles interact in quantum mechanics, the sequence happens in very rapid loops that merge into one experienced reality.

First, you receive data into your brain, from your physical senses as well as from your inner ways of knowing. In any instant you can only take in a very small fraction of all the data that is bombarding your senses every second—for example, your gut telling you that somebody is lying to you.

Then, you use your thoughts to assemble that part of the data that fits together into a representation of actuality, much like putting the pieces of a puzzle together into a final image. Then you use your library of stories to recognise, or project meaning into, the picture on the puzzle you have assembled. This is the reality that you experience.

In Figure 7.1 there will always be aspects of yourself that you are unaware of, and so subject to. The best route to growing bigger is to shift, step by step, what you are unaware of in yourself and subject to, into things that you are aware of and can make an object that you can work with, and then maybe change.

Norman Wolfe[130] uses the metaphor of a cinema. You can think of yourself and the reality you experience as having four sequential steps that change what actually is, leaving what you experience: (1) the white light, which is everything that is in your potential; (2) the film that filters the light, removing almost everything; (3) the lenses focusing what little is left of the light into an image that you can see on (4) the screen, which itself changes the image.

Depending on your religion or philosophy, the white light represents the universal oneness, the infinite universe, Dao/Tao, God—all that can be. The reel of film represents the stories that you are. The film that has already passed the lens is now frozen, these are the experiences you have already had. The film that is still coming is not yet fixed. But it is constrained in what's possible, based on your genes and epigenetics, and the large-scale patterns of the time you are living in.

The lens and screen are formed by everything and everyone around you, enabling you to experience your reality. Unlike in a cinema, these are not neutral, distortion-free flat white surfaces. You have your own unique lens and screen shaping the reality you experience.

One immediate consequence of this analogy is that you can never experience the same reality as anyone else around you.

You also have three ways of changing your future reality. You can work on changing the image in the film before it's formed; you can change the lens; and you can change the screen. Changing the lens and the screen means taking action to change the environment you are living in, to be with different people, or to go on a mutual journey of change with the people you are with.

To know yourself through each of these three lenses means, firstly, growing your capacity for awareness so that you can be aware in each moment of many more aspects of who you are now and who you once were. Secondly, it also means knowing the frames of reference you use to evaluate yourself and your actions.

7.2 You change yourself by looking at yourself

One big leap made in quantum physics was the realisation that the observer and the observed could not be separated: that the act of observing, independent of any measurement, changed (or even created) what was observed. A photon showed up as if it were a wave or a particle depending on what it was 'seen' by.

As soon as you observe yourself by turning your awareness onto one or more aspects of yourself, you immediately change yourself. Who you are now includes who you are in awareness of that part of you that you are observing. Your nature, your capacity for different forms of thought, and your stories about what is and is not acceptable for you to be, shape your self-awareness. So being able to use a well-structured framework makes it much easier to grasp who you are without bias, and to better grow yourself into who you can become.

This is analogous to Picasso realising that the very act of looking at something, in order to paint it, shaped what he saw, and later what the person looking at his painting saw. So if he wanted to represent the deeper essence, he needed to break out of the conventional perspective. Just as physicists realised that, to describe nature, they needed to go beyond the biases and limitations of classical physics.

Keep this in mind, throughout this chapter and the next. You are far more than, and different to, whatever *you* you are currently aware of. You are constantly changing, and every time you focus your awareness on yourself, simply by doing that, you change yourself. Self-identity has a nebulous, uncertain nature, with many parallels to the natural world described by quantum physics.

This means that the full *you* is always different to, and more than, the *you* you can currently be aware of, and there is always more on the edge of your potential to grow bigger. That's the good news. What is challenging for everyone at some point in their life, is the uncertainty of not being able to precisely pin down one single answer, unchanging and valid for all time, to the question *Who am I, and who should I be?*

I'll call this the *naked you* vs. the *dressed you*, borrowing from the concept in physics of dressed vs. naked particles. Every time an electron does its stuff, it's the fully dressed electron. (This is the electron after all the quantum effects coming from its environment have modified its properties. No one ever can see the naked electron.)

How you show up in the world, how others experience you, is always dressed. You experience yourself, dressed by all your stories, the expectations you have of yourself, and the expectations other people have of you. You show up dressed by all your memories, the meaning you make of them, and your hopes and fears about the future.

Growing your capacity for awareness enables you to see more and more clearly everything you are as the fully dressed *you*, and to know that this is the real *you*. The smaller your capacity for awareness, the more likely you are to mistake a small part of your fully dressed *you* for being all you are; or, to seek your naked *you*, which is fundamentally impossible to see.

Your dressed *you* is inherently nebulous, like a cloud changing shape each time you look at it, because each time you look at it you change microscopically your stories, which changes the dressed *"you"*.

This is related to how our memories work. You never actually remember an event, rather you remember the last memory you had of it. Which is why ten different witnesses to a crime give the police ten different, even contradictory, statements. Which is why it is so easy to create completely false memories, as Elizabeth Loftus[29,30] has shown. Our memories are unreliable, and we can easily acquire a completely false memory, either alone or through the influence of others.

The fact that memories are nebulous, changing each time you remember them, is really good news! It means that you are not destined to stay as you are for the rest of your life. You have changed, you are changing now, and you will change tomorrow.

Because you always have untapped potential to change, to grow bigger, in your own unique way, you always have a reason to hope, and you always have work to do in order to turn that hope into fact. The bigger you are as a person, the bigger your capacity to regenerate yourself after any setback, or to address a new challenge that you have never seen before.

If you are feeling too small compared to the challenges you see ahead of you, this chapter and the next will show you how to break that judgement down into the small, actionable steps that you can take to become bigger than the challenges you are facing. In the rest of this chapter, you will see a framework that I have found the most useful to understand who I am, and I believe you too will find it powerful for yourself. The next chapter will show you how to use the framework depicted in Figure 7.1 to continue growing into who you can be.

In the next three sections we will work backwards through the sequence. We'll start with your final step in shaping the reality you experience, projecting meaning onto the puzzle your thoughts have just assembled.

7.3 You are your stories, thoughts and genes

Every time you answer the question *Who am I?* you are repeating, adding to and changing your story. The more nuanced and elaborate your story, the bigger you are as a person.

Over the past few decades research into personality is confirming that, in a very deep sense, your stories are who you are. You have constructed these stories over your life, and they in turn have constructed your personality and the reality that you experience now. You are a dynamic path across time, not a static thing in time. Analogous to quantum mechanics. You construct your stories by distilling the reality you experienced across your life path into scripts defining who you are and what you should do for whom, which then shapes or even creates the reality you experience, which in turn shapes and creates the stories that run you[131,132].

In addition to the stories that you have constructed during your life, and that then construct who you are, the other two elements play an equally important role in who you are: how you think, and your genetic make-up.

How you think, in other words which forms of thought you are more or less fluid in using, determine what you can think about. The kinds of stories that you have access to (out of all the stories you potentially have access to) depend on how fluid you are in each different form of thought. For example, if you are not yet very fluid in using forms of thought around constant flow, movement and change, you will tend to strive towards a fixed self, and then try to stay there.

The more fluid you are in using constant flow forms of thought, the more you can broaden your stories of who you are to stories describing yourself as a process across time, rather than a self that is a fixed destination, or goal to achieve.

The foundation and boundaries to the potential *you* are given by your genes. You cannot change your genes through force of will—not yet, at least. Which of these genes are actually active, i.e. expressed, depends to some extent on factors that you can influence, through your diet, your stress levels, sleep and many other factors. How much most of us can change our epigenetics, i.e., change the expression of our genes during our lives, is relatively limited. This means that our stories and our fluidity in using different forms of thought can at best take us to the edges imposed on us by our genes, with some stretch in their epigenetic expression.

Ubuntu and the observer

> *I am because we are,*

or

> *I am because you are,*

are the two common English translations of the Ubuntu philosophy. This philosophy has much in common with Picasso's art and quantum physics.

Ubuntu recognises that none of us can become human, none of us can become ourselves, without the influence of everyone else around us. Ubuntu reflects the full interconnectedness of everyone and everything. The meaning-making stories that define who you are today have been shaped by everybody who you have interacted with, and the people they have interacted with, going back many generations into the past. This interconnectedness is at the very heart of what it is to be human. It's something to embrace and work with.

Who you are now, and how you show up in the world today, shapes who everyone else around you is, and is in turn shaped by who everyone around you is. This means that who you are—the meaning-making stories that shape you—are not exclusively yours to control.

You've undoubtedly noticed that with some people it's easy to show up as a bigger, better self, and with others it's hard. Much like the observer in quantum physics shapes the specific nature of the photon they observe, your nature is shaped by the people you are interacting with.

Because you are you through other people, the following reasons to hope and ways to grow yourself emerge.

1. You can see yourself with compassion because much of who you are could not have been different, and is due to the time, culture, environment, and family you were born into. Your path from embryo to today required you to create your stories of who you are, using the only raw material you had.

2. You can see yourself in the future with compassionate hope because you now have the power to step away from being subject to the stories around you. Instead, you can see your story more and more as an object to influence and shape consciously.

3. You can choose to spend more time with people who help you show up as your bigger, better self; and less time with those who pull you back into being the smaller person that you used to be.

4. You can begin taking yourself and other people less seriously; you can show up in life more playfully, because you know that the potential *you* is much bigger than your current reality. You can improvise and play with alternative stories.

5. You can work more collaboratively and compassionately with other people, because you can see more and more clearly how who they are has been and is being shaped by the people around them, including you.

6. You can stop blaming yourself and other people for being who they are, and shift your focus to what you can do to step-by-step change the context of your stories, their stories, and how the stories interact with each other.

7. Whilst you cannot become whatever and whoever you want to (because of constraints imposed by your genes, epigenetics, and your past) you can feel hope and optimism that you can become much more than you imagine possible today.

Picture the difference between a traditional landscape, with its strict perspective, and a landscape by Picasso. Then apply it to yourself: you have far more capacity than you can imagine to step out of the strict perspective of who you are and should be, of what you should do for whom, by channelling the art of Picasso. He recognised that a painting is there to interact with the observer, who is as vital to creating the reality of the viewing experience now as the artist was when painting.

To maximise the outcomes it was vital for Picasso to go outside the tramlines of strict perspective. Do the same, and you open up far more power to change yourself and the world you live in for the good.

It was not crucial to your living a good life, up until a few decades ago, to work with yourself more as if you were a Picasso painting than a traditional landscape. In other words, to work with the nebulous changing form or essence of who you are, rather than just your behaviours; and to keep adapting, growing your essence.

It is now essential, because our world is facing global challenges that are so interconnected that there is no way of predicting what might happen in the economy or politics next week, let alone in 10 years. We're living in a VUCA world of volatility, uncertainty, complexity, and ambiguity, which demands you to be more like a Picasso painting and less like a landscape, so you are best able to recognise and grasp the opportunities to act in the face of these nebulous challenges.

7.4 You optimised yourself to overcome your past challenges

It's not just unhelpful, it is also simply wrong to blame yourself for any aspect of who you are today.

You have always done the very best you can to optimise who you are to overcome the challenges in the reality you have experienced. The more skilled you become at using the Adaptive Way (described later in this, and in the next chapter), the more clearly you will see the challenges ahead of you, and the more options you will see for who you can become to overcome those challenges.

If you use the cinema analogy, you will realise more clearly that who you are now, and the reality that you now experience, is emerging and shaped by the reality that you have experienced in the past. Never doubt that you have always done the very best you could do, given the situation you were in at the time. Never doubt that you can adapt; that you can continue to learn and grow new ways of acting and reacting.

Over the course of your life, perhaps even from before you were born, you began learning how to overcome the challenges that you were experiencing. Everything you experienced in your reality was distilled into the essential lesson about how to thrive, and then either added to your existing stories defining who you are, or you added a new story to your library of stories.

Every time you face a new challenge, you decide whether to engage this challenge by reapplying one or more of the stories that has worked for you in the past, or to let go of everything that has worked for you in the past and figure out how to overcome this challenge from scratch.

It clearly costs you far less time, effort, and energy to overcome today's challenges by reapplying what worked in the past. However, that can only work if today's challenges are close enough to your past challenges for the same solution to work.

All life learns to be ruthlessly efficient with energy. If you run out of physical energy, your physical body dies. If you run out of emotional and psychological energy, you are quite likely to sink into a motionless ball of misery curled up on the sofa bingeing on Netflix and Pringles. So taking the risk to create completely new stories from scratch is a high-risk strategy because it has a high demand on both your physical and psychological energy.

So what should you look for, to decide when it's time to take a blank section of film and write a completely new story from scratch? When the challenge that you are facing is an adaptive challenge, not a technical one.

7.5 Adaptive vs. technical challenges

The essence of a technical challenge is that a technique or technology, and mastery of them, is all you need to fully overcome the challenge. A technical challenge can sometimes be extremely hard to master, but that doesn't make it adaptive.

If it is an adaptive challenge, though, you can only rise to the challenge by changing yourself. You will need to add one or more ways of thinking, you will need to change and grow your stories, and you may need to add more subtlety to how you deal with your hardwired nature. Most likely you will also need to do everything described above for a technical challenge, as most adaptive challenges also have a technical component.

In today's world, much of our pain is caused by trying to address our challenges within our current stories by learning new skills, techniques or buying new technology. But all your VUCA challenges can only be addressed if you change yourself. For example, dealing with pandemics like Covid-19 require a fundamental change in who we are being; but almost all effort has gone into medical technology.

We must grow and transform who we are, to build a world we will thrive in.

One adaptive challenge you have is the first job that you were born with: to become someone. You then become someone by changing who you are from baby to child. And this challenge keeps returning throughout your life. Until you get really good at changing your stories, you will fail to overcome your adaptive challenges, and fall short of your goals, because the barrier to achieving your most challenging goals is in who you are, not external to you. So your focus must be inwards on your meaning making, not outwards on others.

One sure sign that you are facing an adaptive challenge is when nothing you try works, and nothing you can imagine trying looks any better. You feel trapped at the bottom of a 20m well, with no way out. You can express your complaints easily (and often do, at least to yourself), but cannot express clearly what you want and what you can do to get it.

If you are a leader of any sort, most of your challenges will be adaptive challenges. You must become adept at changing yourself and supporting others in them changing themselves. Never attempt to change anyone else directly, though; it will backfire. You cannot write a new story for them; all you can do is support them in creating a context they choose because they believe will facilitate them seeing their own meaning making clearly, and allow it to rewrite itself. No company or manager has the right to demand any specific change in anyone else, they can only point out the business needs and implications of those needs.

If everyone adopts the peer-to-peer practices of the Adaptive Way described below, then you have the best available for each of you to adapt yourselves to address these challenges with the least friction, effort, and waste.

You can categorise your challenge as technical or adaptive using Table 7.1, based on the work of Ronald Heifetz[133].

To lead yourself and others through an adaptive challenge, Heifetz identifies five principles. All five are provided by the Adaptive Way practices here and in[134].

1. Look at your stories, assumptions, beliefs, and values. Focus on exploring yourself first, never fixing yourself.

2. Keep the stress levels within a range you and others can contain. Hence the three Evolutesix dojo rules are critical: care for yourself, care for each other,

Technical challenges	Adaptive challenges
Easy to identify.	Hard to identify, and so easy to deny
Easy to solve, best or good practice solutions exist	No existing solution. Can only be solved by changing your stories and thinking, especially your relationships to people, work, and how you see yourself in your roles
Experts can give you the solution	You have to do the work yourself
Only a few changes within your existing stories and boundaries are enough	Change everywhere, especially to your stories and boundaries
It's easy to see and buy into the technical solution	You are unwilling or unable to see the challenge clearly, and that technical solutions are incapable of solving the challenge
The solutions are relatively quick to implement	The solutions take time, demanding repeated prototypes and learning from failing until a viable solution is found

Table 7.1: Technical vs adaptive challenges

and care for the whole[1].

3. Identify the themes that most trigger you and keep these smaller than your trigger threshold so that your defence mechanisms, such as denial, blame, or shame, never kick in. Use the patterns in this book.

4. Take personal accountability for adapting yourself.

5. Pay attention to those voices inside you, or actual people around you, who ask challenging questions.

---

[1]These come from the work of Marilyn Hamilton on what makes excellent cities different[135]. These three are embedded in the city's culture.

7.6 Self-deception and hope

Self-deception is a vital superpower coming out of our stories. *"What? I never deceive myself,"* you may think! Take it from me, you do[2]. We are all very good at seeing what isn't there[136]. We have to be, because our survival has always depended on the capacity to keep hoping for a better future when times are tough.

This capacity for self-deception kept Elon Musk investing his last money into both Tesla and SpaceX, splitting it evenly, even though each needed more than he had in total. His hope and illogical decision in the face of the available facts was essential for both Tesla and SpaceX to keep going for a few months longer. By keeping both going, both benefited from unpredictable lucky breaks.

Paul Ormerod's book[121] *Why things fail* shows that the dominant reason for business failure is bad luck, i.e., unpredictable negative events, and the same applies to each of us. If you can just stay hopeful enough to keep going, if you can keep the business alive when things are going badly, you may still be around when a random positive event happens. Long-term success and failure depend on 'lucky' and 'unlucky' events.

> *Your capacity for self-deception is the superpower behind your success. Never lose this.*

But in other contexts, your capacity for self-deception is your ruin, because you either fail to even see fatal risks, or fail to see them clearly. Our risk-lenses, especially in the chaos during great shifts, are poor—we need better lenses of chaos. The art of being an effective human is learning how to tell the difference between the contexts, and the opportunities and risks[137] in each context. To see clearly contexts where you are harmfully deceiving yourself about the true nature of actuality. To see when it's time to apply the philosophy of *winners quit often* rather than *winners never quit*[138].

This is especially important in leadership roles[139], because other people, perhaps a very large number, will suffer if you cannot tell when self-deception is helpful and when it is harmful. Read more in Section 11.3.

Master all the patterns in this book and you have a better chance of recognising whether your self-deception is likely to help or harm you. These patterns, anchored in the best empirical studies, are designed to guard against self-deception in people like me, and perhaps you, who believe in making the world a better place.

Most importantly you will be able to continue feeling hopeful when facing

[2]This video from Robert Kegan describes how we practice self-deception well. `https://www.youtube.com/watch?v=FFYnVmGu9ZI`

huge odds, or at least continue to act as if you felt hopeful, even if you feel anxiety or despair. The more you can do this, the more power you have to overcome the adaptive challenges that you are facing, and will continue to face.

7.7 Experiences changes your stories, not analysis

Your history, and what you've experienced in your past, is almost irrelevant in becoming who you have the potential to become. This may seem surprising to you, given how much focus there is on analysing past experiences. However, research in psychology is showing with steadily growing clarity how widely different the histories are for people dealing with the same meaning-making stories; and that rewriting those stories depends more on the growth experiences you construct now, and far less on having a deep understanding of your past.

For many, understanding their past is often irrelevant; and may even be harmful, because your memories have become too distorted from your actual past.

This means that there is nothing to stop you from starting work today on creating the experiences that you need to adapt yourself in order to rise to your adaptive challenges. Dive into Chapter 8 to begin doing this work on yourself now, if you want to.

Most of us, though, find it helpful to understand the patterns in our past that have got us to who we are today. I have certainly found it helps me act more compassionately towards myself, my family, and the people who used to bully me at school. So I do invite you to use this chapter and the next to develop understanding. But don't expect that understanding alone will have much impact on you becoming who you can become.

7.8 So who ought you grow into?

Most of the old approaches to developing oneself recognised that there are many paths to self-mastery, wisdom, and enlightenment. Think of a monastery (maybe you enjoy Ellis Peters' Cadfael books); the monk's spiritual development is throughout their daily work. Whether they are reading the Bible, washing carrots, or solving the mystery of a dead body embedded in the ice, it's all part of developing themselves and being of service.

Your work, and the conflict you experience at work, is as necessary a part of you getting to know yourself and developing yourself as reading this book, actively reflecting on your experiences, or any other developmental practice[5,87].

This is very clearly evidenced in all the research into what has made highly successful companies remain so over decades. In them, work contributes so powerfully to each individual developing themselves and their natural talents that the best people want to work there. These are the companies that recognise that fighting the war for talent is a sure way of losing it. It's not a war, it's a garden. Provide all the right conditions, and you will grow top talent out of everything that arrives, and will attract the most ambitious people who are driven by developing themselves. Growing talent collaboratively gives you far better long term performance than hiring talent in a competitive battle.

Knowing whether you are truly developing yourself, or meeting the expectations of other people to be what they want you to be, is a challenge without a simple answer. The best you can do is follow Polonius (councillor to the Danish King) words when he counsels his son Laertes in Hamlet[140]:

> *This above all, to thine own self be true, and it must follow as the night the day, thou canst not then be false to any man*

Despite Shakespeare poking fun at Polonius', this advice has stood the test of time. But what does it mean to be true to thine self? And how can one know oneself? In a sense, because knowledge is always under construction, who you are is always under construction in every moment, and so you will only know how you have been true to yourself looking back. The best you can do in the moment is lean away from your current context and look far into your past and future.

How I (Graham) apply this quote is the same as the way I learned how to ride a motorbike or climb the vertical faces of Table Mountain. On a motorbike, when you go through a corner, the faster you're going, the less you look at the corner, rather you look as far around the corner as possible to where you are heading. Amazingly, by not paying attention to where the motorbike is now and what's happening now, but rather paying attention to where you want the motorbike to be as far into the distance as you can see, you magically avoid all the hazards in the moment.

When I was climbing, whenever the climb got tense, the mantra I used to relax and find a way through was

when in doubt, lean out.

By leaning away from the rock face and into danger, at the point where I was starting to tense up and pull myself into the rock face, I was able to get a better overview of everything else the rockface offered me.

Look as far into your future as you can. Lean out of your immediate panic and look at what else your current context offers you. Do this and you're more likely to recognise your unique path growth, not somebody else's.

And sometimes, you will need to step across a misty void, with nothing secure under you. You will need to leave behind everything that was secure, and what will be secure is not yet in sight. This is a kind of mini-death, leaving your old self behind before you have any idea of who you need to become.

You have two choices. Keep going, or retreat. Choose with your best long-term wisdom.

7.9 The Adaptive Way: How to grow bigger than your challenges

I (Graham) developed the Adaptive Way with colleagues in Evolutesix over the past ten years by integrating many different evidence-based approaches, and transforming them into one peer-to-peer way of interaction. The primary objective was a way based on dialogue that can be used at work, regardless of anyone's beliefs or religion.

Whether you are interacting with your colleagues at work, with your friends and family, or with the different aspects of yourself, these are powerful patterns to harness tension and conflict in service of your growth.

It's called "way", for the same reason Aikido and many others have "way" in their name: this is primarily a way of being and living, not a technique to master. Just as in many of the martial arts, there are patterns to become fluid in. Your end goal is to become so fluid in them that you achieve unconscious mastery, where you are no longer aware of your mastery, and you use just the right variation of pattern in the moment.

The intent and spirit of the Adaptive Way has much in common with Aikido. Both are centred on conflict, and both see conflict as a war *with* oneself that you can use in order to grow in power *to*, not as war *against* another to exert power *over*.

In today's world, our common approaches to conflict are always a net loss. They assume that the only relevant capitals are financial and territorial. That is certainly false today. So even if you win the narrow conflict in the financial or territorial sense—say you get a higher rate of return from some business deal at the expense of other stakeholders—the cost across all capitals leaves you and / or your children worse off long term. Such lose-lose-lose ways of war are long past their sell-by date.

The Adaptive Way is part of the art of war that's needed to defend and grow the capitals of life, both human and natural. And this begins first and foremost with you: master them to grow yourself into the biggest, most developed version of yourself according to your life path and nature.

Again, you need multiple lenses, because the Adaptive Way transcends and includes all the either / or paradigms of common practices. Just as much as the Adaptive Way is a soft, meditative, mindful way of self-development, it is also the way of the new warriors that we need, in order to have regenerative businesses and a regenerative economy. The next three chapters introduce the Adaptive Way, and the forthcoming books, and Evolutesix application programmes, go into detail.

> *Please stay safe whenever you work on yourself and interact with others. Firstly, make sure that the rules of a safe Dojo are well applied, because everyone is willing and able to apply them, and because you have a more adept practitioner to support you in staying safe. Secondly, keep in mind that (like a vulnerable scorpion after shedding one exoskeleton, but before hardening the next) you are at risk of exploitation by any malevolent narcissists, psychopaths, etc. in your orbit. Keep a careful eye open for signs of these. For signs of people who will harness your vulnerabilities to serve themselves.*

CHAPTER 8

You are your stories

We all know that Art is not Truth. Art is a lie that makes us realise truth, at least the truth that is given us to understand. The artist must know the manner whereby to convince others of the truthfulness of his lies.

—*Pablo Picasso*

8.1 Your stories make meaning

We humans are the best at seeing patterns and giving meaning to them by applying one of our pre-existing meaning-making story templates. We only start work on creating new meaning-making story templates, i.e., change our self, when none of our existing ones work for the adaptive challenge we are facing[1].

Because it's so important, it's worth repeating: the reality you experience is created by the meaning making of your stories.

To experience a different reality, you need to change the stories you use to make meaning. Of course, there are very real and hard limits to what you can and cannot change. Simply telling yourself a story that denies climate change, or your height, does not alter the actuality of climate change, nor your height. However, what climate change or your height means to you is shaped by your stories, and you have the power to change these. If you want to do something, but believe that there is nothing you can do, first look at how you can change the stories that create your meaning, a reality you inhabit and are powerless in.

---

[1] This chapter was sponsored by Vet Dynamics UK

Figuring out how to change your meaning-making story used to be a trial and error, hit and miss process. Fortunately, the past few decades in adult development have shown clearly[141] that our meaning-making stories come in distinct categories, or stages, a progression of the clear stages of child development. Each category of stories builds on the foundation of the earlier categories, and forms the foundation of the later category. You can't skip a category. Hence, these categories are commonly called stages.

If you know which category your current stories belong to, you can see more clearly which experiences you need to create for yourself so that you can grow your story templates towards the next category.

No stage is better or worse in absolute than another stage, just as classical physics is neither better nor worse than quantum physics, even though they are sequential. Rather, like classical physics is best at describing what we can say about the world when things are relatively big, and quantum physics is best at describing the world of everything that is relatively small, the same is true of the stages of adult development. Each stage is best at some aspect of being human in human society, each is essential, and requires the previous stage as foundation.

You grow yourself from one stage to the next by chipping away all parts of your old stories that are no longer helpful, and adding new stories that are more helpful in making viable, actionable meaning of the adaptive challenge you are facing. The best way to do this is by creating experiences that give your stories conflicting input so that they rewrite themselves.

There is no way for you to consciously rewrite your stories. The stories are you, they have written themselves up until now, and they will continue to write themselves. There is no way of saying to yourself, let alone to somebody else, *"if you follow this 10-step plan, and work hard, you will get to the next stage in six months."*

In fact, it's more like the joke about the disciple who asked his guru,

> *"Master, how long will it take me to get enlightened?"* To which the master replied, *"probably about 10 to 15 years."* *"And if I work really hard at it, how long then, guru?"* *"Oh, I imagine then it will be completely different. Then it will take you about 40 years."*

Each successive stage is a new paradigm of ever broader and more complex enlightenment. That means a broader and more comprehensive paradigm that sheds light on completely different ways of seeing yourself and others, with completely different yardsticks.

Once you have learnt this new paradigm, you can never unlearn it.

What triggers each step in your journey is a growing awareness that how you describe what is, is not capable of handling what *actually is*. And this creates the drive to break free from your current paradigms and shift into a more comprehensive paradigm, which includes everything still useful in the old paradigm, just as quantum mechanics still includes everything that is useful from classical mechanics, and even becomes completely classical mechanics in certain situations.

In the next chapter, you will see how to use a set of Adaptive Way patterns that I have so far found to be the best at identifying what in my meaning-making story can change, and which experiences can lead it to rewrite itself. But first let's look at the Constructive Developmental Framework (CDF) definition of the six stages of adult meaning making.

Stages of meaning making

The six stages are listed below and depicted in Figure 8.1.

S1: Impulsive mind. Your immediate impulses occupy centre stage and drive you to act almost without any conscious thought. Most people move to the next stage while still children, or at the latest as teenagers. You're unlikely to meet somebody at work who still has their centre of gravity at S1.

S2: Instrumental mind. Your individual needs, and how to meet them, is the central theme of most of your stories. Over 10% of the population remains at this stage throughout their adult life.

S3: Socialised mind. Your stories are primarily centred around what it means to be accepted and valued by other people. The stories now enable you to meet your needs through peer collaboration, whereas at S2 you're more likely to focus on meeting your needs directly or through power over another. Over 55% of the population reaches and then remains at this stage.

S4: Self-authoring mind. Your stories are now centred on the values and unique concept of integrity that you have created for yourself independently of other people's expectations. Approximately 25% of people progress this far. This is the first stage with the full developmental capacity to manage other people effectively (especially knowledge workers), or to fully use the potential of self-governing or self-organising approaches like Sociocracy or Holacracy.

S5: Self-aware and self-transforming. You are now fully aware of all the different aspects of your self-constructed identity, see them all as valid and none as absolutely superior to any others. You are quite comfortable that some of your stories defining who you are are deeply incompatible with other stories of who you are. Your stories, and who you are, are now deeply fluid, enabling you to easily write the new stories that will turn you into whoever you need to be to address whichever new challenge comes your way. Less than 8% progress to this stage.

S6 Stage 6 and any stages beyond have yet to be sufficiently understood, and are beyond the scope of this book.

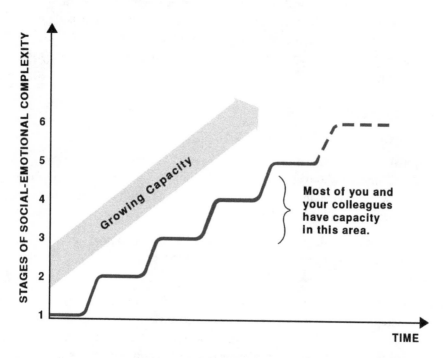

Figure 8.1: Stages of social-emotional / meaning-making capacity growth. Most of you, and your colleagues, are likely to have a capacity in the bracketted range, from entering stage 3 to stable at stage 4. This diagram is derived from Kegan and Lahey[142].

At work you will mostly find people at stages 3 and 4, with a few on their way from stage 2 to 3, or from stage 4 to 5. Very few will have their centre of gravity at stage 5, and even fewer at stage 6. In fact, stage 6 is not yet well understood; there are too few people at stage 6 to have a good enough idea of what it looks like.

Each stage has a clearly identifiable and self-consistent set of stories.

I cannot emphasise enough: having your stories primarily centred on a specific stage does not make you a better person than someone whose stories are centred at any of the others. You will not necessarily be any happier if you are at a different stage to the one you are in now, nor any wealthier. Every society and organisation needs people at all stages, and every stage is essential to meet all challenges.

And remember, the stage is only about your stories; each stage has a wide range of different personalities, different fluidity in the different types of thinking, different hardwired needs, different values and ideals. Useful as it is in making it easier for you to rewrite your stories, never forget that you cannot actually separate your stories from everything else about you. You are one integrated whole, the structures of your thinking, the patterns of your meaning-making stories, all their content, along with your physical body.

Some in positions of influence today are between S3 and S4. Someone who is here has typically differentiated themselves towards becoming unique, but still derives some of their self-identity through belonging to a self-selecting group of people who are similarly different to the general population. In some cases, this is through belonging to a community of expert practitioners in some discipline.

Then you have someone who defines their worth, their self-identity, and who anchors their meaning-making stories in other people seeing them as an expert. There is a huge difference between somebody who is at S4 or beyond and *has* expertise and somebody who has not yet reached S4 who's meaning-making story says

I am *an expert*.

This expert stage encompasses those who are unable to differentiate between *having* expertise versus *being* an expert. They can easily become a barrier to progress because any challenge to their discipline is interpreted as a challenge to their worthiness as a human being—a life-threatening challenge because if you take away the validity of their expertise, it's tantamount to the death of their identity.

All disciplines have this. Expert-stage climate scientists are a barrier to public understanding of the climate emergency; expert-stage economists are a barrier to the adoption of more useful models of our economy; expert-stage lawyers are a barrier to reinventing company law, and so on across all disciplines. (My (Graham) *being* an expert has at times been a barrier to achieving my goals.)

There is a world of difference between people who have expertise (we need many more of these) and people who derive their identity, the validity of their being, from being identified by themselves and others as being an expert.

We have a higher need than ever before for people who have progressed through the expert intermediate stage, retaining all their expertise but no longer identifying themselves with belonging to their discipline. This begins with S4, and then S5, as stages that have an identity, or meaning-making stories, independent of others' expectations.

From S4 onwards you become capable of leading management hierarchies effectively, of leading major change programmes, and in particular leading the change from a traditional organisational hierarchy to a self-governing developmental organisation. From S4 onwards you are adept at working with people from very different disciplines to yours, including those whose discipline contradicts some of your tenets.

But we have fewer people at S4 than we need, and even fewer at S5.

We need more at these stages than ever before because we now have so many large organisations needing significant numbers of people managers and leaders of system transformation. Less than 33% of the adult population ever progresses to these stages, often only towards the end of their working lives, or after retirement. Our current concept of retirement, and age-segregated living, has lost us many of the benefits we need.

Most of the frames of reference that your stories give you are so obvious to you, and so deep inside you, that you can no longer see them. You are unaware that they are there. The ground pattern of Section 8.2 is the best method we have found of sneaking up on your hidden stories and shining a spotlight on them faster than they can run away and hide. Then you can create the optimum experiences for your stories to adapt themselves, and for you to move to the next stage. Feel free to go straight to Section 8.2 if you want to start now.

But no one can just read up on a new stage of meaning making and quickly adopt it. You have to construct it through experiences and reflection. You can, however, learn new forms of thought quite rapidly. We cover the 28 transformational forms of thought in Chapter 9. The more fluidity you have in them, the easier it will be for you to create powerful experiences you need for your stories to rewrite themselves.

Here's an example from one of my clients to illustrate how one of these stages shows up in the workplace, for two people I will call Cathy and Janet[2].

Cathy and Janet both work for the same company and have the same specialisation. Janet is new and on a steep learning curve about how to work in her speciality, and how to work with colleagues. Cathy is new in the role of being the leader of a colleague and is breaking free of her old big assumptions around taking care of people.
Almost everything Janet does is for the first time. She acts from a

---

[2] Not their real names.

frame of reference that says that any sensible person will look to their managers, and anyone with more experience, for guidance on what is expected. Also, any sensible person will also observe closely what more experienced people are doing, interpret that as the way to succeed around here, and mimic them. (Or, as the way to fail around here, and so do the opposite!)

Janet imitates what others are doing, how they behave, dress etc.

Cathy has a very different set of stories to Janet. Some of Cathy's are about independence and avoiding being overloaded by trying to take care of too many other people's needs.

So when Janet is imitating Cathy, or asking Cathy questions, Cathy makes the meaning: *Janet is asking me to take care of her.* Because Cathy is rebelling subconsciously against these old meaning-making scripts imposed on her by her parents, her hidden commitments kick in, and she, misinterpreting the meaning in Janet's words and actions, tells Janet to get lost.

Cathy is beginning to attempt, in a clumsy way, to define her identity independently of belonging to any group by simply adopting the group norms of behaviour and identity.

Janet then makes meaning of Cathy's actions as *Cathy is a cold, demanding, uncaring woman. I need to fix the problems she is causing.* By helping Cathy to bond with the group by conforming to its behavioural norms.

Now we have a perfect spiral of mismatched meaning making, leading inexorably to a dysfunctional working relationship, even though each is doing the very best they can to collaborate.

The most commonly found stage in any organisation is S3, or the socialised mind. This is the stage that society needs most people to be at for society to be stable. It is the central stage that reflects one of our superpowers: the power to live and work together in groups by adopting the common stories as your own.

On the other hand, Stages 2 and 4 are both quite individualistic, so it costs the group far more effort to maintain social bonding of members at Stage 2 or 4 than at Stage 3.

Any healthy group that thrives long term through many major challenges requires enough people at each stage and a way of working with people at different stages. This is a big challenge for companies today.

Judgements and frames of reference

You cannot *not* make judgements. Trying to become someone who is non-judgemental is inherently impossible because the reality you experience is created by the judgements hidden deep in your stories, and that you are therefore subject to.

The best you can do is hold your judgements lightly, as information, not blindly following them.

Your stories are the frames of reference, you use to generate judgements in your reality.

Instead of striving for the impossible goal of becoming free of judgement (because making meaning is evaluating and judging), put your effort into becoming aware of your stories, and how they shape the reality that you experience. Like the film projector analogy, the more you understand how the light, film, lens, and screen all shape the reality you experience, the more able you are to experience with your full potential everything that actually is.

The more you can shift your stories from hidden ones that you are subject to into conscious ones, the more able you are to recognise when one of your stories is past its sell-by date, a frame of reference holding you back. When it is necessary to pull out a different story from your library and use that as a valid frame of reference, or even when it's time to adapt yourself to rise to a challenge you've never experienced before by writing a brand new story.

I sometimes used to judge colleagues as incompetent idiots if they didn't see things my way. Not any more (or at least, not for more than a few minutes) because I now manage to remind myself quickly that the judgement is coming from my frame of reference. It is giving meaning to only the small part that I take in of everything that is happening. Then I can work out if the issue is actuality—the person truly is an incompetent idiot—or my inner reality, shaped and given meaning by my stories. Usually it is a mixture of both!

In the story of Cathy and Janet above, neither sees the whole, unbiased actuality. Each can only work off their own experience of their reality, shaped by their own stories. Each shapes the unique realities they each experience, including the underlying intention they project onto the other. So the "why" that Cathy attributes to Janet's behaviour is not Janet's why. It is, if Cathy ever did what Janet has done, the reason why Cathy would do that. Which has nothing to do with Janet.

Your judgement about why you think someone does what they do comes from your own frame of reference. You may be completely right, you may be partially right, or you may be completely wrong. But either way, keep a very close eye on yourself. Explore how you may be misinterpreting why someone else is doing something. Mis-interpreting because you are looking at them and their actions through the distorting lenses of your own meaning making.

This might be a good time to reflect on where the judgements of Picasso and Einstein came from, both positive and negative, referred to in Section 1.5.

Winning and losing

Beauty is in the eye of the beholder. Marmalade-coloured cats, never hippos, win my animal beauty pageant. But that hippo's mum thinks her baby hippo is the most beautiful being ever.

Nature disagrees with both of us; nature sees cats and hippos as each just right for their niche in the ecosystem, each as vital, integral parts of life on the planet. Nature uses a completely different frame of reference.

Success and failure are also in the eye of the beholder.

There are those who see me as a failure, because 12 years ago I (Graham) stepped away from a rapidly advancing career with Procter and Gamble to focus on using the power of business to combat our climate crisis. Others see me as a success for precisely the same reason.

In the shower this morning I started to judge myself as a failure because I was looking at what I have achieved over the past 12 years. And then I caught myself and remembered that, just a week ago, I'd judged myself a huge success, because I'd inspired and moved people I admired, at a conference in Tuscany. People saw that I have developed, with the Adaptive Organisation that includes the FairShares Commons described in this book, the foundations for a fundamentally new way of doing business. One that is the foundation for combatting climate change without creating even more problems.

I quickly came back into balance, as I became aware of the bigger picture. Firstly, in each case, my judgement was based on a small fraction of everything that I have achieved over the past 12 years. Most of what I have achieved I cannot know about because it lies in what other people have become and done because of how I have triggered movement in them. Secondly, every time I judge myself, or anyone else, I can only do so by comparing what I see to my own unique internal yardstick.

1. What I see depends on which lens(es) I choose to use, out of the infinitely many lenses I could use. Each lens shows a part of what actually is, with some kind of distortion, but none can possibly show all that actually is without any distortion. Every

time you judge yourself as a success, or as a failure, check which lens you are using to look at the data. Then ask yourself, which data is completely hidden by that lens, and which data is distorted by that lens?

2. How I then judge what I see, a distorted fraction of what is, depends on which of my many self-constructed yardsticks I choose to use (Chapter 9, P5 and C6). Every time you judge yourself as a success, or as a failure, check which yardstick you are using. How do you know that that yardstick is at all relevant? If it is relevant, are there other yardsticks that may be equally relevant, and that you also ought to use, because they point to a different judgement? What are all the yardsticks that you need to use simultaneously to minimise the risk of self-deception? (Even if some of them contradict each other.)

There is no absolute success, nor absolute failure, in any part of life, and certainly not as a startup founder, manager or leader. You have succeeded, simply by being born and continuing to breathe until the breath of life leaves you again. At least, I believe that that is how nature defines success for any living being.

Success and failure lie purely in the lenses and frames of reference you are able to use, and in whether or not you give these lenses and frames of reference any validity. Which depends on your stories, and how strongly you believe in them.

I'm getting better at using whatever happens as information about whether

1. what I'm doing is more or less helpful to achieving my goals;

2. or my goals are illusions created by the distortions of my lenses and frames of reference;

3. and not as triggers for feeling hope or despair because I judge myself as a success or a failure.

For example, I came out of the shower this morning feeling relaxed, seeing both success and failure as an inseparable part of what I am doing, which left me calm and energised to continue writing this book.

Judging yourself as a success or as a failure is one of the most common judgements we make about ourselves. Often this judgement is at best incomplete, and at worst totally false. Judging yourself as either a success or as a failure can be the self-deception that enables you to succeed; or that prevents you from succeeding.

Three related topics that hold many potential entrepreneurs back from the results they could achieve lie in their relationship with money[143,144], power[99], and imposter syndrome. These are common challenges for many, and can be very effectively transformed by working on the meaning-making stories that create them via the Adaptive Way Ground Pattern in the next section.

8.2 Grow better, bigger stories

Faced with the choice between changing one's mind and proving
that there is no need to do so, almost everyone gets busy on the proof.
—John Kenneth Galbraith[145]

In this section you will read an abbreviated version of the Evolutesix Adaptive Way ground pattern (GP)[3], which is covered in far more detail in my (Graham's) forthcoming books[134].

The ground pattern is a sophisticated dialogue tool, both for your inner dialogue, and for dialogue with others, to recognise and transform meaning-making stories.

Once you have constructed a newer map that is more realistic and more useful, you will be able to get more helpful answers to your questions *"How am I? Who am I? Who should I do what for? Who can I become as I grow up, and what will help me change, so that I become that next version of me?"*

The Evolutesix Adaptive Way's big advantage lies in the clarity it gives you, because the strict use of patterns separates and so clarifies the often messy mix of all your different goals, activities, feelings, judgements, beliefs, and nature. I (Graham) have found this magical, for myself, and even more so working with others.

Many approaches to developing yourself begin with complaints, as the ground pattern does, but instead then exhort you to declare yourself to just be different or do differently, without providing any viable way of changing the underlying meaning-making stories that are who you are and that create the reality you experience. So they fail, at best; and at worst, are contributing to the growing rise of

---

[3]The sources of inspiration for the Evolutesix Adaptive Way ground pattern include Robert Kegan and Lisa Lahey, *Immunity to Change*[142] and *How The Way we Talk Can Change The Way We Work*[146]; the non-violent communication (NVC) of Marshall Rosenberg[147]; Byron Katie's *The Work*[148]; and *Big Heart Big Mind* by Genpo Roshi[149].

The research described by Timothy Wilson in *Redirect*[150], Steve Salerno in *SHAM*[151] and Miguel Farias in *The Buddha Pill: Can Meditation Change You?*[152] on how ineffective, or even harmful, many of the approaches to behavioural change and self-help are, have guided what I include in the Adaptive Way.

depression and other psychological issues[150].

The ground pattern works because it takes into account you as a full living being, keeping all aspects of what makes you who you are and that shape the reality you experience.

Please hold tightly to the strictness of the pattern at first. Only once you are really fluid at using it strictly are you likely to be able to use it in an improvised jazz fashion, without misinterpreting what the conflict you are experiencing is actually telling you about how to adapt yourself.

GP Step 1: Goals, or translating from Complaints to Aspirational Commitments.

Purpose: Identify your goal(s), or what is important or valuable to you, even better, your underlying needs. We call this an aspirational commitment.

The endpoint of this GP step is having a clear commitment sentence:

> *I am actively committed to (achieving / the value of / the importance of / the need [4] for) …*

You might already have commitments clearly defined, as a clear goal. Some objective or achievement you have already set your sights on. Perhaps the next promotion, getting a pay rise, or whatever. Then finding these commitments is easy.

You also have commitments that are not yet sufficiently clearly defined. So long as there is anything where you are complaining about what is not, rather than talking about what you want that is valuable or important to you, you can benefit from getting more clarity on your commitment by mining them out of your complaints.

Unlike what many managers think, complaints are valuable. Encouraging complaints in order to mine the value in them gives you what you need to develop. Look at complaints as the best that you can do, within your current reality, to communicate to yourself and the people around you that something is not sufficiently fit for purpose. The worst thing that anyone, let alone someone leading a process, can do, is to shut down your talking about what you can feel but cannot yet articulate.

---

[4] Need in this book usually means need in the way Marshall Rosenberg defines it in his non-violent communication. See the list of the more common needs in tables 10.2 and 10.3. The important distinction between needs in an NVC or our ground pattern and common speech is that here a need is yours, inside you, and not linked to any other person. For example, any time anyone says to you "I need you to …", that is not a need. You are not their need. They have a need, perhaps a need for safety, and they are choosing you as a tool to meet that need. Beware of being coerced into becoming their tool. Master these dojo patterns to recognise such coercion. It is very common in how we learn to talk to each other these days!

Feelings are hard data that cannot be put into rational words.

If you are in a meeting, for example, work on any feelings and complaints until you are clear whether or not they are telling you something you must take into account to have any hope of achieving the purpose of that meeting. I (Graham) certainly wish I had been able to do this far better ten years ago in P&G.

Any complaints people have can be translated into an underlying unmet commitment, or need. Start by connecting with your emotions. Most likely you will come up with a number of commitments. Work with one at a time, and start a new ground pattern for each commitment.

To get your commitment into the clearest and most actionable strictness, complete the commitment sentence stem:

> *Therefore I am committed to the goal / value of / importance of / need for....*

Keep your aspirational commitments simple and actionable. Avoid any temptation you may have towards perfection, going ever deeper into abstract commitments, or in integrating multiple commitments into one more abstract commitment. You can easily get caught up in the joy of getting ever deeper insights into your deepest, clearest needs (summarised in the tables of Section 10.3), and remain at the commitment GP step.

If you find yourself staying at GP step 1 in a search for deeper insight and perfection, check if this search for insight and perfection is one of your blocking behaviours of the next GP step. If so, your hidden commitments (GP step 3) have kicked in, and you are protecting one of your vulnerabilities in thinking you cannot move forwards until you have found the deepest, purest commitment.

Keep it simple, approach it playfully with an improv mindset, and move forwards fast, but imperfectly. Be a playful entrepreneur or leader[153]!

Sometimes it feels clumsy to use the full sentence stem. Instead you might want to say, for example, *I'm committed to building my website* or *building my website is important to me*. Sometimes that form is the best way to go. If it works for you, use it. Just keep in mind, especially at the beginning, when you are coaching yourself, mediating between the different voices in your head, using the pure structure prevents you from getting lost in your own circles. It keeps you moving forwards.

Using the words *value of* or *importance of* or *need for* brings three things into sharp clarity:

1. Is it really important or valuable to you? Or is this just something that you have had put on your shoulders?

2. Is there something deeper? The sentence stems *value / importance of / need for* are especially useful when wrestling with a fuzzy set of complaints. They help clarify the underlying needs or values that are poorly met in what you are doing. By stating them clearly then you can go on to identify in the next step why they are not met.

3. Is this expressed clearly as something universal, or at least something that many people will share with you? For example, *I'm committed to being honest* is about you. *I'm committed to the importance of / need for honesty* applies to you and everyone else. This lets you recognise why you have some complaints about others, but instead of trying to fix them, you can now focus on what is in your power to change. You can then explore in GP Step 2 the things you are doing that blocks other people from being honest with you as well. How you are (perhaps unintentionally) demanding that they lie to you.

GP Step 2: From self-blame and shame to self-compassion

Purpose: Begin to transform yourself, by changing your perception of yourself from one of weakness, shame, and blame for your bad behaviours, to one of self-compassion, accepting that you are doing what you do for some good reason.

Attempting to just change your behaviour never works. So long as the reason (usually a good reason, at least within your inner reality.) behind the behaviour remains, you will continue to block yourself from achieving your goals. Maybe with the same behaviour (and then you will feel even worse, and judge yourself even weaker) or with an alternate behaviour. Likely an even more extreme one.

So in this section we begin the journey of mapping yourself, by sneaking up on that reason from behind, so that it does not hide away as it usually does. You will begin by identifying all the behaviours that hold you back from fulfilling the aspirational commitment identified in GP step 1 above. Both what you are doing that holds you back, as well as what you should be doing, but are not doing, and by neglecting to do, you are holding yourself back.

By the end you will have a list of enough of these blocking behaviours to move on to GP step 3, the hidden commitment, as well as clarity on how you feel when you do these blocking behaviours, and how you judge yourself for doing them.

The intention in GP step 2 is to plant seeds for actionable hope by exploring yourself. You will have more clarity on what you are doing to block your aspirational commitments, and why. You will have learnt how to explore yourself by using the hard data in your feelings, and judgements about yourself. Data telling you about the underlying script you use to attribute meaning.

You will be able to accept without judgement, instead with self-compassion, the simple fact that you are doing these blocking behaviours for good reasons. Recognising, though, that some of these reasons, whilst essential and valid in another context (e.g., as a five-year-old) are no longer essential as a 55-year-old!

If you are like almost everyone else, you are doing a number of things that hold you back from achieving your goals. In some ways, you are sabotaging yourself. GP step 2 will help you, and you can help your sparring partner, become aware of what works against your goals, or aspirational commitments.

The objective here is to collect sufficient information for GP step 3, not to compile an exhaustive list of all blocking behaviours. You may find that this list is already partly there, in the complaints you used to identify your aspirational commitments.

If you primarily complained about the behaviour of others, now is the time to look for which of your behaviours might be contributing in some way to blocking you from achieving your aspirational commitment. You may well be the victim of other people's behaviour, out of your control; but there is often something you are doing that contributes to holding you back from achieving your aspirational commitment. Something that is in your control.

All you ever can work on is what is in your control, even if it is only 0.1% of what creates the situation.

This is even more important if your aspirational commitment is on the edge of your circle of influence, like being committed to the importance of leaving behind you a healthy planet for the next generations to live on. For an aspirational commitment like this, the ground pattern is powerful, provided you focus on the fraction of a percent that you own.

Only your words, actions and thoughts can ever be inside your circle of control.

Your focus is on what your behaviour contributes towards your aspirational commitment being satisfied, or that works against that process. Later you will master the different thinking patterns (Chapter 9), especially the transformational ones. The more you master these thinking patterns, the more effective you will be in working on aspirational commitments way outside your circle of control.

Here is the task for GP step 2, blocking behaviours. List as many examples as you need of the following two types of behaviours blocking you from achieving the aspirational commitment you chose in GP step 1 to work on.

Doing. Blocking through action. What do you do, but should not be doing, because it holds you back from fulfilling your aspirational commitment?

Not Doing. Blocking through inaction. What are the things I should be doing to fulfill my aspirational commitment, but I am not doing?

Now you are ready for the task of translating this into a language of personal responsibility.

Look at all the judgements of blame, shame etc. and ask yourself *how would I evaluate myself if I knew that I was doing these for a reason my subconscious believes is good, but perhaps is a reason that is no longer valid, or at least not valid in this specific situation?*

At the very least, suspend judgement of yourself for now, and shift your attitude to one of acceptance and personal responsibility. A language of blame can only get you to dysfunctional New Year's resolutions, as we will see next.

Even if others are 99.999% responsible for what is happening, you still usually have something you are doing that you could change. Differentiate between the part that is in circumstances you cannot control, vs. the part where you do own responsibility. You cannot change something that is a law of physics, or inside the control of another.

So now you have this list of some of your behaviours holding you back from having your aspirational commitments fully realised. Everything you are doing and not doing. Make sure that these are observable, actual, factual behaviours, not judgements or interpretations coming out of your meaning-making stories. Then

> *Leave the behaviours alone!*
> *Do not try to change or fix anything!*

The worst thing you can do is try to change behaviours directly, or to fix anything as if it were a problem to fix. Many other approaches do attempt to change these. Often via a resolution to change, i.e., a new year's resolution!

Such attempts to change, or fix these blocking behaviours, can easily cause you long-lasting harm because they fail to take into account what the behaviours in your list are good for. They fail to take into account the situations where these very "blocking" behaviours are vital to protect you from harm. They fail to take into account what you actually still need them for!

Even if there is nothing you need them for any more, if your subconscious guardian angel still believes you need them, it will do everything possible to protect you by retaining them. In the next GP step you will learn what works when resolutions and fixes fail.

GP step 3: Resolutions to hidden commitments

Purpose: identify which hidden commitments are at the core of your blocking behaviours, because they are actually there to protect you from perceived

harm. Shift from a blame, shame-driven paradigm of resolutions (declarations that tomorrow you will be a different person) to a compassion driven paradigm of exploring your vulnerabilities.

Hidden commitments are what you are committed to avoid or prevent from happening. They are subconscious. They are deeply hidden in the lessons you have learnt about what certain situations or events mean for you and other people; in other words, in the scripts you have constructed throughout your life to generate meaning from meaningless actual facts.

If you are used to Richard Barrett's approach to values[154], these are limiting values; or, if you are familiar with NVC, you can think of these as when you are subconsciously meeting needs related to preventing harm.

Here is an example from when I (Graham) learnt rock climbing on Table Mountain in Cape Town a few decades ago.

I used to climb on Table Mountain. I often felt fear when looking down the vertical rock face, even though I knew it was an easy climb, and I was roped in. Every time I began abseiling, I felt fear.

Feeling that fear is perfectly justified. After all, without the rope, letting go of the mountain means a 500m vertical drop onto solid rock, and certain death. Or, if I'm unlucky, living maimed. So the very last thing I should do is anything attempting to simply make a resolution to not feel fear, or to bully myself to just do it.

That would rob me of exactly what I need to protect myself from falling in another situation where I lacked a rope. It would rob me of the instinct to protect myself going down an open staircase.

What I needed, and did, was a slow process of re-educating my automatic responses in the specific situation while rock-climbing.

I've not climbed for 20 years now, and my healthy fear of falling off cliffs is still with me, thankfully! Of course, it now kicks in again even if I am safely roped up.

Alex Honnold[155], the first person to do a solo unprotected free climb of El Capitan in Yosemite, took over two years to prepare for it. He attempted the climb once before his successful climb and realised very quickly into the climb that his meaning-making stories at that point were not where they needed to be. He immediately aborted the climb. He did not try to push through, or blame himself for being who he was at that moment. All our lives we are doing daily the equivalent to a solo unprotected climb. Trying to simply push against who you are is only going to get yourself hurt, and lead to far poorer results in your startup than you could otherwise achieve.

The hidden commitment is a commitment to avoid or prevent something we believe may harm us. It may be as obvious and natural as avoiding situations where we might fall off a cliff. Or as subtle as avoiding situations where we might be praised.

Your hidden commitments have some value, and should never be just violently squashed. This is why declarations to simply change your behaviour usually fail, and can even be harmful to you. Most resolutions to simply stop doing something you have decided is a bad habit fail because they neglect all the situations where that habit is good.

This dysfunctionality of most approaches keeps many in the self-help industry rich: the approaches fail you in a way that leads you to come back for another.

So until we have explored ourselves thoroughly, understood exactly how we generate the meaning we see in neutral, meaningless actual facts, any declaration along the lines of *as of now I resolve to be different* may well cause harm.

In this GP step we are after your hidden commitment. If your aspirational commitment is your idea of heaven (if my aspirational commitment were always satisfied, my life would be heaven), your hidden commitment is your idea of hell. If this was always in your life, you would be miserable, and seriously at threat of harm and pain. Your hidden commitment is expressed by completing the sentence stem:

I am committed / work hard to avoid / prevent…

To find out what it is they are protecting you from, we need to go through the same door they use to get you to do your blocking behaviours. Worry or fear.

Worry Box   Filling in your worry box opens the door to seeing your hidden commitment clearly. In your worry box you fill in all the bad things you fear might happen if you failed to do your blocking behaviours.

To get at your worry box, take each behaviour in your list of blocking behaviours, and imagine yourself doing the extreme opposite behaviour.

The pattern here is:

Imagine you are doing the extreme opposite behaviour to your blocking behaviour. Really picture it in your head. Take your time to do so and feel inside you. How does it make you feel? If you feel worry, fear or similar, what are the thoughts that cause you to worry?

For example, a common blocking behaviour is keeping silent in meetings until everyone else has spoken, and so sometimes losing completely the opportunity to contribute because someone else has made your point. Now imagine doing the extreme opposite behaviour; immediately you have a thought, blurt it out.

Or perhaps you are one of those whose blocking behaviour is constantly blurting things out immediately, and wish you could keep your mouth shut until after you've thought a bit more, because you keep shooting yourself in the foot with what you say! Now imagine doing the extreme opposite behaviour, keeping your mouth shut until you have really thought it through.

What are the thoughts of worry that go through your head as you picture yourself doing the extreme opposite behaviour? What do you imagine might go wrong? What do you feel as you imagine that?

If your worry sounds like a respectable thing to be worried about (e.g., I worry that my team will be stressed) then you're off-track. If you can be proud to tell others that this is your worry, you are off-track. Remember, this GP step is about finding out what your personal idea of hell is. A sure signal you have found part of your hell is if you feel fear, and feel shame when you tell others about it.

To support you in this, remember, you are here to explore and understand the hidden commitment, not fix it. Certainly not to judge it, but rather to have compassion for the very valid history you have, that made this hidden commitment vital to protect you.

To go from your worry box to your hidden commitment, start by looking for any common themes across a few or even all of your worry box entries. The hidden commitment lies where the largest discomfort is. Then complete the sentence stem:

I am (committed / work hard) to (avoid / prevent)....

Get the sentence as concrete and specific as possible, e.g.

I am committed to preventing any situation where I am seen by others as not smart enough.
Or
I am committed to preventing any situation where I start to feel depressed.

Note that it is perfectly fine to have a hidden commitment to avoid some kind of feeling. We have found it quite common for certain types of feelings, like feeling depressed, overwhelmed, or lonely, to take on a life of their own. And once certain feelings do, merely having that feeling can become the primary threat to you.

For example, I know that once I start to feel depressed, I can very easily get locked into a downward spiral. So preventing this spiral from starting becomes important for my productivity and happiness.

Hopefully you now realise that the image of an internal dialogue between your inner angel and devil is false. All that is actually happening is that you are pulling against yourself, because both your inner angel and your inner devil come out of the same set of meaning-making stories, unique to you. Your aspirational commitments and hidden commitments are like opposing teams in a football match, or in a tug of war, but you are both teams. In any war against yourself, there can only be one loser and no winner.

Part of what makes this a viable map of yourself is, as with any map, putting elements into the map in the same position that they are in the landscape. Recognising when a commitment belongs in GP step 1 or in GP step 3 is an art that is essential, and takes practice with a more experienced sparring partner to develop. Be careful not to confuse the complaints leading to an aspirational commitment of GP step 1 with the resolution to the hidden commitment of GP step 3.

Also keep an eye open for situations where you have two or more aspirational commitments that cannot be simultaneously satisfied with one action. For example, I have a commitment to health, including a good night's sleep each night, and a commitment to excellence. Sometimes I have to choose which aspirational commitment I satisfy. This is quite different to the tension between aspirational and hidden commitments.

The relationship between the aspirational commitment and the hidden commitment is in your behaviour: you intend to fulfil your aspirational commitment, but your actual actions (by which you sabotage your aspirational commitment) follow a well-perfected strategy to fulfil your hidden commitment. To protect you from the harm in your personal hell.

GP step 4: Big Assumptions

Purpose: identify the big assumptions behind the hidden commitments, and that are a subcategory of the meaning-making stories that drive your choices and behaviours.

A "big assumption" is what your meaning-making tells you will happen if you fail to protect the vulnerability that your hidden commitment is committed to protecting. The big assumption is based on past lessons drawn from past experiences which might not apply to you today. Or perhaps only apply in certain specialised situations.

All your big assumptions, along with the stories that still drive you but you are now aware of, are the entire set of meaning-making stories that you use to construct your internal reality out of the inherently neutral facts you take in.

For example, one specialised situation where some of my big assumptions still apply is with my parents. In some ways, neither they nor I have quite accepted that I am now 50, not 15.

The big assumption in the strict form that we use in the Adaptive Way consists of four parts.

1. If I fail to (…my hidden commitment…)

2. The emotional consequence of failing to fulfill your hidden commitment

3. The meaning you give to failing to fulfill your hidden commitment, and / or the meaning you give to the emotional consequences

4. The chain of consequences through to the worst-case end-point.

Using the strict form at the start of your practice will make it easy to use this at work to collaborate effectively, to support each other in peer-to-peer sparring, and even more so to support yourself when using the pattern alone.

You might think, when you say or write down your big assumption, that it is clearly ridiculous. This is very common, and is a first loosening of the hold it has on you. But avoid going too fast, avoid falling into the trap of trying to fix your big assumption there and then. The big assumption is not a thing to be fixed, but rather a mystery to explore and transform into a more mature, wiser and useful meaning making script. One relevant to you now, rather than you way back then.

This is of vital importance. Most big assumptions have some element of usefulness in them. You want to preserve this usefulness at all costs, because it may well be a life-saver. You may have a big assumption saying *If I fail to avoid angering people, I will feel scared and powerless, because it means I will be bullied and hurt, and then I'll be killed.* In some situations this big assumption is realistic and helps you deal effectively with, say, being taken hostage in an armed robbery.

Instead of trying to fix yourself, as if this big assumption is only and always a problem, but never a help to you, approach it from an appreciative stance[156]. In the more advanced Adaptive Way patterns we develop your capacity to use appreciative inquiry as a basis for engaging with yourself, others, and the work of your organisation.

Look at all aspects of this big assumption and yourself. Treat yourself, and everything in your life, as a curriculum to learn from. The five steps in the transformational experiments part of the ground pattern, and the castle move, will support you even more in doing that.

You will often use this ground pattern in dialogue with your colleagues, as well as in self-coaching to mediate your inner dialogue. It's absolutely vital, if you are accompanying a colleague or friend in their journey of self-exploration using the ground pattern, that you never project yourself onto them. Remember always that you are only there to walk with them on their road of self-exploration. You are not there to coach, fix, or heal them.

If you do share your meaning: make it crystal clear that this is entirely yours, shared for the purpose of mutual transparency, and that the other is completely free to reject or use your words in any way useful to them. Making very clear to them that you are sharing an insight into yourself in case that might be useful to them, but not because you have any power to be able to define what another person is.

I cannot over-stress this point. Many of your big assumptions have been created by people taking on to themselves the idea that they have the right and the ability to define who you are, and you then believing them. Be very wary of ever doing something that declares or defines who the other person is.

This is so common when people manage or try to help others. Instead of helping someone learn more about themself, you simply project your own issues onto theirs.

This is why it is only safe to use this ground pattern at work if there is sufficient psychological safety, and everyone is able to abide by the three Evolutesix dojo rules:

1. care for yourself;

2. care for each other;

3. care for the whole.

This is why I cannot over-emphasise the importance of your keeping to a strict form of the pattern until you are ready to jazz with it. The strict form of the big assumption is a sentence structured as follows:

> *If I ... (opposite of hidden commitment, e.g. "If I don't avoid ... "),*
> *I feel (emotional consequence, directly associated feeling),*
> *because it means (the meaning you give to not fulfilling his hidden commitment)*
> *and then ... (your personal extreme consequence e.g. "I'm incapable of living a purposeful life").*

For example,

> *If I fail to prevent any situation where I am seen by others as not smart enough, I will feel small, embarrassed, anxious and depressed,*

because it means that they will judge me as not good enough, not worthy and then I will lose all their respect, will be kicked out of the group, or will have to rely on their choosing to pity me.

Your big assumption has, as its last line, the deepest personal hell that your hidden commitment is committed to keep you out of. Until you have transformed this script, every attempt to fix your blocking behaviours, or bad habits, as if they were problems that could be fixed, will only increase your stress levels.

If your hidden commitment is to avoid a feeling, then your big assumption may need to be formulated differently. For example, if your hidden commitment is,

I am committed to preventing any situation where I feel depressed

then your big assumption may begin,

If I start to feel depressed, it means that I will lose control, spiral into depression, and so become unable to do the work I'm committed to doing, perhaps even do harm to the people and work that is important to me, lose my connection with my sources of energy and life, and then life itself becomes both intolerably hard and meaningless for me.

In this you can see that avoiding the feeling of depression has become primary. It has taken on a life of its own. Because simply beginning to feel that way may easily trigger an avalanche of dire consequences.

The best way to transform your big assumptions is to see them clearly, and then to create experiences for yourself that teach your deepest level guard dogs that the world is now different. Or maybe yours are guardian angels! The problem that they have—and you will need a high degree of compassion to deal with them—is that they are very young and very immature. Some are likely still frozen in your life at five years old.

It is time to send them back to school; create your own unique experiences for them to learn a new script, one that will protect you from real threats today.

Some of your hidden commitments, though, come from hard-wired aspects of yourself. Aspects that you will never change throughout your life, or can barely change. You have most likely accepted your height as something you cannot change; regardless of how much you wish you had a different height, you learn to accept what you have been born with, and develop ways of coping with the disadvantages, and harnessing the advantages.

The same is true with our nature. We all are born with our own unique personal energy economy, as you will see in Section 10.2. And the opposite of the activities we get energy from are those where we need to put energy in, even to do them poorly. These activities are neurobiological vulnerabilities, deep in our hard-wiring, either in our genes, or deep in our past. Any attempt to change them will have no impact, or at best bring such marginal changes that few will notice the difference.

So dealing with your hidden commitments is more than just rewriting the stories of your big assumptions. You also need to recognise when avoiding certain activities is simply part of your nature. You know that doing this activity drains your batteries, requiring you to take time out to recharge them. If you have an introverted nature, you know you need time alone before and after a big event to be able to engage with so many people.

So the advanced approach is to recognise when your hidden commitment is driven by a story you can rewrite, and when it is your nature, and you need to focus on developing better ways of dealing compassionately with your nature.

Sometimes we are asked why we avoid the phrase *limiting beliefs*, preferring *big assumptions* or *meaning-making stories*. The whole concept of limiting beliefs, as it is usually used, carries with it a risk of causing harm.

The issue with labelling a belief as limiting is that we typically only look at the consequences of that belief in a specific context, without including the context itself in our judgement. A belief can be limiting in one context, but enabling in another. The belief itself is not limiting, nor is it enabling; it is the belief in a context that limits or enables you. So we advise against using the phrase limiting belief unless you add the context.

Calling them assumptions makes it far easier to see the role of context. It makes it easier to see that it is an assumption we make about ourselves, others, and actuality. The word big refers to those assumptions that we are unaware of, or only partially aware of. These drive our behaviour without us realising it.

The Adaptive Way is all about becoming ever more conscious of our assumptions, firstly by shifting them from big (we are not conscious of them at all) to small, and secondly by running experiments that make them smaller, until we know all the contexts where they are false, and hence limit us, and all the contexts where they are useful models of actuality, and hence enable us.

By now you should be seeing clearly why many behavioural and self-help techniques are at best useless, and at worst harmful to you. All your assumptions, big and small, and your nature, are who you are. They are your life, as you are living it now. Your hidden commitments are the guardian angels doing their very best to save the life you currently have.

You can choose one of the two exits from the meaning-making stories that currently drive your behaviours.

1. You can creatively find a completely new alternative behaviour that satisfies, in one behaviour, both your hidden commitment to protect your vulnerabilities and your aspirational commitment. We call this, in analogy to chess, a castle move.

2. Or, you run experiments that create sets of experiences enabling you to iteratively get your meaning-making stories closer and closer to ones that accurately reflect actuality, rather than distorting it.

You could also give up on achieving your goal. Of course, if you have come this far, you are highly likely to achieve your goal. But the route is hard. First you need to lose yourself, as you are now, to become a new person.

Exiting your meaning-making cycle

Castle (non-transformational exit)

The castle move is simple to learn. It helps you to achieve your goals without any need to change your big assumptions, or your nature. Two elements are needed to get better at castling yourself. The first is lots of practice. The second is mastering more of the transformational thinking patterns of Chapter 9.

The castle move is useful in getting to your goals even when aspects of you that you cannot change as fast as you would like to hold you back, or perhaps that you never can change because they are part of your biological nature.

Just as you cannot change your height, there are many aspects of your personality that you cannot change. If you have, for example, a genetic predisposition towards depression, hidden commitments that protect you from depression triggers are perfectly sensible. You should never attempt to fix your nature with declarations or resolutions. Instead accept your nature with self-compassion; identify the excessive protection in some big assumptions; run experiments to transform the stories that you have constructed over your life about what it means to you to have depression; and use the castle move to find new ways that simultaneously protect you from depression triggers and enable you to achieve your goals.

Winston Churchill had depression for all of his life. He was enormously successful because he developed alternatives to his blocking behaviours. Alternate behaviours that better enabled him to achieve his commitment and met his need to protect himself from the consequences of his depression.

The castle move is fundamentally about accepting compassionately who you are now, and so finding what you can do to be functional as you are. This is far from fixing. It is not about changing something that is broken, but rather harnessing all you have to be more functional.

The alternate behaviours in the castle move must be ones that still avoid what your hidden commitment needs to avoid.

First, say

> *My reality right now is that I am committed to both: … (your aspirational commitment statement) and … (your hidden commitment statement).*

Then,

> *accepting that this is my reality, are there better ways that I can satisfy both?*

If you are in an organisation or team, you can put into practice what Peter Drucker says: that the central purpose of an organisation is to make your strength productive and your weaknesses irrelevant.

Find an alternative to what you are currently doing that blocks you from achieving your goals. At work this may involve changing how your roles are defined; and in general it often involves asking a third person to take care of certain types of interactions on your behalf, or some other route to harnessing everything that is part of your world to find other paths.

Experiments (Transformational Exit)

> *Walker, there is no path. The path is made by walking*
> *—(Antonio Machado)*

The purpose here is to create experiences that will give you clarity on what you can and cannot change in your meaning-making stories; and that will enable your stories to rewrite themselves, so that they are appropriate to your present and future life, not only your past. So that you steer your actions and your life, rather than it being mis-steered by events and your internally generated reality.

You were born with one big job to do in your life: become someone. You have become someone by writing the meaning-making stories, or scripts, that run you by creating the reality you experience out of what actually is. Together, all your meaning-making stories add up to be your own personal theory of self, or more commonly called, your ego.

You began working on this long before you were born, have continued to work on it each day of your life since then, and you will continue working on it until you either give up, or reach the end of your life. There is always some aspect of you that is ready to grow. That is why we emphasise that the Adaptive Way is a way of life, learnt in a dojo and mastered in practice with colleagues, friends, and family. It is not a one-off training.

The script you currently use to make meaning, including what it means to be you, was written when you were younger, less experienced, and less wise. This is unavoidable, you will always generate your reality by making meaning with stories that are from a younger you. The big difference between the wise and the less wise is how small the time-lag is between the context requiring an update to your script, and the script being updated. For some the lag can be decades. Maybe you are, at 50, still running off the same scripts you had at 20, scripts that began being formed between the ages of five and 15; this is no different to you at 50 uncritically accepting who some ten year old is telling you that you should be, and what you should do with your life.

Before running experiments to test and learn about your unique combination of meaning-making stories, hardwired nature, and your fluidity of using different forms of thought, most people find it helpful to keep an eye on themselves and maintain two lists for each meaning-making story.

1. A list of all situations where you notice your hidden commitment kicking in to protect a vulnerability.

2. A list of all situations that are very close to the first list, but for some reason your hidden commitment stays asleep.

From the difference between the first and second list, you can get some clues to the kinds of experiments you can run to challenge the validity of your meaning-making stories. The more that you can run experiments where you experience situations that are currently in your list 1, but when you try them out your hidden commitment is not active, the bigger your list 2 becomes.

Make sure that these experiments actually deliver hard, experiential data that either validates or invalidates some part of your meaning-making story. Think about what kind of information or data will falsify your big assumption. Then consciously conduct experiments to generate the data that can falsify your big assumptions. Now, let us begin designing a test.

1. Write down the big assumption / meaning-making story you intend putting to the test crisply and clearly.

2. What kind of data will prove one or more of the lines in your big assumption false?

3. Describe in detail the experiment you can run. What will you change in your behaviour, so that you actively do or say something your big assumption tells

you to never do or say? There are various starting points:

- One easy way to find these is to look at your blocking behaviour and worry box. Some of the easiest experiments to design (but hardest to do, and hence most powerful) begin by taking an extreme opposite that you have already listed in your worry box as the basis for your experiment.
- You can also look at the hidden commitment, and just step into a situation that your hidden commitment tells you is going to harm you.
- Look in detail at your big assumption, the whole if-then, and construct an experiment directly.

4. Get support from a colleague to be your sparring partner.

It is vitally important to never ever see the experiment as a way of tricking yourself into changing. You are, at this point, deep in a journey of exploration. Transformation will come later, and easily. For now, be very vigilant defending yourself against your old habits of trying to fix yourself with new year's resolutions. Remember, you are not a problem to fix, rather you are a mystery to explore.

Use a well-designed experiment to explore who you are now, so that you can read clearly the story that currently runs you. Such a well-designed experiment is SMART, as Kegan and Lahey term it. That is, it is a Safe, Modest and Actionable Research Test of your big assumptions.

Safe and Modest. The test needs to be safe and modest. If your big assumption is true, nothing too bad should happen. All consequences should be ones that you are able to cope with, even if the worst-case scenario happens. Use the tools of improv and psychologically safe spaces to conduct experiments.

Actionable. The test should be simple and easy to carry out as part of your daily routine so that you can act soon. Doing, creating new live experiences, is what will transform your big assumptions, not talking nor analysing.

Data-based Research Test. Your experiment ought to deliver real data that truly puts to the test some aspect of your big assumption. You are absolutely not doing this to improve yourself, nor to immediately achieve your commitment (if you do need to improve something now, the castle move can help you find alternative behaviours that are better for your commitment and yet still fully satisfy your hidden commitment). You are here to explore yourself. So only focus on getting data on how you feel or react, how others feel or react, on the "because" reasons that describe what causes your hidden commitment and feelings, or on your final conclusions.

Doing, experiencing and reflecting is the proven way to transform your meaning-making stories, not analysing the past they came from. As Kegan and Lahey write in *Immunity to Change*[142], many of us are in the grip of a fundamentally flawed theory of personal change: that one more self-help technique, insight, or behaviour will be the final key that unlocks you into your new self. Only new experiences that your stories used to rewrite themselves[150,151] will. You don't need any more self-help books or workshops. Run experiments. Do it for yourself with peers like you on the same journey.

Ground pattern example

A participant in a recent dojo illustrated a textbook perfect example of someone who is becoming aware that they have a socialised mind, and is beginning to look for ways of moving beyond this S3 stage towards the self-authoring S4 stage.

Jenny began by describing all the things that she is committed to, and that she complains about. She complains about how sensitive she is to the words and moods of others, how she can be influenced by others, and how dependent she is on the feedback of others. She spoke about how she lacks what, for example, her boyfriend has: certainty about what he wants and who he is. She wishes she had that, so she could feel secure.

We ended up choosing as three sequential commitments:

1. understand myself;

2. respect myself;

3. trust in myself.

She also wanted to have as a fourth commitment, to be stable; but after I challenged that, she realised that stability was already an outcome of the first three, not a distinct commitment in itself. She also saw that it was an unattainable ideal. No-one is ever fully stable; the best we can get to is being really fast in moving back to our stable centre.

We talked about how unhappy she is about being unstable. About one day doing things one way and being one person, and the next day doing things the opposite way and being the opposite kind of person. At this stage, I was tempted to work in a coaching mode rather than as a sparring partner. I realised that if I stepped into coaching mode

I am reinforcing her S3 other-dependence, not supporting her step towards S4. It was also clear that my personal need to help was why my meaning-making stories created an emotion of gentleness, leading to my wanting to help.

This is a risk of going to a coach when you are in the process of moving from S3 to S4. You may well end up with a coach who is themself still too much at S3, insufficiently aware of their own meaning-making stories and stage development to grasp the difference between coaching to meet their own needs versus the true needs of the client. Then you end up slowing down, not speeding up your journey to S4. Learning how to author yourself requires learning that you must independently deconstruct and then reconstruct yourself.

So I chose sparring, not coaching. She chose to focus on her first commitment:

> *I am committed to understanding myself.*

She then came up with four blocking behaviours:

1. not looking at what I need
2. not looking at why I do things
3. looking at the reactions of others
4. feeling selfish if I look at myself and my needs.

For the fourth one, 'feeling selfish if I take care of myself and my needs', I took that as a learning moment to explore the difference between feelings and judgements. Jenny realised very quickly that 'selfish' is not a feeling. It is a judgement. And she rephrased her fourth point now as a judgement, not a blocking behaviour, and from that saw that it was part of her worry box.

So her first worry box line is that she worries

> *others will judge me to be selfish if I look at myself and take care of my needs.*

We then went deeper into her worry box. She began by realising that the actual feeling is feeling stressed and anxious because she thinks other people would disapprove, be annoyed, and much more, if she takes care of herself, expresses her needs and thoughts and opinions clearly. She worries that other people will judge her as a rude person, she's afraid that she will lose empathy, she worries that she will become a different person.

We dived deeper. The worry that she will lose empathy is that if she loses her emotional side, that she will end up feeling less alive. She worries, if people see her taking, not giving, then she will be found out as somebody who is not worthy, because good people always give the best things to others, they don't keep them for themselves. She worries that if she is perceived as rude then that will come back at her as consistent rudeness from others, and she's not sure if she can handle it.

I then asked Jenny to look for the common thread through everything she has been saying. To identify the DNA inside her worry box that points at her hidden commitment. Jenny said

> *I realise that I need other people to tell me who I am. So I do those things that get me the feedback that tells me that I am who I believe I ought to be, instead of doing the things that are right for me.*

This is a classic sentence from somebody who has become aware of their socialised mind state and is beginning the journey towards self-authoring.

Her first attempt at a hidden commitment was

> *if they think I am so, then I will be so.*

We re-phrased that as a true hidden commitment

> *I am committed to avoiding other people seeing (i.e., judging) me as rude, selfish, or lacking empathy.*

Then we got into the meat of the big assumption.

> *If people do see me as rude, selfish and lacking empathy,*
>
> *I will feel horrible*
>
> *because it means that I am that kind of person, it means I must go, and if everyone says it, it means I am a complete outsider. I will then be filled with doubt. I will be angry*

that I'm not who I want to be and who I believed I am. I will judge them to have cheated me, because I trusted them with my sense of self, of worth, and my life and now they're all against me.

It means I'm no good at what I'm doing, they see me as green when I see myself as yellow, and then that will lead to a deep self-doubt of everything that I believe I am and that I want to be, and then all trust in myself is gone. If I don't trust in who I am and all I can do, then it's like pressing the key 'delete Jenny'.

Jenny at this point really understood just how dependent her self-concept is on what other people think and say. If her worst fear of 'delete Jenny' really happened, she saw how she would have to rebuild herself from scratch, and that she was implicitly asking other people to take that decision for her.

I asked her how she felt and what she was thinking at this point. She said

I feel relieved. I'm seeing this as very valuable and deeply honest. I'm also thinking 'Oh God, how do I solve this? Where do I start?' This is not just one problem and it feels a bit scary. But it's fine. It's a bit scary because there are so many things where I have to grow up, and I'm anxious about how to deal with them, but in some ways it feels fine to just accept them as part of the difficulty of growing. However, one barrier is, I have an urge to seem strong towards others and to feel strong; to be an example for others. And so I really want to avoid any situation where I have no control over myself.

After a bit more sparring, Jenny came to a few more conclusions. She realised that just because her partner states clearly who he is and what he wants, does not mean that he has chosen that purely for himself. It is perfectly possible that he has not even yet realised that who he sees himself to be, and what he wants to achieve, is actually coming from other people's expectations of him, from other people's idea of what a good person is or does. She found it enormously encouraging to realise that her deep turmoil and doubts are a sign of her first steps towards her new self-authoring identity.

Jenny relaxed as we discussed how everybody always goes first through a stage of constructing themselves from other people's expectations. This is a necessary precursor to be able to construct yourself from the inside out.

She was energised and encouraged to realise that *she* had built Jenny at her current socialised mind stage by choosing to believe what other people were telling her she should be. She has the power to deconstruct and then rebuild herself again.

As she looked at how the Adaptive Way process of experimentation, of using the tools of improv to deviate from your script, using the action patterns and the thinking patterns, she realised that she had already taken a great stride towards deconstructing who she is and reconstructing her new self.

We closed with me reminding her that she is a mystery to explore, not a problem to fix. That this process of taking bits of her self-identity into her hand, looking at them, running experiments to change them, or to explore them more deeply, will continue for the rest of her life. This is a *Never Ending Story*, like the book of Michael Ende[34]. She always has been and always will be writing her new self.

I saw something important changing in her at the end. Jenny had reached these insights herself, using me as a mirror and lens. She had gained belief in her own ability to do this again without me present. To rewrite her own scripts alone, or in sparring with anyone, without realising it, was a lesson she had now learnt and could reapply for herself alone and with others for the rest of her life.

8.3 Action patterns

There are a large number of patterns in the Adaptive Way, beyond the scope of this book, that are extremely useful in devising castle moves, running experiments, and dealing with the consequences of your nature. These will be dealt with comprehensively in[34].

Two important categories in these action patterns are the Improv and the Luck patterns. Shakespeare recognised that we are but actors on a stage, and this chapter has hopefully enabled you to recognise how deeply true that is. You are embedded in your big assumptions, those meaning-making stories that you are subject to. The more proficient you are at the techniques of improv theatre, the better you are able to improvise your present as it emerges, rather than slavishly following your hidden meaning-making stories.

The second is the set of luck patterns. Luck is crucial to making the most of the opportunities hidden and emergent in a VUCA world. These are based on research showing that the difference between people who see themselves as lucky in life, and those who see themselves as unlucky in life, lies in their meaning-making stories and the consequent choices they make[157].

This ties in very well with the research of Paul Ormerod[121] showing that random evolution is only explanation for why businesses fail that fits a century of data spanning all sizes of business from small to multinational. In other words, the business just gets unlucky. Which is usually a consequence of the leadership team and the business culture having unlucky meaning-making stories. And why Napoleon always used asked whether a prospective general was lucky or unlucky in battle.

8.4 The journey between stages

There is a very good reason why it is difficult for you to grow from one social-emotional stage to the next. What do you think your life would be like if you were so easily influenced, that you immediately believed what anybody said to you about yourself; who they said you must be; and what you should do for them? You would be like a lump of bait waiting for the next shark to come along and gobble you up.

You could not possibly function as a human being in society if you did not have very powerful defences against manipulation. These defences protecting your self-identity from manipulation by narcissists, sociopaths, etc., are very much like a psychological equivalent to your physical immune system. You know all too well, if you suffer from hayfever, just what happens if your physical immune system mis-interprets harmless pollen as a harmful threat to your body. Your immune system goes into overdrive, all your defences kick in, and you end up feeling miserable for no good reason.

Your psychological immune system is just as much a dumb autopilot as your physical immune system is. Every time you try to change yourself, for example repeating a declarative resolution like *Every day in every way I am more confident* you trigger the same psychological immune system that does the vital job of defending you against manipulation from others. So it stops you from manipulating yourself too.

Your psychological immune system is only able to see you in the present. It is incapable of recognising that you are the same person as the person who made the resolution yesterday, nor can it recognise you in five years. So it defends against your resolution to change, or your promise to change for your family, as vigorously as if some narcissistic stranger was trying to manipulate you.

The excellent work of Robert Kegan and Lisa Lahey[81] in formulating this model of the stages of adult development has given us an understanding of how we can temporarily suppress our psychological immunity to change so that we can transform ourselves. This is very much like taking immunosuppressants before an organ transplant so that your physical immune system does not attack the new organ that you need to thrive. Do this, and you will find it easier to achieve your goals and feel comfortable in your skin.

CHAPTER 9

You are your thoughts

I paint objects as I think them, not as I see them.
—*Pablo Picasso*

Before you can make meaning of anything that happens, you need to assemble an image, an inner representation of it, in your thoughts.

The more fluidity you have in using a wide range of different forms of thought, i.e., lenses, the better that this image will be in making you aware of what is important for you, and hide what is not. The better that your thoughts can do this, the more useful and realistic will be the meaning that your stories can make of it.

In this section I will describe the difference between how we think and what we think. You will also finally learn the 28 different forms of thought, or post-logical lenses, that we have mentioned numerous times so far in this book, the forms of thought going beyond simple opposites to complementary pairs; and that you can only begin to develop after you have mastered binary logic.

Contraria Sunt Complementa—Opposites are complementary

is the motto the quantum physics pioneer Niels Bohr chose for his coat of arms when granted the Danish Order of the Elephant in 1947.

By the time most of us have finished our formal education, we have become very good at using logical forms of thought. We know that the opposite of right is wrong. We know that the opposite of true is false. We know that something is either right or wrong, true or false. Never right and wrong, true and false.

Binary logic forms of thought only work if your world is simple, or at most complicated[1]. As soon as your world is nebulous, volatile, uncertain, complex or ambiguous, you need to go beyond binary logic.

As Figure 9.1 shows, the opposite of *true* may simply be *a different truth*. The opposite of a deep truth may well be an equally deep truth, not a falsehood. To make sense of your world and options, you may need to hold both deep truths in your head simultaneously, even though they visibly contradict each other.

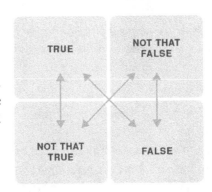

Figure 9.1: Truth square. The opposite of true is not always false.

The 28 post-logical forms of thought are all those necessary to be able to simultaneously hold all the realities needed to make sense of the biggest adaptive challenges you will ever face in your life. Then you will have the most powerful capacity for sense-making anyone can have, enabling you to rise to any adaptive challenge.

We have two kinds of thinking, and these thought forms as well as binary logic can be in both. One, called Type 1, costs us very little effort. Only the thought forms we are extremely fluid in show up in Type 1. Type 2 is much slower and costs us far more effort because we are thinking deliberately. Here we can also apply forms and content of thought that we are still learning to use.

These two types of thinking are described in detail in the excellent book *Thinking Fast and Slow* by Daniel Kahneman[54]. In Type 1 thinking, your thought forms are on autopilot and activate a narrow set of well-used stories. Perfect if you're facing a challenge that you have faced many times before and have the skills you need to rise to the challenge. But a disaster if you only use Type 1 thinking to respond to a VUCA challenge that you have never seen before.

The more any part of your life, but especially your work, involves change, contradiction, or wholes that must be completely included, the more you can only succeed with a sufficiently high fluidity in the 28 forms of post-logical thinking in

---

[1]The Cynefin framework in the list on Page 66 is a very useful way of deciding if your challenge is obvious/simple, complicated, complex, chaotic or disordered[52,53].

Table 9.1. I sometimes call all 28, transformational thinking, even though only the final seven strictly qualify as transformational thinking[2].

A recent example of transformational thinking from me (Graham). There have been times when I have felt all-powerful, capable of doing everything, over the past years starting up Evolutesix. And there have been times when I have felt weak, overwhelmed by the enormity of the task. The thought that keeps me going when I feel weak is:

> *I have power, regardless of whether I feel powerful or weak, and I have weaknesses, regardless of whether I feel weak or powerful. Both power and weakness are in me at all times, independently of how I feel.*

So I can always, when I feel weak, act just as I would if I felt powerful because the power is in me anyway.

Since I'm not all-powerful, my weaknesses are always present, and regardless of how strong I feel, I should avoid acting strong if I'm actually weak in that area. For example, if I want to pick up a 285kg motorbike, acting as if I were powerful, this is only going to hurt and embarrass a 67kg me. In starting up and filling my roles in Evolutesix, I am best able to do what is good for Evolutesix if I constantly check whether my feeling of power is leading me to ignore the warning signs that I'm getting something wrong.

A root cause of many mistakes we make is when your capacity for Type 2 thinking is not enough for the VUCA challenge we are facing. When you are in this situation, you will at best make a poor decision, and at worst blow your organisation up, because you failed to recognise this as an adaptive challenge.

A common example of this in business occurs when something works, or fails to work. A leader sufficiently fluid in these 28 thought forms knows that, in a VUCA world, the right strategy and process can lead to a harmful outcome due to bad luck; and the wrong strategy and process can lead to a beneficial outcome. Such a leader does not misinterpret success or failure as evidence for the strategy and process being right or wrong, when in fact it has been caused by luck / bad luck driven by a VUCA context[121,158]. (See Figure 9.2)

Post-logical thinking, at its highest level, is seeing that the 27 years of impris-

---

[2]Otto Laske, pioneer of using these thought forms practically in business, these are called dialectic thought forms. I have mostly avoided using the word dialectic in a book about economics to avoid adding in any interpretations you associate with Marx's dialectics. These thought forms are pure forms, and have nothing to do with the content or meaning of Marxist dialectics. Of course, Marx used these forms himself.

Figure 9.2: Cause-effect square in a VUCA world, and the role of luck.

onment on Robben Island ahead of you (if you were Nelson Mandela) might be part of your becoming the statesman, capable 27 years later, of leading South Africa through an awe-inspiring transition. Seeing that you are a prisoner and a leader, without any contradiction between the two, and still being fully a prisoner and fully a leader.

Post-logical thought forms are all about grasping opposites, contradictions and paradoxes to create transformation. Like seeing sources of hope in our fears, in our enemies.

9.1 28 post-logical thought forms

The 28 thought forms (see Otto Laske's second volume[6] and *Metathinking*[159] by Nick Shannon and Bruno Frischherz for full details) extend the binary logic of true-false into forms of thought to enable you to get ever better at grasping the nebulous, VUCA actuality you live in. The better you can use all these forms of thought and logical thinking, the closer your reality can match the subtleties of actuality.

Once you are fully fluid in these forms of thought, you fully grasp that unceasing change is normal, not exceptional. There's always more to what you're looking at than you can see; contradiction, conflicts, oppositions, paradoxes, anomalies etc. are inherent, with no way of reducing them to binary logic. Everything is part of a bigger whole, connected to multiple different things, nothing is isolated or independent. And there is always potential for transformations that you cannot see or predict from where you are now because there are always more lenses, perspectives or input needed to fully grasp actuality than you are using.

When you look at the 28 thought forms in Table 9.1, you may recognise them all and think that you already use them all with a sufficiently high fluidity. Very few people really have the capacity to use all 28 thought forms with full fluidity when facing challenges. No matter how good you think you are, you can grow in mastery.

You can only learn how to use these 28 thought forms fluidly through dialogue with other people. I (Graham) initially tried mastering them solo and found that whilst I made good progress memorising the thought forms, a hundred times more fluidity developed through dialogue with others because they have different worldviews and use the thought forms differently.

These thought forms have been uncovered, over thousands of years, by all the world's different philosophers and religious thinkers. Otto Laske has distilled out this complete set of 28 thought forms, in four groups of seven each, summarised in Table 9.1.

Context: these are thought forms that you use to fully grasp the static aspect of actuality. If you are only able to use context for forms, inner reality will be static, although perhaps extraordinarily complex.

Process: these are thought forms that you use to fully grasp opposites and simple changes or processes from one state to another. Process thought forms create an inner reality that far better represents the movement, change, and paradox of actuality.

Relationship, or relatedness: these thought forms go even further, giving you the capacity to grasp what is common, and the relationships between aspects of actuality that at first sight seem to have nothing to do with each other. They also give you the capacity to recognise relationship as an element of actuality in its own right, independent of any two specific things that are in relationship.

Transformation: the most advanced forms of thought, build on the foundation of context, process, and relationship thought forms. These transformational thought forms give you the capacity to rise to the biggest adaptive challenges.

To get an idea of where you are, print out this table, and keep an eye on which forms of thought you are using during the course of a week or two.

	Process (P$_i$)	Context (C$_i$)	Relationship (R$_i$)	Transformation (T$_i$)
1	Permanent movement	The parts within a whole	Limits of separation, existence of relatedness	Limits of stability, harmony, durability.
2	Including opposites	The whole, its equilibrium	Value of bringing into relationship	Value of conflict for development
3	Composed of interpenetrating opposites	Structures, functions, layers of a system.	Critique of neglecting relationships	Value of developmental growth
4	Patterns of interaction	Natural hierarchy of layers of a whole	Relatedness of different frames of reference	Evaluative comparison of systems in transformation
5	Knowledge always under construction, never absolute nor complete	Stability of a system in its functioning	Formal structure of relatedness	Bringing multiple systems into balance with each other
6	All always in motion; a form not thing.	Frames of Reference, traditions, ideologies	Patterns of interaction in relationships	Open equilibrium systems in constant transformation
7	What is embedded in a bigger process.	Multiplicity of contexts	Constitutive relationships	Integration of multiple perspectives

Table 9.1: 28 forms of post-logical thought, based on Laske[6].

These thought forms are devoid of content. Think of them as more like a modern kitchen full of all possible equipment, enabling you to create all kinds of dishes and tastes from common and unusual ingredients, because you can work at all scales, from molecular up, with all kinds of changes and transformations, and by bringing into relationship ingredients never connected before. (For example, Odyssey, the chef at Granny Dot's, where Jack and Graham have written part of this, has just introduced us to pumpkin leaves with peanut butter. Surprisingly delicious!)

Cooking is assembling a puzzle in food. Your thinking is assembling reality as a puzzle out of different pieces from actuality. Each piece of the puzzle becomes an element of the content of your thinking, and by making meaning through your stories of the final assembled puzzle, you end up with your experience of reality.

If you use equipment unsuited to the shape and nature of the puzzle piece you are about to assemble, you will end up bending, squashing, or stretching it to force the pieces to fit together. So you end up with a distortion of the puzzle.

Similarly, if you use an unsuitable or clumsy thought form to grasp a piece of actuality and bring it into your awareness, you will distort it. But, because you have distorted it at first contact, you cannot realise that you have created a poor representation of actuality in the assembled puzzle that is your reality.

In other words, whilst you believe you have grasped what is actually happening, you have not. You have created a distortion that you cannot see.

Sense-making is the name we give to the process of assembling what you are aware of into a complete representation of actuality. If you have distorted this representation because you lack the necessary fluidity in the appropriate thought forms, the next stage of meaning making will be even more distorted.

Rising to your adaptive challenges becomes easier the more fluid you are in using all 28 thought forms. You become better at recognising clearly the meaning-making stories that run you, the big assumptions that you are subject to, and then creating the experiences you need for your stories to rewrite themselves.

The better you can do this, the more effectively you can lead yourself through life, and your organisation and staff to success.

9.2 Process, movement thought forms

To oppose something is to maintain it.
—*Ursula K. Le Guin*

This quote from Ursula K. Le Guin is, for me, a most thought-provoking quote. I have realised that some things I have done to try to oppose the causes of climate change are instead making it harder for us to get to a viable human society with an economy that works with, not against, nature's economy.

Consider, as you read this chapter, what these process thought forms can show you about how your actions are maintaining the very things you are trying to change. After all, one of the best ways to maintain something is to resist it!

To compare the first two sets of thought forms, process and static context, imagine you are about to hire someone. Is it the decision point that you focus on, and the gap in the organisation chart? Then you are using static context thought forms.

Or is the decision point for this recruit simply one fleeting stage in a sequence moving towards an ever higher-performing workforce? And so no decision can ever be *right*, but only just one step in a journey that began a long time ago, and will continue deep into the future? Then you are using process thought forms.

You may hire the best person to raise your team's overall performance. But immediately anything changes, for whatever reason, that may no longer be the best person to raise the performance. The team may change for external reasons, because its work changes, because someone else in the team changes, whatever.

So process thinking makes clear that you can never hire the right person if you only hire for the job you need filling now. But if you hire people who bring skills you need now and can adapt themselves, can learn new skills, and can bond well with others, you will continue to have a good team as things change over time.

P1: Permanent movement. You are using this thought form when you are aware that everything is on a journey from past to future, changing all the way. You're using this thought form, when you are aware how the past is part of the present; and even the future is part of the present.

For example, the more aware you are of how your thoughts about what might be in the future actually shape your choices and experiences in the present, the better you are using this thought form.

Permanent movement, P1, also includes awareness that things are constantly changing into their opposite, or the complementary component of a complementary pair. E.g., the bigger an organisation grows, the closer it gets to collapsing and shrinking as it outgrows the strength of the structures holding it up.

P2: Including opposites. This is where you shift from *either-or* into *and* thinking. A classic example of this was developing the concept of servant leadership: the recognition that the leader is also there to serve their followers, in ways that enable the followers to deliver better results. Traditionally, people thought that it was the follower's job alone to serve the leader. Applying P2 made it visible that each is serving the other. Similarly, managing your manager is an application of P2.

Just as in a complementary pair, there's no victory of one over another here, rather it's just the inclusion of opposites to construct a greater whole.

P3: Built of opposites. This is the next stage, building on P1 and P2. This is a foundation of complementary pairs in quantum physics. Here, you go beyond merely including opposites into seeing how something is inherently constructed from opposites. For example, juggling is built up of the opposites of gravity pulling down and the juggler's hand pushing up. An electron is inherently and irreducibly both particle and wave, even though classical physics cannot allow any entity that is simultaneously both.

You, your organisation, and society as a whole, works, has strength and stability because the whole is constructed from what we would normally see as opposites. If you try to fix yourself, or your organisation, by removing parts that you deem "bad", you may wreck something that you value because everything is built of apparent contradictory opposites that are both required.

P4: Patterns of motion and interaction. P4 is about patterns of motion, where two or more distinct things have a pattern of motion relative to each other. For example, as the leader, you may get angry with a colleague, leading them to make a mistake in their work through nervousness, leading you to then recognise your role and apologise, or just getting even angrier with them. If this only happens once, all you need is P1. Usually, though, this is a pattern of behaviour that the two of you have got into. Each of you is in constant movement versus the other in a clear, distinct pattern. Just like the earth is in a pattern of motion around the Sun.

P4 is the thought form you are using when you really understand what that pattern is and what causes it, as Newton did when he thought that the force of gravity caused the Earth to rotate around the Sun, and as Einstein did even better when he realised that there was no force of gravity, rather a closed circular pattern in curved spacetime where the earth and sun moved relative to each other without any force of gravity, but with an apparent interaction mediated by the curvature in the geometry of spacetime.

P5: Knowledge under construction. You are using this thought form whenever you are able to see clearly how something that you know is just knowledge that you have actively constructed, and because you've actively constructed it, it can never be complete and absolute actuality. It is always part of your internally constructed reality.

The choices you make about what elements to add to your knowledge construct, and how, always have some practical shaping driver. You construct knowledge because of some practical use you want to put it to, and this use is a consequence of your meaning-making stories. Maybe you are just a collector of knowledge, like a stamp collector wanting to have enough of it to arrange in beautiful patterns and present to others; or, you want to use the knowledge to beat other people by exploiting a weakness.

The better you are able to use this thought form, the better you are able to recognise that what you have until now taken as an absolute, that that is the way the world is and has to be, is your personal construction determined by your practical needs emerging from your meaning-making.

This is especially true for any knowledge you have about yourself or any other person. That knowledge is always a very sparse representation of who that person actually is, and is something that you are constantly and continuously constructing and reconstructing.

Similarly, once you see an organisation as a living being, you realise that you can never know it, rather you are constantly constructing the best approximate knowledge that you can. Disciplines like economics, or any social and physical sciences, are always a body of partial knowledge under constant construction.

P6: Always in motion, a form not a thing.   Picasso got this right, when he said

> *If I paint a wild horse, you might not see the horse ... but surely you will see the wildness!*

He recognised that if all you do is think of a horse as a thing, you miss almost everything that differentiates a horse from an identical statue of a horse.

A horse is always in motion, not random motion, but motion within some form. If you think of yourself, or your organisation, or society and its economy as a whole, as a thing that you can understand in itself without movement, the ebb and flow of interaction, all you can grasp is a shadow frozen in time. Rather, it is not a thing, but a form, an entire collection of certain allowed motions, changes, processes, etc., that together give the form of a wild horse. One moment that form looks like a thing, the next moment it looks like another thing, or a process, or a relationship.

Whenever you are unable to see the form, but only a concretised "thing" instead, you miss 99.9% of what you can do to lead change. Seeing yourself, or the legal structures to incorporate a business as a non-human legal person, as things you can only accept or reject, rather than forms that are always moving and changing, is one of our biggest barriers to creating an economy that works for you, for our planet, and for profit. Concretising what is actually a fluid flowing form into a thing is one of the cognitive weaknesses holding us back.

P7: Embedded in bigger processes.   Expanding P6 to everything, you see that a whole is itself a form in constant flow, composed of ever more forms themselves in constant fluid flow. Everything is embedded in a larger flow and composed of entities in a smaller flow. You can only really use P7 after you have mastered, and can use fluidly, all the previous process thought forms.

So to understand anything happening in your life, you need to look at all the flows that you are embedded in. These might be processes that began in your childhood, a process of change and movement that has got you to where you are now. If you don't look at the entire sequence of changes, and choices, you will misunderstand what is happening to you now, and very likely choose poorly out of the options you have.

Even more, what happened to you in your childhood is a consequence of all the processes of your parents, and of all the other family members around you, from the moment they were born. Without having enough understanding of these even bigger processes, you are likely to misunderstand what is happening in your life now, and which option ahead of you is the wisest to choose.

Even more again, all of that is a consequence of the processes going back generations. Which is why many traditions around the world ask anyone taking a decision to look at the consequences of that decision over the next seven generations.

The economy, stupid is a phrase coined by James Carville, a US political consultant, in 1992, in response to a question. He clearly recognised in this response the importance of taking into account, for even the smallest of questions, the consequences of all the processes we are embedded in, up to the very largest.

9.3 Context, structure thought forms

The next seven thought forms are static structures and constructions. If you are about to hire somebody, and look at their university's ranking in the current tables, the courses they studied and the results they got, you are using context thought forms.

Just as the process thought forms do not deal with context and structure, these thought forms do not deal with processes of movement and change, nor with the inclusion of opposites to create something new that is different to just the opposite put together. Nothing changes in any of these thought forms.

C1: Parts within a whole.   The better you can use this thought form, the better you can understand any part of a whole, because you have grasped the context that the whole gives to the part. For example, you are a part of a bigger whole, a family, or a group of friends. How is who you are shaped by being part of that family, or group of friends? How do you in turn shape them?

Whenever you only think of yourself or anything else in isolation, you are quite likely to misunderstand what is actually happening by neglecting the shaping influence of being part of a bigger whole.

Becoming aware of all the different parts that make up the whole is vital in creating a better reality out of actuality. For example, recognising that I am built up of many different parts helped me see my digestion as one part, my blood and blood vessels as another part, and my brain a third part that all need to be taken into account to understand my depression. So whenever something is happening, and you suspect that you haven't grasped enough, always look for additional parts that you may not be looking at, and the larger context that you're not yet seen clearly.

C2: The whole.   If you're looking at the whole as a whole, where each individual part is more background, you are using this thought form. You are using this thought form, when you recognise that the team as it *is*, is composed of all the people in it, so introducing one new person to the team might lead to a completely new team dynamic, not just a slight modification.

When you ask yourself whether your team is a big enough whole, or rather you should look at the organisation as the relevant big enough whole, you're using this thought form.

The emphasis here is really on zooming out until you have identified the biggest whole necessary to grasp what is going on, and an understanding of how the essence of that whole emerges.

C3: Structures, functions, layers of a system.   Sometimes the whole might just be a random jumble of parts, as if you had taken a box with all the pieces of the car kit and looked at the contents as a whole. Yes, it is a whole car kit, but it is far from being a whole kit car.

A whole car has all the same pieces, but arranged in a hierarchy of parts. You have a hierarchy from the bottom to the top, beginning with the tyres and ending with the roof; you have a hierarchy from front to back, beginning with the head-lights and ending with the taillights; and you have a hierarchy of function, such as the brake pedal activating the servo motors activating the hydraulics activating the brake pistons which squeeze the pads against the discs leading the tyres to slow down.

C4: Natural hierarchy within a whole.

C4: Natural hierarchy within a whole. Going one obvious step further from C3, you realise that any functioning whole has a natural hierarchy of layers and functions. Even if you tipped your box of car pieces onto the floor of your garage in a pile, gravity would impose a natural hierarchy. Any piece that was not strong enough to support the weight of the pieces above it would deform until what was left was strong enough.

The better you understand the natural, essential, hierarchical arrangement of parts within a whole, the better you can figure out what is going on, and what to do about it. For example, without understanding the natural and necessary hierarchies within organisations, some misinterpret the emerging approaches to dynamic or-ganisation design and governance like Holacracy and sociocracy as hierarchy free. They can still be hierarchical, just the hierarchy allows it to be context-dependent and locally adaptable, rather than identical in all contexts and requiring approval from above to change.

Such essential hierarchies are hierarchies of complexity, rather than hierarch-ies of person. For example, if I go to an excellent doctor, we both recognise that there are two hierarchies simultaneously present: I am at the top of the hierarchy of knowledge of my experience of my illness, and the doctor must accept that to be a good doctor. They are (I hope) superior to me in understanding health and illness, and the ability to see a successful treatment in the data of my symptoms. Blindness to either of those essential hierarchies will lead to a substandard or harm-ful outcome. As the permanent damage one doctor caused to my (Graham's) left ear is testimony to.

C5: Stability of a system.

C5: Stability of a system. One question that led me to the content of this book illustrates C5:

> *what is keeping our dysfunctional system stable in its dysfunctional-ity?*

because I recognised that our economic and business systems have proven enorm-ously difficult to change, despite decades of intense effort by very many people.

By asking what keeps the whole system stable, even though it's widely recognised as dysfunctional, enabled me to understand why more regulation, more effort on values-based leadership, and more corporate codes of conduct were at best going to make marginal differences. We need to pull out the pins of shareholder primacy that keep the system stable.

Even worse, by fighting against the system with those pins in place, we might even maintain the system. Picture a tug-of-war; the very fact that you have two teams pulling against each other is what keeps the rope off the ground and stiff. Or, consider the punitive justice system used in most countries. That system is kept stable because all the opposing elements reinforce each other. No part of the system can change unless the whole system changes. Changing the whole system is what South Africa did, e.g. via the Truth and Reconciliation Commission, which prevented a countercoup.

Until you are viewing a system sufficiently holistically, with an understanding of what keeps that whole as it is, you have little chance of generating any change to the system. C2 and C1 are two thought forms used in the ground pattern of Chapter 8 to understand who you are, and grow into who you can be, by triggering the very instabilities needed for who you are to become a process of growth, not a static identity.

C6: Frames of reference. This is one of my favourites, and you have already read these words many times throughout this book. Every single time you make a choice, that choice is based on an ordering of options determined by the C6 frame of reference you are comparing each option against.

A common misunderstanding of Darwin's survival of the fittest is that it means survival of the strongest. Any business leader using that as their frame of reference will build an organisation and strategy around overpowering enemies with strength.

However, a business leader who understands evolution recognises that the frame of reference Darwin used is that *whoever is the best fit to their particular business context, and is most able to adapt as that business context changes, is most likely to survive.* Using this, they will choose, depending on the bigger picture (C2), to collaborate, compete, or some mixture of the two (P2, and perhaps P3 in some cases). By using this different frame of reference, from exactly the same actuality, they follow a different strategy leading to different choices.

Until you look at the options you are choosing between, and the frame of reference you are using to evaluate those choices as one complementary pair, you have an insufficient grasp of what is happening. This is especially true whenever you are judging yourself, anyone else, or any situation. If you fail to take into account the frame of reference that is always part of any judgement, you are taking a blind step, which in the worst case may cause irreparable harm to you and your business.

The game of paper, stone, and scissors is a perfect example; which beats which depends on the Frame of Reference, rather than being an absolute property of the paper, stone or pair of scissors.

C7: Multiplicity of contexts. As with P7, C7 depends on all the other context thought forms and takes them onto the largest possible stage. C7 is when you are easily able to look at multiple contexts to see and work with more of actuality. These different contexts may well have nothing to do with each other or may also, from another perspective, be different parts of an even larger context.

For example, you may have a direct report that is delivering substandard results. You recognise that you need to look at them in the context of the team they are part of and the organisation that that team is part of. So you realise that part of their performance problem lies in how the roles are split between themself and their colleagues, and so you modify the role definitions and accountabilities.

You also realise another distinct context is their family life, even bigger, all the team members' family lives, that each one arrives at work still part of each of their family contexts. Any worries or joys in their family contexts are shaping what they do at work.

Then you think how each of them is carrying their own personal context of internal meaning-making stories that tell them what to do. Without fully understanding what this context is telling them to do, you will be missing some vital intervention needed to address the performance issue.

Throughout all these context thought forms, the more fluidity you have in each and all of them, the better grasp you can have of what you are actually dealing with in any instant.

9.4 Relationship/relatedness thought forms

These thought forms span all kinds of relationships between all kinds of entities, not just human relationships between people.

R1: Limits of separation. You are using this thought form when you are aware that two things that might each appear to be unique and completely distinct, are actually connected and have common ground. Even more, if you actively say that two things are connected, even though everybody typically thinks they are separate, and then look for the common ground, you are using this thought form.

Most isms originate in an inability to use this thought form. Racism lies in an inability to see that someone of a different skin colour shares as much or more common ground with, than difference to, every other human being.

Businesses collapse, and nations collapse, when their leaders lack sufficient fluidity in R1 to recognise the limits of separation and fail to stand sufficiently in the common ground that connects individual businesses and nations.

No single nation can thrive if the polluting CO_2 from all nations changes the atmosphere's insulating properties to the point where the global economy collapses, because much of the earth ceases to be viable for human life. An inability to use R1 is a root cause of many of today's intractable problems.

R2: Value of bringing into relationship. You are using this thought form when you see clearly how it becomes valuable to connect two things that are separate. For example, the standard limited company separates, with a very hard boundary, investors from all other stakeholders. Using R1, you see that the common ground of all the stakeholders lies in all of them being stakeholders in the same business, with a stake in the business's success.

R2 then shows you how changing how businesses are legally incorporated, to bring the stakeholders into a relationship with each other where all are part of steering the company into the future, and sharing the wealth generated, has enormous value. You eliminate many losses from the artificial and costly fights between them, and you bring into business decision-making, for the benefit of the whole business, information that only one stakeholder category may have. Enter the FairShares Commons.

R2 plays a role in developing yourself and enabling your meaning-making stories to rewrite themselves, by enabling you to see the value in the relationship between different aspects of your self that you have, up until now, believed were distinct.

This thought form is vital for economists to develop a real understanding of how an economy actually works. Without a deep understanding of the value created when individual and collective meaning making, and social processes and economic choices, are brought into relationship with each other, no broad theory of an economy can be developed.

R3: Critique of neglecting relationships. You have already seen examples of this thought form in the above paragraphs, where I criticised the fact that many academics and leaders in economics and business fail to see clearly how all the different stakeholders in every business, and of course the economy as a whole, have to do what they do because of the relationships.

Whenever you recognise that actuality is far more deeply interconnected than the reality you are able to perceive, and where you refuse to accept that a disconnected reality is enough to get a good enough idea of everything important that is actually happening, you are using this thought form.

When you point out the complexity that is missing by ignoring its relationships, and the absolute necessity of including that complexity to be able to decide what to do next, you are using R3.

R4: Relatedness of different frames of reference. In C6 you are thinking about a frame of reference; how an awareness of the frame of reference and the judgement made against the frame of reference is equally necessary to understand your judgements and choices.

Using R4 you see clearly how different frames of reference are related to each other. These might be different frames of reference inside yourself, or differences in the frames of reference you and your colleagues are using when faced with the same choice.

Imagine you are part of a startup leadership team needing to take a decision on whether to bring in venture capital (VC) money, borrow from the bank, or bootstrap on cashflow. You might all use C6 to give your choice, with the reasons why you think that is the best decision and the frame of reference you use to define best. Each person may well have a different choice, set of reasons, and frame of reference.

Now you start looking at what the relationship is between each frame of reference, and for the common ground uniting all the frames of reference. By doing that, you may end up with a larger frame of reference that gives you one single choice which everybody agrees is the best.

That will be a very different discussion to the one many leadership teams usually have: just arguing until one option is left standing, without ever understanding the frame of reference each person is using in that argument.

Better leadership teams surface first each frame of reference and argue about those until they find one to use.

The even better leadership teams uncover the hidden relationships between all the frames of reference, integrate them into a bigger inclusive frame of reference, and take a decision on the common ground.

You are also using this thought form when you are able to recognise the relationship(s) between different individuals' value systems, and between different cultural value systems, even though the actions taken to express the value systems may be completely different. For example, in some countries it is polite to blow your nose (e.g., UK, Germany, US), and in other countries it is polite to sniff (e.g., Japan). The two conventions are related by common values: respect for other people, harmony, and social cohesion.

R5: Formal structure of relatedness.   The quote from Ursula K. Le Guin at the start of the Process section points at this. There is an underlying structure in the oppositional relationship between those supporting a system and those fighting against the system. For example, consider the battles between a trade union and a company. There is a formal structure that relates them, in that both exist because of the apartheid-like way companies incorporate, denying stakeholder relatedness.

Neither the union nor the company can achieve their objectives because they are trapped in a *relationship* that lacks those objectives.

In many cases the formal structure of relationship maintains the status quo, even though huge effort is put into the fight against the status quo. The way forwards is to recognise the formal structure of the relationship and decide to step beyond that and invent a new structure. This is what the FairShares Commons does for the relationship between stakeholders, and between different kinds of capital.

The structure of a relationship may be so much part of the background, that it becomes invisible, or worse, unquestionable. Much like fish in water do not even see the water giving structure to the relationships between all purely water-based lifeforms. Any that were able to consciously recognise and question water as the only structural basis for the common ground of all aquatic life might figure out how to become flying fish.

R6: Patterns of interaction in relationships.   This thought form is what you use when you've used all the earlier relationship thought forms, and grasped the existence of patterns due to the relationship in how entities interact.

You can begin finding ways of influencing without direct control if you are able to tap into these patterns of interaction.

The pattern of interaction might be one of opposition, it might be one of collaboration, or a mix of the two. The big difference between this thought form and P4 is that here your focus is primarily on the relationship, whereas in P4 you are blind to the relationship and only looking at the pattern of interaction. So those who are only fluid in P4 find it far more difficult to subtly influence what is happening around them, and may only be able to make progress by using power over others.

R7: Constitutive relationships. Many relationships are old. The relationship existed long before any of the individual elements even existed; the relationship shaped, or even created, the elements, rather than that the elements created the relationship only after coming together.

For example, a marketplace has pre-existing relationships going back many thousands of years, long before any specific buyer walked up to a specific seller. This pre-existing relationship shapes what the buyer and seller each do.

In apartheid South Africa, the relationship throughout the entire lifetime of a specific white and a specific black was predefined long before birth.

The relationship shaped the life experiences of a black baby and a white baby born at exactly the same time in the same hospital. When they meet for the first time, perhaps at 40 years old, they are already in a pre-existing relationship.

Even if they first meet at 70, standing next to each other in an enormous queue of people snaking backwards and forwards waiting to cast their vote in the very first election in post-apartheid South Africa, that pre-existing relationship has shaped who they are and what they do.

Recognising the pre-existing independent relationship enables them to interact from a place of compassion of how the pre-existing relationship has caused what they experienced, instead of directly blaming as if each person had complete freedom to develop the relationship from scratch.

If you are married, you and your spouse entered into a pre-existing relationship going back millennia that has shaped how each of you show up together. Similarly when you join a hierarchical organisation.

This is why it is so hard for a couple to change themselves and their behaviour within the relationship; why it is so hard to restructure from a hierarchy to a sociocracy; the generations-old pre-existing relationship shapes what you do.

9.5 Transformation thought forms

Now we get to the transformational thought forms, the seven most powerful ones to address our global challenges. But, until we are sufficiently fluid in context, process, and relationship, we can't become fluid in the seven transformation thought forms.

The Dunning-Kruger effect (Section 10.5.11) applies, in that many people imagine that they can use these thought forms. While cognitively they understand what is written, they lack the fluidity they need in all the thought forms to recognise what these thought forms really entail. They are not good enough to know how weak they are, and so imagine that they are good, or at least average.

T1: Limits of stability. There is no stability across all time and space, let alone anything smaller. You are not stable, your relationships with other people are not stable, nor are the companies that you work in stable.

When you recognise that there are limits to stability, you can begin to work with them. You can begin to accept that a relationship may break down because there is an inherent limit to the stability of that relationship over time or under external pressures. Then, you can more easily recognise the difference between not having done enough versus the impossibility of maintaining the stability of that particular relationship.

The more aware you are of the limits of stability, accurately and in detail, the better you can identify what to do to maintain the stability, if that is important; the better you can accept disharmony as inherent, without taking it personally; and the better you can understand why the system may be so easy to knock into instability. The more fluid you are in using this thought form, the less personally you take disharmony or changes in your life, and the better you can begin to tap into instability.

T2: Developmental value of conflict. This is a tough one for those of you who have a need for harmony in your nature or meaning-making stories. The developmental value of conflict is a thought form at the heart of this book. You grow as a human being through conflict, and your business grows through conflict.

You are using this thought form if you have a conflict and react with joy because you know that the simple existence of conflict means that you have potential to develop yourself, and likely the other person has potential to develop themselves.

You are using this thought form when, instead of your pain leading you to manage or resolve conflict quickly, you stay with the conflict, or even broaden it to include even more elements. You do that to be able to identify all the developmental golden nuggets buried in the conflict.

Living organisations today that really know how to mine and refine conflict are the ones most capable of transforming themselves and their collective meaning making, so that they thrive long-term because they remain a superb fit to their business drivers, no matter how fast those business drivers are changing.

T3: Value of developmental growth. T3 goes even beyond recognising that conflict can have huge value, into recognising the value of development. All the chapters in this part are about the value that you can get by developing your stage of meaning-making stories, and your cognitive capacity to use the 28 thought forms fluidly. The other parts of this book are about the value of the same kind of development of our business systems and our economy and society as a whole.

You are using this thought form only when you go beyond simply saying that there is value in development, into actually describing what that value is; describing what needs to be done to trigger and guide development to access that value.

Business leaders who are insufficiently fluid in this thought form have difficulty keeping all the existing operations running unchanged, and delivering the cash needed to keep the business alive, whilst simultaneously leading the transformation needed for the business to adapt to its changing drivers.

Business leaders who are really good at this recognise when the old divisions between structures, processes etc., are no longer fit for purpose, and the potential in integrating parts of the system that have previously always been separate, in ways that lead to higher stages of complexity. For example, the shift from running a business selling books to running a platform that sells everything, as Jeff Bezos did.

T4: Evaluative comparison of systems in transformation.   The final four thought forms are the most challenging to even begin using, let alone use fluidly; yet they are essential to transform our society and its economy to one that works for everyone, for our environment that we all depend on for life, and for the profit essential for our economy to function.

You are using this thought form, when you compare our current business system with the kind of business system that will emerge if every single company was incorporated as a FairShares Commons, and measure them against multiple frames of reference to judge which system is better for what outcome.

You are using this thought form when you fully grasp how each system can contribute helpfully or harmfully to dealing with the challenges we face. If we have a system including a tax on carbon pollution, how will that be a better or worse system than a very different one based on legislation mandating a zero-carbon economy powered by hydrogen and renewable electricity? What other structures and processes are relevant; how does each compare to the other; and which frames of reference have relevance in order to evaluate them?

I was using this thought form when I looked at how freedom as an institution has transformed individual satisfaction and development, then took that as a guiding template for how we might transform business systems composed of very large numbers of individual non-human legal persons.

T5: Bringing multiple systems into balance with each other.   Thought form T1 introduces you to the limits of stability that trigger transformation of systems. Far more challenging is to bring systems, and even multiple systems, together and into balance, using T5.

You are only using this thought form if you've really grasped in sufficient detail, complexity, and holistically, what each system entails, and what it really means to bring the systems into balance. Given that living systems are, to a high degree, inherently nebulous and unknowable, if you are more aware of what you don't know than what you do know, you may be beginning to use this thought form.

You are using this thought form well when you're very aware of where each system is coming from, the contexts, including the dominant meaning-making stories that were concretising each system. And when you're very aware of just what needs to be preserved of each system's functionality while you are bringing them into balance with each other, even as you recognise that that functionality may be toxic for the final balanced system.

You are using this thought form well when you're using multiple frames of reference to evaluate your choices against, and meta-frames of reference to evaluate the frames of reference in order to decide which ones are helpful and which ones are harmful.

T6: Open systems in constant transformation. The previous transformation thought forms are blind to how all systems are open in some way, inseparably part of bigger systems, and in constant transformation. The earth is far from being a closed system. There is a constant flow of energy into the earth from the sun, and up until a few decades ago a constant equal cooling radiation of energy from the earth out into space. The growing carbon dioxide pollution in the atmosphere is upsetting this delicate open system balance by reducing the outflow of energy. Like a car with a radiator blocked with dirt, the engine is starting to overheat.

So when you're busy working on transforming the system, you need to use this thought form to fully grasp what it is that you're working with and what the consequences might be of any change. If you think that the system is closed, and you neglect to take into account what needs to be done outside the system with inflow and outflow, you will fail. On the other hand, if you can take into account how the system is anyway in constant transformation, and nudge it along more quickly where that helps, and slow down where it doesn't, you can begin to work magic.

You are using this thought form when you grasp both the opportunities and the risks in opening the system more, or in new areas, or closing the system where it is currently open. Linked to this is understanding what the necessary self-identity is of the system and what maintains it, and therefore that needs to be preserved as you work on the system.

You are using this system when you fully grasp how its openness and inherent transformations might affect you and your business, and therefore what strategy you need, and how you execute that strategy with excellence. All the while tempering what you do knowing that everything is inherently nebulous and your knowledge is under construction (P5).

T7: Integration of multiple perspectives.   This is the most challenging thought form of all for anyone to even begin using, let alone to reach high fluidity in using unaided.

This thought form lies at the heart of Cubism, relativity, and quantum physics. Few people even begin developing the capacity to use this thought form, let alone use it fluidly. Fluidity in T7 is essential for anyone playing a pivotal role in guiding our social systems and institutions, especially economic and political, into a future that can work for the many by addressing all our global challenges.

Insufficient fluidity in this thought form is what leads experts to try to use their formalism even harder, not realising that the very attempt to use formalistic approaches is the problem.

You are using this thought form when you both use and dispense with using formalism in addressing the challenges. You are using this thought form when you use multiple, often contradictory, perspectives to understand what is happening. This is a challenge for people who have self-authored an integrity with one specific perspective on what integrity is, where that very integrity prevents them from seeing clearly the full complexity of what is going on.

How hard this is, is apparent when budding physicists are learning quantum physics. Quantum physics works because it is filled with multiple conflicting perspectives. To truly grasp what it means for an electron to be both a particle and a wave, to be at a point in time and spread out, is challenging even for the most advanced physicists. So early on, budding physicists learn that the equations really work, and how to use them to predict correctly how to build a smartphone, even when they haven't yet understood how these conflicting perspectives can ever come together to yield equations that work.

You are using this thought form well when the difference between actuality and the model you construct to represent it—reality—is immediately and always apparent to you. When you grasp precisely when not to trust your own experienced reality, but look for other complementary realities that might shed more clarity on what actually is.

This is where you realise just how deeply connected everything is. That trying to separate structures, processes, individual and collective meaning-making, etc., and deal with each alone can never really work.

9.6 Executing with excellence

You may enjoy wrestling with these thought forms and developing your fluidity for the sheer pleasure of mastery. After all, mastery is one of the topmost human needs, and meeting that need is a source of joy for almost all of us.

I hope that most of you will go beyond intellectual mastery of the thought forms and into practical mastery by applying them in business. To deal with our global challenges and build a better world we need many more people who are able to do their work with excellence because they are highly fluid in all the thought forms.

Even more so because these thought forms are at their most powerful when used in dialogue with others; and you can only develop real mastery through dialogue with others. You need their use of a thought form before you can see clearly what is missing in yours.

Keep going, even if you cannot see where you are going, think you are making no progress towards any of your goals, and the effort of trying is unbearable.

I (Graham) used to row at school and university. As an oarsman I learnt to give all I had to reach a goal that I could not see until after I had reached it. I learnt to row until every muscle was in exhausted agony; and then just keep going, with little clarity on just how much further it was. (If you've not seen rowing, or rowed yourself, only the cox looks forward, the rest face backward.) Perhaps that helps me keep going now, even though I cannot see the finish line.

CHAPTER 10

You are your nature

The meaning of life is to find your gift. The purpose of life is to give it away.

—Pablo Picasso

God grant me the serenity to accept the things I cannot change, the courage to change the things I can, and the wisdom to know the difference.

—Reinhold Niebuhr

10.1 Your nature just is; or is it?

The serenity prayer of the American theologian Reinhold Niebuhr (1892 – 1971) captures the nebulous balancing act of getting to know all the elements of who you are and growing yourself into who you can become.

The first step in your process of experiencing your reality depends on your hard-wiring. You cannot change most of this, and those small bits that you may be able to change may take an entire lifetime for very little change.

Unchangeable aspects of you are all those directly anchored in your genetics; other aspects of you affected by your epigenetics may or may not be changeable.

You have limited room to change anything anchored in your physical body either. Especially your physical brain. For example, the psychiatrist and nuclear brain imaging specialist Daniel Amen speaks[1] and writes[160] of how your physical

---

[1]See his TEDxOrangeCoast talk.

brain determines the reality you experience.

If you are dealing with OCD, depression, anger, panic attacks, etc.—much that is usually dealt with via psychotherapy or medication—it may well be your brain's wiring that is the cause. All your behaviour is merely the symptom of the cause.

Which is why behavioural interventions can easily be cruel, because the behavioural symptoms can never be wished away. There will always be some symptom of the root cause. For example, you may have had an innocuous fall when young, one that no one even remembers, that caused physical trauma to your brain, which now shapes the meaning making you're capable of, causing your behaviour.

Two people with identical behaviours, or sharing the same visible characteristics, may have fundamentally different brain activities behind them. And so they require fundamentally different kinds of coaching, scaffolding at work, etc. to change their behaviours.

Be very aware of this with anyone trying to help you from a purely behavioural paradigm; especially if you are trying to help yourself by bullying yourself into new behaviours!

We recommend you focus yourself on what you absolutely can do, which is to get to know the difference between your nature and your meaning-making stories, and then modify your meaning-making stories to work *with* your nature in an ever more subtle, compassionate, and productive way. And check out emerging approaches, e.g., in neuroscience on rehabilitating your brain after damage.

If your nature has given you exceptional natural talents in responding immediately and creatively to unplannable crises, don't waste your time in trying to become good at planning predictable processes. If your nature has given you exceptional talent and energy at connecting with people, don't try to become an analyst sitting alone with vast tables of data.

10.2 Your personal energy economy

There are some activities that you will find naturally give you energy, and some activities that you will find invariably drain you of energy. Look at these carefully over the course of at least a week, and you will get useful clues to what I like to call your personal energy economy.

Manage your personal energy economy scrupulously, and you will find that you are happier and more productive. I have found the following approach, based on Jung's work, very effective because it is so simple that everyone can remember it. This is a language about how to maximise flow; to understand yourself and each other through talking in a non-judgemental way. This is not at all intended to be an accurate measurement of your nature!

To get a good enough idea of your natural energy economy, think of the different kinds of tasks that give you or take your energy across the following four categories:

Exploring If you get energy from always doing new things, from creating on a blank sheet of paper, you are naturally an explorer. Most likely you lose energy if you need to use a process more than once or twice, or go on holiday to the same destination for the third time. You have a high need for significance, to see the big picture, and want your work to matter.

Vibrant If you get energy from meeting people, from talking about what excites you and what excites them, and you love seeing people getting energised with shiny eyes after talking to you, you most likely have a vibrant energy. Most likely you lose energy if you need to pay careful attention to detail or draw conclusions from deep analysis. You have a high need for movement, to see growth, and want diversity in experience.

Context If you get energy when a plan of action is thought through in advance, so that everyone can see what needs to be done, when, by whom, then you are likely to be naturally high on context. You have a high need for connection, to be grounded, and want to understand everything that is and needs to happen.

Systems If you get energy by spending time alone, working with facts and data to get to the right answer, you'll score high on systems in your natural energy profile. You likely lose energy spending lots of time with large groups of highly diverse people, especially if you are required to move them using your charisma and working intuitively with what's happening in the moment. You have a high need for certainty, clarity on what needs doing, and want to avoid mistakes.

Caution: never think of yourself or others with sentences like *I* am *an Explorer / Vibrant / Context / Systems person / type*. Only use these as a language to identify clearly and talk about the characteristics of activities that give you energy, compared to those that you need to pump energy into. Read more on why most type indicators are seldom helpful, and can be harmful, in section 11.3.2.

Any well-functioning organisation needs people across all four energy dimensions. None of them is inherently better or worse than any others. Whatever your natural energy profile is, if you try to be someone else, you will end up less happy and less productive. If you mistakenly see your natural energy economy as stories that can be changed, you are likely to end up frustrated and disillusioned because you haven't changed, despite all your effort.

As with any economy, you can only be successful when you work with, not against, its true nature.

In Table 10.1 is a simple way of getting an initial idea of your natural energy profile. Take this just as a starting point, and each time you find yourself doing something that gives you energy, or something that drains your energy, add that data to this profile to get a better handle on your natural personal energy economy.

Explorer   *total:*
Vision, Ideas, Big picture
Dynamic, bubbly, intuitive
You get energy starting things
Decision making: Intuition, reflection first

Vibrancy   *total:*
Variety, Growth, Participation
Passionate, extroverted, excited
Great at meeting new people
Decisions making: through dialogue with others

Context   *total:*
Timing, Delivery, Perception
Compassionate, team player, sensory
You get energy by getting things done with others
Decision making: guided by one of more senses

Systems   *total:*
Process, Data, Quality
Detailed, orderly, introverted
You get energy completing things
Decision making: Analytical, data first

Table 10.1: Quick test of your natural personal energy economy. Distribute 100 points across all 16 lines under the headings, in the way that you think best matches the kinds of activities that give or drain you of energy. Give more points to activities that give you energy, and fewer points to energies that don't, and no points to activities that drain you of energy. Ignore any effect from what you have learnt to do well; focus on what naturally gives you energy. Then add up your points in the four lines under each energy to give your final score for that natural energy type.

The higher your score in the four energies, the more that these activities are natural energy givers for you. You could call your highest energy your sun energy, because the more time you spend doing activities of this type, the more energy pours into you. (Double check that you have avoided giving high points to something you have had to learn to do well and efficiently, but that drains your energy.)

If you have one (or maybe two) that are significantly lower than the others, and you know that spending more than 10% of your time doing these kinds of activity leaves you drained, you can call this your battery energy.

The other one or two neither give you energy nor drain you of energy, and we call these your moon energies.

Some people score very highly on one and very low on another; and some score more or less the same across all four types of energies. None of these is better or worse. It just means that your natural energy is different to somebody else's, and your task from now on is to continuously work on putting yourself into environments where you can play to the strengths of your natural energies.

For example, I (Graham) am naturally very high on explorer energy, extremely low on systems, and moderately low on context. I got huge amounts of energy in the very early activities of creating this book, but the final activities of proofreading, polishing, and checking all the resources exhausts me. I quite gladly spent a month's holiday doing the early exploration and creation of the book, and returned feeling refreshed and energised. As we moved into the book's later stage, I relied more heavily on Jack having a higher systems and context natural energy.

Take this to heart. Focus on maximising your natural energy, and finding other people whose energy complements yours to take care of the activities that drain you. They will be very grateful because they will find that precisely these activities that you get energy from other ones that drain them.

10.3 Your needs

Your natural human needs are linked to your natural energies. In Table 10.2 you'll find a list of the needs that show up as most important to people across a wide range of studies[2].

What I find striking, looking at these needs, is how poorly designed our workplaces are at meeting them. Altruism, for example, has been clearly recognised as a fundamental human need. It's a superpower of humanity, enabling us to thrive

---

[2]The needs, feelings, judgements etc. tables here have been compiled from a wide range of sources over the past decade, many from the NVC community[147,161,162] started by Marshall Rosenberg. Go there for more good stuff.

better by bonding around shared stories. Yet how many workplaces lack any systematised opportunity to thrive by meeting people's need for altruism?

Perhaps the most important human need is the need for hope. How well does our economy do at meeting your need for hope? How well does your organisation do at meeting the everyone's need for hope?

Primary general needs	Primary Work Needs
Hope	
Health	Purpose
Security	Autonomy
Community	Mastery
Fairness	Relationships
Bonding	
Altruism	
Playfulness	
Celebration	

Table 10.2: In this table we list the top human needs identified in biological and social science research. The work needs are also general needs, but are met through some kind of work.

In Table 10.3 you will find a comprehensive table of human needs. I find this table very useful, and I hope you will find it useful in understanding your hardwiring, and how that shapes the reality you experience.

It is especially useful to make better sense and meaning of how you and your colleagues show up at work. Almost everyone will agree with you that these are valid human needs, even if they have a different order of importance to you.

Money is nowhere in the table of human needs.

Money is merely one tool we have at our disposal to meet the needs listed in these tables. And it is seldom the only tool that can meet these needs. As this book shows, we have removed much of the power that we have to use business to solve the global challenges we're facing, because we've designed our businesses and our society so heavily around the one tool called money that many mistake it for a need.

We all differ from each other in some way in how important each need is to us. Some needs in the table will have such a low importance to you that whether it is met or not makes no difference to you. Other needs will have such a high importance to you that, if those needs are not met, you will experience extremely strong feelings. Sufficiently strong that you will either be almost irresistibly driven to act to get your need met, or will need all your strength to not act.

> One of my (Graham) highest needs is freedom. This is very closely related to my natural explorer energy profile. If I do not have enough freedom, I will break out sooner rather than later, whatever the cost, to meet my need for freedom. Over the course of my life I have become a little better at enduring situations where my need for freedom is not met, but I will never ever be able to do that naturally. It will always cost me energy.
>
> And one of my needs (Jack) is self-expression. My self has always been non-binary and amorphous. When I was younger, I cursed God for my long sleepless nights, nights that seemed like days, days that seemed like months, for placing me in *"the dark woods, the right road lost"*[163], not knowing who I was or who I was supposed to be. But now I'm thankful for being non-binary, for I marvel at life's wonderful diversity, I listen to the rain, I understand what it means be male and female, to be accepted, rejected and hated, to be despaired and fulfilled. To fulfill my life's potential, to be a full human being and to help others do so, it is important for me to self-express, whatever my self is.

Many needs are strongly driven by your hardwired nature, and failing to get these needs met sufficiently well will at best leave you less productive and happy than you could be, and at worst will take you into dire consequences like burnout.

To identify which needs are most important to you, keep track over the course of a few weeks: 1) when you experience feelings in the table of positive feelings (Table 10.4), these are reliable indicators that one of your or more of your important needs is being met; and, 2) when you experience one of the feelings in the table of negative feelings (Table 10.5); again, this is a reliable indicator that one or more of your important needs is not being met. In both cases, note down which feelings you experience, and which needs your feelings are telling you about.

Keep doing this and over time you will build up a good understanding of which of your needs are really important to you. Some are part of your hardwiring, and will remain important throughout your life. These needs, whilst part of your hardwiring, are age-dependent, and your personal ranking and weighting will change throughout the course of your life.

Even better, some needs are primarily anchored in your stories, and your stage of development. These will change as you grow.

Table 10.3: Comprehensive table of needs.

achievement	connection	mutuality
best use of energy and time	acceptance	nurturing
knowledge of self	affection	respect
self-development	appreciation	self-respect
spirituality	belonging	safety
	company	security
autonomy	cooperation	stability
choice	communication	support
choose dreams	closeness	to know
choose goals	community	to be known
choose means to achieve goals	companionship	to see
freedom	compassion	to be seen
independence	consideration	to be heard
space	consistency	to understand
spontaneity	empathy	be understood
to listen	inclusion	trust
	interdependence	warmth
meaning	intimacy	honesty
awareness	to love	authenticity
challenge	to be loved	integrity
clarity		presence
co-create	celebration	physical wellbeing
competence	appreciate life	air
consciousness	appreciate accomplishments	breath
contribution	celebration of life	comfort
creativity	commemorate grief, loss	emotional safety
discovery	share joy	exercise
contribute to others' well-being	share pain	light
efficacy		material security
effectiveness	peace	movement
growth	beauty	nourishment
hope	communion	physical contact
learning	ease	protection
mourning	equality	reconciliation
participation	harmony	rest/sleep
purpose	inspiration	right temperature
self-expression	order	safety
self-worth	play	sexual expression
stimulation	joy	shelter

to matter	humour	touch
to make a difference	charge one's batteries	water
understanding	fun	
	letting go	
	recreation	

10.4 Your emotions and feelings

Your emotions and feelings are part of the data that you use to make sense and meaning. They are hard data, coming from a superbly designed instrument, your mind and body, as a way of evaluating potential opportunities to meet, and potential threats to, your needs. Feelings and emotions are your best guide, telling you what needs are important to you, and if they are met or unmet.

You have a few fundamental feelings; the rest are emotions that you construct from your meaning-making. For simplicity I typically call both feelings, but sometimes the distinction is important. You can read more about how you create most of your emotions through your meaning-making stories in Lisa Feldman Barrett's book[164]. In short, many of the feelings that many believe are universal actuality, experienced by all the same way, are more each person's unique inner reality, dependant on your unique life path.

Unfortunately, we seldom develop the vocabulary to name the precise emotion or feeling we have. If we can't name it, we can't use it for its prime purpose: to identify clearly which specific need is met or not met, and therefore what to do about it. Imagine how different your life would be, and even how different economics would be, if everyone had been taught how to use this at school!

It's never too late; start today putting into practice all the words in Tables 10.4 (positive, energising feelings) and 10.5 (negative, energy-draining feelings) below.

Table 10.4: Feelings anchored in positivity.

affectionate	hopeful	gleeful	delighted	composed
compassionate	expectant	intense	glad	centred
friendly	encouraged	invigorated	happy	content
loving	free	keyed up	jubilant	cool
open hearted	glorious	lively	mirthful	expansive
sensitive	optimistic	passionate	merry	fulfilled
sympathetic	confident	perky	overjoyed	zestful
tender	cheerful	surprised	pleased	mellow
warm	empowered	upbeat	tickled	quiet
engaged	open	vibrant	exhilarated	relaxed

absorbed	proud	helpful	blissful	relieved
alert	safe	grateful	breathless	satisfied
curious	secure	appreciative	elated	serene
engrossed	excited	filled	enthralled	still
enchanted	adventurous	gratified	exuberant	tranquil
entranced	amazed	joyous	radiant	trusting
fascinated	animated	moved	rapturous	refreshed
intense	ardent	thankful	splendid	enlivened
interested	aroused	touched	thrilled	nurtured
intrigued	astonished	inspired	ecstatic	peaceful
involved	dazzled	alive	peaceful	pleasant
inquisitive	eager	amazed	at ease	rejuvenated
glowing	ebullient	awed	at peace	renewed
spellbound	effervescent	motivated	calm	rested
stimulated	energetic	wonder	carefree	restored
	enthusiastic	joyful	clear headed	revived
	exultant	amused	comfortable	wide-awake
	giddy	buoyant	complacent	good-humoured

Table 10.5: Feelings anchored in negativity.

afraid	aroused	repulsed	baffled	sad
apprehensive	angry	sceptical	bewildered	blue
concerned	cross	disquiet	dazed	depressed
dread	enraged	agitated	hesitant	dejected
fearful	furious	alarmed	lost	despair
foreboding	hot	discontented	mystified	despondent
frightened	incensed	disconcerted	perplexed	disappointed
mistrustful	indignant	dissatisfied	puzzled	discouraged
on edge	irate	disturbed	torn	disheartened
panicked	livid	ill at ease	disconnected	downcast
petrified	mad	muddled	alienated	downhearted
scared	mean	perturbed	aloof	empty
suspicious	nettled	upset	apathetic	forlorn
terrified	outraged	rattled	bored	gloomy
wary	resentful	restless	cold	guarded
worried	upset	shocked	detached	hopeless
annoyed	aversion	startled	disenchanted	melancholic
aggravated	animosity	surprised	distant	miserable
bitter	appalled	troubled	distracted	morose
dismayed	contempt	turbulent	indifferent	mournful

disgruntled	disgusted	turmoil	numb	solitary
displeased	dislike	uncomfortable	passive	sorrowful
exasperated	bitter	uneasy	preoccupied	sorry
frustrated	hate	unnerved	removed	regretful
impatient	horrible	unsettled	tepid	remorseful
irritated	horrified	upset	unconcerned	unhappy
irked	hostile	confused	uninterested	woeful
pessimistic	repelled	ambivalent	withdrawn	wretched
vexed	embarrassed	bereaved	up tight	ashamed
devastated	vulnerable	chagrined	grief	bowled over
flustered	heartbroken	lonely	guilty	hurt
fragile	mortified	broken hearted	heavy hearted	self-conscious
tense	helpless	fatigue	anxious	in despair
beat	cranky	insecure	burnt out	distressed
leery	dead beat	distraught	reluctant	depleted
edgy	reserved	dull	fidgety	sensitive
exhausted	frazzled	shaky	lethargic	harried
shaken	listless	unsteady	sleepy	irritable
yearning	spiritless	jittery	envious	Tired
nervous	jealous	weary	over-excited	longing
worn out	overwhelmed	nostalgic	pain	restless
pining	agony	stressed out	wistful	anguished

Judgements dressed up as feelings

In normal speech, we all often talk about our judgements and our feelings as if they were the same. For example, you might say

I feel insulted.

That is a judgement, an evaluation, you have made, not a feeling that you have.

By calling it a feeling, you will find it far harder to recognise which of your stories has led you to evaluate somebody else's words or actions as an insult. Insult is a meaning that your stories are making, that you then attribute to the other person, even when the other person intended to insult you. What better way of winning than refusing to make the meaning of insult that the other person wants you to make, and instead making meaning from compassion for the other person's weakness, or simply laughing out loud because you've made a humorous meaning.

I (Graham) experienced this clearly when a former direct report got into an arm-wrestling match with me. Recognising that they were deliberately trying to provoke me into a fight to prove that I was justifiably their boss, I made meaning of what was happening on that basis. So I did not get angry, did not enter into a fight, and thereby demonstrated paradoxically that I was justifiably their line manager. It has taken me quite some time to develop this capacity. I don't yet have it always, everywhere, with everyone.

The better you get at distinguishing cleanly between true feelings and judgements dressed up as feelings, the better you will be able to know yourself, understand other people, and collaborate with them.

Table 10.6: Judgements that can be incorrectly dressed up as feelings.

Accusation	Attack	Domination
accused	aggressed	beaten
blamed	attacked	boxed in
caught out	crushed	bullied
dragged in	harassed	coerced
hurt	humiliated	cornered
let down	insulted	interrupted
pressured	intimidated	mothered
misunderstood	mistreated	obliged to
neglected	offended	persecuted
overloaded	provoked	put down
	trapped	used
made to feel guilty	threatened	stifled
Denigration	**Deception**	**Rejection**
abused	betrayed	abandoned
diminished	cheated	excluded
distrusted	exploited	misunderstood
dumb	grassed on	neglected
horrible	hard done by	rejected
patronised	let down	unappreciated
ridiculed	manipulated	unheard
stupid	trapped	unimportant

unworthy	unseen
sullied	unsupported
taken for granted	unwanted

10.5 Your biases

This section on biases is hard to allocate uniquely to any chapter. Your biases are a mix of your hard-wired nature, your meaning-making stories, and your fluidity in transformational thought forms. However, because they are deep and hard to change, I have decided to put them into this chapter.

We all have our own unique mix of biases but there are some biases that we almost all share, because they have a central role to play in being human. Robert Cialdini has done an excellent job describing these in his book on influence[165].

In this section I summarise some of the most common biases. Keep an eye on yourself, and check whether one of them is shaping the reality that you experience and leading you to take decisions that are not in your best interests. Learn how to harness your biases to serve your interests, those of people you care for, and the needs of your organisation. Learn how to subtly protect yourself and others from your own biases, and those of others.

Warren Buffett and Charlie Munger, the founders and partners of Berkshire Hathaway, one of the most successful investment companies, attribute their success, in part, to rigorously checking their investment decisions against these common biases.

You can think of these biases as both lenses that you look through and frames of reference to evaluate against. As lenses, they create the reality that you see or experience. As frames of reference, they decide for you which decision to take. When those decisions have at least some rightness, these biases are helpful to us. When these decisions are harmful, and we often don't even realise that until way too late, sometimes never, our biases are not our friends.

To thrive as human beings we need these biases. They are all the Type 1 thinking of Daniel Kahneman[54], which gives us quick decisions and cost very little energy or time. For most of human history, and in any technical challenge, this has been enough. However, in today's nebulous world filled with adaptive challenges, we need to be more than ever before on our guard against our cognitive biases kicking in inappropriately.

One excellent clue that your cognitive biases may be kicking in inappropriately is if something just doesn't feel right in your gut.

Then stop, and use Type 2 thinking. The other thing to do is to remember all these biases and force yourself in all decisions to check whether one or more of them is active before you take the decision.

Hope-seeking bias

Hope is one of our most important needs. So when times are tough, when we cannot see a better future ahead of us, and hope has deserted us, then we are easy pickings for anyone able to sell us hope. Our hope-seeking bias is both what enables us to overcome overwhelming odds, and prevents us from pivoting into a different direction when we ought to.

> Over the past 15 years, I (Jack and Graham) have often felt very little hope in me. The hope that I have has kept me going on the one hand, because I've continued to deeply believe in what I'm doing and that what I'm doing is a necessary part of creating a viable regenerative future for us all. And, my hope-seeking bias on the other hand sometimes led me astray, seeking for sources of hope in others.
>
> This has led me to occasionally spend time with people whose display of energy and confidence fooled me into believing that they knew better than me. Invariably I very quickly discovered that there are no gurus truly worth following. At least, none of those who declare themselves to be gurus and seek followers. I learnt that my bias towards seeking hope was sometimes leading me astray.

Jack and I have written this book with the intention of generating and amplifying hope in all of you reading this book. We certainly believe that everything in this book is either what we need to be able to rise to the global challenges facing everyone, or it is at least a useful step towards what we need. We are consciously tapping into your bias to look for reasons to hope in order to accelerate the transformation of business that we believe is necessary.

Equally, your hope bias can easily be tapped into by the unscrupulous seller of expensive fake remedies. If you have lost hope, for example, of ever finding a way out of the pain you are in, anyone with charisma and the right words to trigger feelings of hope can convince you to give them what they ask for.

Throughout history there have been the sellers of snake oil, offering hope of a cure to those with an incurable disease, tapping into all your biases in order to get you to buy what they're selling.

In times of crisis, whether it's just your own internal crisis, or the crises everyone on the planet is facing, whenever you no longer feel hope, and find yourself leaping at anything that triggers feelings of hope in you, notice that jump in feeling hopeful and pause for a moment.

Ask yourself what has actually triggered that feeling of hope; are being manipulated through any biases in this section; and: if all you had were the naked facts, without any of the emotional catalysts used by the seller of hope, would your feeling of hope have jumped just as much?

Comparison bias

This is at the heart of so much marketing, and influences many of your purchase decisions. Ever wondered why international coffee chains offer the range of products they do, and manage to sell at the prices they sell at? Comparison bias is deep in almost all of us, and leads us to decide what is the best option based on the comparisons we are making in the moment, not on what is really best for us.

Comparison bias happens most easily in people who have little or no fluidity in recognising the frame of reference they are using, thought form C6.

Comparison bias is kicking in when you automatically decide that the most expensive item must be the best quality, or the best for you.

Comparison bias kicked in every time I (Graham) bought anything expensive, like my motorbike. Eleven years ago I took the decision, over the course of many months, to buy a new motorbike worth €15,000. At the dealer, looking through the list of all the optional extras, I ticked off many of the boxes. Each added €200 here, €300 there. By the time I'd finished, I had committed myself to another few thousand euros.

If I had decided first, without any knowledge of the motorbike's base price, whether I truly benefited enough from any optional extra for it to be worth the price, there are some that I wouldn't have chosen. But because €300 looked small to me compared to €15,000, my comparison bias kicked in and took the decision for me.

In business, comparison bias is often called the sunk cost fallacy. You take the decision to keep working on a project, or to keep your startup going, because you look at the incremental cost of doing just the next step compared to the far larger cost that you have already sunk into the project or your startup, instead of comparing it to everything else you could spend that money on now.

Because it looks smaller, you decide to add that extra bit of money and keep going.

Reciprocation bias

Reciprocation bias has enabled human beings to become the dominant life form on the planet because it powers our long-term collaboration. The very first humans thrived because if one hunter brought home an antelope, he would share it with everybody, knowing that at some point in the distant future, when he came back empty-handed, somebody else would share what they had brought home with him.

So most of the time reciprocation bias serves us extremely well.

As our society has grown in complexity, reciprocation bias has evolved with us. Now, we remember people who did us a favour many years ago and continue to honour the obligation to do them a favour.

Reciprocation bias is, even if we know we are being conned into something, almost irresistible. Every time I collected my motorbike from a service, the garage owner would always give me something small that he thought would be useful to me. I knew that these were never of any great cost to him, but reciprocation bias left me feeling obliged to return the favour by remaining a loyal client. I saw my relationship with him to be one of loyalty and obligation, not a mere transactional business relationship.

By getting a free gift, regardless of value, our reciprocation bias kicks in and compels most of us to give back more than the unsolicited gift.

Think about how often you will cross over the road if your radar detects any possibility of a charity collector intending to give you something small in order to manipulate you into giving them what they ask for. (This is why I seldom accept food samples in the supermarket. I know how easily that leads me to buy something I would have never otherwise bought.)

Reciprocation bias is also at the heart of effective negotiation. If one party has made a concession, reciprocation bias creates internal pressure in the other party to offer an equally valuable concession. Again, you can see that without reciprocation bias we would never be able to collaborate, and we would never be able to start up organisations nor function well with colleagues that we have little in common with.

Dealing with reciprocation bias is easy to describe, and very hard to put into practice. First, listen to your gut instinct. If your gut is telling you that somebody has given you something to manipulate you, it might be right. Maybe a narcissist. Then, realise that the enemy is not the other person, but rather your own meaning-making story compelling you to reciprocate when given a gift. Because the other person has given you something to manipulate you into giving back, not out of true reciprocal generosity, your story telling you that you have to give back to them is now invalid, at least in this deliberately exploitative context.

Use these situations, and the ground pattern experiments described in Section 8.2, to create a set of experiences that rewrite your meaning-making story to one that now says that you reciprocate only when somebody has given in generous, collaborative, reciprocity, not if somebody has given manipulatively.

Commitment bias

Commitment is a central dimension of trust. If somebody else says that they will do something, and they reliably then do it, you will have a far higher level of trust in them than if they regularly say they will do something, and fail to. So commitment bias is a very necessary and powerful story for humans to live by. We experience internal pressure from our stories to stick with what we have previously committed to, and external pressure from our family and colleagues to stick with what we've committed to. This pressure can become very powerful, including people cutting off friendship and ostracising you from the group.

The problem is, we make commitments now with the best information that we have, and then get trapped by our commitment bias to stick with that commitment even when new information emerges which, had we known it at the beginning, would have led us to making a different commitment. Without commitment bias, we would have no hesitation in making a new choice that was better.

Commitment bias is why companies large and small fail. A certain project becomes the company's holy grail, or perhaps just one manager's, and money continues pouring into it long after there is evidence that it will never pay off.

Commitment bias is why some people continue to invest time and their emotions into friendships that have been one-sided from the start.

> After I (Graham) slipped and hit my right hip on a stepping stone, I realised that I was feeling emotionally far worse than the pain in my hip warranted, and asked myself why. I first said, because I'm blaming myself for taking a risk when I can little afford it. Why did I take the risk? Because I was in a hurry to get back. Why was I in a hurry to get back? Because I had taken far longer than planned. Why had I taken far longer than planned? Because I had needed to do some strenuous climbing down a near-vertical drop, after going seriously off-route. Why had I gone off route? Because once I had started going off-route to try to reach a new path by going forwards, my commitment to keep going was stronger than the wise voice in me saying that I ought to turn back to where I was last on a path.

Consistency bias

Consistency bias is another dimension of trust, and can be friend and foe. Consistency means that you do the same thing each time you're in the same situation. Other people can then trust you to behave in predictable ways in the future, once they realise that you subscribe to the stories of consistency. Consistency bias is another reason why executives can easily lead their companies into collapse. We've always done it this way, and we will continue to do things this way.

As we mentioned in Section 1.3, Kodak invented digital photography, but failed to change its focus from chemical to digital as fast as consumers changed their behaviours. Commitment bias and consistency bias together led Kodak to continue to strive towards ever better chemical photographic film long after the electronics world had clearly recognised that digital photography was the way of the future. Because the electronics companies had no chemical photography, they were able to make an unbiased decision.

Consistency bias is also why it is so hard for you to change your stories, or to grow from one stage to the next. You experience huge internal distress, and external pressure, every time you begin changing one of the meaning-making stories that run you. This is especially true as you try to move from S3 to S4. Remember, S3 is called the socialised mind, because this is the category of meaning-making stories that is the very best at creating large, collaborative, stable and reciprocal collective relationships. No early tribe nor modern community can survive for long without enough people at S3. Keep this in mind when you begin running experiments to create the experiences you need to rewrite your stories; keep an eye open for when consistency bias keeps pulling you back into your old stories.

Consistency bias is also one of the greatest barriers to acting in time to prevent the impending climate crisis. It keeps us using limited companies, even though they cause problems. Consistency bias creates internal distress at the changes in attitude and behaviour needed. Part of our intent in writing this book is to make it easier for all of us to recognise when our meaning-making stories are holding us back from making the right choices, and doing what we know needs doing.

The better you get at chipping away at your consistency and commitment biases, the easier you will be able to decide and act appropriately in the adaptive challenge that our climate crisis is.

And, the better you'll get at enabling other people to take the right action despite their consistency bias.

By keeping a careful eye on which story is compelling you towards consistency, you will develop the capacity to recognise when it is a foolish consistency and when it is a wise consistency. A foolish consistency is likely present when you are about to do something to be consistent, even though your intuition is telling you that you ought not.

Social proof bias

Society plays a huge role in shaping us and our decisions—as Ubuntu says

I am because we are.

The category of meaning-making stories we call S3 fully recognises the power of truly belonging to a group of people who help each other in a reciprocal way. A consequence is that we tend to believe whatever the general opinion of others is, is true. Others can be millions who have a certain opinion, or simply one other person.

I (Graham) have lived in a number of different countries with widely different cultural and behavioural expectations. When I moved from Italy to Japan, I was extremely attentive to what I saw the Japanese doing, and to the best of my ability mimicked what I saw people around me doing. That's how we learn as a child what the right thing is to do, and is often the best way to learn how to behave according to the norms and expectations of any culture that you have just landed in. Far better, in my mind, than the many examples of tourists I've seen having no idea of what offence their behaviour has triggered in the meaning-making stories of the host culture.

You can harness social proof bias to support you in transforming those stories that no longer serve you well. For example, Robert O'Connor ran an experiment with young socially withdrawn children. (I wish that I had been part of his experimental group. I usually was, and to this day tend still to be, the shy person standing on the edge of the group.) O'Connor made a range of short films each showing a solitary child watching a group of children doing something together, and then joining in, to everyone's enjoyment. He found that simply showing the film once transformed their behaviour, and the transformed behaviour remained when he returned six weeks later.

Put this into practice when you run experiments for your meaning-making stories to have the challenging experiences they need to rewrite themselves. The more that your stories see that other stories of how to behave are more successful, the more the old stories will weaken and new ones will grow in their place.

I (Graham) know that social proof bias, along with consistency and commitment bias, are part of why I have continued for the past 12 years to focus on developing the approach described in this book. Having committed to this, quitting my career with Procter & Gamble, and having invested heavily, social proof is a big part of what keeps me going. I have a group of people around me who believe in what I'm doing. This keeps me going, despite other evidence and people telling me that I should give up and go back into a normal job. I believe that social proof bias here is helpful, as in many startups and disruptive innovations, because it carries you through that stage where the established majority still dominates.

Equally, social proof is what keeps cults going, and holds us back from acting on our climate crisis despite overwhelming evidence.

Social proof is often far more powerful than any factual proof. If we have enough people around us who are saying the same thing, and acting in a certain way, social proof keeps us acting and behaving in the same way.

It says that the more people there are, the more that that way of acting or that opinion must be correct. And so in the face of change, consistency bias traps people where they are, and they tend to gather only with people who believe what they believe and act in the way they act so that social proof supports them.

Social proof bias is the reason why, in our modern cities, large groups of people can see a crime happening and not intervene.

The best-known example of this is the murder of Catherine Genovese in New York, whose killer attacked her three separate times over a 35 minute period. She finally died from the stab wounds, despite screaming for help, with 38 witnesses.

Because each of them was seeing their inaction as proof that they personally needed to do nothing, nobody did anything. Had one begun doing something, social proof would then compelled another to do something, until all were coming to her aid.

This is why the first to act, for example, the first follower in a startup is crucial for the success of any founder's endeavour.

If you are ever in a situation where you need help from a large group of people, for example as a project initiator or start-up founder, you are far better approaching specific individuals and asking them to do something specific for you then sending out a general request for support to the universe.

Uncertainty avoidance

Uncertainty avoidance is a standard measure across cultures and individual human natures. Most people find uncertainty to be highly discomforting, and to be avoided. Uncertainty avoidance is anchored in both your nature and your meaning-making stories. People who have a very high explorer energy almost always have a low uncertainty avoidance, and often an affinity for uncertainty.

> I (Graham) experience this. I would never have begun studying theoretical physics, moved into management with Procter & Gamble, and then begun developing everything that is described in this book, if I had a high uncertainty avoidance. Nor would I have moved to so many different countries. However, my affinity to uncertainty has come at a cost. Living now in Brussels, none of my school friends are anywhere near me. Every time I've changed countries, my relationship with everyone I had got to know in the previous country shifted to no more than occasional birthday wishes on Facebook.

Get to know how strong your uncertainty avoidance tendency is. The higher it is, the more stress you will experience when facing the inherently uncertain, nebulous challenges that face us in today's world. An adaptive challenge brings with it even more uncertainty than the most uncertain technical challenge because we are required to embrace a journey across a completely uncertain and nebulous void to becoming someone with a new self-identity.

Nothing triggers our uncertainty avoidance bias more strongly than the journey across the void from who we are now, which has given us all the success we have enjoyed up until now, to the person we need to become. After all, we don't even know what that person might be like, how they might act, how they might feel, or even if we can get across the void to become that person. You need to recognise your uncertainty avoidance tendency and figure out how to counteract it through experiments if you are to successfully rise to the adaptive challenges you're facing.

Reward vs. loss bias

As Warren Buffett and Charlie Munger say,

Show me somebody's incentives, and I'll tell you how they will behave.

The difference between our reward bias and our loss bias is one of the reasons why human beings do not take the rational economic decisions assumed in neoclassical economics. In one study a group of students filled in a survey about their preferences for chocolate bars. A while later some of the students were invited to attend a different research programme, and at the end were all rewarded with a Mars bar. This group was carefully selected to have a 50% preference for Snickers, and a 50% preference for Mars bars. As they left the room, they were given the opportunity of exchanging their Mars bar for a Snickers bar. Very few of the people who preferred Snickers were able to overcome their loss avoidance bias to give back the Mars bar in order to receive a Snickers in return.

> I (Graham) see the far stronger power of loss avoidance bias in many of my decisions. This is one of the biases that feeds into the sunk cost fallacy. If I change my path now, after everything I have invested in it, I will lose everything that I've bought with that investment of time and money. And so loss avoidance is one thing that keeps me going down this path and investing more, even if it might be wise to stop, accept all the losses, and move on to something completely different. Growing up in Africa, one of the earliest stories that I can remember reading, or perhaps it was even my father reading the story to me, was a story about how to catch a monkey. Take a pumpkin, cut a small hole in its side, hollow it out, and fill it with seeds. And then tie the pumpkin to a tree. If the hole is small enough, when the monkey puts its hand into the hole and grabs a fistful of seeds, its fist will be too big to come back out of the hole again. The pressure to avoid losing these precious life-giving seeds is so strong that the monkey will often stay trapped until caught or even killed.

Loss avoidance is often very useful, because if we lose something valuable to us, it may not be replaced. Reciprocity bias has power because it needs to overcome loss avoidance bias to get us to give things away. However, loss avoidance bias is harmful when it traps us into foolish decisions. Like staying with something that we know, even if it's not what we really want, because the pain of losing what we have feels more powerful than the anticipation of what we might get.

Liking bias

Liking bias says that if you like something or someone, you tend to minimise, or not even see, their faults. Equally, if you dislike something or someone, you tend to see their faults even more clearly and magnify then.

This is especially relevant in a work context, especially for young managers and start-up founders. The tendency to hire or promote people that you like, because you are not seeing sufficiently clearly whether their strengths and weaknesses truly make a good fit to your company and the tasks that they need to do.

Liking bias is at its most powerful for people who are at S3, where their mean-ing-making stories are part of the socialised mind category. A central theme of S3 stories is the necessity to be like everybody else in the group, and to be liked by everybody in the group, in order to be accepted.

Managers and leaders need to be constantly on their guard against liking bias. Whenever you hire somebody into your organisation, or promote that person, take enough time to gather information on whether that person is truly a good fit for the tasks, and for the organisation's culture. Keep your eyes open for when liking bias might be hiding relevant information from you.

Liking bias is also a very powerful driver for your success in your career, get-ting helped, or staying out of jail. For example, in one study of jail sentences, it was found that defendants who were rated as attractive were twice as likely to walk free from the courtroom as those rated as unattractive. In another study of hir-ing decisions, it was found that how well-groomed the applicant was was actually a stronger driver for the hiring decision than the job qualifications, even though the interviewers believed that the job qualification was the dominant frame of reference they were using to take a decision.

People can manipulate you by using your liking bias simply by indicating that they like you. As soon as somebody makes it clear that they like you, reciprocation bias may kick in, along with social proof, so that you start to like them. And then you're a sucker for whatever they want to do with you.

If you have just met someone, especially in a sales situation, keep an eye on how strongly you like them. If you have any indication that you've developed a stronger liking for this person then you typically do for somebody like that, then be very wary about whether they are deliberately manipulating you into liking them, knowing that your liking bias will then prevent you from seeing all the negatives. For example, why you should not buy what they are trying to sell you, because it's not very good.

Authority bias

Authority bias comes in a light and a strong version. The light version kicks in when somebody tells you to do something and gives you a reason for doing this. Authority bias, coupled with social proof bias, makes it far more likely that you would do what they tell you, or give them what they are asking for, regardless of whether the reason has any validity whatsoever.

Simply by using a sentence that has some kind of reason and logic to it, your brain makes a quick decision on whether it might be worth the effort of Type 2 thinking to really look at the reason, think through whether it has any relevance to the request, and whether it holds water or not. All too often your brain decides to just go with the bias so fast that you don't even have the opportunity to decide consciously.

Be cautious when somebody gives you a reason why you should do what they ask. Much of the time the reason may well be valid, but sometimes it's not.

The strong form of authority bias is how you react to any authority figure. I know for myself, somebody who has the credentials or dress or behaviour of authority triggers my authority bias in one of two ways. Sometimes, I suspend judgement, and tend to do what they say because they are an authority figure. At other times, I tend towards doing the opposite simply because they are an authority figure. Neither is sure to be wise.

The best defence you have against undue authority bias is to stop yourself whenever you are interacting with somebody who either is, or is pretending to be, an authority. Ask yourself, if exactly the same information was being given to me by somebody I had never met before, who looked like me, and who dressed like me, would I do what they're saying? Even more strongly, if somebody I had formal authority over was giving me this message, would I do what they're saying?

The second thing to do is to ask whether this person truly is an authority, and are they sufficiently expert. Ask yourself how this authority is rewarded. And then ask yourself whether you can really trust them to be acting in your best interests.

And apply this to anything you do today because your younger self said to.

Superiority-Inferiority bias

The Dunning-Kruger effect[166–169] plays a huge role in organisations. Combine the Dunning-Kruger effect with some of the other biases above, such as authority bias and uncertainty avoidance bias, and you have a perfect storm. Throughout this book, as you read about how various myths about incorporation and the economy have become concretised in the reality you experience, imagine how often the Dunning-Kruger effect has created the crises of our reality today.

The Dunning-Kruger effect is behind many of the myths of superiority and inferiority that pervade your life. Put simply, it is that almost everybody thinks they are average.

This is accurate if your skills, competencies or capacities are indeed average. It is an unhelpful distortion if they are significantly below or significantly above average. And it is disastrous if somebody whose skills, competencies, and capacities lie way above average is reporting to somebody who is way below average. It is toxic for the junior person, and toxic for the organisation as a whole, because choices will be made that are wholly inadequate for the challenges being faced.

You can only accurately evaluate how competent you are if you are sufficiently competent in the skill in the first place. If you are not competent enough, you don't know what you don't know, and you don't even have a frame of reference good enough to evaluate your competence. So you will typically overestimate your confidence.

Reinforced by the other biases, and even more so if you have personality traits that tend towards confidence, optimism, or narcissism.

Vice versa, people who are really good often evaluate themselves as inferior, about as good as everybody else, because they are so good they have a highly precise and evolved frame of reference, which they use to evaluate accurately the remaining gap between themself and the very best in the field.

Way too often in expert fields, someone who is not competent enough to recognise their own incompetence also has very high self-confidence and the ability to project that self-confidence. They will invariably convince those around them that they are the best and end up in positions of authority. They are even able to convince people better than them!

Anyone who is too incompetent to be able to accurately evaluate their competence, will make error after error, blame those errors on people around them and on circumstances, without ever realising that the problem lies with their own competence. Combine this with authority bias, and especially an expert stage of self-identity, and dumb decisions will be made.

The toughest thing to do is recognise clearly what is happening, if you are working in such an inverted competency hierarchy and judging yourself as inferior. The best way to target this is to simply be aware of the Dunning-Kruger effect, raising the standard of competence of everybody[168], and to replace any kind of management accountability hierarchy with a human capacity hierarchy (defined in Section 12.6), where positions are filled using a Sociocratic consent process (Chapter 14).

Scarcity bias

So much of what I (Graham) have done has been driven by scarcity bias, sometimes where the actual scarcity of something led me to see it as far more desirable than it actually was for me, or where something actually was scarce, and because of that my focus narrowed down onto only that part of my reality, ignoring everything else that was plentiful. Either way, scarcity bias has been behind many of the mistakes I've made in my life.

Scarcity bias was part of an accident I had 15 years ago on my motor-bike on the Nürburgring in Germany. I'd ridden over from Brussels to spend a couple of hours on the ring during the open sessions at the end of every day. There was about enough time to get ten laps in, and so as usual when the eighth lap arrived I pulled off the ring. My rule always was to never ride the final lap or two, because that's when tiredness and overconfidence come together to dramatically increase the risk of an accident. Not just in me, but in everybody else on the ring.

However, on that day they were four Ducatis ahead of me and I could see that they were about to head off for a lap. I thought, in a week's time is the Motorrad training weekend on the ring. These are the last two laps of practice that I can get in, so I'd better get these two laps of practice in so that I'm just that little bit better prepared for the train-ing session. The lens of scarcity bias made these final two laps seem so incredibly desirable that I saw nothing else. I was not seeing clearly the abundance of eight laps that I already had ridden that day, the many laps that I would ride in a week's time, and a lifetime of laps ahead of me.

Halfway around the ring, on the Exmühle 90° right-hander, I banked over just a little bit further than the bike could hold, and the wheels slid out in a classic lowsider.

If I had to have an accident, that could not have been a better accident to have. I was also unbelievably lucky in where I had the accident; the ambulance crew, parked 15m away, was with me within 20 seconds. They were already starting the engine and entering the track before I'd finished hitting the barriers; and, because it's a steeply banked curve, by the time my body hit the barriers I'd already scrubbed off much of my speed; and because I hit the barriers with my body parallel, the impact was spread across my entire body.

I walked away from that accident with nothing broken, no lasting damage except to my ego, and was back on a borrowed motorbike the following weekend to take part in the training session.

That accident was also really good for me in two other ways. First, it really brought home to me the abundance of innovation potential that I had ahead of me in my life, and the role I could choose to play in the crisis that humanity was entering.

It brought home to me that, whilst I had the potential for a good career in Procter & Gamble, I would never be truly proud of myself at the end of that career. I realised I was staying at P&G because of scarcity bias. Scarcity bias led me to think that there was very little that I could do that would earn money, so I'd better stay with what I had even though it was not what I really wanted to do, nor was it anywhere close to the biggest difference I could make in the world. It had very little to do with what I had chosen as my core purpose in life, which was to make a difference towards the climate crisis and what we now call the sustainable development goals (SDGs).

That accident may well have been the best thing that happened to me, and to everyone who has found value in what I've done over the past 11 years, and perhaps for you reading this book now, because it broke the spell that scarcity bias had had on me.

Scarcity bias, like all the other biases, has been and still is a vital tool enabling us to thrive.

When it's right, we can make quick decisions, spending very little time, by using Type 1 thinking. Very often, scarce items are more valuable than plentiful items.

Facebook, Google, and all the others know that the scarcest resource in the world today is your attention. They will use every trick in the book to convince you that you absolutely need to look at the next post because it is scarce. FOMO, Fear Of Missing Out, is an example of scarcity bias.

Scarcity bias also kicks in with non-material values, such as freedom. If you have a freedom that is valuable to you, and that freedom is even slightly curtailed, you are very likely to overreact because of scarcity bias. You may well recognise this in yourself as you were growing up, or if you have a teenage child.

And so we react more intensively than warranted. Whenever you find yourself reacting way more intensely than is reasonable, you have been hijacked by one of the biases.

If you find yourself wanting something very intensely, check whether scarcity bias has kicked in. Auctioneers are very good at setting the stage for scarcity bias to drive your behaviour. A few years ago many countries around the world held auctions for access to the 4G spectrum. In some countries these auctions were carefully designed to make full use of these biases. The result was that the large cell phone providers paid far more than they ever had before for access to the new bands.

Dealing subtly and compassionately with biases

The challenge dealing with all these biases is that they compel you to act through your emotions. You are seldom aware in time of the Type 1 thinking, or of your hidden meaning-making story. And because strong emotions tend to shut down cognitive, Type 2 thinking, just knowing about these biases from reading this book will help you in 1% of cases.

Your biggest defence against you manipulating yourself, or somebody else manipulating you through triggering the stories behind your biases, is to get really good at slamming on the brakes whenever you feel strong emotions driving you towards a specific decision or action.

At that point, the Adaptive Way pattern called Psycho 1 is a powerful defence. In Psycho 1, you simply ask yourself,

> *if I did not feel the way I do, what other decision would I take? What else would I do?*

In the case of scarcity bias being the story that is triggering disproportionately intense feelings, ask yourself what you want this for. Is it something that will truly benefit you if you possess it? Where the benefit is bigger than whatever it will cost you to get? If not, think seriously about walking away, especially if there is any intuition telling you that you are in the hands of a master at using your biases to get you to comply with their needs.

Recent research into food cravings, and other kinds of addictions, show that physical needs for food, or physical addiction, is less important than we thought. When you feel a strong craving for chocolate it's unlikely that your body is telling you that it needs something in the chocolate. It's far more likely that you had two fleeting thoughts in quick succession: something triggered a fleeting thought of chocolate, immediately followed by your conscience saying no, and before you became aware of either of those thoughts, a bias kicked in and triggered an intense emotional craving for chocolate. Your bias did register both fleeting thoughts and concluded, for example, that if chocolate was something that was forbidden or restricted, it was scarce and valuable, so you had to be forced to get some. Now!

This is similar to willpower. Old, less valid research suggested that willpower was some kind of finite resource. That on average you had enough willpower in your tank to take only five tough choices each day. So, if you were sitting in a business meeting, where you needed to take five tough decisions, not to attempt to use any willpower to resist eating a plate of biscuits in front of you. We now know that this research is wrong. Willpower is not like a fuel tank that gets used up, it's an emotion influenced by scarcity bias.

As soon as you feel the stress of resisting the plate of biscuits, or the stress of being in conflict around a tough decision, your brain narrows in on, say, calmness as a scarce resource. This triggers the overreaction in your feelings that makes it so difficult to resist the temptation to eat the biscuits. Once you recognise that will-power is a feeling triggered by your meaning-making stories; is neither a fuel tank that gets drained nor a muscle that gets exhausted; you have the power to recognise that: either somebody else is deliberately triggering your biases to get the decision they want; or something deep in you is triggering your biases.

Step away from those feelings by using psycho 1, use the space you get to remember that willpower is a feeling, and broaden your awareness from the narrow focus on what you're feeling now and the single decision in front of you, to the coming week, year, or even the rest of your life. Actively look at everything that is abundant in your present and future. (I'm glad I can occasionally do this; I'm working hard, though, to become consistent.)

CHAPTER 11

You are one

People aren't just people, they are people surrounded by circumstances.

—*Terry Pratchett*

11.1 Who are you, are you big enough?

You've maybe heard or read many times over that you cannot solve a problem with the same thinking that created it (Einstein). In the language of this book, you cannot solve an adaptive challenge with the same Size of Person that created it.

In this book the phrase Size of Person (SoP) is your total three-dimensional capacity, as described in the previous three chapters: to fluidly use the 28 transformational thought forms; how far along the stages of meaning-making you are; and your capacity to work subtly and wisely with your hardwired nature, including your capacity to manage your emotional state.

Figure 11.1 shows how the chapters of this part integrate. In it you can see how your behaviours are driven by your aspirational commitments (to achieve your goals) and your hidden commitments (to protect your vulnerabilities). Both of these are a consequence of who you are, including your nature and SoP. If your behaviours are blocking you from achieving your aspirational commitments, you have two options: either a Castle Move, an alternate behaviour that delivers simultaneously what your aspirational and hidden commitments need; or transformational experiments that chip away the invalid aspects of your meaning-making stories.

I cannot emphasise enough that there is nothing inherently better or worse in

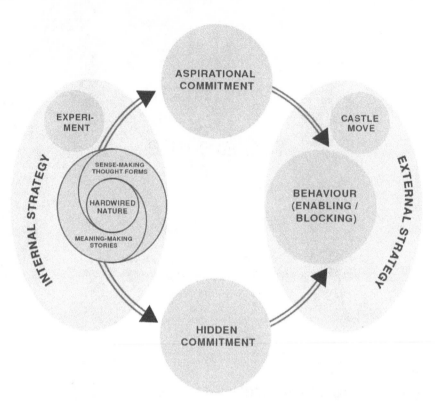

Figure 11.1: How your inner SoP generates your experienced reality and drives your behaviour, as a competition between your commitments to achieve your aspirations and protect your vulnerabilities.

having a bigger or smaller SoP. There is nothing inherently better, or to be proud of, in having your meaning-making stories centred at a later stage in the sequence described in Section 8.1.1. Just as an elephant is not inherently better than a virus.

The adaptive challenges we are facing are bigger than any challenge anyone has faced before. These challenges are as big as the planet, have time horizons of centuries, and are inherently nebulous, volatile, uncertain, complex, and ambiguous. Humanity needs enough people across all sizes of person to address them.

Whoever you are and whatever your role, the bigger you are, the better you will rise to the challenge. Many are too small for these unprecedentedly large challenges, especially those experts who are at the expert intermediate stage of self-identity.

The better you know the stories that you use to shape your reality and give you your self-identity, and the better you are at then rewriting those stories, the more likely you are to shape a future reality that addresses the challenge.

The greater your fluidity in the 28 transformational thought forms, the more likely you are to be able to work with the irreducibly nebulous, complex, or even chaotic nature of the challenge without falling victim to harmful either / or logic. You will be able to apply the kind of thinking that transformed physics into quantum physics.

The more subtlety you can use in rising above your own unique nature and biases, the more likely you are to address the challenge according to its actual nature, rather than according to your own.

In fact, I will go so far as to say that we would not have crossed the edge into our current climate emergency, nor any of the other existential crises humanity faces over the coming century, if the people who had shaped neoclassical economics, and applied it to our society, had been bigger.

Today, none of us is big enough for the challenges we are facing. We need to grow.

Sense-making

In conversations that the two of us have had writing this book, about many economists and their research articles, we often come across evidence that they are not big enough for their work in the world. Especially they lack sufficient post-logical thinking capacity.

If a thought form is not available to an economist, they won't see some aspect of the economy. All 28 thought forms of Chapter 9 are needed to really grasp the true significance of trends; what the signals visible ten years ago were telling us about today; and what the signals visible today are telling us about 50 years in the future.

Or consider a focus on data and formal manipulation of that data, rather than what lies behind the data. Your data is never neutral, your opinions on what matters, what data to gather, and how, shape the data before you even begin measuring. Your opinions come out of your meaning-making stories and the thought forms you can use fluidly. And the better you get at recognising which stories and thought forms are shaping your opinions about which data you need, the more chance you have of recognising when you need completely different types of data.

The essence of the scientific method is identifying opinions, and testing them, which makes clear how much in many of today's disciplines are more like the cargo cults described in Section 2.7.

If you are not fluid enough in the transformational thought forms, you may well be force-fitting your ungrounded opinion on the economy into logical right or wrong choices. It doesn't matter how precise your data is, if the thought forms you are using are insufficient to gather useful data and see clearly what you can and cannot use it for.

If you are highly fluid in these 28 thought forms, you'll be constantly aware that the economy is never absolute, it's always nebulous, because it is always under construction and, equally, your knowledge of it is always under construction and lagging behind the economy.

Meaning-making and experts

Too many experts, economists included, use just one lens in making meaning and only one frame of reference in evaluating. In Chapter 8 you read about the different stages of meaning making that human beings can go through in sequence. Later stages allow you to grasp different types of stories, and to create your own stories with less and less dependency on the stories of others.

One stage that may well partly cause the distrust that many have for experts is the expert stage halfway between S3 and S4, Chapter 8. Recall, if you are at this stage, you make meaning and shape your reality based on others recognising you as an expert. So any challenge to your discipline means an identity crisis.

In physics, it took a couple of decades for quantum physics to establish itself as a new domain of expertise, and so a group for socialised mind and expert stage folk to derive their identity from. The people who were able to move first were those who had progressed beyond the expert stage. Over time, they formed a new group that others could join as expert members, while those who could not eventually retired and left active work in physics.

A big driver of your meaning making, in addition to the stage that your meaning-making stories are at, are the different cognitive biases described in Section 10.5. The Dunning-Kruger effect (imposter syndrome), or inferiority-superiority bias, authority bias, consistency bias, and uncertainty avoidance bias all have a significant effect on anyone who is sought out as an expert, and wearing a label of authority like professor or consultant or executive.

The book *The Econocracy: The Perils of Leaving the Economy to the Experts*[124] points very clearly at the impact of too small SoP individuals in positions of power over others and the discipline.

The authors refer to the economics profession as an elite, disconnected from the rest of us and our day-to-day use of our economy as a tool to do the job of provisioning[1]. The emergence of such an elite is often a consequence of a large

---

[1] The Econocracy is one of many tangible and transformational outcomes that emerged from the global dissatisfaction, beginning around 2001, of economic students with the validity of what they

enough community of people whose sense of self-esteem and identity comes from shared stories of being experts recognised and validated by the other experts in the field.

Very much as in Ubuntu (section 7.3.1), this becomes a self-reinforcing closed community. Any challenge to the expertise is identical to a challenge to the identity of the community as a whole, and specifically any individual that is challenged.

This is a stage that every professional discipline goes through as it evolves and that a number of human beings go through. Applying thought forms T1, 2, 3, and 4, this is nothing other than the necessary conflict and loss of stability necessary to transform the economics discipline to the next stage with the adaptive capacity capable of rising to our crises. Embrace the tension and conflict, it's your friend!

You can do this, if you remind yourself every time you feel triggered at a challenge to your expertise, that this challenge has got nothing to do with you, or your legitimacy to have expertise. The strength of your trigger is most of the time simply valuable data telling you about deeply hidden meaning-making stories that you are using to construct your self-identity.

So economics is today at the same exciting time that physics was a century ago; on the edge of an equivalent great shift to the shift from classical to quantum. To leap across the chasm between economics as it has been, and economics as it will be, economics needs big economists, just as physics needed big physicists.

If your work includes balancing and coordinating across multiple systems, for example multiple institutions across the economy, politics, and society, you need to be big. Else the Dunning-Kruger effect may well bite you!

> I (Jack) would not be here writing this book with Graham without the following response to a paper that I submitted to a peer-reviewed journal early in my career. Even though the reviewer's response was clearly painful for me, with hindsight I can see how the meaning-making story shaped the reality of my life.
>
> I had discovered an error in the deductive logic of a fundamental model in neoclassical economics. Not knowing anything about the expert stage of identity, I naïvely assumed that my discovery would be welcomed by the economics discipline, so we could correct an error and move forward. My worst 'fear' was that somebody would point out the logical error that I had made, which I would've welcomed, since it would have made me a better economist.

were being taught.

Instead, I received a terse, three-word letter of rejection:

How dare you!

I asked myself what is wrong with the economics discipline if a very simple question on the internal logical consistency of a small building block of economic theory generates a thermonuclear emotional response.

(I wish I had then known how my meaning-making stories and the referee's meaning-making stories created the reality that each of us experienced.)

I was buoyed by the always-helpful advice of my football (American) coach, Frank deFelice:

Success is defeat turned inside out.

Indeed, I turned this defeat into success by sketching on the back of the rejection letter, a new story that would (hopefully) transform the economics profession and how we educate our economists. This new story created, three years later, the first edition of *The International Journal of Pluralism and Economics Education.*

In 2015 I was invited to speak at the Rethinking Economics Conference in London, because of my research work and as the journal's founding editor; I met Graham, and this book is the consequence.

This book that you are now reading never would have happened without that rejection letter, and so if you derive any benefit from reading this book, then that rejection letter may well have been the best thing that ever happened to me.

Take hope that your journey and the difference you can make in the world will be bigger and quicker than the journeys Graham and I have had to get to this point. You're building on everything in this book, and in the books listed in our bibliography, and much more. You're bringing your own genius to play, surfing on a rising tide of many more. Ubuntu at work again.

Every successive improvement and expansion in quantum physics has described even better what we see happening in nature. Regardless of which philosophical interpretation a physicist finds most plausible, all physicists use the same equations and make the same predictions of what will happen. Predictions that have consistently proven extraordinarily accurate.

It's high time that we develop the same rigour in our studies and paradigms of business and economics. We may never be able to pin down which is the right interpretation of what an organisation is or is for, but if we manage to get the same experimental rigour into business and economics, we will at least know what works.

The way forward is to repeat what physicists did a century ago. Recognise that the different philosophies of quantum physics primarily exist so that we can feel secure in our meaning making. As soon as physicists only focused on using quantum physics to make smartphones, GPS devices, and many other products that we depend on today, all physicists agreed.

We need to get to that point in business and economics. Way too much still depends on opinions that have as much anchoring in what actually works in organisations and businesses as the air anchoring the clouds I'm currently looking at above the mountain across the valley.

11.2 Who you are now vs. who you are

Recall, from Section 6.4, that most of our economy is non-ergodic, even though most of economics assumes ergodicity. As we introduced there, this has huge implications for who you are, and what it means to "find oneself".

Who you are is the integration of every influencing event in your experienced reality along your life path; which may well go back a number of generations. It's not for nothing that many ancient customs take into account seven generations. Think: *I am my life path and the meaning-making stories that I have internalised because of that life path.*

Who you are not a static thing. So you never can "find yourself" and then stay true to that self forever, unchanging. Nor ought you put your life on hold until you have found yourself. Because who any of us is is a process across time, not a static thing in the here and now. Who you are is continuously being changed through your relationships with others and your environment. You are an open dynamic system in constant transformation. (This applies all the thought forms of Chapter 9 to see your self across, rather than in, time.)

Who you are now is the integration of your entire life path within your experienced reality up to now: every influence, every experience you have made meaning of; and, to make matters even more challenging, also the integration of your expectations about your life path into the future.

You truly are unique.

No-one else has had your life path ever before, nor will any one else ever have your life path again.

And since that is common for everyone, around 8 billion people, it also means you are also not unique! You being unique and not unique is yet another complementary pair.

So often we all limit ourselves by looking at ourselves in the moment through a narrow lens that excludes almost all of who we are across all time, saying something like *I am a …*; and then identifying who we are with those words—across all time, all people, and all situations.

Equally we often delude ourselves that we are far more than we are in exactly the same way!

Any self-declaration in time beginning with *I am …*, and any declaration another makes about you beginning with *You are…* cannot precisely describe all that you are across time.

This life path perspective is missing in most approaches to identity and belonging. Identity groupings (e.g., gender, culture, nationality, etc.) of people around some common ground at a point in time (the present, or some past milestone) have validity; and yet miss the uniqueness integrating each individual's entire life path across time.

Some of you may identify with some past milestone, e.g. where you've come from (*I was born a …and so I am a …, but you were not, and so you are not part of my identity group*); or maybe with where you are now (*I say I am a …; you also say the same; so we're the same, and are members of my identity group*). Both of these lenses on self-identity have full validity within one frame of reference, and neither is complete in all frames. Each emphasises one aspect of common ground by hiding complementary aspects of uniqueness, and common ground with others.

And so arguments between people and members of an identity grouping about someone *being a …or not* usually produce only emotions, seldom understanding, let alone resolution, because they fail to see how those differences and similarities are created by the lenses used and the narrow focus on one characteristic, at one time, rather than each person's full being across time.

You are a unique integration of your life path to now and into the future.

And you have multiple types of common ground with many other people. Choose for yourself the groups you identify with.

And you have some common ground with everyone alive today, with everyone who has ever lived, and with everyone who ever will live.

Coming back to the crises of today then. Whoever you are now, however you evaluate yourself, and however daunting your journey may seem, I see two reasons to stay hopeful.

- Whoever you think you are after reflecting on those questions and reading this book, you're already far more than that. None of us ever can be fully aware of everything that we are. We are always more aware of part of who we are, and unaware of some other part. You are a lot like a Picasso painting, there's always far more to you than whatever you are currently seeing.

- Also, like quantum physics, as soon as you focus your awareness on yourself, you immediately change yourself. Who you are, as you become aware of yourself, has already changed. So who you think you are is always one step behind who you are. I find that a very powerful reason to hope that I am already someone even more able to rise to the adaptive challenges I am choosing to face, and already even more someone that I will enjoy spending the rest of my life with.

Remember, you are unique.

No-one else experiences the same reality you experience, and so no-one else can be who you can be.

And who you are being can continue to change, as it has changed so far, so that you can be who your world needs you to be.

11.3 Why most self-help approaches aren't helpful

To change your being, you may turn to one of the many self-help approaches. Some work, some do not, and some cause harm.

For example, the Losada ratio of flourishing people having three to six times more positive emotions than negative, often cited in positive psychology, is wrong[170]. Mindfulness, which does good for many, can also cause harm[152]. People have ended up needing to be hospitalised because of mindfulness training. Many self-help approaches are like the cargo cults of Section 2.7—they have similar visible rituals to ones that work, but lack the hidden engines.

All approaches to development and growth need to be treated with a high level of self-aware caution. Including everything in this book.

Declarations don't work

One recurring theme in self-help is pumping yourself up. Self-help is full of admonishments to look yourself in the mirror each morning and say something like

Every day, in every way, I'm getting better and better.

Look at some well-known, popular programmes built around a charismatic individual exhorting you to tell yourself you can do it, and making good money for their founders and key staff members; even though their foundation is luck, not a method that works[150] to drive change. And even worse, some are so flawed they are actively harmful.

A very effective route to going under in the turbulent stresses of modern life is simplistically declaring that you are awesome, instead of the hard but effective work of dismantling the scripts that tell you otherwise, then using experiences in the areas you do well in, and those you do not, so the scripts rewrite themselves.

If most self-help actually worked, there would be few people trying out a new technique every year. The self-help industry protects itself, because the implicit mantra is, *if you failed to help yourself, it is your fault, because you didn't do it right.*

The whole industry of self-help, weight-loss, motivation etc. is filled with approaches that, in themselves, are inherently incapable of delivering reliable, long-lasting benefit. Only a few lucky people experience long-lasting benefits. Lucky, because the benefits come from some other cause than the self-help approach.

But because the industry has become so good at persuading you that failure is your fault, not theirs, the response of most people is to blame themselves, and then buy another book or course.

You can read a lot more about why most approaches at best do no good, and often do harm, apart from those that involve you recognising and changing your stories in *Redirect* by Timothy Wilson[150] and *SHAM: How the Self-Help Movement Made America Helpless* by Steve Salerno[151].

The empirical evidence for what really works, without risk of harm, and that leads to sustainable growth and transformation, shows that it is all in the meaning-making stories that shape our thoughts, our feelings, and trigger our actions; and our fluidity in transformational thought forms.

To change or improve yourself, it's no good to just counter-declare yourself to be different to who your stories declare you to be. Counter-declaring like this can cause harm.

Typologies need a pinch of salt

Type indicators have become popular over the past couple of decades. I recommend that you avoid all type indicators with fixed categories, such as the MBTI and Enneagram. Many are a modern equivalent to the cargo cultists: they look evidence-based, they give you an illusion of understanding, a feel-good factor, but that's all.

There is growing evidence that these type indicators are too generic to be really useful[171], let alone help you grow into who you can become. Rather, you shape yourself to fit into whichever box a test has put you into. If you end up believing, and adopting as your own, the meaning-making stories of a specific MBTI or Enneagram category, you may well narrow and slow down your development towards *your* next meaning-making stage.

More recent approaches do not allocate you to a box with a label, but rather tell you how high or low you score on a few dimensions. One example of this is the OCEAN (Openness, Conscientious, Extroversion, Agreeableness, Neuroticism) set of traits.

These have a usefulness as a language to communicate clearly within your inner dialogue and with others. OCEAN is now well-validated, but, no matter how validated, they (including everything in this book) are limited, because no model can never capture the full nebulous, unknowable being that you are.

So reject all type indicators and profiles that claim to tell you who you are—yet have all 7.9 billion unique human beings in just a few boxes. Take all with a pinch of salt, some with a couple of tonnes. Each of us is unique. There is no one else just like you.

Why coaching can stunt your development

Much coaching is surface-level behavioural: it is there to change your behaviours so that you can achieve your aspirational commitments. Or, far worse, so that you can achieve someone else's goals, often your boss's.

Behavioural coaching based, not on castle moves, but only on simplistic attempts to change your blocking behaviours without understanding the vital role they are playing in protecting vulnerabilities in your big assumptions, and without understanding the developmental process that you go through as you progress from one meaning-making stage to the next.

So whilst you may temporarily succeed in delivering your immediate goal, your vulnerability is likely to feel more threatened, and come back with an even stronger way of protecting itself. That will simply hold you back even more from your next goal, and from developing yourself into who you are intended to become. It will hold you back from becoming authentic.

You are also likely to end up feeling even more stressed, and in even greater need of coaching. A wonderfully self-perpetuating business model, if ever I saw one.

Too few coaches out there are sufficiently fluid in all 28 thought forms, especially the specific transformational thought forms T1 to T7. A coach must have sufficient fluidity and stage of development in their own open meaning-making system to effectively and safely engage with your open, transforming meaning-making system.

Just as you saw that S4 is the earliest category of meaning making sufficiently independent of the need to belong to a group and follow its norms to be able to manage others, so too is S4 is the earliest category able to coach another as a different but equal being.

If you are being coached by someone with less fluidity than you have, or at a less complex stage of meaning-making, your coach's smaller capacity is more likely to just pull you back to their SoP. Only a coach with a bigger SoP than you can support you to grow your SoP.

So choose your coach with a high degree of caution. If your gut instinct suggests that they don't get you, or they are misinterpreting as resistance your attempts to pin down and clarify a nebulous sense that something is wrong in their understanding of you, it may be time for a new coach.

Of course, sometimes you will be wrong. Sometimes Dunning-Kruger is at work, and you are simply not yet big enough to grasp what the coach is doing. Sometimes your own psychological idiosyncrasies are creating an inner reality that is so distorted from actuality that you cannot see clearly.

This is why I believe that the best approach to development is through your work, in a structured peer-to-peer dialogue, using a common language and patterns, with your colleagues or peers, e.g. the Adaptive Way (strictly applying the three rules of safety: care for yourself; care for each other; care for the whole). This is also the only approach that can scale to reach enough people in the decade we have left to build the regenerative businesses and the regenerative economy needed to address our global crises.

As the old maps used to say, proceed with caution, for there be dragons ahead. But only by proceeding can you tell whether these are the beneficial dragons of some Asian cultures, or the threatening dragons of European cultures.

11.4 Self-protection

Never forget that you have every right to protect yourself. You will live with the consequences of your choices of who to follow; which practice to incorporate into your life; who to allow into your life as mentor, coach, or guru.

Keep in mind, about 1% of the population has narcissistic personality disorder, another 1% has strong psychopathic tendencies. What better job for them to find prey than providing professional help? Keep your eyes open.

Apply the PT Barnum test[136] to anything or anyone that in any way is attempting to tell you who you are. Much in the typologies, the self-help industry, spiritual development, astrology etc. fails the PT Barnum test.

The Barnum test captures how easy it is to write a description that appears to be specific about a few people, and yet that most people believe accurately describes them. This has been demonstrated time and again in research. In the first study, a paragraph (like those you find in type indicators) was given to a full cross-spectrum of university students of all types and natures. They were asked to rate this for how accurately it described them, on a scale from 1 (not at all) to 5 (this is absolutely and uniquely me). The average was 4.3.

This shows how easy it is to write or say something that looks specific, but is in fact so general that it fits many extremely well. These are the kinds of things used by people who want you to feel special, or to manipulate you; and that are behind some type indicators, and more.

We are all very easy to fool, especially those of us trained in the sciences. We learn to think that everything is rational and, whilst nebulous, is never malicious. Stage magicians are often a far more reliable judge than scientists of whether something is a con, playing on our human capacity for deception, or for real. Listen to them too!

Deeply mistrust any mystical explanation of some phenomenon, if the same phenomenon can be reproduced by a magician using sleight of hand and misdirection.

Protect yourself by keeping in mind that you are the only person who can ever have the depth and breadth of understanding to define who you are, let alone who you ought to become.

Certainly no colleague or manager has the capacity, let alone the right, to play God: to attempt to define who you are or should be.

Anyone who says to you anything beginning with

you are … (annoying, lazy, clever, kind, successful)

may well be playing God over you. Even if they are just saying that as a colloquial form of expressing their personal admiration, rephrase it. What they are actually saying is that their meaning-making stories attribute this quality to what they are seeing of you. Whilst they are saying it's about you, it's actually more about them.

I recommend that you read *Experiencing the Impossible: The Science of Magic* by Gustav Kuhn[172], *Paranormality* by Richard Wiseman[136] and *The Buddha Pill* by Miguel Farias and Catherine Wikholm[152] to get an even better idea of the different ways you can be fooled, and what you can do to protect yourself.

For me, the bottom line is that it is *my* life, *my* experienced reality generated through *my* meaning-making stories that I have to live with. I choose.

11.5 Accepting or rebelling against who you are

Your very first job in life, from the moment you were born, was to grow up into the biggest, shiniest self that you could become. This job stays with you throughout your life. Your primary job is to be yourself, and continue to grow into who you can become, in this nebulous, VUCA world.

Accept and work subtly with everything that seems to be part of your unchangeable core essence. It is as futile for you to try to change that, as it was when King Canute deliberately demonstrated the futility of even a King trying to hold back the tide. Part of your unchangeable core essence includes, for example, sounds you can distinguish easily but others cannot (e.g. *l* vs. *r*), and even emotions you can experience, but others cannot, because the environment, including beliefs and culture, you grew up in, as well as your early childhood experiences, gave you a different neural connectivity to another.

Rebel against any part of you that is not part of your core essence and is creating a distorted experienced reality contrary to your core essence, or that is taking you down a path towards long-term harm.

Your real challenge, as you undoubtedly know, is how on earth are you going to tell the difference? Unfortunately, there is no easy way. This has always been a challenge for each of us and will remain a challenge for the rest of our lives. I have found it useful to combine constant experimentation, using improv to try out different possible steps for me to take in my development, moving forwards with whatever seems to work, and never taking anything as right.

Picasso's art, as on the cover, is relevant to this. There is no right perspective to take in deciding who you ought to become, and there is no single you that you ought to become. You are a flowing river, not a static thing. Like his art, there are infinitely many possibilities ahead for you to become. Of course, there are limitations and boundaries. You cannot become someone that is contrary to your core, unchangeable essence. But within that space, you have infinite possibility.

This story of my journey may help you by illustrating what I'm talking about.

> I (Graham) have tried to gain weight, and especially to put on more muscle. From around 10 years old until around 40 I tried everything I could. Multiple different eating regimes, different exercise routines, heavy weights with few repetitions, light weights with lots of repetitions, rowing, cycling, rock climbing, the works.
>
> None of them led to sustained weight gain. I have always been a tall skinny guy.

The driver behind all this effort was a deep assumption that I was not OK as I was. Recall, I grew up in South Africa, where sport and physical prowess is the most highly prized quality at school. Even more so, I went to a boys-only school, where sporting achievement was the route to respect and acceptance from my peers. So from a very young age I learnt that until I had muscles and excelled at sport, I was nothing.

Now I've given up trying to gain weight. I've ceased blaming myself for not trying hard enough, because I now know two things. First, the stories I believed are not true everywhere, always, with everyone. I have respect because of who I am in total, regardless of how much muscle that total includes. Secondly, there are unchangeable limits to how much muscle I can gain. My body is what it is.

Believing that I could have the body I wanted if I tried hard enough, and therefore, it was my fault for not trying hard enough, was just setting myself up for failure. Now my attention is focused on right health, which means eating and exercising well. I have accepted that that means staying at a lightweight 67 kg at 6 ft 2″ height.

Even more, I have transformed myself by re-writing my stories. Now I am proud that, at 55, I am as slender and healthy as I was at 20. The only physical issues I now have are back and knee injuries—ironically caused by training beyond my nature's limits, with weights that were simply too heavy for me.

Treat yourself with at least as much compassion and kindness as you would anyone that you cared deeply for. Most of us, though, find it extraordinarily difficult to see ourselves through such a lens of compassion and kindness, and refuse to allow ourselves to simply be what is deeply embedded in our nature, and unchangeable.

The better you get at applying the quote from Reinholdt Niebuhr on page 226, the better you will be able to harness the unique strength that your nature gives you, and the less you will waste those strengths in futile rebellion against the weaknesses that they bring with them.

All the patterns in this book, and in all the forthcoming books, are useful in enabling you to do that. Stop bullying yourself, and instead accept with kindness and compassion your nature. Stop bullying yourself, and instead explore your meaning-making stories, and then create experiential experiments so that they rewrite themselves.

11.6 Being yourself with others

I find the quote by Terry Pratchett at the start of this chapter a very neat way of describing the philosophy of Ubuntu (Section 10.5), and what we discovered in Section 7.2, that you always show up as your dressed self.

You cannot switch your self-awareness on or off consciously. (I use awareness and consciousness[2] as nearly synonymous.) Once you have become aware of something, you cannot actively become unaware. Equally, if you have no awareness, you lack even the awareness to begin the journey to becoming aware.

What is currently in your self-awareness changes slightly your self-identity, because it changes which of your stories is in the driving seat. Since you cannot decide now to shut down your awareness of yourself. It's a bit like telling someone *now whatever you do, do not, under pain of death, think of a pink elephant*. The very attempt to not to think of the pink elephant is itself a thought of a pink elephant, and so they think of and see a pink elephant. (Every time I edited this I ended up seeing a pink elephant too.)

Because you are self-aware, your self-identity in any instant is "fully dressed". It's the self you get after all the different elements of your self-awareness have acted on each other.

In that sense, you are actually never your "naked" self. You are always the you after all the bias and distortions coming from your self-awareness have done their work. It means that who you are is always under construction, never ever fixed.

You can take huge hope from this because it means that you can make some very easy changes. Just changing what in yourself you are aware of already begins to change your self-identity.

If you are in the grip of anger with a colleague and become aware of this, you change, and anger loses some of its grip on you. Then becoming aware that you are much more than your anger; that you have anger now in this moment, which is quite different to seeing your being as angry, loosens the grip even more. Step even deeper into awareness that your colleague is also far more than just a target for anger, they are everything a colleague can be, including at this moment one who has done something that triggers anger in you.

Then suddenly you've regained your self-identity as a fully conscious human being, and are aware of your colleague as another different but equally fully conscious human being. You've stepped from a smaller self-identity into a bigger one.

---

[2] In my opinion, consciousness is simply the emergent property of a fantastically complex system, our huge brain of neurons, neurotransmitters, etc. I find myself in awe of just how much more must be possible in this universe, if a sufficiently complex constellation of protons, neutrons and electrons is able to be aware of itself and understand protons, neutrons and electrons.

Notice how this is exactly what I recommend you use to prevent being manipulated through your biases in Section 10.5

This also means that Ubuntu 7.3.1 acts on an individual level, as well as at a societal level.

I (Graham) show up quite differently with two different work associates. With one, I'll call him Mike, I usually feel calm, energised and optimistic. With the other, I'll call her Sarah, for a long time I felt energised as well, but also frustrated and irritable. With Sarah, at first I tried working on my stories. What was it in my stories that was reacting to what she was doing? I tried various experiments, I tried various improv approaches, I tried everything described in Part III and more. Nothing worked, nothing changed, increasing my frustration and irritation every time we worked together.

Through a process of elimination, it became clear to me that what was happening lay neither just in me, nor just in her. Most of what was happening lay in the archetypal relationship between someone with my essence and category of stories, and someone with her essence and category of stories.

The relationship exists independently of us, shaping each of us; who I am and who she is in that relationship is shaped by this third, independent entity, the relationship. By recognising that the dressed me is created by the relationship, and the dressed Sarah is also created by the relationship, it made it very clear that, for me to change how I was showing up, and the reality that I was experiencing, it was essential for her to change herself, so that both of our dressed selves became different. Then a different type of relationship could emerge, reinforcing our changed selves.

I realised just how much of who I was, was there because of who she was, and that neither of us were to blame. This enabled me to look at Sarah and myself with a high level of acceptance and compassion. With the balance and peace that that gave me, I took the steps to change the kind of work we were doing together to one that would enable us both to be effective, given the reality that each of us shapes for ourselves in response to the other person.

Keep this firmly in mind when you are working with your colleagues. If there is someone who frustrates or angers you, maybe it's neither them, nor you. Maybe they are only this way with you, and you are only this way with them. So don't blame yourself, and don't try to fix yourself, in isolation. In the same way, don't blame the other person, and don't try to fix them, in isolation. Each of you is shaping each of you through the kind of relationship that has you in its grip. You will learn a pattern called deconstructive conflict in Section 13.7.1, which is the most powerful pattern I have ever found to enable you to transform who you are, and your relationships at work.

Recall what I wrote in Section 7.4. The meaning-making stories that shape who you are your superpower versus all other life forms on the planet. Even more powerfully, the stories of a tribe, a sports club, or the community of people that constitute a business, are their collective superpower.

Human beings could never collaborate the way we do, to overcome challenges that are bigger than any single human being, without the collective stories that unite us. These collective stories enable us to see the common oneness that unites us.

Just as in quantum physics, where no particle is an independent isolated entity, but rather where the properties of every single particle are shaped by every other particle around it and shape every particle around it, your personal stories create the collective stories of the groups of people you are part of and are in turn shaped by the collective stories.

There is no way of teasing apart your story from the collective story.

Nor should you ever try to. This is a core message behind applying the lessons of quantum physics and Picasso's art to ourselves. If you try to separate yourself from everyone and everything around you, if you try to separate your story from our stories, you will lose the very superpower that you need to overcome the challenges that you, and we, will face in the next ten years.

When we are with others, we tend to put ourselves into boxes, we put other people into boxes, and none of those boxes are ever all you are. The better you understand your stories, the better you get at guessing the stories that are running somebody else, the better you'll get at recognising when your way of being and meaning-making have put somebody into a box. *Leadership and Self-Deception*, an excellent book[139] by the Arbinger Institute expands fully on this.

If you read it after reading this book, you may suspect what I suspect: that their "in-the-box" is what I would call S3 meaning-making, and their "out-of-the-box" is what I would call stepping into the bigger box of S4. Since S4 is just a bigger box, you may need to step out again into the next bigger box of S5, and then into the even bigger box of S6. So you are always in a box—the question is, is it big enough for the task at hand?

11.7 Bigger than one: from you and me to us

Each of us is part of a much bigger whole than any of us can easily imagine. We are one life out of countless many living organisms on one bluish planet revolving at 19 miles per second around a sun that provides us with all the energy that almost all life on the planet uses.

For most of human history, life demanded far less from the planet and it's limits. We have now grown so big that we have hit the limits to growth[173]. We've hollowed out Kate Raworth's doughnut[12] until no dough is left, only us nuts.

A thread throughout life, that I hope is clearly visible throughout this book, is that what we all have in common with all other human beings, and all life on the planet, is far bigger than the dominant logic of today sees. This common oneness is far more important in each of us being able to survive and thrive than the uniqueness of any of us.

To move forward, we now need an Ubuntu philosophy to take centre stage, rather than an individualistic philosophy.

Once we do this, we will start multisolving[7], as Elizabeth Sawin of Climate Interactive has named those single actions that simultaneously solve multiple problems. For example, replacing a coal-fired power station with a combination of photovoltaic panels on everyone's roofs, wind turbines nearby, and local storage of electricity in the form of hydrogen, compressed air, or any other form, is multisolving.

It contributes towards solving our climate emergency, and it solves health issues, reducing the burden on health insurance and medical practitioners of the many problems caused by pollution. It increases the lifespan of our buildings by reducing the impact of pollution, including acid rain. It reduces local unemployment and poverty by providing work that is best done by large numbers of small businesses rather than one big power plant, and so on.

The better we are at using all 28 thought forms, at recognising that the common ground that unites us is far more important than the uniqueness that divides us and that all our problems are interrelated, the easier it gets for us to find one quick and affordable action that is a multisolution.

We cannot see everything that a multisolution will solve until after the fact, but just knowing that they exist and that we can find them is part of what gives me hope.

One organisation that Evolutesix has supported, including incorporating it as a FairShares Commons, is UniOne. UniOne is a business and a movement that provides safe spaces where wide ranges of differently unique people can come together and stand safely in their common oneness and, at the same time, without any loss of self, in their diverse individual uniqueness.

This is at its most powerful when highly diverse unique organisations and cultures find a way to come together and collaborate on the common oneness because they retain the full power of their individual uniqueness. Until nations and their politicians can do this sufficiently well, we are unlikely to move forward on the political contributors to our global crises.

Until different businesses can do this, we are unlikely to move forwards on the business contributors. But at least we have now ways of incorporating that make this natural, like the FairShares Commons.

11.8 How will you measure your life?

Take a moment to imagine that you are now at the end of your life. Maybe only the end of your working life, or the end of whatever phase of your life you are in now.

Sitting there at your life's end, looking back, how will you measure your life?

This is the topic of the excellent book[174] by Clayton Christensen, aptly entitled *How will you measure your life?*, which strongly influenced me (Graham) in 2009 when I first read it, and the Adaptive Way. The book is based on the lecture he gives to his business school class at the end of every year, where he shows how to apply everything that he has taught about business strategy and disruptive innovation[45] to oneself.

I recommend that you sit down, perhaps at the end of every year, and imagine that you are sitting at life's end. You are now looking back over your life and measuring it. How will you measure it? Which measures, or frames of reference, will you use? What evaluation will you give to your life? What were the major choices you made, the important actions you took, that created this life?

You will likely be tempted to do this in the present, writing about what you will do. Avoid that. Seat yourself firmly in the future, at the end of your life, and write as if you had already done it. (See *giving an A* in *The art of possibility*[175].)

Think about which measures, or frames of reference, are really important to you now. Think about how they may change from now until the end. And then take that as the best set of measures you can use now as you imagine yourself measuring your life.

Part Four

Organisations

Let's look at the organisation as a living, meaning-making being, just like you are, except that each cell of an organisation is
a human being. It depends on humans to act as its eyes, ears,
and mouth. Using this lens, you can see what ought to change,
across all aspects; from legal incorporation as a free company,
e.g. using the FairShares Commons, through having tasks and
roles structured using dynamic governance, to developmental
inter-personal and intra-personal interactions.

CHAPTER 12

Organisations are living beings

Organisations exist to make every individual's strengths
productive and their weaknesses irrelevant.
—*Peter Drucker*

12.1 Why we need business

Three central elements of modern life: capitalism, scientific research, and manufacturing, are at the centre of the huge increase in humans thriving. They succeeded in turning the scarcities in financial capital, intellectual capital, manufactured capital, and food into the abundance many of us enjoy today. I (Graham) remember my Granny saying that the modern invention that had improved her life the most was the indoor bathroom, with hot and cold running water.

Business, as currently designed, has done phenomenally well. There is more than enough money, food and housing for every single person in the world to live a better life than the nobility could four centuries ago, and way better than anyone could 4,000 plus years ago.

However, business as it's currently designed is no longer fit for purpose. It's clear that we are facing two new, interwoven drivers that, unless used to trigger a fundamental reinvention of business, will continue to grow as threats to each of us today and in the future.

1. The first driver is the abundance that modern business has created is growing less and less evenly distributed. Global inequality between rich and poor continues to grow. The fact that in 2020 a disabled man starved to death in

Britain because changes to the disability support system left him unable to afford food is a smoking gun signal. We need a way of distributing our global abundance more evenly, i.e., an economy that provisions all.

2. The second driver is the environmental and social capitals, the foundational capitals for all life, including yours, are being severely overspent. We are eating into our capitals so fast that we are close to the point of irreversible civilisation collapse. We need a fast way of regenerating, i.e., growing, all these capitals.

Failing to act on these drivers means the end of this cycle of human civilisation, just as previous civilisations have been ended by the same drivers[176]. The Roman civilisation ended because they needed more environmental resources than their environmental capital base could provide, like the children of a wealthy family spending all the money accumulated by their parents, rather than spending only the sustainable income generated by working the capital.

How did we get into this mess?

Perhaps the first multinational recognisably similar to the multinational of today was the Dutch East India company. This company was incorporated by charter of the Queen, to address the biggest scarcity of that time: financial capital. Up to then, anyone engaged in business had to either provide the capital needed to start the business themselves, or obtain it from their friends and family.

The driver for creating the incorporated organisation was the growing demand in Europe for spices, tea and other limited commodities from distant lands. The cost of building the multinational business necessary to transport these valuable commodities from Asia required more financial capital than any single family could gather through their relationships with their trusted friends.

Given that driver, an incorporated business capable of attracting risk capital from strangers was the answer.

The limited company as we know it today has been perfected to solve the adaptive challenge of creating trust between people who do not know each other. Sufficient trust for them to risk some or even all of their wealth in the enterprise of complete strangers.

If a stranger walked up to you in the street and asked you to give them 50% of your total wealth, to be locked down for the next 20 years in a risky endeavour, what would you answer? The collective answer society has built up over the past four centuries is the modern private and public limited company.

The problem we have today lies in just how well business was designed as a tool to do the job of attracting financial capital. To do that, it was designed to maximally multiply financial capital, without any balance across the other capitals.

Of course, in our new design, we need to keep all the good things that business and capitalism brings us, as we redesign it to eliminate all the harm. This means expanding the design of business to one that multiplies, i.e., regenerates, all capitals.

12.2 Why we need organisations

To do together what cannot be done alone. To rise to challenges bigger than the strength of one person, and to attract, multiply, and distribute the scarcest valuable resources. Or, as Gabriel Grant puts it[177], we need organisations to maximise our individual and joint capacity for self-determination; i.e., fully human organisations, the *Humanocracy*[178] of Gary Hamel and Michele Zanini.

Human organisations are as old as the first hunter who went out with a friend and set up a deliberate ambush to bring an antelope home for dinner.

If you think of what human beings are good at, none of our physical strengths are anywhere near the best in class in the rest of the animal kingdom. None of us come anywhere near the long-distance endurance of a migratory bird, nor the top end speed of a cheetah, nor the sheer strength of an elephant, or the power-to-weight ratio of a flea.

What we excel at is organising ourselves into teams, and our tasks into sequence, because we are best in class at picking up on other people's emotions, and bonding together into communities or working teams by using stories to build common ground and common purpose. Organisations have existed since time immemorial. Whenever we have faced a challenge beyond the strengths of any individual human being, we have organised until our collective strengths have been big enough to overcome the challenge.

Strong as the woolly mammoth was, it was no match for a large group of humans working together in an organised way. Stories bonded everyone together, while planning and strategy created clarity on who was doing what.

The biggest challenges that humanity faces today are so big that they affect every single human being alive on the planet today and far into the future: wide-scale pollution, resource depletion, social fragmentation, and all the crises those are creating. We now have no choice other than to take a blank sheet of paper and recognise that the driver for our organisations has fundamentally changed, and that we need to re-conceive the organisation completely.

Especially the act of incorporation into profitable business organisations.

The Germans have a wonderful phrase to describe a fantastical animal that gives you everything you need: an egg laying, sheep's wool, and cow's milk producing pig. Usually this phrase is used to insultingly refer to something as an impossible fantasy.

But over the past 400 years we have managed to create in our business organisations just such a thing.

The business organisations we have are fantastic mythical entities that used to give us everything we could possibly imagine. Now we need to invent the next version, one that does it without ravaging our resources and polluting our planet, but instead regenerates all our capitals.

Enter the organisation as a living being.

12.3 The Living Organisation

I find it very helpful to look at organisations as living beings. Norman Wolfe describes this well in his book, *The Living organisation*[130]. Meaning-making stories are the essence of the living being. These form the difference between a living being like you are, and a living system like a forest, a tree, or even your kidney. Organisations are whole living beings, with a meaning-making capacity emerging from their culture.

Here are Norman's thoughts, as a special guest contribution.

The Living organisation is a major shift in thinking, a change of mindset, a true paradigm shift. It is the shift tneeded for us to achieve organisations where people flourish, and business fulfills their true potential of being a force for good in our society. Yet, none of that was behind the creation of The Living organisation® Framework (TLO). Over the course of a 50-year career leading numerous organisations and having the honor and privilege of consulting and advising many other leaders, there is one truth that rises above all others. A leader's most sacred responsibility is to ensure the organisation creates the outcomes needed for it to grow and thrive. Said simply, above all else a leader must ensure results are achieved.

The question of how best to accomplish this responsibility was the core reason for undertaking the creation of The Living Organisation Framework. It was clear to me that something new was needed, especially as organisations became larger and more complex, as was the environment they operate in.

I also knew that asking a leader to just give up control of the outcomes and trust a new way of leading would never work. While it may be attractive and garner great interest, in the end no human will give up control of that which they are responsible for.

This led me to answer the question, if controlling outcomes using traditional management practices were actually hurting the organisation, what other ways can a leader ensure success.

This was the foundation for creating the ARC Framework. Outcomes are the results of the dynamic interaction of Activity, Relationship and Context energy, and while traditional management practices focus mostly on Activity and ignore Relationship and Context, the real leverage for creating outcomes is to manage Context.

The shift in paradigm is moving from seeing an organisation as a machine of activity to seeing it as a living being defined and guided by its context. Shifting a paradigm is never easy. It creates internal tension because it is counter instinctual. It goes against everything we ever learned on how to be safe and successful.

An example many may relate to is learning to ski. Everything my instinct knows about going down a steep hill is to lean back into the hill. Leaning forward down the hill will only lead to severe disaster, maybe even death. Dredging down a snow-covered hill on foot is a real drudgery and exhausting.

A much more effective way to get down is on skis. Skis work best when you weight their tips, as this is where you have the most control. It allows you to get down the hill faster with much less effort. The problem is you have to learn to lean downhill, which as we said is something your whole being screams, *"NO, don't do it, you will die."* It is counter instinctual.

The same is true for learning to lead The Living Organisation.

Learning to let go of managing through Activity, and instead manage through Context, is like leaning downhill. Managing through Context will get you greater results, faster with less effort, while providing you the control you need to ensure you fulfill your responsibility.

Learning to lead through Context does not require you to give up what you know, only add on to and expand it.

That is what this book will provide you. A new set of skills that will enhance your ability to create the results that will ensure your organisation grows and thrives. And allow you to do it with more ease and less effort.

Look at the table of our topmost needs, Table 10.2 on P231 and you will see how many of those needs lie in this meaning-making essence of you as a living being. How important to you are your needs for hope, purpose, mastery, or autonomy? Your needs for community, belonging, or altruism? These all show how much of you is anchored in your meaning-making stories. These shape or even create the reality that you experience. All of your skills and capabilities are put to use within the limits and constraints imposed by your meaning-making stories.

The same is true in any organisation. How everything gets deployed to deliver results depends on the dominant meaning-making stories of the organisation and those of each of its individuals. I experienced, during my time (Graham) in P&G, how the dominant meaning-making stories were more powerful in shaping business choices than the purpose statement hanging on the wall.

You, and your organisation, experience a reality that is first and foremost created by your meaning-making stories. You read about the primary power of your meaning-making stories to really understand why you are doing what you are doing, and to change yourself, in Chapters 7 and 8.

Add in the theme of Chapter 4 on how taking the concept of an incorporated organisation to the logical consequence of it being a non-human legal person, and you will readily see why the lens of an organisation as a living being is now essential.

You never can know any living being exactly, so your knowledge of your organisation as a meaning-making being is always under construction (thought form P6). So you can't hope to gather data, then analyse, and then adopt good practice, let alone best practice. Instead, you need to constantly act in small, safe ways; observe how the living being reacts; and then act again[52,53].

Seeing an organisation as living integrates the eternalist and nihilist (Section 2.5, Page 38) "meaningness" views of organisations. An organisation is an inherently nebulous complementary pairing of what is inherently meaningful and knowable with what gets meaning given to it by each of us in an inherently nebulous way. There is no structure or process that can ever eliminate this nebulosity, i.e., no eternalist approach to organisation design. Equally, no laissez-faire structureless, processless (nihilist) approach can work well either.

What you see when you look at your organisation is not what it actually is. How other people are when you are around is not all they are; and you are not the same when others are around you. Very much like quantum physics, observers—your context and others—shape you. This is inherent, not a gap that can be closed by technology, skills, or trying harder.

Following equation 12.1, Wolfe's equation, defined[1] by Norman Wolfe to cap-

---

[1]This equation may well be a useful phenomenological model, or even a useful metaphor, rather than

ture the essence of the living organisation, you can see that the biggest lever you have to deliver with excellence lies in the individual and team meaning-making stories. Context in the equation is these stories, the fluidity in transformational thinking, and the subtlety in managing their emotional states and hard-wired natures.

$$OP = [A \times R^2]^C \qquad (12.1)$$

OP **is output-performance.** These are the business results you deliver, and that are the central reason for your startup to have any right to exist. If you do not deliver the results that society needs with sufficiently high efficiency and profit, your business will rightly experience stress. Then it's up to you to mine and refine the stress for what it's telling you about how you need to either adapt or die. Every business leader's single most important objective is delivering results.

A **is activities.** This is everything around your organisation's activities. Which organisation design you choose falls here. Whether you choose vanilla sociocracy, Sociocracy 3.0, Holacracy, Management 3.0, or you construct your own set of adaptive structures and processes to turn the activities of individuals and teams into business results, everything that is directly around activities lies here. The activities variable includes most of what in integral theory lies in the visible upper right and lower right quadrants.

R **is relationships.** This covers both how individuals are in relationship to each other as human beings, and how different roles and parts of the organisation are in relationship to each other. Most of this variable lies hidden from sight. You do not know exactly what is happening here, and never can know. This variable is inherently nebulous and volatile in nature, because as soon as you look at a relationship, you begin changing it.

C **is context, i.e., meaning-making stories.** Context here is primarily hidden, and even more inherently and irreducibly nebulous, volatile, uncertain, complex, and ambiguous than relationships or activities. Context cannot be any less so than that of each individual's meaning-making stories; rather, putting all individual stories together as multiple complex open systems makes context orders of magnitude more nebulous and VUCA. To lead an organisation to success today, you need to be fluid in all 28 thought forms.

Compare this equation with the six capital types your business depends on, listed in Section 3.1.1. The activity arena is the only one that has a medium to strong

---

a physically precise equation. Even if you don't buy it as exactly true, at least rent it for the duration of this paragraph is a useful metaphor.

dependence on the financial capital. The relationship, and even more so the context arenas are heavily—perhaps only—dependent on the human capitals.

This is why, as we have shifted from a manufacturing to a knowledge economy, and are now moving on to a wisdom economy, the role of human capitals has become far more important to the success of your business than financial capital. So you need far more power *with*, and far less power *over* people, in all four organisational strata (Section 12.7), from the inner individual to the inter-stakeholder.

Since a company is there to multiply capital, it's time to build the multiplication structures and processes for human capital. (And of course natural capital, because then you automatically have a regenerative company for all capitals.)

An essential element is to keep the meaning-making stories driving R and C as visible as the cash flow. Turn them from hidden stories that you are subject to into visible stories that you can make objects of reflection, and that you can transform. You see in more detail how to do this in Chapter 17. In brief, it's adapting and reapplying, to the meaning-making stories of organisations, everything you saw in Chapters 7 and 8 about how to make your own stories visible objects of reflection that you could transform.

Doing this well requires sufficient fluidity in all 28 thought forms, and the ground pattern. In the next chapter, you'll see how to modify the ground pattern to use it effectively in an organisation to surface and then rewrite all meaning-making stories, from every single individual through the teams and verticals, to the entire organisation's meaning-making story. Having sufficient fluidity is vital for any organisation design consultant to work with the inherent nebulosity of an organisation. Lacking it, they will either propose too little structure or will concretise into structure prematurely.

To chunk this down into small enough components to handle, below are a few useful simplifying lenses.

12.4 Conscious Leadership

What is conscious leadership? Is it about the stage of the leader's consciousness, and the kind of leadership of that stage; and then developing yourself to later stages?

I think it is that; but even more: it is the art of leading other conscious, living, meaning-making beings. Both individual human beings as well as the organisation, a non-human living being.

Looking at the organisation and people you are leading as fully conscious opens up a different lens on conscious leadership; and this book is here to make it easier for you to put that into practice.

12.5 Organisational Energy Economy (OEE)

Two of your capitals, when they are in flow and delivering results, are physical energy and psychological energy (Section 3.1). Both are vital for you to do work, and so the single most important thing for you to manage with loving care is your energy. Managing your physical energy is socially more acceptable: if you are physically tired, it's socially acceptable to go to sleep, eat some nourishing food, and exercise.

It's less socially acceptable to take care of your psychological energy, let alone to show the signs of an impending draining of your psychological energy. And yet, if your psychological energy collapses, you will fall far short of your potential until you have rebuilt it. It also takes far longer to rebuild than your physical energy. This is why it is so important for you to get really good at managing your personal energy economy (Section 10.2).

The same is true for your organisation as a whole. As a living being, the physical energy and the psychological energy, i.e., the meaning-making stories, as individuals and as a whole organisation, is the primary capital you convert into results. It is a regenerative capital, and will regenerate so long as you care for it well.

You can have an organisation with perfectly structured roles to optimally execute tasks, but if the energy required is not there or is going primarily into other areas, your organisation will underperform because it is not managing its energy as lovingly as living beings do in nature.

Robert Kegan[81] has introduced the concept of Job 1 and Job 2. Job 1 is what you are doing when you deliver results that build the business. Job 2 is everything else that takes up your energy and effort, and that takes energy and effort away from delivering business results. Job 2 is everything that individuals need to do in order to protect themselves, look good, or survive an organisation environment that is toxic to their human nature. The more that you are putting energy into Job 2, the less you can put into Job 1.

Most of the clients I (Graham) talk to very quickly recognise that people in their organisation are wasting between 30% and 80% of their energy in Job 2.

By looking at an organisation first and foremost as a living being, and recognising that the psychological and physical energy is the foundation for everything in your organisation delivering the business results that your organisation exists for, it becomes perfectly clear that the topmost priority is minimising the amount of energy that is unproductive, i.e., is used up in Job 2, and unavailable for Job 1.

A psychologically safe workplace, where less than 20% of anyone's time and effort is going into Job 2, is the foundation of an organisation that thrives long term, attracts the best talent, and develops all the talent it has into the best.

You and your organisation can rise to the adaptive challenges you are facing and feel hopeful for the future. Divert half of the energy you and your colleagues are currently putting into Job 2 into first making the workplace safe, then into other elements of this book. You will continue to deliver at least the same business results that you are currently delivering and will grow the organisation's performance with no extra time or effort.

You will very quickly create a virtuous spiral, where the amount of energy going into Job 1 steadily increases as the organisation becomes more effective at converting human energy into business output.

Ideally output that regenerates all capitals.

In analogy to the personal energy economy of Section 10.2, think of this as your Organisational Energy Economy. Inefficiencies in your organisational energy economy must be eliminated, and you need to be a superb organisational energy economist to deliver results. If you want to found a startup, you need to continuously increase your mastery both as a personal energy economist and as an organisational energy economist.

This is the business equivalent to the National Happiness approach of Bhutan that you may have read about.

Some very successful firms have used their staff's and all other stakeholders' happiness as the primary strategy. For example, Henry Stewart's *Happy Computers* in the UK[179], who make clear that the central managerial accountability is to ensure that their reports are happy, because happy people are more productive. Oh, and their hierarchy is built bottom up: individuals choose which manager they think will be best able to manage them.

Even in a modern Holacratic Sociocratic organisation, the lead link's central accountability is to build a container for everyone in the circle to have as much energy available for Job 1 as possible and converted into output as efficiently as possible—in other words, to be happy as a living human being at work.

More examples are described by Rüdiger Fox in his book[180]. He applied the concept of the Corporate Happiness Index to turn around an ailing aerospace company in Germany, as well as later companies he has led.

The topmost task of any startup founder, business leader, and everyone else working in an organisation, is to keep a careful eye on where the energy is both helpful and wants to flow, and then help more of it flow and multiply itself. In fact, this is your topmost task in your life.

Watch where your energy wants to flow, get some idea of whether that flow is helpful or harmful to your growth as a human being, and to growing an adaptive, regenerative business. And if it's helpful, get more energy flowing.

12.6 Integral Organisation

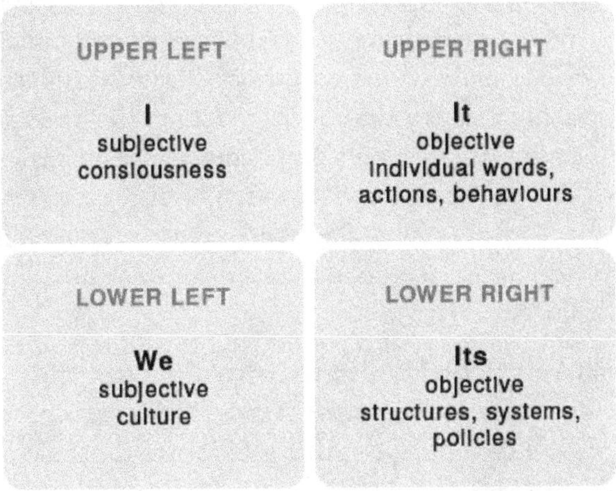

Figure 12.1: The experienced reality of work, the mental space that each person's work occurs in[6].

UPPER LEFT	UPPER RIGHT
I subjective consiousness	**It** objective individual words, actions, behaviours
LOWER LEFT	LOWER RIGHT
We subjective culture	**Its** objective structures, systems, policies

20 years ago, early in my career with P&G, I (Graham) came across the phrase *Culture eats strategy for breakfast.* I learnt to see culture as the final determinant of turning energy into results, after purpose, strategy, structure, processes, people etc. have done their bit. The longer I work in organisations, the more I realise just how true that is, and more importantly, the implications for how to create organisations that thrive in the face of adaptive challenges, and to build a better world.

If a proposed change to the structure, strategy, etc. of an organisation is contrary to the meaning-making stories (culture) which shape and create the reality experienced by all stakeholders, the change is almost certain to fail, and may even break the organisation, no matter how much good the change might bring.

In just the same way that you will usually fail to change a behaviour that your meaning-making stories tell you is wrong, or even harmful, regardless of how logical the new behaviour is.

The diagramme in Figure 12.1 illustrates how it all ties together. This is the standard diagramme from Ken Wilber's integral model. This captures quite clearly why culture is the biggest lever, and why I regard an organisation as a living being.

Upper Right (UR): Visible Individual All the output your business delivers lies in the upper right quadrant. This is the quadrant where all visible activities of every single individual and the organisation lie. All output is ultimately individuals turning their energy into output through acting, and what they do is driven by the other three quadrants. Every action is compliant with the forces of the lower right, lower left, or upper left quadrants.

Lower Right (LR): Visible Collective Lower right is the other visible quadrant. This is where everything tangible related to your organisation lies. Your visible organisational structure lies here, your organisational chart as it stands on paper lies here, your explicit rules and policies lie here. In any of the Ocracies the circle structure, and the explicitly stated role domains, accountabilities, and drivers lie here. Your explicitly declared company strategy lies here. This quadrant drives compliance through the use of explicit rewards and punishments to impose adherence to prescribed structures, processes, and relationships. The Management Accountability Hierarchy (MAH) describes the organisation when you look at it through a lens showing this quadrant.

Upper Left (UL): Hidden Individual Upper left is where individuals' unique meaning-making stories, values, biases, personal energy economy lies; along with everything else that is hidden and nebulous. If everything you do in your personal upper right is fully in accord with your upper left, all of your activities are compliant with your meaning-making essence as a human being. Your conscience, sense of guilt and shame drive one side of your compliance; your sense of joy, mastery etc. drive the other side.

Lower Left (LL): Hidden Collective Lower left is where the organisation's culture lies, your collective meaning-making stories, as well as the nebulous, invisible organisation structure and hierarchy that enables you and your colleagues to deliver results despite visible organisation structures, hierarchy, rules and regulations that block you from delivering results. The actual, implicit company strategy lies here. Upper right actions are often compliant with lower left. If you look at it through a lens that highlights this quadrant, you see an organisation to be a Human Capability Hierarchy (HCH).

Culture eats strategy for breakfast summarises clearly that the driving forces are far stronger in the hidden, left than the visible lower right quadrants. The primary driver of what you and your colleagues do at work is everything that you cannot see, is nebulous, and where the only data that you have lies in your nebulous feelings.

The biggest lever you have to improve your business output is a nebulous, invisible one.

These quadrants capture perfectly how inherently, irreducibly uncertain and nebulous any organisation is. Each organisation is at once inseparably both lower right and lower left, and each quadrant apart has validity. Looking at this through the lens of a quantum physicist, they look analogous to the complementary pairs of a photon.

Some approaches look at an organisation as just the lower right MAH, and everything lower left is a consequence of the lower right. In other words, once you get the visible organisation design, hierarchy, roles and circles, policies, and statutes of incorporation right, as an MAH, the organisational culture will fall into place.

Other approaches say that once you get the organisation's culture to be healthy, the most effective and efficient organisational design, an HCH, will emerge.

Looking at this as a quantum physicist, I can only conclude that an organisation is both HCH and MAH; and more, in an inherently nebulous, unknowable fashion.

Perhaps we never can describe clearly what an organisation is, but only what we can say about what it is; just as physics is the study of what we can say about what is, not the study of what is.

Similarly, the best we can say about an organisation is that it is somehow both lower left and lower right, in a nebulous, contradictory way that we will never be able to pin down precisely in all dimensions and details. Just like an electron.

If you choose to look at your organisation through a lens that gives you maximum knowledge of the lower right, you will have the least or even no knowledge of the lower left. And vice versa. They are complementary pairs.

The best you can do with such complementary quantum pairs in physics is defined by Heisenberg's uncertainty principle. There is a similar analogy to the uncertainty principle at work here too. Just as the uncertainty in quantum physics is an inherent uncertainty in nature, so too is this an inherent uncertainty in the organisation. The organisation itself does not and cannot consciously know everything that is happening in the lower left quadrant. As soon as you even look at the lower left quadrant, it will change, and what the lower right quadrant is actually driving in behavioural compliance of individuals will immediately begin changing away from what it was.

Looking at organisations as living meaning-making beings integrates lower left and lower right, just as looking at yourself as a living meaning-making being integrates upper left and upper right.

If you want better results, you and all your colleagues need to become more effective and efficient at converting your human energy into results. This means you need to work with the internal reality of the workplace that each of you constructs from the hidden individual and collective meaning-making stories.

Lower left compliance in most workplaces is a more powerful driver of your internal workplace experience and your actual productivity than lower right compliance (culture eats strategy). Perhaps the only workplace where lower right compliance is a more powerful driver is in slavery, and similar workplaces.

Look at the difference between the experienced work reality of each individual, i.e., their inner workplace, and the outer workplace that lies in the upper and lower right quadrants; it should become immediately clear to you how inherently nebulous designing the optimal organisation is. You simply cannot measure everything important, and not everything you can measure is important, as Einstein would have put it. Even more, once you have measured it, or even talked about it with a consultant, it has been changed by the process of measuring.

This also makes clear that improving results has relatively little to do with skills and competencies and far more to do with the developmental nature of each individual, covered in Chapters 7 to 11. All the work that you and your colleagues do comes from the self-constructed reality of each of your inner workplaces.

Another consequence of this is that there is no empirical justification for segmenting the members of your business into distinct categories like employees, managers, customers, investors, suppliers, family and community etc. The organisation as a whole is both lower left HCH and upper right MAH like any other living being, a constantly nebulous, undefinable flux shaped by the interactions of all stakeholders with each other across all four quadrants.

To do justice to what an organisation actually is, especially in today's world where we need Adaptive Organisations with their full power and developmental capacity, we need to re-examine all of our current stories of what a workplace is, from the legal stakeholder level structures, the visible and invisible MAH and HCH, and each individual's developmental essence as a living, meaning-making being.

As you structure your organisation, by looking at it as a living, meaning-making being, a scaled-up version of yourself, it ought to be clear that any mismatch between an organisation's structure or process and the organisation's stories will be expensive, at best, and at worst lead to collapse.

12.7 Four layers, three dimensions in an organisation

In many ways the Adaptive Organisation and the Living Organisation are synonyms. I refer to a living organisation when I want to emphasise the nebulous, impossible to pin down essence of a living, meaning-making being. I refer to an Adaptive Organisation when I want to highlight the driver for that organisation to exist lies in its capacity to rise to adaptive challenges that require changing the collective and individual meaning-making stories creating the organisation's reality and identity.

If you look at an adaptive living organisation only through the lens of complex adaptive systems, you are blind to these meaning-making stories as the most powerful things that shape the organisation's reality.

Since most of these stories are hidden, you can only get at them if you use the living organisation lens, pay very careful attention, and do a lot of subtle detective work to deduce them without causing major disturbances in the process.

Four layers

An organisation has four layers, the lowest four layers listed in Section 2.8.

4 Inter-organisational How stakeholders at the big picture level are dealt with. First and foremost here is the choice of legal incorporation, and then the processes used during general meetings and any other forum where stakeholders and the company interact with each other. The FairShares Commons incorporation is the best I currently know of for almost all kinds of entities, except perhaps a pure trust, or a wholly owned subsidiary of a FairShares Commons.

3 Inner-organisational How work gets done, and tasks deliver results. This spans how tasks are organised, the organisation design and power hierarchy, the visible decision-making processes, in fact, everything that is sometimes narrowly defined to be "the organisation". Sociocracy, Holacracy, and other forms of dynamic organisation design or governance do this well.

2 Inter-personal How individual human beings interact with each other, their relationships, and how they bond into teams to pool their collective energy and activity into delivering bigger results than any one of them could ever have done alone. The Evolutesix Adaptive Way for teams increases the organisation's effectiveness really well.

1 Inner-personal How individuals and groups of people interact, how they develop themselves, and how they are in relationship to each other. The Adaptive Way for individuals also does this really well, covered in Part III.

Looking at these four layers through the living organisation lens, you can see that each layer contributes in different ways to the three elements of Equation 12.1. Each layer is essential for the entire organisation to be fully alive. If any layer is constrained in its freedom to live, the organisation as a whole is constrained in its capacity to thrive and deliver the output expected of it.

Each of these four layers and the interfaces between them must be optimised for whatever challenges we are facing. Most of our past experience is in optimising them to face and thrive in a world of technical challenges, experience holding us back now, when building an adaptive living organisation that can thrive in a world of adaptive challenges requires a very different optimisation. An adaptive living organisation, with all layers at full strength, is the ultimate learning organisation[181].

Regardless of whether your organisation is only optimised for technical challenges or also for adaptive challenges, these four layers can only change within the constraints imposed by your organisation's meaning-making stories.

This is especially relevant if you are leading an organisation that's optimised to overcome technical challenges, and have decided to transform all four layers to become an Adaptive Organisation with the potential to thrive in the adaptive challenges ahead of you. You are unlikely to be making this journey unless you work simultaneously on making the meaning-making stories of the living organisation lens visible, growing them to become bigger and more adaptive, and only changing any of the four layers within the boundaries of your stories.

I have seen many well-intentioned leaders recognise the imperative for their organisation to become an adaptive one and dive headfirst into the deep end of changing only one of these four layers, immediately rolling out the flavour-of-the-month approach from the top down. All too often these attempts crash and burn, because the meaning-making stories of the individuals and the organisation as a whole do not support this approach, or they support the "why and what", but not the "how" of the path of change[2].

One example that comes to mind is typical of many. The organisation was a small consultancy, formed by a group of people in their early 30s who had a very clear vision to create a company that was different to any traditional consultancy. In many ways they were at the cutting edge of visionary experimentation towards Adaptive Organisations. The personal energy economics (described in section 10.2) of the founders was superbly complementary. During the very first meeting I had with them, I pointed out how they could form a superhuman if they figured out how to put Peter Drucker's dictum fully into practice, by organising and collaborating in such a way that their strengths were made fully productive and their weaknesses irrelevant. They could have been the model case study of an adaptive living organisation.

Unfortunately, their living organisation had other deeply hidden and more powerful meaning-making stories in it. These were stories about what it meant to succeed and fail, stories about vulnerability, safety,

---

[2]Organisations are clearly not ergodic. Where you are now depends crucially on the path you took from where you were, and very little on the characteristics of where you were and where you are.

> and security. Stories harming their aspiration to flourish by standing together in their common oneness in ways that supported each individual's uniqueness.
>
> The organisation imploded less than a year after they began seriously implementing Holacracy, leaving a shadow of its full potential still living. The living organisation's dominant hidden stories created the reality that everybody experienced, and it was not one that people were willing to live in.

I've experienced this time and time again in organisations that I have worked with, and people who I've spoken to.

On the other hand, the success stories I've heard fall into two categories. Either the meaning-making story of the living organisation was big enough and ready enough for the change destination and path, so it welcomed the change and the change worked. Or, the change or the path did not fit into the organisation's meaning-making story, and the change agents recognised this soon enough to dial back the change to something that did fit within the living organisation's meaning-making story. And then step-by-step grow the story just before taking the next step along the path to organisational change.

How adaptive is your organisation?

If your organisation is going to thrive because it can rise to the adaptive challenges ahead of it, you need to know how adaptive it is. The rest of this chapter will enable you to understand just this.

Darwin recognised that whenever any life form no longer fits the context and need, or driver, of its niche in the ecosystem, the conflict created provides both the direction and the motivation for change. In the language of Darwin's time, this was the meaning of survival of the fittest. It had nothing to do with how many currently perceive his words, that the stronger and more aggressive you are, the better you will survive. Darwin was quite clear that if the best fit to a niche in the ecosystem lay in altruistic collaboration, the species most able to collaborate altruistically would thrive.

The conflict in and between these four layers contains valuable data on where you and your organisation are poor fits to the driver of your niche in society and its economy. The bigger your adaptive capacity, the more likely you are to be able to mine and refine this data to evolve at least as fast as your niche is moving.

There is conflict within each layer. (And, more complex, between layers.)

1. The stakeholder arena, where the conflict between the different stakeholder interests and meaning-making stories.

2. The task arena, where human energy gets transformed into business results.

3. The interpersonal arena, between two or more people in an organisation. This is where the organisation's culture is created and is the primary shaper of the reality that the organisation as a whole experiences.

4. The personal arena, the conflict inside you between the different facets of who you are.

All four conflict arenas are at the heart of the challenges humanity is facing. Until we figure out how to do what nature has done so well from the beginning of life on the planet, namely mine and refine conflict as the driver for how to evolve to face the adaptive challenges, we will fail to sufficiently address our climate crisis.

I am optimistic, because we already have clarity on what to do in each of these four conflict arenas. We already have more than enough success stories of individuals and organisations who have used one or more pillars to increase their organisation's adaptive capacity. An excellent example of someone practising this, harnessing conflict individually and in his organisation, is Ray Dalio[96], the founder and CEO of Bridgewater, one of the world's largest hedge funds.

Three dimensions

The capacity needed for a living organisation to be healthy in all four layers requires the right structures and processes in each of the three dimensions of Figure 12.2. The following three chapters deal with each dimension in turn.

The key message to keep in mind as you read each of those chapters: to create an Adaptive Organisation, or Teal, or whatever name you prefer, you need to aim for Level 5 on each axis.

Take psychological safety, for example. Some organisations attempt to deliver that by working on the culture—the human axis. Yes, that's where psychological safety lies; but you cannot create long-lasting antifragile psychological safety if your roles and tasks dimension is less than Level 2 Self-Managing; nor if your incorporation is anything less than a Level 2 worker coop. And even having both of these on level 2 is barely adequate for psychological safety.

If you really want antifragile, long-lasting psychological safety—at the level you need to maximise the Job 1 energy—you need to strive for Level 5 incorporation (Free company / FairShares Commons) and at least a self-directing Level 4 in roles and tasks.

This is why so many efforts to create humane, self-managing, or deliberately

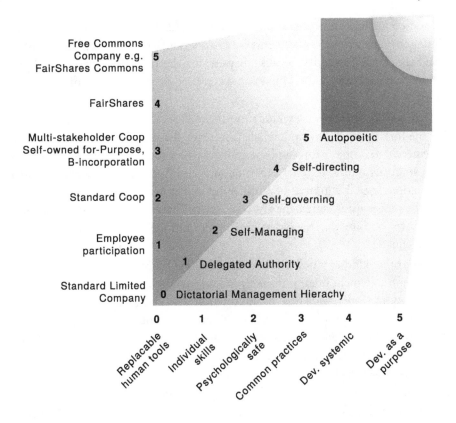

Figure 12.2: The three dimensions of an organisation. Most of the possible points your organisation could sit at are at best only stable for a short period, at worst extremely fragile.

developmental organisations fail. They act in only one dimension, maybe two, but miss the third. Most commonly the incorporation is the missing dimension.

Move forwards on all three; moving far on just one or two is recklessly fragile.

12.8 The vision and purpose problem

Losing connection with the source (Section 13.2), the driver to becoming a living being, is the reason why many organisations have run into trouble with their purpose and / or vision statements in today's world.

Very few businesses have a vision statement that is of any use in creating an organisation with long-term viability. Most vision statements are visionless. They say something like *we want to be the best in the world.* There's nothing wrong with aiming to excel, but vision statements are dysfunctional in facing the global adaptive challenges we all face today, because they create a sharp divide between everybody inside the organisation / the winners, and everybody outside the organisation / the losers.

Such vision statements exclude most possibilities for collaboration, and meeting the human needs of bonding, altruism, etc., listed in Table 10.2. Any vision statement that is not inviting and energising to every single stakeholder in the business: staff, customers, suppliers, their families and descendants, the communities and nations they live in; is at best unhelpful and at worst harmful. By excluding sharply, such a vision statement sows the seeds of business collapse from day one. It's not for nothing that the oldest organisations in the world are centred around all stakeholders.

The other kind of vision statement articulates clearly some ideal better world. This vision statement is far more likely to lead to long-term viability, and to invite contributions from a wide pool of stakeholders who all sign up to that vision of a better world. The problem with such a vision statement is that it easily becomes concretised. The vision statement takes on an independent life of its own and continues to drive, unquestioningly, the activities of the business and everybody in it, long after its sell-by date.

Purpose statements are a significant improvement on many vision statements that are out there. For example, during my time (Graham) at P&G's stated purpose was *improving the lives of the world's consumers.* That clarity of purpose was one of the initial attractions for me of working there. A consequence of that clarity of purpose was the very clear recognition that the consumer was boss. If the consumer data pointed at one option, and an individual in senior management demanded that the team choose a different option, we seldom needed much discussion, once we had solid data on the consumer preference.

However, the longer I worked in P&G, the more I began to realise just how the choices we were actually making were also being shaped by a dominant hidden story. This dominant hidden story was meeting the quarterly investor expectations, and delivering total shareholder return (TSR). It became clearer that this quarterly TSR focus was sometimes leading us to make choices that were not truly in the interests of the world's consumers today, next year, and seldom good for future generations.

That purpose statement was very close to being a driver statement; it was implicitly anchored in the external world. But because it lacked a clear articulation of the external context and need, it was nearly impossible to recognise when the dominant TSR story was, so shaping the reality we experienced that it was no longer anchored in meeting the external need; and no longer aligned with our purpose.

The current push towards for-purpose enterprises is a huge step forwards vs. the traditional approach of not defining a purpose in the statutes, leaving it to be deemed as TSR. We can do even better: the evolutionary enterprise with the explicit driver. This addresses an Achilles heel of for-purpose and perpetual purpose companies: what happens to a perpetual purpose company when something big changes in the context and need that that purpose exists to meet, if it loses connection with that driver?

12.9 First drivers, then objectives and purpose

The rise of the for-purpose organisation is one of the most important developments over the past decade. In most countries, company law makes clear that an organisation exists to fulfil its purpose, and the executives' fiduciary duty is to maximise the organisation's capacity to fulfil its purpose.

However, few founders have their organisation's purpose clearly stated in the legal documents of incorporation. And so, when things have ended up in court, lawyers and judges have needed to come up with a definition of what the implicit purpose then is. Given the nature of the neoclassical economics meaning-making story, the default was that the organisation's purpose was to maximise total shareholder return.

More founders are now perfectly clear that you cannot leave defining the organisation's purpose in the hands of lawyers after things have gone wrong. You must express it very clearly before you even incorporate it.

When Dee Hock[182] was creating Visa during the 1960s to bond all of the world's players in the emerging credit card industry, he was able to do that because he had a very clear idea of the context and need, making it easy to define a purpose that aligned all stakeholders.

Hock later coined the term "chaordic" to describe the process he used to find the purpose of Visa and create the organisation. He had realised that in nature, the best evolutionary leaps emerge right on the boundary between order and chaos. He recognised clearly that evolution anchors itself in the immediate context and whatever is needed within that context. I read his book, *One from Many: Visa and the Rise of Chaordic organisation*[182] every few years, and every time I read it I uncover deeper brilliance in his insights.

The starting point of Dee Hock's Chaordic Organisation I call *the driver*, to my knowledge first named as such in Sociocracy 3.0[183]. The driver comes before any purpose. The driver is the combination of the current environment and the need calling to be met. The purpose is then trivial: to always meet the need, within the constraints and possibilities of the current environment.

Anchoring yourself and your organisation in a driver, rather than a purpose, keeps the organisation at the emergent edge of evolution. The driver statement is a tool enabling an organisation work with its evolutionary purpose (see Frederic Laloux's book *Reinventing organizations*[184]).

Explicitly stating the driver in the statutes addresses a weakness in almost all purpose statements I have seen: the loss of contact with the changes to the driver the original external founders' first concretised into a purpose. In the worst case this loss of contact means a business putting all its resources and energy into continuing to fulfil a purpose long after the driver has ceased to exist, the purpose irrelevant, and so becoming a zombie company eating investors and staff.

We are strongly for going beyond a for-purpose company to an evolutionary enterprise, where the company's strategic objectives and legally anchored objects are stated in terms of the evolutionary driver.

12.10 Changing a living organisation

> *One is led to a new notion of unbroken wholeness which denies the classical idea of analysability of the world into separately and independently existing parts. We have reversed the usual classical notion that the independent elementary parts of the world are the fundamental reality, and the various systems are merely particular contingent forms and arrangements of these parts. Rather, we say that the inseparable quantum interconnectedness of the whole universe is the fundamental reality, and the relatively independently behaving parts are merely particular on contingent forms within this whole.*
>
> —David Bohm, Physicist

Given everything that you have read so far, you might be asking yourself,

so how on earth do you even begin changing an organisation?

As Jack and I were writing this book, the above quote from David Bohm was very present in what we were doing. David Bohm later left physics and pioneered a dialogue process that enabled people to experience their common interconnected oneness as primary. Not the only physicist to move into dialogue processes!

Do you see an organisation as primarily many individual human beings that just happen to be in and serving it, or do you see an organisation as primarily the web of interconnections and activity, in which the people who are there just happen to occupy key points in the interconnected oneness? Do you see an organisation deriving its nature because of the people, or the people deriving their nature because of the organisation?

The reality you create and experience in your organisation, especially in any attempt to change it, will depend on which meaning-making stories you use.

It has become clearer over the past few decades that it's often far more accurate to say that the reality of an organisation is the indeterminate, spread-out continuum of interconnections; the processes that move and change things from A to B; the relatedness of different aspects; the relationship between the people; the interactivity between people and between roles; and how all of that can be and is in constant transformation.

This means that when anything needs changing, the biggest levers to create that change, and therefore the place to start, lie everywhere. The most powerful though lie in the collective and individual meaning-making stories, and growing each individual's Size of Person.

Compare that to the change process that you typically find today in organisations, primarily centred on the people. Often starting by replacing the CEO.

The corollary of this is the belief that we need to pay individual CEOs extremely high remuneration packages.

If the whole organisation's interconnectedness is the fundamental reality, and the relatively independently behaving people are merely particular forms within this whole (multiple thought forms from Chapter 9 are used here), then it doesn't really matter which CEO is in place, so long as they have the right developmental Size of Person, skill set, and motivation to be a strong connector in the CEO role constituted by the pre-existing relatedness created by the organisation. The CEO themself is just background. The foreground is everything else, including the entire organisation as a living being.

The behaviour of individuals derives its nature from the whole, as an expression of the whole. Paradoxically, this actually makes it easier to work with behaviour in organisations when changes are needed.

To improve results, especially for the long term, shift from looking at individuals to looking at the whole as a living being, and as an inseparably interconnected nebulous intangible ecosystem.

First of all, because it eliminates the entire paradigms of individual blame and shame. This immediately shifts, into productive effort, all the time and energy people put into preventing themselves getting into situations where they might be blamed for something, protecting their vulnerabilities, looking good at work, impressing the boss, etc.

Secondly, instead of a large number of managers and HR professionals trying to get to grips with every single individual in the organisation, and how to change each individual in the organisation, the focus becomes setting up an organisational condition that naturally has the behaviour you need because that behaviour is simply the most probable behaviour. The behaviour equivalent to a particle in physics moving in a straight line because no force is acting on it.

Just as you read in Chapter 7.4 about having optimised who you are today as the best possible living being you could be to overcome the challenges of your past, so too your organisation as it is today is optimised for its past challenges. Not for its current challenges, let alone its future challenges.

Unless your organisation is firmly anchored in the external challenges of today, you run a high risk of disappearing in the near future. If you want it to thrive long-term, you cannot do better today than anchor yourself in the best possible understanding of the challenges that the future will bring.

This means anchoring your organisation in a relevant driver statement: the external context and need your organisation chooses to meet. Regularly check for changes in the external context or need, and immediately update the driver statement to match. Put an expiry date (or expiration in the US) into your driver statements, to trigger that checking process on regular intervals. Without an expiry date, it's all too easy for you to lose sight of the original driver, concretise the purpose that comes out of that driver, and then continue to act on the purpose, even though it's no longer as relevant to your success (thought form P6).

Changing existing organisations to this way of working is, in many cases, a bigger challenge than starting a new organisation. Changing requires you to first get your company back to zero before you can build it up to a new place. Once your organisation has been running for any significant length of time, you have investors on board, the story that defines who your company is and how people interact with each other has embedded itself and attracts people who reinforce that story.

Figure 12.3 depicts what often makes surviving a change impossible, and how many things behave when you try to change them. You can see here the path that many organisations will go on. The organisation begins at zero and climbs in an S-curve to wherever it is now. The vertical axis represents profitable business output. The x-axis represents staff engagement, and how much energy they are putting into their work.

You can see in the upper curve, with the arrow going back, that initially em-

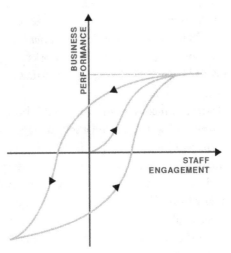

Figure 12.3: Hysteresis. As staff engagement, motivation and Job 2 energy loss changes, this is the path business performance moves along over time: from funding the startup to maturity, then the response to a threatening change, and the recovery. Or collapse, more likely, as few businesses ever recover from the leftmost point.

ployee engagement and effort drops significantly before there is any measurable impact on business performance. By the time the curve has dropped far enough for senior management to have clear data that something is seriously wrong, average engagement has gone through zero and continues to plummet.

By the time the consultants have been brought in, analyses have been made, and a plan of action is in place, staff engagement is even lower. If it is a good plan, staff engagement begins to rise. But, critically, it rises along the lower curve. It does not go back along the upper curve. This means that while staff engagement begins to move towards the positive, it needs significant growth before there is any business-relevant increase in output.

In many businesses the wealth of social capital (patience, trust in senior management and the investors, etc.) and financial capital has already been so far depleted before action is taken to get productivity above the line, and back into sustainable profit, before the company collapses.

This is why it is very hard, after you have cast the first foundation stone, for any of the approaches described in these chapters to fix the problems. Start when you found the company, not when you finally realise you are in trouble.

It is also important to guard against any of your cognitive biases, leading you to believe what is false[136]. You may only have one, at most two attempts; do not waste them. Protecting yourself against sleight of hand, illusion, and the seductive appeal of false certainty[172] is an ongoing application of thought form P6; and gets harder the more your business drivers are Cynefin complex or chaotic.

A book that shaped my thinking on how self-governing could deliver extraordinary business results, and that guided me (Graham) when I took over the section in Beijing P&G, is Tracey Kidder's, *The Soul of a New Machine*[185], the story of how a team of computer geeks in a skunkworks program created the 32-bit minicomputer that could have built the bridge for Data General to become a successful company in today's PC era.

I strongly recommend you read this book if you are working within an existing company, and want to build a self-managing team, especially if you have the hope that this will be the positive disruptor that turns your whole organisation into a self-managing team. The book tells the story of how the team leader, Tom West, created a story within the team where they were or on a hero's journey to save the company from the recently released VAX of Digital Equipment Corporation. The book also tells the story of the brutal political battles he needed to fight to make sure that the team was protected from the rest of Data General.

The team's success in delivering what nobody thought could be delivered, their beating (time, resource usage, and final profitability) the official team developing what management had intended would be the VAX beater, lay in Tom West running the team according to some of the principles we have just discussed.

I believe that a key reason why Data General was unable to use this success as its bridge into being one of today's most successful companies in the computer world lies in its management not recognising the power of this way of working. And I believe the reason for that lies in it having a traditional incorporation. Read the update, published 20 years after the team delivered its computer, in Wired[186].

Just one story of organisations failing because they have been optimised to rise to technical challenges. We will never be able to rise to the global adaptive challenges we are all facing today if we continue trying to do the same as we've done before, only harder. Throwing more money at our current adaptive challenges is only going to make them worse, unless we work with our businesses as adaptive living beings.

CHAPTER 13

Your organisation is its people

Every child is an artist. The problem is how to remain an
artist once [you] grow up.

—Pablo Picasso

13.1 Where your organisation is: human

The six stages of organisational development given here were developed by one of us (Graham) and Bernhard Possert. You will be able to read more about these in a forthcoming book, and can download the latest white paper on these from us, or access the online diagnostic via our websites[1].

The list below gives you an idea of where your organisation is now.

5: Learning as a purpose. Development in its own right is a purpose of both the organisation and the individual, with developmental activities extending as far beyond formal organisation boundaries as is helpful. The organisation is designed in full recognition that only an open system in continuous nebulous, unknowable transformation can provide the high level of learning needed to fully fulfil the organisation's and individual's learning purposes.

All employees participate systematically in improving the processes to promote development. People invite others to trigger them, in order to support development by creating developmental tension and conflict situations. Challenging assignments and colleagues are actively sought in order to pro-

---

[1] This chapter was sponsored by the Consorticon Group

mote individual development. People stay within their roles only as long as they are developing, subject to business needs.

4: A learning system. The organisation works on all the collective meaning-making stories, continuously refining them according to context, strengthening them where they are a helpful representation of actuality, and chipping away at them where they are a poor, unhelpful representation of actuality. The organisation uses a common language and has clearly articulated principles for development. Everyone has the duty to surface tension, conflict, potentially dysfunctional or misaligned behaviours, using developmental and neutral languages like NVC and deconstructive dialogue, and then process them to facilitate development.

The organisation's values and principles are laid down clearly, and misaligned behaviour is treated seriously using structured dialogue processes to facilitate development. Hierarchy of power, age, expertise, background, etc. does not automatically give legitimacy to opinions, rather they are evaluated according to an appropriate frame of reference and the content. Conflicts are seen as a source of development, and there is a clear process to learn from them.

3: Common learning practices People are matched to roles according to the fit: Size of Role vs. Size of Person, the person's natural energy versus the role's requirements, the person's skills versus the role's requirements, and any other consideration relevant to the individual and the organisation maximising their capacity to thrive as independent living beings.

Leadership shares vulnerability, actively role models and strengthens the entire organisation as a psychologically safe space, where showing emotions is safe and supported. Exposing your limitations is encouraged and safe. Errors are actively harnessed, in the cultural norms, and in the structures, processes, and policies, for their developmental potential. Everyone, and the system, supports each other in achieving their personal goals. Structured practices and dialogue patterns are used for giving and receiving feedback.

2: Psychologically safe for personal development. How meaning-making stories shape the experienced realities, and how they can hold someone back, is understood and applied in personal developmental processes. People have an understanding of their personal developmental goals, and implications of these, in all three axes and actively work on developing themselves.

People know how to get support for their personal development from their peers, mentors, and coaches. People are able to recognise and evaluate when they are acting defensively, the vulnerability that their meaning-making says needs protection, and can foster a positive climate to engage in this. Social skills facilitating interaction, cognitive depth, and other areas of personal development are visibly and clearly recognised as necessary to progress in the organisation.

1: Individual skills, strengths There are various organisation level programmes and support to foster individuals developing their personal strengths. The diverse workforce's uniquely different talents, and the consequences that these differences have, is valued and actively turned into productive strengths using development processes. People have competency or skill developmental goals, and the organisation knows which skills they expect their employees to be able to use at which level of competency.

0: Short-term gain. Differences are not accepted let alone valued. Development is not part of work, it's a waste of time and money. People are either good for their job or not, they are an anonymous and easy to replace resource without any loss to the organisation from firing and hiring. The organisation is psychologically dangerous, with significant amounts of individual's energy going into Job 2, protecting themselves, including the need for significant amounts of recovery time outside work.

13.2 Source

At the beginning of anything new is a source[187]. Every startup needs one person, sometimes two, very rarely more, to be the source. The source plays a critical role at every potential transformation point in the company's journey. For Apple, Steve Jobs was the source. When Steve Jobs was fired from Apple, there was nobody who was capable of picking up the source role that Apple needed—someone with the exceptional farsighted view of long-term trends that Steve had. Apple shrank steadily until the company rehired him. With the source back in the company, the stream of innovation began flowing again.

The role of source is partly inside and partly outside the company. Their primary accountability is to anchor themselves far enough into the cloudy, nebulous emergent future. They must anchor themselves outside, not inside the company. And this must be something that is so natural to them as a living being that they cannot do otherwise.

In that sense, the source may well be the same person for multiple companies, or business units in a conglomerate. In P&G, I (Graham) met a few people who were extraordinarily powerful sources and worked across multiple business units.

One who I knew and admired was the source for products that turned into billion-dollar brands across many of P&G's business units, from dental care to nappies.

In the traditional world of startups, most sources run at a fraction of their capacity, because they are the founders of one startup and spend huge amounts of time doing everything necessary to start up the business operations. This means we can be very hopeful that we will find ways of dealing with our impending crises as soon as we focus, as I propose in this book and am doing via Evolutesix, on investing in and incubating regenerative ecosystems of adaptive living businesses.

Because all the businesses are using the same FairShares Commons approach, along with multiple elements we will cover in this chapter, a single source can do that role for many companies in the ecosystem. Once the source has sufficient clarity on what it is they are seeing in the nebulous future as a potential business concept, and can tell the story of the emerging future sufficiently concretely and visibly for the first follower to engage, people start coming together.

Every business begins with a meaning-making story flowing from a source person. Every successful business change begins by transforming the old story into a new one.

13.3 Coming together

This is where foundations are laid for a successful Adaptive Organisation to form and deliver the business concept with excellence through multiple pivots and transformations—or not.

People come to an organisation because its central story connects with enough of their individual stories and inner motivators. So long as enough of their personal meaning-making story fits within the organisation's meaning-making story and its tangible structures and processes, they are highly likely to stay and contribute value. So at the beginning of any organisation, the more clearly and unambiguously the source is able to craft and communicate the organisation's central stories (in other words its deep evolutionary purpose), the more likely the source is to have just the right people coming together to bring the organisation to life.

I (Graham) have seen the source disappearing like a stream vanishing into a hot desert, in my own startups, and in companies that I have consulted for, because the founding team coming together resulted in individual and collective meaning-making stories that could not fully embrace the message the source was bringing.

Sadly the source themself often sows the seeds for this, because they do not always have a large enough Size of Person to be able to do the job that a source is there to do.

Mining and refining inner and interpersonal conflict from before a founding team even begins to talk about working together, through until long after the founding team ceases to work together, is the best way of creating thriving startups. Do this with the on-the-job, just-in-time, accelerated development of team and individual performance (at no extra cost and no extra time) described in Section 13.7.4.

If you are a source, a founder, or anyone else forming a team, there are two questions you need to ask. Get good answers to these questions, and the probability that you will fly is high. Get poor answers to these questions, and the probability that you will tank is equally high.

Individuals. What natural talents, spread of personal natural energies, and skills do I need on the team? What minimum and maximum Size of Person (SoP) is appropriate for the adaptive challenges we will be facing?

Teams. What is the right balance between team and individual perspectives, and what do we need to do to turn the individuals into a team?

Comparisons of teams and organisations that consistently deliver top-level results show that most businesses get the answers to these questions wrong. The role of individual talent is seriously overrated.

A team of competent but average individuals will typically outperform the same number of top talented individuals who haven't really bonded into a team. So if you are a source, or a team leader of any nature, emphasise bringing together people who can function quickly and effectively as a single team because their meaning-making stories and Sizes of Person match, rather than a collection of prima donnas who struggle to bond into a single team.

Make sure that you have one or two people on the team who cannot not open their mouths, even if it lands them in trouble. During my (Graham) time transforming Edgetalents (a strategy and organisation design consultancy specialising in impact and social enterprises in India, Kenya, Brazil and Colombia), we had a couple of people who were really good at bonding and bringing harmony to the team, and a few who did not hesitate to open their mouths. This combination brought just the right mix of conflict to make sure that we missed nothing important, and the team dynamic to then mine and refine the value that conflict.

In that team, we initially had very clear boundaries, with everyone knowing who was on and who was off the team. As we grew, that clarity weakened, and it was a reason why performance began dropping. As you form your team, be ruthlessly clear about who is on the core team and who is not. Be equally clear in the startup's early phase that you have the best chance of success only if the team's nucleus is committed. Not just committed in their alignment with what you're trying to do, but most importantly in all their working time and much of their private time. Be very wary of trying to succeed with a large team of people each working less than half of their time.

Paradoxically, just as you would expect from a book using relativity, quantum physics, and Cubism as a guideline to how we should think about business, the best teams need a few people who are absolutely not team players.

You can read more on why focusing on hiring the right individual is far less likely to give you the team you need to deliver excellent results in the HBR article of Diane Coutu[188] on why teams don't work, and by Bill Taylor on why great people are overrated[189,190].

A wide range of different studies have demonstrated clearly that the star's performance, whether it's a top-performing CEO, a Wall Street analyst, or a startup founder, has far more to do with the team around them, and the company's culture, structures, and processes than with their own individual talent. For example, Groysberg[191] looked at 1,000 star analysts at Wall Street investment banks. He saw without any doubt that whenever any of them changed firms their performance dropped immediately and stayed lower than before; except if they changed to a firm that had overall better teams, culture, structures and processes; or if they took their entire team with them.

The other significant exception was when a woman changed companies. Perhaps more women these days are inherently better at landing in a new team and facilitating the team bonding better, thereby increasing everyone's performance. So if you are an investor, you may well do better investing in female rather than in male founders, at least until everything in this book becomes standard practice amongst everyone.

And if you are a founder or source or any other kind of team or circle leader, take hope from the evidence that the war for talent is a myth[192]. There are more than enough highly talented individuals around. Don't waste your time or money trying to find the one person that you imagine will be so talented that they will fix everything that is a mess in your organisation. Attract people who can bond quickly to become one high-performance team.

And then focus your effort on growing a living organisation.

13.4 Growing a living organisation

Sadly most startups, and businesses attempting to transform themselves towards becoming an Adaptive Organisation, focus on the activities variable of Equation 12.1. Traditional companies train people in yet another flavour-of-the-month skill or organisational redesign, or perhaps change from one software to another, typically hiring a consultant specialised in a single aspect of the Activity variable. Sad, because this is the smallest lever you have to do your job of delivering superb business results.

The biggest lever that you have lies in transforming each individual's meaning-making stories and those of the whole team: the Context, or C variable.

Linked to this, your second biggest lever is in developing high-performance collaborative relationships between people as living human beings in your organisation. Relationships that are highly collaborative, in the sense of reciprocal helping (Section 13.6.3), and that have high interactivity (Section 13.6.3).

This means focusing your efforts first on the human dimension, and putting in place the minimum viable structures and processes to support your activities. Get your effort into the culture, how people relate to themselves and each other; take into account the problems of relational loss and the rapid scaling of relational complexity as organisations grow, described in Section 13.6.2.

13.5 Personal arena

We've already covered most of what you need at work to understand yourself, and to grow yourself, by harnessing the internal conflict you experience. So in this section, we will assume everything that has already been covered in Chapters 7 and 8, and only cover the essential additional factors that the organisation needs to provide you with.

Psychological safety

The most important factor that the organisation needs to provide you with is psychological safety. In your private life, psychological safety is part of what you need to construct yourself. There are many ways that you can do this in your private life, both by rewriting your own meaning-making stories and by making decisive choices about who you spend time with. Sometimes you will be in situations that are beyond your capacity to create psychological safety alone, and will need to turn to others for support, maybe even lawyers.

Amy Edmondson in her excellent book *The Fearless Organization*[158] writes about the competitive edge organisations have when they take care of the psychological safety of everyone working in the organisation. This applies the words of Peter Drucker, that the purpose of an organisation is to make each individual strength productive and their weaknesses irrelevant, to the organisation's job of to minimising the energy invested in Job 2, and maximising the energy invested in Job 1.

Management by fear is an absolutely certain recipe for the death of any organisation facing adaptive challenges. You as an individual living being, and your organisation as a collective living being, will never have the adaptive capacity you need unless you have psychological safety.

Creating psychological safety requires action on all three axes of Figure 12.2. It is simply not enough to work on the culture, and other aspects of the human dimension; better, but also not enough to bring in self-management on the roles and tasks dimension, if you still have a limited company or similar. You must incorporate at least at Level 2 to have some level of robust psychological safety, better at Level 3.

Only at a Level 5 fully free company do you have fully antifragile psychological safety. I strongly advise everyone starting up now to go straight to Level 5. If you cannot, look carefully at what risks that brings. Risks that may prevent you from building the better world you intend to; because you cannot build a better world on the foundations of any incorporation that treats companies as if they were property.

Also choose wisely on the Roles and Tasks axis. You have psychological safety if you have a say over who can exert power over you, whether through their role or their person. If managers / lead links are simply appointed you have at best fragile safety, because you cannot easily protect yourself if, say, a narcissistic person is allocated power over you. This is why some implementations of Ocracies fail.

Peak adaptive performance

Otto Laske and I described what happens at the individual level during the change journey towards Holacracy or sociocracy, drawing on my experiences in P&G China, where I used what I know would now call self-organising team dynamics, in my own businesses and as a consultant.

Every challenge that you face in an organisation will put you into one of four Zones versus your Size of Person (the combination of your dominant meaning-making stories and your fluidity in using all 28 transformational thought forms).

Zone 1, Comfort zone. In Zone 1, you are able to deal with the challenge completely within your Size of Person. In a sense, the challenge is smaller than you are. You have more capacity for transformation thinking than is necessary to fully overcome the challenge, and the challenge fits completely within your dominant meaning-making stories.

So the challenge will feel easy and natural to you, without any stress.

Zone 2, independent growth zone. If you are in Zone 2, the challenge is marginally bigger than you are. To rise perfectly well to the challenge, you need to exert yourself to use forms of thought that you have begun using, but are not yet fully fluid in using. The reality that you need to shape and experience is just within your grasp, because you have already begun developing the appropriate meaning-making stories.

So you can support yourself in fully rising to the challenge. You will feel some level of stress, but on the safe side. So long as less than 40% of your work places you in Zone 2, you will feel stretched while you are rising to the challenge, proud of how you have grown, and the results you've delivered at the end.

Zone 3, assisted growth zone. If you are in Zone 3, the challenge is bigger than you are. To fully rise to the challenge and deliver the results that business success needs you to deliver, you will need to use thought forms that you are only able to use if somebody else supports you. You will also need to use meaning-making stories that are just off the edge of your current set of stories, but so long as somebody else is able to support you, you will be able to build a bridge into the void.

With support from others, and of course from your organisation's structures and processes, you will just be able to deliver adequate results. You will feel stressed, perhaps anxious, during the process. But, at the end you will likely feel exhilarated and proud that you have accomplished something that at first seemed beyond your capacity. Even more so because you can see how overcoming this adaptive challenge has led you to change yourself into someone that you are proud to now be.

Zone 4, panic zone. If you are confronted with an adaptive challenge that places you in Zone 4, find a way to delegate the challenge up, down, or sideways within your organisation, or to somebody outside your organisation. If a challenge is so much bigger than you that it places you in your Zone 4, it requires transformational thinking fluidity and meaning-making stories that are beyond your grasp, even with the best possible support that your colleagues and an organisation can give you.

So regardless of what you or anyone else does to support you, you will fail, unless you hit a seam rich in the ore of underserved luck. Someone else must pick this up. If you are the CEO, that means finding consultants you can really trust, or perhaps relying on your board.

You will be at peak adaptive performance if your challenges place you in exactly the right mix of Zone 1, 2 and 3 for you. If you are leading a team, or are the lead link for a circle in one of the Ocracies, keep a very careful eye on the challenges that each individual and the team as a whole is facing, compared to each individual Size of Person. Do your best to keep yourself and everyone else out of Zone 4, and well supported in Zone 3. This will maximise the energy in Job 1, and minimise the energy in Job 2. Also compare this with Section 14.2.1 on divided teams.

Think about yourself and your colleagues in your organisation. Your feelings are your most reliable guide to which zone you are currently in. If you are feeling completely overwhelmed, if you think you are so far in over your head[193] that you know that you are going to underperform because you lack something essential, you are most likely in Zone 4.

If everything feels easy, if you feel no stress at all, then you are most likely in Zone 1. Usually a technical challenge places you in Zone 1 or 2.

You may also be in Zone 4 and feel no stress at all because you have failed to recognise the challenge's inherent nature, and so see yourself as fully capable of rising to the challenge. This is most likely an adaptive challenge so big that you cannot even recognise how much bigger the challenge is than your Size of Person. This is one of the most common causes of business leaders making atrocious decisions. They are facing an adaptive challenge that requires a Size of Person so much bigger than they are that they do not even understand that they haven't understood the challenge.

There are only three possibilities here.

1. You and your company may get lucky.

2. You find out that the challenge was so much bigger than you are when you find out far too late that you've made decisions that have led your company into collapse.

3. Or, ideally, you have a colleague who does have sufficient Size of Person to grasp the true nature of the challenge, and you trust them enough to listen to what your colleague says. Then, together, you may be able to find a way forward that will enable your company to rise to the adaptive challenge and thrive.

Zones 3 and 4 are not always easy to distinguish alone. In both cases, if you have recognised that the challenge is significantly bigger than you are, you will recognise that you need the support of somebody else and your organisation's structures and processes. To truly tell the difference, you will need to get the input of somebody who has these challenges within their Zone 1, and who knows you well enough to be able to evaluate how big the adaptive challenge is versus your current capacity for transformational thinking and meaning making.

If your work requires you to be in Zone 3 for more than around 20% of the time, or it requires you to be in your Zone 4 at all, it's vital for your health, and for the short and medium-term success of your organisation, that you find your way to handing over all Zone 4 and enough of your Zone 3 challenges to somebody else.

Peak performance needs the right balance of zone 1, 2, and 3. Just what the balance is depends on your unique individual mix of cognitive biases, psychological makeup, transformational thinking capacity, and meaning-making capacity. It also depends on how strong the scaffolding is that your colleagues and your organisation provide to support you as you grow yourself into the void.

The more that everyone in your organisation sees it as a living being, where its meaning-making stories are the biggest lever to lift results, the easier it will be for you to get the scaffolding you need to spend more of your time in Zone 3, 2 and 1.

However, the more that your organisation's meaning-making sees it as a complex system, perhaps as a highly complex machine or software system, the less capacity you will have to support yourself in Zone 2, let alone get the scaffolding you need to support you in Zone 3.

This is especially important if your organisation is changing from a traditional vertical management accountability hierarchy to any of the newer, agile approaches[2]. Such a change journey can very easily put everyone so deep into their respective Zones 3 and 4 that the entire organisation's productivity drops well below the minimum survival threshold.

If you want to read up more on this, these four zones are derived from the original Vygotsky zones of proximal development[194,195]. Originally applied to the development that takes place during childhood, I find the concept equally applicable to adult development.

The workplace is not for changing others, nor for therapy

I cannot stress this enough. Your boss, your colleagues, and your organisation have absolutely no right to demand that you change or grow in a way that they desire. None of them is you, none of them will live with the consequences, none of them is a god, even if they believe they are!

You are the only person who has decision authority over your developmental path. You are the person who has to live with the consequences of all of your decisions about growing yourself, and you are the person who has the best possible insight into all the hidden meaning-making stories that shape who you are today.

---

[2] Some of these are becoming known as Teal. I've chosen not to use the name much here, as there is a gap between how the word is often interpreted and what is needed to be truly at teal.

You are the only person with the right to look at who you *might* become, and choose to start the journey towards becoming that person.

If organisations, or your boss, or colleagues, demand that you become someone, they are overstepping the mark. What is perfectly acceptable is for them to request unambiguously that whoever is in a specific niche of the organisation is a sufficiently good fit to perform well. If who you are is unable to perform sufficiently well, then the organisation must give you that feedback unambiguously, and the organisation has the responsibility to work in partnership with you to figure out whether or not this is an adaptive challenge that is part of your life path. If it is, then the organisation must offer you whatever support it is resourced to offer, to ease your growth, if you choose to.

If this is not part of your adaptive path—which is your decision, not the organisation's—or the organisation does not have sufficient resources to support you adapting yourself, it's important for both you and the organisation that you either move into a niche that does fit you, and that you can perform well in; or that you move to another organisation with a niche that you fit well into. Anything else is disrespecting the organisation's right as a living being to perform at its best, and grow into its unique potential, or disrespecting your right as an equally living being to thrive and grow into your unique potential.

Finally, the personal arena of an Adaptive Organisation is also not there to give you whatever therapy you may need to deal with large trauma or mental health issues. Of course, the better an organisation is at everything in this book, the easier it will be for you to perform, regardless of your unique nature and life history.

A good example of this is the UniOne Foundation. Working there I (Graham) saw how high some people were on the autism spectrum. The skills that they brought were highly valued, and the way that UniOne ran and was organised enabled them to be fully themselves and maximally productive. There's no reason why you can't do the same thing for yourself and your organisation.

Life-threatening organisation designs

Many approaches to organisation design are at worst toxic to the living organisation, or at least weaken it considerably. Even the modern approaches, such as Sociocracy, Holacracy, Agile, etc. can be perfect enablers of an organisation thriving as a living being; or can be toxic; depending on the meaning-making stories behind how they are deployed. Some approaches more clearly recognise that the essence of an organisation is alive, similar to a beehive, with an intelligence and meaning-making story way bigger than that of any individual; and others less clearly.

The more the story creating an organisation design paradigm exclusively focuses on the visible structures and processes (activity variable of Equation 12.1, or lower right visible collective in Section 12.6), the more toxic it is likely to be to an organisation's living, meaning-making aspects (context variable, or lower left hidden collective in section 12.6).

And if the powerful in an organisation impose a story on a quadrant that fails to add value to any of the other quadrants, let alone suppresses it, the organisation as a whole will suffer.

The meaning-making story dominates, as you saw in Equation 12.1.

Some Ocracies recognise this more clearly. The human being is always seen to be speaking from a number of roles, including the permanent role that all humans have in the living organisation, as its senses and voice. And especially that, in a living being, very often what is happening is so nebulous that there is no rational way of putting it into words; it can only be felt. You feel when something is emerging or is wrong; and then you must be able to object to a proposal, not because you have a rational reason why not, but simply because it feels wrong to you in your core role as the living organisation's representative.

This is the same as recognising that you are not primarily your bones, muscles, and energy supply. You are primarily the meaning-making stories that you use to shape the unique reality you experience.

13.6 Interpersonal arena

Delivering results together is the difference between a high-performing team, and the same individuals who happen to be in the team. Doubtless you can think of sports teams who didn't have any specific star player, yet consistently outperform teams that have a couple of expensive Prima Donnas yet were unable to play as one team.

To understand where your organisation is on a scale from zero adaptive capacity to full-spectrum adaptive capacity, look at how effectively all types of interpersonal conflict can be immediately and rapidly surfaced without any blame or shame. Just as in nature's evolution, the task of everyone in the organisation is to mine the interpersonal conflict for the valuable information it's giving you on how to maintain or even increase your fit to the external drivers.

In Chapters 7 to 11 you dived deeply into who you are and how you are anchored in the meaning-making stories you have internalised through your life. You learnt how to iteratively transform your identity to get ever better alignment with actuality. This chapter will hopefully whet your appetite to master those chapters even better, because they are the prerequisite for the interpersonal layer of an adaptive living organisation: superb capacity for working effectively with the current self-identities of all stakeholders, and using work for further self-development.

For example, take the work of Brene Brown (e.g. *Rising Strong* or her TED talks) on blame and shame. Any level of blame or shame directed towards you for being who you are, or doing what you have done, reduces your adaptive capacity, and so reduces the results you can deliver for the business. If you are leading an organisation, especially if you are leading a change towards any or all of an Adaptive Organisation's elements, every single time you blame or shame someone pushes that person deeper into their Job 2, leaving less energy available for a success.

Everything in this section revolves around understanding, and then increasing, your individual capacity working with your colleagues, and the capacity of your organisation as a whole, to mine and refine tension and conflict. Doing so will extract the nuggets of gold telling you about who your organisation currently is, and who it needs to become, to perform in your current context.

The physics and art of work teams

Creating a high-performance team and organisation is as much physics as art. The physics has much more in common with relativity and quantum physics than it does with Newton's classical physics. The art has much more in common with Picasso than it does with a traditional landscape painter.

There will always be aspects that are nebulous, that you cannot know about. Aspects where, as soon as you do something to know, your doing will change the very aspect you need to learn about. So you'll still not know!

If you are a business leader, there is no way back to a safe and predictable life. If your business does not deliver output, and deliver it efficiently, it will soon die. Businesses exist to deliver what is needed by society, within the context of their niche in society. Everything else is there to support delivering. This output can span a very wide range, not just the number of widgets you make or your total delivered cost of making them. Also, always remember that profit and shareholder returns are not primary business results. Profit and TSR is a consequence of delivering excellent business output with high efficiency.

Because the first seven years of my (Graham's) working career was in theoretical high-temperature particle physics, I naturally have looked at everything I've touched since then through the lenses of a particle physicist. I am always asking myself how the final performance of an entire business can be improved by working on the smallest particles that make up that business, and their interactions or forces between them.

I've long seen that external regulations to change the behaviour and output of business sectors are much the same as changing the properties of, for example, a bucket of water by heating it, cooling it or putting it under pressure. Of course, that can change the bucket of water into a block of ice or a nebulous cloud drifting away in the wind, but you're not going to create a diamond by doing that.

If you need a diamond, you need to change the individual particles from water molecules to carbon atoms, and you need to change their interactions, from weak Van der Waal's to strong covalent[3]. The same is true in your organisation. If you need your organisation to deliver better results, you are far more likely to get there with less effort by working on the individual elements, how they interact, and the overall context they are in, and trying to work via pressure and temperature.

Research in high-performing teams supports this.

Take the difference between a diamond, and the graphite in a pencil. Although both are the same pure carbon atoms, the relationships between the atoms, how they are arranged, and the kind of interaction that results from that, differs. The diamond is extremely hard; the graphite is soft and slippery. In graphite the individual carbon atoms only interact strongly with neighbouring carbon atoms in their 2D plane, and outside the plane through weak interactions. In diamond, they interact strongly in all three directions.

This is a lot like many organisations. Team members only interact strongly with those team members on the same team or silo, and weakly with anyone else. I know this only too well from working within P&G; although I believe that P&G was one of the best companies around at recognising this problem and actively enabling individuals interaction across the entire organisation.

A diamond is quite different. The entire diamond, no matter how big it gets, is one single crystal. The carbon atoms interact strongly with all the carbon atoms they can. This is what makes a diamond so strong.

Develop high-performing teams as a physicist would. Focus on the interaction between people, and support each person developing their skills, their fluidity for transformational thinking, and their meaning-making stories.

During the early start-up days at Evolutesix, our focus was on developing the Adaptive Way component of the Adaptive Organisation. Two colleagues, Marko Wolf and Adrian Meyer joined me in London

---

[3] Van der Waal's forces are very weak forces between molecules together; they are easy to break, which is why water melts at 0°C. Covalent forces are way stronger, and hold atoms together to form molecules, which is why water only breaks up into hydrogen and oxygen with both a catalyst and 500-2000°C temperature.

for two weeks of intense work trying out the Adaptive Way prototype on ourselves, and improving it to bring to others.

After ten days of hard work, with just a few days left to finish everything, we decided that working in a different environment would do us good. So we all headed off to a nearby National Trust stately home and continued working while walking through the grounds, and enjoying tea and delicious scones in the café.

Approaching midday, the discussion became both heated and drained of energy. In particular, between Adrian and myself. Marko put his hand up and interrupted the conversation, asking

> *Which meaning-making stories are active in each of us right now?*

I said

> *you guys have both given a significant amount of your precious time and money in coming here, I must honour your gift by giving back far more value through what we develop in the Adaptive Way. And, my meaning-making story is that what I already know and can do is not very valuable, so the only way I can honour your gift is by giving you in these few days* everything *that I have mastered over the past years.*

Adrian replied, with a sense of immediate ease and a grin of recognition,

> *The story alive in me right now is a typical story for many consultants—we insecure over-achievers. I'm looking at our relationship as an archetype client-consultant relationship, so I need to take whatever you give me, digest it, and give back to you something that is more powerfully insightful and helpful to you. So every hour that we spent talking, stays with me as an additional hour of digesting and processing, and perhaps an hour discussing that with you. In addition, I also judge that whatever I am able to do is never quite enough, and prize achievement very highly. This combination of insecurity and*

over achievement means that I only begin to think that I've done enough long after I have actually done too much. The more you give me, the worse my life becomes.

Marko was grinning broadly by now.

I probably don't need to tell you what's happening inside me; you know it already. My background is philosophy and other aspects of the human dimension, I don't have a business background. This conversation is triggering in me stories of not having enough value to contribute, and questioning my place.

So the more that I see the two of you ratchet everything up, the more I judge myself as having no place here, but very much want to have a place here, and so look for anything and everything I might possibly contribute to add to what you are doing.

All three of us grinned, realised how each of our vulnerabilities, and our strategies to protect our vulnerabilities, were colluding with each other to make things worse for us all. Despite us all thinking that what we were doing was our very best to achieve our common goal of creating an Adaptive Way program sufficiently polished to bring to clients, what each of us was actually doing was far more about job 2, defending our self-esteem. (Notice how the stories pick up on a number of the biases of section 10.5, such as reciprocity bias, social proof, and commitment.)

At that point, we realised three very important things.

Firstly, that we had just experienced the power of the Adaptive Way in action. Even though we were still relatively clumsy at using the Adaptive Way, within ten minutes of Job 2 kicking in, we had registered that our emotions were telling us that something else was happening. Recognising the tension that each of us was experiencing, we shifted gear into understanding what was actually happening, and using the Adaptive Way to use that data to get us to focus back on the result we were trying to deliver together.

Secondly, each of us realised that we had just done an impromptu experiment to challenge our meaning-making stories. We had learnt just how much our meaning-making stories were giving us a distorted, dysfunctional reality. We had just had an experience showing that a more functional story was that each of us was bringing in more than enough value to settle everything.

And finally, Marko reminded us of the objective we had set ourselves on the first day.

It was immediately apparent to each of us that we had actually passed that goal two days ago. What we were doing now was a combination of perfectionism and developing the next module. In the absence of any consumer data to tell us what was actually better or worse, and what was needed next!

We immediately decided to stop, celebrate what we had achieved, and go out and test with real consumers the current stage of our Adaptive Way prototype.

Relationship scaling

When I was at school, maths exams regularly had questions along the lines of

if a team of 10 people take 10 days to dig a trench to lay an electricity cable, how long will it take a team of 20 people to do the same job?

At school, you get full marks by saying it would take 20 people five days.

In business, though, it is quite clear that the answer is often 20 days.

Jeff Bezos and Steve Jobs are both known to favour small teams. Amazon has a metric for team size based on how many pizzas it takes to feed the team for a meal. More than two, and the team should be split. Why is it that individuals in larger teams deliver weaker results than the same people do in smaller teams?

One reason is relational loss[196]. In a larger team, each individual's uniqueness and unique contribution becomes less visible to all others, and each has less support and interaction than they need with key people. This is also linked to social proof bias, Page 244.

The more people there are in the team, the more likely somebody is to keep quiet when they see a risk, or not take action when they see an opportunity, especially if that means acting alone or convincing everyone. The bigger the team, the more courage it takes to go against the group opinion, especially for the many at S3 or S2.

There is also information overhead; the effort needed to get all necessary information to and from everybody, coordinating everybody, and maintaining psychological safety. This scales nearly exponentially because the number and complexity of relationships in the team scales nearly exponentially. You can see how this goes as follows. The left column is the number of people in the team, and the right column is the number of relationships of each size in the team.

No. people	Self	Dyads	Triads	Quads	Total
1	1				1
2	2	1			3
3	3	3	1		7
4	4	6	3	1	14
5	5	10	10	1	26
7	7	21	35	15	78
10	10	45	120	126	301

Table 13.1: Table showing how the number of each type of relationship and the size of the largest relationship scales with team size. You have the relationship of each person with himself, each group of two, three, and four people, and so on.

You already get the picture looking just at dyads (pairs), triads (threes) and tetrads (fours). As you can see from the Table 13.1, as your team size grows, your relational overhead to maintain high performance grows nearly exponentially[4].

The perceived loss of support in larger teams coming from relational loss means that larger teams are even more stressed in rising to adaptive challenges than they are in rising to technical challenges.

Simply adding three more people to a team of seven increases the number of relationships nearly four times. So if you want to take a team on a journey towards becoming an Adaptive Organisation, you are far better off doing it with small teams of fewer than ten people.

Relational overhead depends on the absolute number of people in the team, not on how many days each person is working in the team. This is why startups are far better off, once they go beyond four people, to have a smaller number of people working full time, rather than a large number of people working part time.

---

[4] If you want to extend this table for your team, the formula for the number of different combinations of k people out of a team of n people, the Binomial Coefficient, or n choose k, is $\frac{n!}{k!(n-k)!}$.

Interactivity and reciprocal helping

I (Graham) co-led, during my time with P&G China, one of the best teams that I have ever worked in. It delivered excellent business results and work was fun. It was easy to feel that this was a high-performing team because there was a constant crackle of excitement and energy whoever I was interacting with. And I was interacting with everybody. We were tasked with fundamentally reinventing the laundry process for our low-income markets. Hari Nair, my counterpart in product research, and I were motivated by the impossible deadlines to get the first minimum viable prototypes done in time for the next scheduled senior management meeting and launch window.

We brought in the global design company IDEO, and the Indian innovation and marketing consultancy, Ray+Keshevan. The combination of these external partners and our internal cross-functional team members lead us to repeatedly do the impossible. Where typical project teams took four or more weeks, we were taking two or fewer.

We knew it was a high-performing team because you could feel its energy in every interaction, whether we were together in a meeting in one of our offices in Beijing or Singapore, or with the consumers in the Philippines who were testing the minimum viable prototypes, or sitting down together in the evening over a meal and a few drinks.

Two other significant characteristics were that we were in a small core team of seven, working either full time or more than 50% on the project; and everybody was talking to everybody and helping each other constantly, at work and outside work.

Collaboration is reciprocal helping, as Edgar Schein describes in his book *Helping*[197]. Reciprocity bias has been core to humans thriving, enabling us to bond together into collaborative groups (Page 241). The more performance you expect from your team, the more reciprocity in helping each other you need. And all reciprocal helping depends on how well everyone in the team is able to interact.

Research on which characteristics correlate with high-performing organisations show that the more staff interactivity there is, the higher the performance[198,199]. This is one of the few clear correlations with performance across many different measures. It's only natural when you look at an organisation as a living being, where the reality experienced is shaped by the whole organisation's collective meaning-making stories. The more everybody in the organisation interacts, the stronger the stories become, and the easier it then becomes for people to collaborate.

So if you want to evaluate your organisation, or one that you are about to be hired by or consult for, have a look at the interactivity. The less there is, the worse the business results will be compared to the potential, because the reciprocal helping will be lower. If you are leading an organisation, and you want better results, one area you have to take loving care of is the amount of interaction between members of your organisation and the quality of that interaction.

Surprisingly the research showed that it didn't matter much whether the interaction was while working together in project teams on specific tasks, or conversations over lunch, or tea breaks with colleagues you don't normally collaborate with. More important was how much interactivity there was in the team in total, that every person was interacting with every other person. How people were interacting was what mattered, not the content of their interaction. Again, looking at an organisation as a living being composed of lots of people like you, bonded into a community, it's no surprise that our strengths as social human beings are still the dominant strengths in our companies.

What makes it so difficult for people to interact effectively, harnessing the power of reciprocal helping to deliver the business strategy with excellence? If I think back to my time with P&G, I mostly found it very easy to collaborate with colleagues across the organisation. It's very clear to me that all my successes lay in people who I had helped then helping me in return, or vice versa. Reciprocity bias bonded us together into a very powerful, informal, flat organisation that tunnelled through all the barriers between silos and hierarchical position. Much like quantum physics, the real power of P&G to create disruptive innovation lay more in this emergent, hidden, nebulous human capability hierarchy, than in the visible management accountability hierarchy.

One of my first actions when I took over responsibility for a section in the Chinese organisation was to invite one of the best-connected women in P&G, Kathy Felber, to rapidly ramp up the amount of interactivity between my fledgling Chinese R&D section and the rest of the world. The team was so hungry for this that she returned home sucked completely dry. Kathy was also leading the annual weeklong training programme, and because of her visit to China and getting to know just what the team there were capable of, she then started bringing people from the Chinese organisation to deliver training in the US, and ironed out some barriers for the new Chinese recruits attending training in the US.

Interactivity, and specifically reciprocal helping, only exists when there is sufficient psychological safety. Collaboration within an organisational hierarchy is one of the most psychologically contorted arenas there is, because, if I help you, then psychologically we're stepping into a parent-child transactional relationship, with me is the parent and you as the child. If ten minutes later you are then helping me, then our relationship inverts to one where you have the role of parent and I have the role of child.

It works when the formal boss is helping the formal subordinate, as then the relationship is aligned formally and psychologically. But when the formal subordinate is helping (=leading) the formal boss, the two relationships oppose each other.

All of us function best when we are in a constant relationship with another person. We have difficulty functioning when the very relationship itself is emergent, flipping from one type to another according to the context that we are in, independent of both people in the relationship. Given our very normal human needs for stability and consistency, this kind of nebulous relationship triggers our psychological defence mechanisms, our Job 2.

This is also what makes it so hard for some bosses to collaborate effectively with their subordinates, especially those yet to reach S4.

How much psychological safety do you experience in your organisation? If you are in a leadership position, and someone very junior in the hierarchy offers to help you do something that they can see you need help in, are you able to accept their initiating help?

If you are in an Ocracy, how easy is it to truly interact with your colleagues and help each other reciprocally? Whilst that is at the heart of how these organisation designs are meant to work, in some organisations the individual stories of each person prevent them from doing this kind of relationship flipping.

There is no better piece of evidence for the way that any kind of interactivity increases reciprocal helping the research of Pentland[198,199].

> ... we advised the center's manager to revise the employees' coffee break schedule so that everyone on a team took a break at the same time. That would allow people more time to socialize with their teammates, away from their workstations. Though the suggestion flew in the face of standard efficiency practices, the manager was baffled and desperate, so he tried it. And it worked: [average handling time] fell by more than 20% among lower-performing teams and decreased by 8% overall at the call center. Now the manager is changing the break schedule at all 10 of the bank's call centers (which employ a total of 25,000 people) and is forecasting $15 million a year in productivity increases. He has also seen employee satisfaction at call centers rise, sometimes by more than 10%. Any company, no matter how large,

has the potential to achieve this same kind of transformation.

Pentland identified three aspects of the interaction between team members. These will be no surprise to you, now that you look at your business first and foremost as a living being.

Energy The most important is energy. No surprise there! The more exchanges there are, and the more that these exchanges raise the productive energy of individuals and their relationships, the better the productivity. The more that dialogue patterns, such as deconstructive dialogue on Page 328, are used to give each other the scaffolding you need to stretch deep into your respective Zones 2 and 3, the more productive you will be. The more that you can use the ground pattern yourself to transform your meaning-making stories and increase your adaptive capacity, the more productive you will be.

And the more that all of these combine to reduce the amount of energy you put into unproductive Job 2, the better the business results you and your company will produce. This is where bringing in the radical transparency of ongoing regard and deconstructive dialogue can really drive your productivity[196], provided of course it emerges naturally because you have a psychologically safe space. Not because you mandate with power that everybody uses these patterns.

Engagement The more evenly distributed the activity and energy is across all the team members, and all their relationship combinations, the better the performance.

Exploration The more that there are team members who go off on random explorations outside it, the better the overall performance. So make sure that your team has one or two people with naturally high explorer energy, and recognise that the issues caused by the times they are not there, or their struggle finishing tasks, is a small price to pay for the overall boost in performance that they bring.

Engagement and exploration are somewhat like complementary pairs in quantum mechanics. The more you are one, the less you are the other. But, truly high-performance teams find a way to switch themselves from the paradigms of either or into the paradigms of both.

This is one of my (Graham) personal challenges. I have a somewhat introverted nature and a high explorer energy. So it's very easy to go off exploring, not so easy for me to finish things nor to regularly and consistently interact with everybody. So I block off chunks of time for structured interactivity and plan in limits to how much time I spend on that, limits to how much time I spend on exploring, and layer them like a slice of mille-feuille cake.

Seeing an organisation as a living, meaning-making being composed of people like you, human meaning-making beings, the sequence of energy, engagement, and exploration probably seems quite obvious. The research of Pentland and his team now shows just how much of a performance boost comes from this[198,199], with the following hard data coming from their research.

- The number of face-to-face interactions accounts for a full 35% difference between the high and low performing teams.

- Up to one interaction within the team every five minutes increases performance; beyond that, it starts dropping.

- In a typical high-performance team, whole team interaction uses around half the time spent interacting, the rest is in pairs and a little in triads.

- When speaking in the group, members use time efficiently and fairly across the group, primarily listening and not speaking.

- Social time is a core driver of team performance, often accounting for more than 50% of positive changes in communication patterns.

The interactivity research has also confirmed from a different perspective that talent is overrated. Getting smart, talented people onto your team is far less a driver of productivity than getting your team to increase their interactivity.

The problem with stars is that they tend to talk more than others on the team, and tend to listen less, both of which reduce interactivity and performance. Even more so, highly charismatic people are only helpful to performance if they use their charisma to increase the quantity and energy of interactivity between all team members by facilitating it, rather than driving it themselves.

The research shows that interactivity is at least as important as all the other factors together that are typically believed to drive team performance. So if you are starting up a company, and raising the level of interactivity is not one of your topmost activities, you better have somebody really good supporting you in this area. The big reason to be hopeful, in your capacity to build a highly productive Adaptive Organisation, is that interactivity is a learnable skill, as well as an adaptive challenge.

This is also a very important lens to look through as you choose which approach to dynamic organisation design to deploy, or to create your own unique flavour. Anything that reduces the human energy in the interactions between people as human beings will push towards lower business results. Do as nature does, and find highly creative ways of integrating all the different elements and layers of the living system, in ways that maximise the human energy that is transformed into business results.

Stories and culture

Since the essence of a living being is the meaning-making stories that shape the reality experienced, an Adaptive Organisation needs to go beyond the level of psychological safety and interactivity needed for reciprocal helping in an organisation that is designed to deliver excellent business results while only facing technical challenges. An Adaptive Organisation needs the step change in psychological safety and interactivity to make the hidden stories and culture visible, to become a deliberately developmental organisation that deliberately develops its collective meaning-making stories.

In your organisation, do you feel that it's safe to talk openly about your feelings? If not, your organisation has its hands tied behind its back in trying to rise to adaptive challenges. As you read in Chapter 10 your true feelings are hard data that will tell you if something is not right. (Caution if you or other people are using judgements dressed up as feelings; these are distorted data. They come from your unique inner reality, generated by your meaning-making stories attributing meaning to a small biased segment of actuality.)

The more playful your organisation is, the more likely it is to grow and adapt. If you are a playful entrepreneur, evidence is that you are more likely to thrive[153].

A playful South African company, Blueprints, has pioneered a way of making the desired stories visible and memorable to all in a playful, visual and intuitive way. These are captured as a measurable equation that can be monitored monthly to track how well the business is living its stories.

The BBC[200] successfully used humour during WW2 to counteract the internal Nazi propaganda, to keep those Germans who were against the Nazi regime connected with themselves and the common ground all humans share.

Thinking and deciding together

A few decades ago the airline industry realised that the interpersonal arena was where a number of accidents and near misses were taking place. The worst happened on 27 March 1977 on the Spanish island of Tenerife. 583 passengers died when a KLM 747 collided with a Pan Am 747.

This crash might have been prevented if the KLM pilot and co-pilot had had the right interaction in the interpersonal arena. Instead of using all the information they each had to think and decide together, the captain overruled the co-pilot and flight engineer. Most likely authority bias played a significant role, because the captain was the head of the KLM pilot training, with the authority to pass or fail the co-pilot in the next training session.

The consequence was big changes in standardising the interactivity between flight crew members and the control tower. In particular, authority bias is explicitly counteracted by the elimination of all authority-reinforcing patterns of interaction. For example, in some languages the word *you* comes in two or more variations, depending on relative rank and authority. Flight crews today are not allowed to use anything except the rank neutral peer-to-peer version of *you* if they are not speaking English to each other.

The more the arena of interactivity is psychologically safe, the more that everyone can bring to bear their most powerful level of transformational thinking fluidity, and the better the decisions.

13.7 Personal and interpersonal arenas

We put these two arenas together in this chapter because you use the same dialogue-based "mining technology" you have covered in the ground pattern of Section 8.2 to extract the valuable information buried in human conflict, whether the conflict is within you, or between two or more of you.

Deconstructive dialogue

For the ground pattern to work at its most powerful, you need to introduce deconstructive dialogue and ongoing regard. These are the two most powerful tools to mine and refine the valuable gold from the raw conflict you have with your colleagues. Deconstructive dialogue can also be called deconstructive criticism, feedback, or exploration, depending on the specific situation.

A colleague once gave me some constructive criticism, saying

Graham, at times you can be such an intellectual terrorist.

I immediately felt both anger and fear, triggering thoughts of fighting back, themselves a consequence of the worry that I might lose my belonging to the group. Since I was co-founder and MD that was not likely, but even the slightest hint of a threat and the guardian angels put their ballistic missiles onto red alert.

He then proceeded to give me some well-intentioned, but actually harmful, feedback. Harmful for me personally and for the company, because it was just not actionable by me, and significantly reduced my capacity to lead. All that his feedback did was reinforce the very meaning-making stories that were leading me to behave that way.

Now, a decade later, I know how to translate that feedback into developmentally useful language using the ground pattern, especially by embedding clearly my needs, true feelings, and judgements into the translation. Back then I was still learning how to do this, and whilst I did OK, it was still a catch-22.

Take care when you are giving someone feedback: you are not a god, you lack the ability to define who someone else is. Rather, when you give someone feedback you are partly—maybe even only—talking about yourself and your own meaning-making stories. What you are actually saying when you give feedback is that when someone else does and says certain things your internal meaning-making stories attribute, or create, meaning (e.g. "intellectual terrorist"). Rephrase what you normally say using the clean language of NVC[201]: what was actually said or done in pure observable facts; how you feel; what you think; your judgements cleanly distinguished from your feelings.

Use the opportunity to both express your clean feedback and to get information on how you generate reality through your own stories. Then both of you can explore your respective meaning-making stories (and your natures and forms of thought) as part of the discussion. You can work together to uncover how your stories and natures are banging into each other, like two icebergs, hidden from your sight. Through that you can both figure out how at least one, and most likely both, can grow, and perhaps you can figure out a joint castle move that will keep both of your hidden commitments satisfied.

A deconstructive approach is hugely powerful and minimises the risk of making a grave error when you are giving feedback in a power hierarchy.

This approach is also extraordinarily effective when you are in a power game. By actively exploring, or deconstructing, how you and the other person are making meaning, you will take distance from yourself and the other person, helping you remain centred. You will continue to see them from a compassionate stance, as full human beings, with their own unique set of big assumptions driving their behaviour. You will remain clear on what is yours and what is theirs.

We often look at criticism and encouragement as a polarity of being fed carrots or hit with sticks. Deconstructive criticism opens up ways of being hit with a carrot and then eating it, of seeing complementary pairs when before you only saw exclusive opposites.

One of our Adaptive Way participants, Sharon, is in the leadership team of a 50-person company. She recounted a situation she had had on the very day we covered deconstructive criticism for the first time.

Three people in my team had simply not done what they should have done during the week. Nor did they communicate in advance that there was an issue. But in our meeting last week we all agreed that we would do it, that we would bet on the 50% probability of getting a 'go' for the product launch. Not on the 50% risk of a delay. I criticised their lack of ownership, their laziness, and their general gap as middle managers in the company.

As we explored what might be happening, in particular what the three people's stories might be, and how they might be banging up against Sharon's stories, she had a big insight:

I know they are uncomfortable making assumptions. I suspect that no answer is better for them than a wrong answer based on false assumptions. Also, up until now I have stories around avoiding conflict, so I have never openly challenged their fears. More, I may have reinforced the danger of giving a wrong answer that triggers conflict with the founder.

Sharon, a few days after the dojo, invited the three for her first attempt and led them through deconstructive dialogue. In the following dojo she reported back saying

It was really clumsy at first, but now we have bonded to-

*gether far more strongly as a team, I understand far bet-
ter how to help them deliver, and they understand far better how I see the world. We are wasting less effort, have less
stress, and are delivering better than ever before.*

Deconstructive exploration is not a simple language pattern. Rather, it is a lens you look at yourself and the other person through, where you use everything in the dojo to get the best possible grasp on what is actually happening, at all levels, clearly distinguishing between yourself and them. Deconstructive exploration is very much applying the core lenses of quantum physics and Cubist art to yourself and your interactions with your colleagues at work.

Looking through the deconstructive lens at someone you are about to criticise, you see the following clearly:

1. Your view likely has some value. You may even be completely right that the other person is wrong.

2. Your view may not be complete, and / or may not be accurate.

3. The other person's view may have some value. At least it makes sense to them within their set of meaning-making stories and way of constructing their reality, and so through using deconstructive dialogue each of you can learn something about their meaning-making stories.

4. Your criticism may come from a difference in constructing reality, and so cannot be effectively addressed until both of you understand each other. This can cover all their commitments, their hidden commitments, and their meaning-making story.

5. So there may be multiple different and valid realities at play here, which means that their view is vital for you to evaluate how 'right' your criticism actually is.

6. Since your internal tensions are the driver for your growth, now you have the chance to use tensions inside and between each other to open up even more avenues for growing your capacity, both individually and as collaborators.

7. The whole focus is on exploring each other, or sparring, not on fixing the other person. This generates huge psychological safety, because both sides know, so long as they stay within the pattern of deconstructive dialogue, that the dangerous forces of blame and shame[202] are excluded.

Comparing deconstructive criticism to constructive criticism, you can see a number of differences.

1. The biggest, and most important difference, is that in deconstructive criticism you both have the chance of learning something that leads to growth. Rather than only the other person learning what your reality imagines they are, or have done wrong. Which may have no relevance to their reality, or even actuality. It may be purely in your mind!

2. What you learn in deconstructive criticism comes from a more accurate view of all that actually is, rather than your own limited reality emerging from your own meaning-making stories.

3. You see the other person as a whole person, you are outside your box[139]. You see them and their unique way of constructing reality, with their own meaning-making stories; and that their way may be just as valid (or invalid) for them as yours is for you.

4. Instead of seeing the truth as something you alone possess (especially an issue if you are their manager, the lead link, or a subject matter expert, and identify with your role or expertise), you see the truth as something that spans all of: you, them, your relationship, and the external context.

5. In deconstructive criticism you see that quite possibly neither of you gets it, so you are a curious explorer; versus constructive criticism attempting to educate or correct someone who fails to get it, with you as a flawless teacher, or judge and jury.

6. We normally view tensions and conflict as an issue to manage away, whereas a deconstructive stance says

    Yay, we have a tension! Vital raw material for our self-reconstruction activities. Now we both have even better chances of transforming ourselves.

7. Deconstructive applies all three Evolutesix dojo rules: care for yourself, the other person, and the whole.

8. Deconstructive criticism is active, not passive. You go in with a spirit of curiosity; you are anchored in not knowing.

Of course, the outcome of deconstructive criticism may still confirm that your point of view is completely correct. It may well still be, if you are accountable for who is on the team or in the company, that you still follow through your decision to, for example, fire the other person. Deconstructive dialogue is absolutely not about ducking your accountability. It is about living up to your accountability in the biggest possible way, maximising the number of options available to you to deliver better results by, at the same time, with no extra effort or cost, developing yourself, others, and your entire organisation from an adaptive perspective.

A final tip: I have found it very helpful to look at what anybody else does through the lens of them doing it for themselves, not against me. Even if what they have done works against me, they are doing it first and foremost to meet their needs, not to obstruct me in meeting my needs.

Ongoing regard

One Adaptive Way participant, Tania, had a central meaning-making story:

> If I make mistakes, I will feel vulnerable and insecure because it means I can't do a good job of making the best of my life, and then my life is not worth living.

This big assumption drove Tania's behaviour strongly when deciding where to go on holiday but was absent when she took big life-changing decisions.

Tania's development took another step a few weeks later, sparring with William. He said

> Tania, you are so strong, you don't need to worry about this.

I interrupted

> William, that comment sounded to me like it came from a need you have to be seen as helpful. It risked reinforcing Tania's big assumptions and potentially creating new big assumptions.

Neither had seen ongoing regard, so we went into a quick explanation of why it is actually harmful to praise someone with a "you are" statement. Such "you are" compliments are the root causes of many of our big assumptions later in life, because by praising somebody with the sentence stem *you are*, you're acting as if you have godlike powers to define who they are, when in reality all you can do is project your own making meaning-making stories onto them.

William thought for a while, responding with

> *This has really made so much clear to me. About what has created my big assumptions. I will never say that again to anyone, and certainly no-one reporting to me at work or in my family.*

"You are so strong / clever / beautiful ... " is an example of how so many of us typically try to help someone who doubts themselves, is in pain, etc. It is also how we commonly support someone developing a new skill, or a child growing up.

Saying something like *"I am worthy"* to ourselves, perhaps in front of the mirror each morning, is just the same as someone else saying it to you. It seldom improves your sense of self-worth for longer than a few minutes.

Such statements are the origin of many of your big assumptions, one cause of imposter syndrome, that most common of challenges which many of us face. Most of the work you now need to do to deconstruct your big assumptions is a consequence of the well-meaning praise of people who care about you, and your own attempts to assert yourself to already be someone else, by saying *You are....*

When I pointed this out, saying

> *Tania, this kind of helping is actually harmful because it can reinforce the very big assumption you are trying to break down,*

she replied

> *but it feels so good, I got a definite lift from what William has just said to me.*

> *Yes,* I replied, *and next time you try to achieve your commitment of speaking from your intuition, your big assumption of avoiding mistakes will be even stronger. Because you now have strengthened your big assumption that you need to avoid anyone ever seeing anything in you that is weak or makes mistakes. You have become just a little more dependent on others for your self-identity. You are giving other people the power to define who you are, and your worth as a person. But no-one has the power of*

god to be able to do that sufficiently well.

This makes a lot of sense to me, Graham. I can see why big decisions have become easy, but small decisions are still quite hard. It's the small decisions that still trigger the big assumptions coming from other people's ideas of who I should be.

This illustrates why we never ever do anything with the intent to help or fix someone in the Adaptive Way. Ongoing regard is the only language for feedback in an Adaptive Organisation.

It also illustrates why it is so important to give people feedback, positive and negative, in ways that clearly distinguish between the praise / critical feedback giver's own meaning-making stories (which are creating what they value, and hence what they believe needs to be said in praise) and the praise / critical feedback receiver's nature, meaning-making, and qualities.

Ongoing regard is a form of nonviolent communication, whereas conventional praise is a form of violent communication. Violent, because it imposes your way of making meaning onto the other person as if your personal meaning-making was objective actuality, rather than just your own personal internal reality.

The pattern for ongoing regard has two forms: one when you are recognising the value you got from someone else's actions or words; the second for when you want to express your admiration of a quality you see in another.

1. Recognising the value you perceive in another's words or actions. *"John, thank you for spending an hour with me going over the proposal for the client, because it helped me see the potential pitfalls for the client."*

2. Acknowledging the inspiration you get from another. *"John, so often after talking to you I understand the issue far more deeply and see the complexity more clearly and simply. I admire the way you think and talk to me."*

Notice how much more effective this is than simply praising John by saying *"John, you are so clever."*

Ongoing regard is far harder than simple praise because you need to think about yourself and the other person. Which means it is invariably far more valuable to the other person. How often have you discounted praise because you know the other person has not really grasped you, but is just throwing out a standard phrase?

Most importantly, ongoing regard invites both parties into transformation.

Each can use the ongoing regard as input to their own experiments to transform their big assumptions. Neither is at risk of the words reinforcing old big assumptions, nor at risk of new ones being created.

After you have read all of this, you may be wondering whether coaching has a role to play in an Adaptive Organisation. It has a role to play, but far far smaller than most would think; and keep in mind the warnings of Section11.3. The most powerful and efficient way of spending your money is to train everybody in the organisation to use peer-to-peer developmental practices like the Adaptive Way.

Public agreements

A public agreement is *very* different to the rules and policies that are used in and outside work to force people to behave inside a narrow range, regardless of their meaning-making stories. This is easiest to see in an example.

> In one small Adaptive Way dojo we had Rob, Tania and Cathy as participants, and myself as sensei. We brought the following hidden commitments into our sparring:
>
> **Graham:** *I need to avoid any situation where I am not seen as the smartest person in the room.*
>
> **Rob:** *I need to avoid conflict in myself or with others. If I don't, we will all get emotional, and then I risk being deserted. So whenever conflict begins I feel discomfort and start smoothing it over.*
>
> **Cathy:** *I must avoid being in the centre of attention, I must avoid showing off. If I don't then I'll feel lonely because they will all think I am arrogant.*
>
> **Tania:** *I must avoid making mistakes, or any situation where I might fail, not use my time wisely, or not take full advantage of all the opportunities in front of me. Otherwise I am a waste of space on the earth.*
>
> It is clear that, if we had been colleagues, each of our hidden commitments would trigger the defensive blocking behaviour of each of our hidden commitments! Each of us would invest energy into Job 2, thereby taking energy and time away from delivering results.
>
> Company rules, policies, etc., will not help. If anything they will drive the issues underground, making them show up to protect our vulnerabilities in ways that are even more damaging to our capacity for

reciprocal helping, and with each of us suffering in silence.

The following public agreement complements rules and policies. It gives a far better alternative for any behaviours anchored in nature or meaning-making, which are vital for a developmental organisation of Level 2 upwards:

> *When we have a work meeting we will give each other space to speak. Each of us will have a specific meeting nudger, who will 'activate' what the other might need to say, but be hesitating because of their hidden commitment. Once activated, the right to talk or not goes back to the person with the hidden commitment.*

We also discussed how, over time, we might add more to it, like building in pauses so that each could listen to any quiet internal voice prompting some different action.

Most importantly, we would consciously support each other in running experiments to transform each of our big assumptions until they no longer had power over us.

Whenever there is something we see as 'wrong behaviour' there are two responses to maintain group stability and cohesion. Either we create laws, policies or rules to regulate behaviour, with the intent of punishing those who break the rules and rewarding those who follow them. Or we create public agreements, with the understanding and intention that they will be broken. When, not if, they are broken, we react by exploring with curiosity each other's meaning-making so that we can each grow. The best way to do this is with the pattern of deconstructive exploration in Section 13.7.1.

One reason why some organisations fail in their attempt to implement Holacracy or sociocracy effectively is a lack of true public agreements for human interactions. Our society, especially in the Anglo-Saxon worldviews, is designed around policies, rules and laws, not public agreements.

By bringing in public agreements to an organisation or community, you provide part of the scaffolding needed for those who naturally gravitate to rules to better use deconstructive exploration instead of enforcing rules, and to extend their Zone 3 deeper into their developmental boundaries.

Be careful to never use public agreements as if they were rules or policies. If a rule is needed, use a rule.

The difference can easily be felt, but it's hard to describe. If you feel pressure, shame, or a sense of blame, then quite likely public agreements are being abused as covert rules.

Public agreements create a sense of curiosity and exploration, with more psychological safety to be who you are now, with all of your behaviours, so that you can safely explore who you can become. But they are only agreements so long as each person voluntarily agrees that they are useful to their own developmental path.

Any public agreement imposed by someone with more power, or perceived to have more power (whatever the source and legitimacy of that power)—rather than co-created by both parties based on their individual development paths—is a rule hiding behind the mask of a public agreement.

Any sense of external force, reward, or punishment points at this actually being a rule, not a public agreement. Then declare it to be a rule.

For example,

> *we will always arrive on time for meetings, or put a Euro into the biscuit tin*

is a rule. Even if you call it a public agreement. However,

> *we will strive to arrive on time for meetings, and when we do not we agree to explore, with a sparring partner who we feel safe with, what in each of us (nature and meaning-making) and our organisation's structures, processes, and culture led to late arrival; and even why arriving on time was important.*

is a public agreement.

What's most important is that the public agreement has absolutely no promise to change behaviour, no punishment for not changing; rather, it is an invitation to explore what could grow. Maybe you change your behaviour now; maybe it takes five years to change a deep big assumption; or maybe the organisation needs to change. Or maybe we just need to accept that arriving late is an inherent downside of a highly valued strength—for example, the strength of optimism.

Group coaching, not individual

In their book *The Art of Possibility*[175] the Zanders described the difference between superb musicians who never quite manage to create music that moves people, and musicians who do. The musicians who do move people pay attention to the music's long line, not each individual note. They recognise that it is sometimes necessary to play individual notes imperfectly in order to get the long line of music right, and through the imperfection of those notes communicate the more important underlying message and energy of the long line of music. Their music is alive. Those who never quite make it focus so much on playing each note with perfection that the long line of music lacks life.

Over the past two decades the individual coaching industry has exploded, both in the form of one-on-one executive and life coaching, as well as in the form of workshops run by highly charismatic individuals.

Delivering business results has common ground with moving an audience with music. Just as that works better if the musician plays the music's long line, not individual notes, so too is money usually better spent on improving the long line of the team as a whole, not each individual. Spending company money on wholesale individual coaching is at best an inefficient use of resources; and at worst harmful.

If you are starting up a company, taking an existing company on a change journey, or just aiming to increase its performance by 10%, you are usually better off spending the amount of money on everyone than on hiring an expensive coach just for the CEO. Get everybody better at using the ground pattern for themselves and peer-to-peer sparring with each other as part of their work: using deconstructive dialogue; and ongoing regard; to mine and refine the conflict between each other.

The best way of doing what good coaching is there to do—namely surface and grow meaning-making stories—is as an integral part of work. As part of how colleagues collaborate with each other, i.e., reciprocal helping, where everybody recognises that an essential element of work is using what is happening today to grow capacity to do better tomorrow.

Where coaching individuals is most likely to pay off long term is strictly developmental coaching of key change agents, tasked with leading by example. Support them to increase their fluidity of transformational thinking. This will help them to shift their entire category of stories to the next stage of meaning-making, and increase their capacity to manage their emotional state and subtlety working with their hardwired nature, so that they can embody the new way of being and interacting flawlessly. Ideally do this before they even begin their work.

As we've seen, research into high-performing teams and organisations is now showing that the level of interactivity between all team members is an excellent predictor of team performance. It is far more strongly correlated with high-performing teams than the presence of excellent talent in a few individuals. See for example this summary in Harvard Business Review[188] from which I have taken the following:

... the HR department will set up training to (hire and) develop the

"right" people in the "right" way. The problem is, this is all about the individual. This single-minded focus on the individual employee is one of the main reasons that teams don't do as well as they might in organizations with strong HR departments. Just look at our research on senior executive teams. We found that coaching individual team members did not do all that much to help executive teams perform better. For the team to reap the benefits of coaching, it must focus on group processes.

CHAPTER 14

Your organisation is its tasks

Chaos is found in greatest abundance wherever order is being sought. It always defeats order, because it is better organised.
—*Terry Pratchett.* Thief of Time

This chapter has been written to complement whichever of the many excellent sources you choose to use to approach organisation design, such as sociocracy or Holacracy. I have given the collective name of Ocracy to refer to the multiple practical implementations that have emerged from the philosophy of Auguste Comte in a neutral way that recognises the enormous value of any approach that enables a community of people to self-manage, self-govern or self-organise; and to emphasise the huge common ground they all share.

In the previous two sections, we've looked through the lens of organisations as living, meaning-making communities of living, meaning-making individuals. This lens enables us to see clearly the physical and psychological human energy that is converted into business results.

Energy is the most important element of an organisation to understand, if you need to improve performance, or the capacity for regeneration.

There are only a few types of organisation forms common today. You have the classic dictatorial hierarchy; the common organisational pyramid, which in larger organisations becomes a matrixed pyramid; a few flat teams without any hierarchy; and fewer self-organising flex-flow teams, which have a functional hierarchy that changes according to the immediate work context. Those of you familiar with the Spiral Dynamics[203] classification of worldviews, value systems, and the associated organisation designs, summarised in Table 14.1, will recognise these. Spiral Dynamics is an excellent model and well worth gaining some familiarity in. Note that there are differences between the original of Beck and Cowan[203] and the Spiral Dynamics Integral that combines it with Wilber's integral work[105].

No organisational form is absolutely better or worse than any other, and each is ideally suited to certain types of challenges. For example, the dictatorial hierarchy can be the best organisational form if you have a small team dealing with the tasks of a technical crisis over a very short timeline; if you wake up in the dark at 3AM to discover that your house is on fire, for instance.

The classic pyramid and matrix organisations are only good at the roles and tasks of standardised production and iterative improvements.

The approach that's best suited to delivering excellent results against large scale adaptive challenges is a flex-flow organisation design.

For any organisation to be fully adaptive, it needs to have a flex-flow approach to roles and tasks, be excellent at mining and refining conflict to regenerate all human capitals, and of course be incorporated to support both of those.

14.1 Where your organisation is: tasks

I, (Graham), have developed, together with Bernhard Possert, a classification scheme and diagnostic to evaluate where your organisation is on a scale from zero, dictatorial micromanagement, to autopoietic.

Category zero, dictatorial, is definitely a dictatorial hierarchy; categories 4 and 5 are definitely flex-flow. The middle ones build a fluid bridge from the classic pyramid to flex-flow.

5 Autopoietic. The external driver (context and need) that gives the organisation a purpose is what matters, not preserving the organisation for its own sake. The organisation is supported in gracefully dying by the rest of the ecosystem, especially all direct stakeholders, when the driver has changed beyond a level that the organisation can follow.

The organisation actively collaborates with other organisations in a larger ecosystem (which may, for instance, be all the circles in a large-circle circular economy) in order to maximise the entire ecosystem's capacity. The boundaries between organisations in the ecosystem, ecosystems, and stakeholders, are recognised as fluid and permeable. Everything is clearly recognised as multiple open nebulous systems in constant unpredictable and unknowable transformation. The inherent complementary pairing of competition and collaboration is a foundation of all business activities.

		SD	SDi	Characteristics
8	Holistic self	Turquoise	Turquoise	Focus on collective individualism, holding a multiplicity of perspectives, navigating a world with inherently nebulous, unknowable elements.
7	Integral self	Yellow	Teal	Awareness of oneself within the world and cosmos. Integrate all layers 1-6, embracing functional hierarchies, focus on achieving needs through balance and development.
6	Sensitive self	Green	Green	Social democracy, pluralism, belonging to a caring community, power with, human rights, dialogue and consensus, emphasise the group needs over own needs
5	Rational self	Orange	Orange	Drive-strive, each individually plays the game to win, rationalism, meritocracy, market-driven. Focus on materialism and civilisation.
4	Bureaucratic self	Blue	Amber	Order and purpose keeps everyone safe, there's one right way to fit in, follow the rules, position not person hierarchies, discipline, inner stability, and faith will lead us to live well together and have good lives.
3	Power self	Red	Red	Power is what matters, do and take what you need through power, find and keep your place in the pecking order, focus on being a hero, power, glory, and revenge. Sacrifices to the power gods.
2	Magic, animistic self	Purple	Magenta	Egocentric, impulsive, magical thinking, a focus on placating the spirits. Wisdom of the elders, ancestors, of myths, and spirits.
1	Instinctive self	Beige	Infra-red	Survival. Narcissistic. Focus on basic needs. Catastrophe thinking. Use whatever strategies work, regardless.

Table 14.1: Brief overview of Spiral Dynamics , with the colour schemes of Beck and Cowan's original model in column SD, and Spiral Dynamics combined with Integral theory of Beck and Wilber in column SDi.

4 Self-directing. The budgeting process is flexible and continuous. Leadership can only step into autocratic decision power, limited to specific cases and clearly defined by the whole organisation, including at least staff, board, and investors, often with input from other stakeholders.

Organisational strategy emerges through a cooperative process across the organisation, bottom-up and top-down. Teams decide for themselves who enters the team and who is ejected from the team involuntarily, individuals take decisions to move to another team after some form of consultation with their existing team. Most overhead functions and decisions occur within the teams. Roles, especially leadership roles, are filled by a democratic process.

3 Self-governing. Leadership, which may be in the form of an anchor circle, as found in the Ocracies, focuses on a balance between the needs of individuals and the whole, spending time on systemic enablers that support self-governing, interactivity, clarity, alignment, and direct coaching.

Clear principles and rules for self-designing structures and processes are used to constantly and locally optimise the organisation for the immediate driver. Everybody can, and does, start a process without requiring permission from any hierarchy, to change any structures and processes to improve them and enable them to function well at work.

2 Self-managing. Everyone is aligned across the organisation, with the top-level strategies and central key performance indicators. The whole organisation has a common language about value and waste, which is used to increase value creation and minimise waste.

There are common systems implemented to enable self-management of constellations of roles and the teams that fill them. Each individual has clearly defined roles including clear decision domains and clarity and authority on decisions within those domains. Teams manage and distribute their work themselves, not looking to a formal hierarchical boss to do it. Everything is structured in teams or circles.

1 Delegated authority. Experts are hired because they know things better than their bosses, and managers are comfortable with following the guidance of their expert direct reports, whilst retaining where necessary the decision authority on how to integrate the guidance across multiple domains of expertise in order to meet consumer needs and other business drivers.

Project management systems are well implemented and practised, enabling different types of experts to collaborate and deliver results together. Individuals and teams define for themselves how to tackle the goals they are given. Each employee is seen as an expert within their role, and given an appropriate management for their expertise to be maximally useful to the organisation and to flourish.

o **Dictatorial micro-management.** Employees are seen as inherently lazy, so their managers have to keep careful control of them, with powerful rewards and punishments, or they will stop working hard. Management, especially the CEO, is the only source of predictions about the future, and has sole accountability to generate detailed strategies and execution plans for the business to generate profit in that future.

Management has all the power needed to exert sufficient control over all employees under them in the power hierarchy to keep them strictly executing the plan laid out by management; but if something turns out to be wrong at the end, it's then typically the employee's fault, regardless.

The boss always knows better, so even if you think you have a better solution, you keep quiet about it. People are not hired for thinking, so they should only act after their boss tells them what to do.

Where do you think your organisation is across these different categories? Most will find that they are spread out across a few. For example, if you are in category five, autopoietic, you will certainly have some of the best project management systems and practices around and score highly in Category 1.

The category you are most likely in, at any given moment, is your centre of gravity. You will recognise that you're doing some characteristics from a higher category, but not sufficiently well, nor for sufficiently long, to regard that as a stable centre of gravity.

Equally, if your organisation has certain kinds of gaps in lower categories, you have foundations with weakness that may prevent you from succeeding, even though your organisation as a whole is striving upwards.

Any more than occasional, limited elements of category zero indicate that your centre of gravity is still category zero, no matter how much you believe it is higher.

Keep in mind, if you are in a leadership position and use this as a frame of reference to evaluate where your company is, you are quite likely to put your organisation in a higher category than an external, anonymous, and unbiased controlled survey across all your staff.

14.2 Requisite organisation design

In Chapter 7 I described the never-ending process of how you can get to know who the ever-changing you is, across (1) how you think, (2) your stage of meaning-making story, and (3) your fixed nature. In Section 11.1 we introduced all three of these together as your Size of Person (SOP).

In this chapter we have the Size of Role (SOR). This is defined by the decisions requiring the most fluidity in how you think, the most complex stage of meaning-making stories, and the greatest capacity to manage your nature and emotional state.

Elliott Jaques observed over decades, both employed in organisations and as an academic, the characteristics of organisations that were highly successful in highly challenging business environments. He saw in them what he named requisite organisation design: designing organisations as human beings require them to be, in order for them to be able to perform at their best. Sadly he passed away in 2003, but his work lives on in the Requisite Organization Institute[1], co-founded with his wife and colleague, Kathryn Cason.

In a requisite organisation everybody is in a role that is approximately the same size as they are: SOP = SOR. Neither the Size of Person nor the Size of Role should be too much bigger or smaller than the other. Otherwise, there will be problems.

If you are working in a role that is much smaller than your Size of Person, one of two things will happen. Either you will get bored out of your mind, and end up suffering from bore-out, which is just as debilitating as burnout. (Both are becoming seen as work-induced depression.) Or, to avoid getting bored out of your mind, you will immediately set about increasing the complexity of your role until it is at least as big as you are, and gives you the challenge you need to be at peak performance.

Your organisation will suffer in both cases. If you increase your role's complexity, you may well end up doing work that no one else in the team or even the organisation can follow, and may not even be meeting any of the current drivers. If you are the founder or the CEO, you will end up trying to lead your people, perhaps even your entire business concept, into places they are not yet ready to go. Quite likely your organisation will implode.

Equally, if your role is way too big for you, you are either going to end up burning out, as you valiantly try everything you can to cope single-handedly despite being in over your head, or you will trim the role down to your size.

Again, in both cases, your organisation will suffer. If you burn out, you will be

[1] https://www.requisite.org/

underperforming for however long it takes before you and your organisation realise what is happening, and for the time it takes for you to heal. You may well be out of action for many months and still cost your organisation your fully loaded employee cost. You may find that you carry the scars of burning out for the rest of your life and that your career is never what it would have been if your manager, or lead link in a self-governing circle, had never put you into a role too big for you.

In the worst case, no one, not even you, recognises that this is not your problem, but rather, it is work-induced depression caused by your management allocating you to a role way bigger than your Size of Person. In this case, you will likely blame yourself, absolving the manager or lead link of all accountability, and simply accept being fired for poor performance, or resign in a depression.

In the worst case, this can lead to employees dying by their own hand[2].

It may be even worse for your organisation if you trim the role down to your size.

Whether you are in a single person expert role or the CEO of your company, if you oversimplify the inherent complexity, ambiguity, uncertainty or volatility of your role, you will simply have no idea about the possibilities in front of you for your business to survive or even thrive. You will quite likely kill off your company, because your decisions are limited to an insufficiently complex set of choices for the situation you are in.

Just how much bigger the role can be than your Size of Person (SoP) depends on how much scaffolding the organisation can provide for you to stretch deep into your developmental Zone 3, as described in Section 13.5.2. The better this scaffolding gives you psychological safety and capacity to recognise and talk about your feelings, and the more you can mine and refine conflict to work on your own development, both in skills and the three SoP dimensions, the better off you are.

A requisite organisation requires both the developmental stage and the task organisational stage to be matched, and to develop in lockstep.

Failing to do this is why organisations that attempt to progress far along the organisational axis towards self-governing, but without sufficient progress developmentally, either rapidly fall back into traditional management practices or implode. Equally, organisations that attempt to bring in developmental practices, without progressing at an equal pace towards self-governing, begin haemorrhaging the most developed members of staff. The sweet spot is the valley shown in Figure 14.1.

This valley has good news for you, whatever type of organisation you are in. There is a simple small next step you can take, deeper along the valley, wherever

---

[2] The nonprofit Minds at Work in the UK was founded by Geoff McDonald, former Unilever Global VP HR, and others to address mental health issues in the workplace.

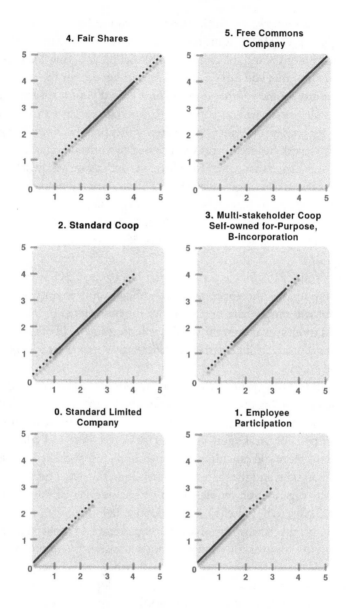

Figure 14.1: The valley of continuous stability as organisations grow their capacity along the two axes of human development and organised task execution. Each square shows the viable valley for that level of incorporation. Solid diagonals represent systemic stability, dotted lines fragile stability dependent on the leadership to maintain.

you are now. Even a Management Accountability Hierarchy lying at the bottom left can easily introduce simple Adaptive Way patterns, like giving effective feedback, and take a step towards becoming a developmental organisation. You can introduce simple self-management patterns that take you a step towards becoming self-organising.

Each little step will bring benefits, and ease taking the next step, up to the limit of what your incorporation can sustain.

If you have already stepped far along the self-governing organisation direction, pay vigilant attention for any signs of stepping beyond what the current meaning-making stories can support, or beyond what your organisation's developmental stage can keep within everyone's Zone 3.

It is very easy for an ambitious change agent to lead, without realising until it is too late, that their organisation has gone too deep into self-organising, forcing people into their Zone 4. This is the panic zone, where you cannot perform regardless of how much support you have from both the organisation and outside, and all you can do is either shut out what is so far beyond your Size of Person, or leave.

Either way, you are likely to be highly stressed and harmed, and equally so the organisation.

Everyone in your organisation will be best served if they are all fluent in the Adaptive Way patterns, at the very least in the Ground Pattern and the first few in each category of the 28 thought forms.

Once everyone is fluent, you are far on a journey towards becoming a developmental organisation. To reach the highest levels as a development organisation you also need the power of self-organising.

If you are a change agent, or the CEO leading the transition away from a person-centred hierarchy and shifting a company towards Holacracy, you have a make-or-break role in developing this adaptive capacity in every individual and team. Best to do it by introducing structured patterns of dialogue, so that it happens as part of work, at no extra cost, time, or effort.

Your job leading change spans all four layers. You will be supporting individual social-emotional and cognitive development; interactivity and reciprocal helping; self-governing organisation design and processes; requisite matching of task to individual; and changing the shareholder structure to one that enables and doesn't hinder this.

So developing high performing teams, whether in a traditional company or modern self-governing teams (circles, as they are more commonly called) demands far more than has ever before been expected of a team coach, employee or leader today.

Divided teams

Organisations are intended to be good at chunking down[3] the complexity of roles, but sometimes the complexity is inherent and irreducible. When it is, you cannot divide it down into simplicity. Whoever fills these roles must be big enough to grasp the full complexity.

Also, anyone within a team or circle who has a smaller SoP than the whole team's SoR may cause the entire team to function at a lower size than required for its task.

When a team, or circle in an Ocracy, needs to take a decision, the team as a whole must be at least as big as the entire driver and decision. So either every single member must have a big enough SoP, or each member must be psychologically able to recognise and take a decision they have not fully grasped.

Most teams have a few members at a bigger or smaller SoP than the team centre of gravity. This is called a divided team, and has important implications for how the team can rise to their largest challenges, especially adaptive ones.

In trying to understand who your organisation is, the first question you should ask is whether the team leader or lead link has a bigger or a smaller SoP than the team's centre of gravity. If it's bigger, and they have sufficient respect from the rest of the team, they will be able to provide the developmental scaffolding to support the whole team to take decisions that are bigger than its average SoP.

However, if their SoP is smaller than the centre of gravity, you had better hope that the team leader has the humility to follow the team. I have so often seen team leaders who have a smaller SoP than the people they are leading, but have the formal or personal power to overrule the others in the team. This leads eventually to the team taking overly simplistic decisions that cannot reliably help the business to survive, let alone thrive.

Usually only an outsider with a sufficiently bigger SoP than any individual in the team can recognise which way round it is divided, because of the Dunning-Kruger effect. The team itself, and its members, unless they have proficiently applied everything in this book, probably won't be able to tell the difference.

The ideal team, or Ocracy circle, is composed of people of more or less the same size. This ideal is rare in any team bigger than three people. More normally the team is divided. And then you need to have interpersonal relationships and psychological safety such that the team as a whole takes decisions at a SoP = SoR, regardless of the SoP of whoever has formal authority over the team or decision domain.

---

[3] Taking a role, or task, that is too big to do and breaking it down into smaller ones (chunks) that can be done.

In such a divided team, the few individuals with a larger SoP than the team's centre of gravity are recognised and explicitly tasked by the team with growing everyone's SoP.

14.3 Sociocracy, Holacracy, etc.

Sociocracy and its various forks emerged from the philosophy of Auguste Comte. He recognised that governance in modern society could no longer be based on in-herited or appointed power. Thus was born the philosophy of sociocracy, which loosely translates as *society governing itself*.

The first practical implementation of the sociocratic philosophy in an organ-isation was in a school in the Netherlands, founded by Kees Boeke and Beatrice Cadbury Boeke during the Second World War.

Since then an ever-growing number of organisations have recognised that being at an appropriate level along the journey towards full self-organising, appropriate for their business context, increases their business results and staff well-being.

Ted Rau, co-founder with Jerry Koch-Gonzales of *Sociocracy for All (SoFA)* and authors of an excellent book on implementing sociocracy, *Many Voices, One Song*[80], describes it well in the following guest contribution.

> Since we spend so much time in organizations, why not make them a place where we can thrive as humans, and contribute positively to the world we want to live in?
>
> The founder of sociocracy in its modern guise, Gerard Endenburg, a former student of the Boekes' school, sees the essence as *no one ig-nored*. SoFA translates that into *everyone's needs matter* and *everyone's voice matters*.
>
> Sociocracy is a practice of equality and it can have a positive impact on everyone.
>
> - It creates space for personal growth because you have self-responsibility and trust-filled relationships with others.
>
> - We can meet people's needs through organizations, including autonomy, competence, relationships, contribution, belong-ing, and meaning.
>
> Sociocracy is *one* framework of many that allows us to hold complex-ity while generating more ability to act in ways that are healthy for us and the planet.

And at the same time many early adopters of self-managing, self-governing, or even self-organising, methods added their own flavour to what they do. So now you have a wide range of approaches, including Holacracy[79], sociocracy[80], and Sociocracy 3.0[183,204], with close relatives in the agile approaches.

All have value, all have advantages and disadvantages in specific contexts, and all have passionate adherents.

One challenge some transitions to an Ocracy face, that this book addresses: whenever anyone in an organisation still has S3 elements to their meaning making, they must either have actual people as role models creating new norms for the group, or become part of a large group that already consistently practices these norms.

This means that in any organisational change journey, the role of real live human beings in shaping the group's meaning making (lower left), and the meaning making of each person (upper left), can never be fulfilled by structures and processes (integral lower right).

There are now a large number of excellent websites and books filled with everything you need to build your own unique flavour of Ocracy, or to apply one of the existing approaches, so I've not repeated what others have already done better.

14.4 Task and role arena

Here I touch briefly on how to build the structures and processes your organisation needs for tasks and roles, integrated with the other three layers of an Adaptive Organisation: intra-personal, inter-personal, and stakeholder incorporation.

After all, to actually get many people to work together does require some way of organising tasks and roles, and some way of mining and refining conflict and tension, in order that the organisation continuously improves its fit with the external drivers whose need it exists to meet[4].

---

[4]Specialist books about each approach include: Sociocracy in *Many voices, one song*[80] by Ted Rau and Jerry Koch-Gonzalez; Holacracy in Brian Robertson's[79] book; and Sociocracy 3.0,[183] by James Priest, Bernhard Bockelbrink, Liliana David and many others in the S3 community[204]. Books on the theme of creating such organisations include Frederic Laloux's *Reinventing Organisations*[184,205] and *New work needs inner work*[206]. There is much more, e.g., Appreciative Inquiry and Open Space Technology; the Chaordic Organisation approach developed by Dee Hock; Decentralised Autonomous Organisation (DAO); and the Open Organisation. There are so many good approaches out there that it's best for you to choose what seems right for you and your organisation in your current context.

Minimum viable structures and processes

Recall that I regard an organisation as living, as represented by Wolfe's equation, $P = [A \times R^2]^C$. I find looking at the smallest unit of an organisation, the human being, a good model for the journey of an organisation.

When you were first conceived, you were one embryonic cell, somewhat like the founder and source of a startup. Then you were two cells, and then four. At this stage, none of your cells had distinct roles, and there was no hard structure like a skeleton. All four cells were simultaneously taking care of themselves, each other, and the whole.

As the number of cells grew, the minimum viable level of differentiation in roles, and the minimum viable structure, was implemented to fit the needs of each stage of growth. Your body grew with amazing speed and efficiency, extracting the most results from the least investment in structure.

At some point you were born, and even then the structure of your skull had not yet reached its final shape. You grew in size and complexity. Your brain only reached full adult complexity around the age of 25. Your Size of Person continues to grow long after that.

All the distinct growth stages you went through were exactly right to give you just enough structure for you to maximally adapt to the life conditions you were in at the time, and to get your energy flowing.

The same applies for any business as a living being. Your topmost priority is to maximise the free energy available to convert into business results. That needs all the capitals to be present in viable quantities and flowing. Build the right organisational structure for the stage you are entering.

After all, the first liver cell in your body did not have the full structure of veins and arteries of an adult liver. Avoid building a highly developed structure before you are close enough to needing it.

Energy flows when, where and how it wants to flow. The very essence of your organisation, because it is a living being, is the nebulous, unknowable, and uncontrollable energy flowing and transforming into business results. Just the right amount of structure and process definition is needed to maximise energy flow and conversion into output. Keep a very careful eye on where energy is and isn't flowing, and adjust what is happening to get it flowing and converting everywhere.

Also keep in mind what we covered in Section 12.6. The workplace reality that you experience is your inner workplace, not the tangible outer workplace. Work with all quadrants in Figure 12.1 to bring your organisation to life. There are a number of approaches that have proven very useful in creating minimum viable structures in organisations. You will find a number in these references[206–210].

Multiplicity of roles

In every organisation, everyone plays a multiplicity of roles. In an Adaptive Organisation, this multiplicity is made explicit, so that you can play these roles with full recognition and support from your colleagues and organisation.

In an Adaptive Organisation all members of staff are simultaneously executives, workers, leaders and followers. Even more so, as you'll see in the next section, customers, suppliers, family members and the community you live in may also be executives, workers, leaders and followers for your company.

Making this explicit means that nobody is disempowered from interacting wherever and however they can add value to the organisation. It also means that the organisation can expect everyone to be an effective executive and care for the whole organisation as a meaning-making living being, whatever your most primary role or stakeholder category is.

It means that the newest hire's, or the most junior person's perception, of what the organisation needs from its people must have a systemic place to be heard. In addition to any visible, explicit role you may have in the organisation's lower right quadrant (either a Management Accountability Hierarchy or a Functional Accountability Hierarchy), you and everyone else always has a number of hidden, implicit roles in your organisation's lower left quadrant (Human Capability Hierarchy).

Think about this perspective in a meeting, for example, a governance meeting. It is clear that you are always sitting there with both explicit and implicit, visible and hidden organisational roles. You may feel a tension in one of the explicit MAH-/FAH roles that the meeting is explicitly about, you may feel a tension in one of the implicit HCH roles, or even in both. This is the same as quantum mechanics: what you see when you look at the roles is not the same as what the roles actually are.

The better scaffolding is enabling you to speak as clearly as you can to bring the tension into the meeting so that everyone can mine and refine it, the better the organisation is at being fully adaptable.

Keep in mind that the most pivotal tensions often begin as a nebulous feeling, pointing at a deeply hidden tension, not yet open to any articulation, let alone one that anyone else is able to see sense or logic in. The single most important tension to mine and refine may well be the one that cannot be articulated any more clearly than someone simply saying

> *I feel a tension listening to this proposal. Something doesn't feel right, and I cannot articulate what it is. I request ... (time / a sparring partner / discussion and debate on) to get to a point where we can articulate something more clearly.*

Are executives born or made?

Since everyone needs to be effective in all roles, both explicit and implicit, part of your journey in an Adaptive Organisation is to continuously increase everyone's effectiveness.

Peter Drucker came to the conclusion that effective executives are made, not born. He found that every single top executive who he met had had to learn how to be effective. Every single one had had to learn how to be more subtle with ineffective elements of their nature, biases, and meaning-making stories. His excellent short book, *The Effective Executive*[25], albeit written in the 60s, is as relevant in an Ocracy of today as it was in the Management Accountability Hierarchies that predominated when he wrote it. Peter Drucker was, in my (Graham's) opinion, one of the pioneers of today's trend towards Ocracies and the Adaptive Organisation.

Drucker has summarised the common characteristics of effective executives.

1. They ask *what needs to be done?* Which means they stand more often in a place of ignorance and curiosity, not in a place of certainty; and actively keep looking at the context and needs for anything new or changing.

2. They ask *what is right for the enterprise?* Doing this well requires fluidity in all thought forms, especially C6 (Frames of Reference).

3. They develop action plans. How and what they do here depends on where the organisation is, in the categories of Section 14.1.

4. They take responsibility for decisions. Regardless of which category your organisation is, taking responsibility for decisions in your domain is the minimum. And in any HCH or FAH you always have a decision domain.

5. They take responsibility for communicating. This applies to any and everyone in any organisation. You are all executives in many senses.

6. They are focused on opportunities, rather than problems. For many people, this is a big challenge. Problems are usually so much easier to lay out clearly, and have clearer ways of solving them. Opportunities are often inherently nebulous.

7. They run productive meetings. Well, yes.

8. They think and say we, rather than I. This is an art, not a science. It is all about the art of facilitating human beings to bond together, to feel energised, and to engage in the reciprocal helping that creates the collaboration needed for high team performance. So sometimes it's important to say I, and at other times it's we.

Of course, his work ought to be read together with complementary work, say by Margaret Wheatley[31,32] which played a pivotal role in my (Graham) journey towards this book. And keep in mind, where you find contradictions between them, that the opposite of a deep truth may be another quite different deep truth.

UniOne and nebulous

Of course, the characteristics of being an effective executive in an Adaptive Organisation have some important nuances. The most important is that in an Adaptive Organisation we inherently recognise that much is nebulous and cannot be pinned down, because the organisation is inherently in both lower left and lower right quadrants. These quadrants are complementary pairs, as in quantum mechanics.

An Adaptive Organisation, for example, harnesses both the uniqueness of each individual and the common oneness of everyone—the full complementary pair—to be truly one living organisation and part of one business ecosystem. (Read more on creating living regenerative business ecosystems in Section 17.2.)

In a traditional vertical hierarchy, the dominant meaning-making stories are likely to be concentrated on individual uniqueness. Stars will be disproportionately fêted and rewarded (even though the research that you read about in Sections 13.6.3 and 13.3 proves that the star's success is primarily a consequence of the whole organisation in which they are embedded).

So in these organisations, the most long-term effective executives are those who explicitly restore the natural balance between uniqueness and oneness that characterise any living being. They say *we* far more often than *I*.

In an Adaptive Organisation, you need to work out when it will serve best to emphasise the uniqueness that you or a colleague brings—then say I. Or, if it serves the organisation better to emphasise the common oneness—for example, to note the common ground that you are all standing on as representatives of this living being—say we.

During the course of my working life, I (Graham) have been criticised almost equally for using I, and for using we. You most likely will be too. Every single criticism had validity, as had my choice in the first place. This is another classic example of the nebulous, quantum, or Cubist essence of an organisation. I can always speak with the voice of we because I am part of what is common to all of us and represent it just as much as any other individual can represent oneness from within their own unique meaning-making and reality.

Equally, each person criticising me could only experience my words in terms of their own unique inner reality.

The more comfortable everyone is with the nebulousness of organisations and language, the easier it gets to hear the intent behind the words and to choose words that make that intent easier to hear. As with any Picasso painting, both the painter and the viewer jointly shape what the viewer sees in the painting, or hears in the words, or perceives in the actions.

Seeing an organisation as a living being, filled with nebulous complementary pairs that cannot individually and simultaneously be pinned down precisely, requires equal effectiveness in head and heart. Equal effectiveness in using conscious thinking (especially transformational thought forms, not just binary logic) and using intuition. And equal effectiveness in applying hard empirical data, and crossing unknowable chasms using nebulous clouds of intuition as your stepping stones.

As Einstein said,

> Not everything that is important can be measured, and not everything that can be measured is important.

Or as Peter Drucker points out, data is not the foundation of your data-based business decisions, opinion is.

You begin with an opinion, likely anchored in your intuition (i.e., anchored in your biases, nature, and meaning-making stories; limited by your capacity for transformational thought forms). An opinion on what you are dealing with, and so what kind of data will be useful to you in generating useful options to choose between, and driving your choice. This opinion is created and limited by your Size of Person. Any data that does not fit within this Size of Person you won't look for; and, if it is given to you, you may not be able to fit it into your reality.

Very few of us are equally and sufficiently good in intuition and thinking—most of us are naturally more talented in one or the other. If your natural talents lie predominantly in the visible explicit lower right MAH/FAH, then you need to develop your comfort with aspects of your organisation that you may well find highly uncomfortable. Find a colleague who is naturally talented in this area, and a route for both of you to use the tension between your natural talents to then develop into two legs that your organisation can run with; rather than you trying to be one single super leg that your organisation can only hop with.

14.5 Scaffolding to stay out of the panic Zone 4

Deploying the scaffolding described here will benefit all organisations, but it is essential for any organisation aiming to become Level 5 in each three axes of the Adaptive Organisation model. To determine what scaffolding is needed, by whom, and when, ask two questions.

1. With which SoP do circle members, individually and collectively, put their competencies to work?

2. Therefore, what Job 2 supports do the work structures and processes need to provide, individually and collectively, in the three elements of Size of Person?

The work of a leader, change agent or coach, anyone with a lead link role, etc., goes beyond what is typically expected of a team coach today because people are challenged at many levels by the identity paradox created by working sometimes as a peer, then above, and then below the same colleague. Leaders work now spans all six layers of Section 2.8, at least the first four layers described in Section 12.7.

In any organisation, management, or the anchor circle and lead links, has the accountability to both construct this scaffolding and to match the Size of Person to the Size of Role . This is an absolute imperative in an Adaptive Organisation. The anchor circle (i.e., equivalent to the leadership team in a traditional organisation) and, to some degree, everyone, works constantly on constructing the scaffolding that the circles use on a day to day basis.

For each developmental stage a different scaffolding is needed.

1. In Zone 1, continue to do what any good organisation does for each stage.

   - S3: clarity on the expectations of physical others, and feedback from them. (NB: this needs to be physical others, just role clarity fails to deliver what the meaning-making identity needs.)
   - S4: roles where you act according to your personal values.
   - S5: fully developmental and self-organising in your immediate organisation space.

2. In Zone 2, where work requires individuals to stretch up into their current growth zone, you can then usually self-support given the above. You are at your best if you also have

   - S3: strong personal bonding with other circle members.
   - S4: alignment, clarity and buy-in to the big picture across all peers.
   - S5: roles demanding constant stretching, growth in maturity and flexing of your full meaning-making range.

3. In Zone 3, work requires a size beyond your capacity to self-support, but you can act if given sufficient support from the organisation's structures and processes, and your colleagues.

- S3: you need peer to peer coaching practices you fully trust in, and that all your peers also use effectively. Processes that are the cultural norm and expectation, not just policy.
- S4: a peer group of individuals that you recognise as being of equal or larger Size of Person to yourself, and so you trust them as human beings to be able to give you useful feedback on your integrity and value system. Others may give you feedback that you deem useful.
- S5: Peer to peer exchange of a deeply mutually developmental nature

4. In Zone 4, the size required is completely beyond you. No scaffolding exists.

In Section 13.7.3 we described how public agreements are one type of scaffolding. Hopefully this section makes more clear the imperative of using such scaffolding whenever your organisation brings in Holacracy, Sociocracy or any other self-governing approach.

Since this support must be an integral part of all work processes, a peer-to-peer developmental scaffolding is needed for any self-governing organisation design to truly work. Any organisation benefits, of course, whether agile or even a traditional management accountability hierarchy. But as long as a self-governing organisation lacks the capacity to change the organisation design at all scales, such peer-to-peer developmental scaffolding will always be less effective.

CHAPTER 15

Your organisation is its incorporation

There is only one way to see things, until someone shows us how to look at them with different eyes.
—*Pablo Picasso*

Modern business, the tool that we have invented to meet our needs, is no longer good enough. That we are stuck dealing with many issues is visible in the plethora of conflicting opinions in business theory, politics, and economics, on what to do; and the growing number of fudges to keep business as usual going.

This is like the situation in physics and art a century ago. It suggests that we are asking fundamentally wrong questions, like when Rutherford asked where an electron is (Chapter 2).

It is time for the capitalist business concept to transform. As you've seen before in this book, transforming capitalism needs transformational thinking and us to transform our meaning-making stories, to bring together apparent opposites and integrate them into completely new complementary pairs. Just as Picasso and Einstein did.

To build a truly Adaptive Organisation that performs regeneratively over the long term, and to mine and refine all the conflict in order to extract valuable data on how it no longer fits into its niche in society, we need a new capitalism, where all stakeholders are members of the organisation.

Borrowing from quantum physics, this means reinventing the elementary particles of incorporation and how they interact. These elementary particles are the shares and the shareholders, interacting via the rights and obligations embedded in the shares they own.

15.1 Where your organisation is: incorporation

As always, I use a scale from 0 to 5 so that you can map out where your company lies on the stakeholder and incorporation axis. Each is a concrete meaning-making story category, developed in consultation with Rory Ridley-Duff of Sheffield-Hallam Business School. This ranking is a lens designed to shine a clear light on a progression from the company as the property of a narrow group of people, to do what they want with, through successively greater levels of freedom and inclusion of broader groups of stakeholders and needs, up to complete freedom and broad appropriate inclusion.

On this scale there are jumps. The level 5 Free / Commons is, I believe, the first incorporation form suited to Tier 2 consciousness, called Teal in Reinventing Organisations[184] and Yellow in Spiral Dynamics[203]. (See Table 14.1 on Page 343.) There is a jump from Level 3 to 4 to 5. Level 3 is spiral green, Level 4 is green with a little yellow, and Level 5 is cleanly yellow or teal.

There is a huge amount of good in the progression we have already made to Level 1, 2, and 3 companies. To build the regenerative, or at least sustainable, economy we urgently need, now is the time to take the next step. I hope that this scale will inspire you to step your organisation up one or more levels. If you are using deliberately developmental practices, or dynamic governance for roles and tasks, anything less than Level 3 makes these fragile.

If you aspire to antifragile Teal for your organisation, get yourself to Level 5 incorporation, then strive for Level 5 on the other two axes along the viable valley. Any organisation below Level 4 on each access is inadequate and too fragile for the critical task we have today of creating a thriving society in a thriving natural environment. If you want to build a future-fit, regenerative, circular, or Teal organisation, go for Level 4, ideally 5 on each axis. Especially the incorporation axis.

5: Free Commons of productive capacity.

The organisation here is consistently and integrally a free non-human person, across all domains. As such, it is free to act in an optimum way to benefit the entire ecosystem it is in, including having the freedom to choose for itself when it is right to change or even when it has reached the end of its life. Without this, no organisation's task and role design can progress beyond self-directing, let alone reach being an autopoietic member of an ecosystem.

This applies at all scales, from each individual through to each company. Members are free to opt out, and each member within each scale and between scales forms complementary pairs. There is a constant dance between the roles of the individual and the collective at the next scale up, between roles, needs, and offers between members with each scale and between scales.

Stakeholders engage in the governance of a commons of productive capacity, and represent all capitals touched, using a stewardship paradigm that takes the probable needs of future generations of beneficiaries into account in any decisions. Everyone recognises that the commons is bigger and longer living than any of them. Appropriate sanctions are in place for stakeholders that fail to fulfil their fiduciary duty of care towards the Commons.

At Level 5 growing all capitals and sharing surplus capitals equitably to all members investing any capital is deep in the practices and culture. A Level 5 company is regenerative in all ways for all capitals and stakeholders because that is the kind of company it is, not because of any regulation nor any incentive. Some Steward-owned companies will have some elements of a Level 5 company[211], but lack the leap out of all concepts of ownership, or the all-capitals required to naturally form regenerative ecosystems.

This is the best legal incorporation for an investor or founder wanting to protect the long-term integrity of their intent, values, and purpose; and especially any impact, regeneration, circularity, or sustainability outcomes. Because it is a free incorporated being, bad actors cannot later seize control.

This is the first Tier 2 incorporation level, suited to a Teal or Yellow organisation.

4: Governance and wealth sharing across multiple stakeholders.

Has multiple stakeholders, representing all the capitals relevant to the business. All stakeholders receive an equitable benefit across multiple capitals and all invest the capital(s) of that stakeholder category in the company's success. All capitals count as 'skin in the game'[28]. Individuals can be in multiple stakeholder categories.

Intellectual property is treated as a commons (either closed only to members, or open to the public), curated by the company, and available for use by the originators of that IP, even if they cease to be members. You cannot be alienated from your IP.

All wealth generated is shared equitably, and in particular, any appreciation of the company's market value as a whole is partially distributed to the holders of investor shares as an increase in the market value of their shares, and partly to the other shareholders in the form of investor shares.

Decisions in general meetings are taken using at least a weighted decision-making process that minimises the possibility of overwhelming the needs of any stakeholder group. Ideally, decisions are taken using a consent process.

This is the highest Tier 1 incorporation, perhaps with a tinge of Teal / Yellow. The standard FairShares company is an excellent example. Some Steward-owned companies are also at this level[211].

3: Multistakeholder Coops/For-purpose/basic Steward owned/Self-owning

A company falls into this Level if it is still within the meaning-making story of a company as an ownable good, but is half-way out of that paradigm towards being a free commons with all-capitals growth and sharing. It may be structured with a trust, or similar, that has voting rights, and trustees or stewards who are selected for independence and capacity to take wise long-term decisions according to the company's interests and values as laid out in the statutes.

The statutes and split of ownership between the stewards, the trust, and other shareholders is such that the company as a whole cannot be sold in any normal sales process. One possibility where it might in effect be sold would be if its larger purpose requires it to change how it is incorporated, and so it is sold into another incorporation that is also at least at Level 3, steward owned or self-owning. Depending on the details[211], it may have elements of Level 4 or Level 5.

It may be a multistakeholder cooperative, but not yet fully FairShares. Some incorporated benefit corporations may be here, not at level 1; some standard cooperatives may be here if they also have clear mandatory vetoes to the sale of the company, and changing any purpose and sale-related aspects.

I see John Lewis as a level 3 company, along with many others, such as Robert Bosch and Zeiss, that are formally owned by a trust that serves to benefit a broader set of stakeholders than just the financial investors. These are a vital step towards the commons. Perhaps you could consider them a hybrid of a narrow Commons and an owned company.

The Scott Bader Commonwealth Ltd is another excellent example of a Level 3, tending towards a Level 4 company. The original founder, Ernest Bader, wanted to ensure that his Quaker values continued, and so put all his shares into a trust, with all colleagues as trustees. Their trustee obligation is to act in the company's best interest for the present and future.

B-corp incorporated companies (not just the certification) often lie at Level 3.

The paradoxical shadow side of these initiatives is that, because they act within the myths of Section 4.4, especially the myth that shareholders own the company, their very laudable efforts at making business a force for good also increase the strength of the myths. A bit like a tug of war against yourself, fighting a meaning-making story whilst staying within the story makes the story stronger.

2: Cooperative, Employee-owned company.

One of the oldest and best alternatives to the limited company. Likely most of you have a cooperative nearby, either a worker coop (most of the shares are in the hands of the staff stakeholders) or a customer cooperative (most of the shares are in the hands of customer stakeholders). The cooperative has been, and still is, an essential, and very powerful counterweight to the limited company. More in the next section.

A disadvantage of the cooperative form is the difficulty attracting risk capital; and the risk in general meetings of having only one stakeholder type in the decision making.

1: Employee ownership (Limited company, etc.)

You have an employee stock ownership plan, all staff behave consistently according to your clear corporate values. Sustainability and corporate social responsibility are business strategies, not tangential exercises. Companies with B-corp certification, but still incorporated as typical limited companies, can lie here. They may do superb work, and act as superb role models; but it is fragile, subject to the financial investors agreeing. All it takes is enough voting power in the hands of an extractive investor, and everything can go out the window in an asset-stripping spree.

0: Standard limited company, or analogous organisation.

Most companies, such as private limited or public listed companies; impact companies; standard non-profit organisations, non-governmental organisations are here. For up until the second half of the last century this seemed good enough, because we could not see the harm it was doing.

This legal form is unsuited to a Level 3 or above developmental organisation or self-governing organisation. Attempting to go Teal on these two axes in a Level 0 incorporation is a highly risky, fragile endeavour.

For those into spiral dynamics (Table 14.1 on Page 343), you cannot build a Spiral level 7 Teal culture and operations on a level 3 and 4 (red-blue) foundation.

15.2 A share is a package deal

Recall from Section 4.4 that business is full of myths, concretised meaning-making stories believed to be absolute legal truths.

One of these myths is that shareholders actually own the company. Rather, the shareholders own an abstraction called a share, a package deal of rights and obligations[76]. These rights and obligations are the building blocks you use in constructing a business capable of doing the job at hand; for example, to build a regenerative economy. Like any set of building blocks, you must assemble them in the right way for the job you need done, regardless of how others have assembled theirs. So if you want a regenerative business, assemble the blocks to multiply all capitals and protect all stakeholders from exploitation.

There are six primary building blocks.

Liquidation rights. Shareholders come last if the company folds. Shareholders have the right to residual assets after all other obligations have been paid.

Income rights. The right to receive a share of the dividend in return for your investment, if there is a surplus that the directors decide to distribute.

Appreciation rights. If the company's total value grows, the value of your shares may grow.

Voting rights. The right to engage in governance in a general meeting.

Transfer rights. The right to transfer by selling, or in some other way, your shares to another person.

Information rights. The right to information about the company's policies, practices, and performance.

There are a number of pre-packaged deals, differing in countries around the world, and each may have different subtleties and flavours. But there's nothing sacrosanct about any of these package deals. Each is just one meaning-making story concretised in law.

That concrete is not irreversibly solid; it is just as nebulous as the story that created it.

In most jurisdictions, there is some freedom to build your own specific package. For example, voting rights: a share can have no votes or many. In a cooperative, it's one person one vote, regardless of how many shares they have. In a traditional plc, it's one share, one vote. In France, recent legislation has made automatic what has long been possible: people who hold their shares for longer than two years get a double vote. Belgium intends introducing multiple voting rights from 2020.

Appreciation rights can be capped; for example, Enspiral in New Zealand has a 15-times cap on appreciation rights.

The standard package deals in most countries range from trusts, through co-operatives, to private or public limited companies. The FairShares Commons company we propose can be constructed sufficiently well as simply another package deal that integrates the most desirable elements of the full range into one super package. Of course, to get to a perfect FairShares Commons, company law needs updating.

Each of the traditional package deals below, common examples of incorporation at levels 0, 1 and 2) has advantages and disadvantages.

Public limited liability company If your company has shares that anyone can buy or sell on a stock market, it is most likely this.

> Public limited liability companies are superb tools to attract and multiply large quantities of financial capital. They have superb strength at convincing strangers (and large numbers of strangers in today's crowdfunded companies), who don't usually even first meet in person, to trust this non-human legal person with their money.

> This is huge. Trust, the deepest foundation of human society, has been externalised from real humans into a non-human institution that is a legally concretised story.

> These companies have been a superb engine in raising the standard of living of a number of us reading this book. Sadly they have proven to be equally powerful tools to increase the gap in financial wealth between big investors and the rest because they are designed to multiply only financial capital.

> Typically in public limited liability companies, every share that you buy comes together with one vote in decisions in any general meeting of shareholders. In a one-share, one-vote scenario, a decision taken in the annual general meeting (for example, how much to pay the executives, to sell the company, or buy another one) is the opinion with the most money behind it.

> The problems we are facing today are a direct consequence of decisions taken because they met the needs of the money-majority, and were contrary to the needs of other stakeholders.

> Investors are the only stakeholder category active in the company. Other stakeholders can only become active by buying shares, thereby also becoming members of the investor category. Usually, though, they won't be able to buy enough votes to have any meaningful weight in an annual general meeting.

Private limited liability company Many companies begin life as a private limited liability company and become a public limited liability company when they are successful enough to warrant going public via an initial public offering (IPO).

The governance processes here are typically the same as in a public limited liability company. Investors are the only stakeholder category active in the company. Other stakeholders can only become active by buying shares, but with the same caveats as for public limited companies.

One important difference though: in most jurisdictions, new investors buying into the company need to be known and approved.

Employee-owned limited liability company This is a restriction on the limited liability company, one where the voting shares of the company are in the employees' hands. Even better is if the shares are in a trust that all employees are members of.

The big benefit of an employee-owned company is that all staff can now align their needs with those of any investors and the company as a whole. If the employees take significant risks, such as accepting a 50% salary cut during an economic downturn, they know that they will all share the benefits in capital gain and dividends when the economy picks up. Employee-owned companies have proven significantly more resilient in the face of setbacks than investor-owned companies.

Worker cooperative The next kind of company, going back to the Rochdale Pioneers, is the worker cooperative. Just like an employee-owned limited liability company, a worker cooperative has both limited liability and the shares in the hands of the staff.

One difference here compared to the Level 4 FairShares or Level 5 Free company, e.g. a FairShares Commons, is that in a coop wealth shared is with the staff only, whereas the FairShares shares wealth back to all stakeholders and investors of all capitals.

The important differences to a limited company are a consequence of a very different underlying story. The story shaping the reality of a cooperative puts the group of people working together and the business results equally on centre stage. Governance is now one person one vote, regardless of how many shares you have.

In this case, decisions in a general meeting get taken according to the opinion with the most people behind it. However, they are more likely to take multiple perspectives into account, and some are using the latest dialogue approaches to achieve consensus.

Employees are either the only stakeholder category active in the company, or the most powerful category. Investors can have shares, but they are usually limited to some small fraction of the total capital invested and have limited voting power.

Customer cooperative The customer cooperative is very similar to the worker cooperative, except that now the dominant stakeholder category governing the company is the customers. Everything else written above for the worker cooperative applies here too.

Social enterprise Social enterprises have also grown rapidly over the past two decades. Social enterprises typically use one of the above forms, although in some countries there are now specific social enterprise company structures available, such as the Community Interest Company in the UK. The significant difference in making a business a social enterprise lies in the meaning-making story that underpins it, which puts the benefit of a target segment of society as the primary reason why the company exists. So any company can be a social enterprise, so long as the company purpose clearly state this social benefit, and legally bind the company executives' fiduciary accountability to serving this purpose.

The stakeholders with the power to govern the company will then be defined by whichever form of company is chosen. Choosing the right set of stakeholders is a very important part of making sure that the social enterprise remains true to its values and objective(s).

Charity Depending on the country, a charity may use a specifically defined charitable legal form, or one of the legal forms above. In either case, the company is structured to concretise the reality shaped by a story as being of service to some disadvantaged stakeholder or other form of public benefit[1]. Because they exist to directly provide benefits to targeted segments of society, charities usually benefit from special tax regulations, both for the charity and for the donors. Charities operate under trust law. Donated money either goes to a core funding of purpose or a specific trust for that group's campaign.

Trust A trust is much broader than, but in some ways has common ground with, a charity, in that it exists to serve some specific non-business objective. A trust

---

[1] https://www.gov.uk/guidance/public-benefit-rules-for-charities#about-public-benefit

is completely constrained to serve whatever need it was created to serve, and no other; and to stay completely within the values and principles defined by the trust founders. A trust is governed by trustees who are elected or appointed and must vote in accordance with the principles of the trust. A trust may be legally incorporated as a charity, for example, the National Trust in the UK is a registered charity.

All company forms are mythical beasts that we have invented. We, through our individual stories and the stories that we've invented to underpin these companies, have created the reality that we experience today[2].

Even though these are all merely concretisations of stories, over time we've lost sight of the story. And now we believe the concretisation is the only possible actuality, rather than our invention.

15.3 Reinventing the company

There are two essential lenses to use to see both what a company can become and what we need to do differently to incorporate Level 3, 4, or 5 companies.

Separate past from future, money from power

If you look at the rights above, you will see that they fall into two different types: rights anchored in the past, and rights anchored in the future of the company, covered in Chapter 4.

In the traditional package deals, the past and the future are locked together. You invest money in the past and buy the whole package of rights locked together. Even though there's no inherent connection between your right to benefit from the wealth that the company has generated in the past, and your capacity to wisely steward the company into the right future for the company.

Recall, governance rights are anchored in the company's future. They give the shareholder the right to engage in steering the company wisely into the future. We can justifiably design a company on the basis that the stronger your connection to the company (not how much money you've invested), the more governance rights you ought to have—for example, anyone who has owned shares for less than six months has no voting rights, but if you've owned them for over a year, or a number of years, you have a multiple of voting rights.

This makes sense when you look a bit more closely at the fact that, even if there is only one single shareholder, they do not own the company in the same way they

---

[2]For German speakers it's worth reading Jo Aschenbrenner's book[212].

might own a bar of chocolate. Because the company is a non-human legal person just as much as the shareholder is a legal person, company law requires even a single investor to keep it at arm's length. They cannot directly use the company and its assets as their own. It's time to take that really seriously.

There's also nothing fundamental in the idea that the holder of a share can only get the share by buying it. After all, in most countries the law no longer allows citizens to buy the vote. You can see how silly the idea is that only investor stakeholders get the right to vote, by thinking how silly it seems today that only male landowners once had the right to vote in England. For example, the Fonterra Co-operative Group Limited, New Zealand's largest company and responsible for around 30% of the world's dairy exports, issues shares only to member-farmers, at one share per kilogram of milk solids produced annually.

Today you earn your national vote through being a citizen in good standing and satisfying certain eligibility criteria. This is part of the foundation of your freedom of self-determination, your freedom to follow your own purpose in life, and for you to develop as is best for you as a free human being.

We can concretise this same meaning-making story in our companies. Base voting rights on stakeholder citizenship, including the strength of the stakeholder's long-term commitment to, and dependence on, the company. Then the company is free to develop as is best for itself as a free-living non-human being.

In contrast to governance, the financial rights, (liquidation, income, and appreciation), are anchored in the past. Depending on how much wealth the company generated in the past, you get some percentage.

A hard separation of the future from the past is at the core of a FairShares Commons and any other free company.

- The people who steer the company into the future all have a strong commitment to the company's future, and fully recognise it as a living being and a fully free non-human legal entity.

- The people who benefit today from the wealth that the company has generated over the past are those stakeholders who have contributed to that wealth generation through any investment of any kind of capital.

Multiple capitals and returns on investments

Financial capital is not the only capital, and the investors of financial capital are not the only stakeholders investing with risk. Depending on which meaning-making story you use, in other words, which frame of reference you use to give meaning to the risk of your investment, you may see an investment of money as being a lesser risk than your investment of ten years of your life as a founder of a company.

After all, if a regular investor gets none of their money back on one investment, they are likely to get it back many times over on another; they can earn money in multiple ways to make good on their loss. On the other hand, until everyone owns a Tardis with a capacity for time travel and to regenerate themselves, there is no way that you will ever get back 10 years of your life. The human capital investment of years of life, by founders and other people working for the company, may be a higher-risk investment in their frame of reference than the investment of money is in the investor's frame of reference.

Equally, nature has invested significant resources in our economy, which will take millions of years to regenerate naturally. The risk of natural capital investments to human life, especially the investment of waste absorption capacity, is now a major risk to all life on earth. Were businesses and our economy designed around all the risks of all stakeholders across all their capitals, we would make different decisions.

The foundation of an incorporated business is risk-reward. Any risk investment is rewarded, in proportion to the risk, with returns. We are now in a world where we must recognise the investment of all kinds of capital, and the risk that each investor is taking, on an equitable footing. Risk is defined by the meaning-making stories, which means working with the interpretation of risk of each stakeholder investing in each kind of capital.

The reward may be in exactly the same capital and currency invested, or there may be some floating exchange rate mechanism between capitals and currencies. The financial wealth that's generated because of the investment of all the capitals needed for a business's activities is part of what must be equitably shared across all stakeholders, in a proportion that balances the relative perception of risk. The financial wealth generated by a business includes both the surplus that the company can generate and the appreciation of the company's value.

The current allocation just to the investors of financial capital, and none to the investors of any other kind of capital, is part of what gives us the dysfunctional rent-seeking we have today.

15.4 FairShares companies

Few companies can start, scale, and deliver results sustainably over the long term without the investment of external financial capital. To be attractive to financial capital, a company must balance the risk that investors take locking their wealth into the company for many years by offering the possibility of a greater reward. (Recall from Section 6.4 on ergodicity[120] that this is not simple probability.)

The company must also be trusted, which means offering investors the right to information, and votes in the general meetings as well. If you give someone some of the power to steer the company into the future, and enough of the wealth that you hope to generate, they may believe they can make the gamble pay off on average.

Peter Drucker, one of the few people in the past century who deeply understood what businesses are for, pointed clearly at why a business needs to be a Fair-Shares Commons. He stresses customer centricity, that every business exists to deliver something that customers are prepared to offer more for than the total delivered cost. In Procter & Gamble during my (Graham's) time, the phrase

the consumer is boss

was regularly invoked in business decisions. This made it relatively easy to use consumer research data, not the HIPPO (highest-paid person's opinion) as the basis of business decisions.

The different CEOs running the company during my tenure regularly repeated this message, making clear that we should think of them as de facto reporting into Procter & Gamble's consumers.

However, there were many decisions where that was clearly not the case. Decisions around the long-term sustainability of our products were quite clearly too heavily driven by meeting the quarterly expectations of analysts and shareholders. As were some decisions around buying other companies, retrenchment, or selling off parts of P&G, discontinuing or starting a product line.

Customer centricity in many companies can only drive choices within small bubbles, constrained by the immediate investor needs, without any direct dialogue between customers and investors. Any company that truly wants customer centricity must retain the power of a customer cooperative to have the customer's voice in the largest decisions taken in a general meeting, directly talking with the investors and staff.

Claiming customer centricity as core to your company is extremely fragile if customers lack adequate direct voice and power on the board and at the general meeting level. (The idea that consumers have sufficient voice and power through withholding purchase fails today, and I doubt if it ever really worked.)

This is equally true for any other stakeholder group you claim to be part of your purpose, whatever your organisation. If you are bringing clean wood-burning stoves into Kenya, do you have people using your stoves on your board and in your AGM, with voting rights?

Equally, many companies say that their staff are their greatest asset. And yet, when you look at large scale decisions affecting staff, many treat them as a disposable, and they even show up on the balance sheet as a liability. Very few companies keep track of the asset value of their real human capital.

If a company is going to truly regard staff as part of the company's asset base, the staff need to have an equitable power to govern the company, and an equitable share of the wealth generated, compared to other voting stakeholders. The company needs to have both the strengths of an investor-centric limited company and a worker cooperative or employee-owned company.

These days companies are also competing with each other for talent, looking for suppliers that will share business risk with them, and asking their end customers to play a central role in building the business's success. For example, without the core value creation role that the end users play in companies like Facebook or Google, those companies would be worth a minuscule fraction of their current value.

Today, companies are more and more dependent on the non-financial capital that is invested. The FairShares company developed by Rory Ridley-Duff, Cliff Southcombe, and colleagues[213], and my integration with the Free Company to form the FairShares Commons, recognises the risk that all investors of all capitals are taking. The FairShares company is designed to offer all investors of all capitals an equitable reward for their risks, and an equitable power in the large-scale governance decisions taken in the general meetings on behalf of the company.

> I (Graham) gave a talk in 2018 on the FairShares company at a conference at the RSA in London marking 10 years since Lehman and Northern Rock triggered the 2008 financial crisis, using LTSGlobal (2013) and Evolutesix as examples. One participant was a senior civil servant, who came up to me afterwards to thank me for what I'd said and the hope that my talk had given him: *Graham, I am often in talks that begin the way your talk did, pointing out one or more of the problems we are facing, and the way that companies are a major part of the problem. Yours is the first one that did not end by asking us, civil servants and politicians, to first change the law. Yours is the first to end with the message that there is nothing stopping us addressing these problems now with existing company law.*

As you read the rest of this section, keep that firmly in mind. The essence of everything I'm describing can be created in almost all jurisdictions. You may need a little bit of creativity to find the route within the company law of your country to turn the same essence into a specific incorporation. For example, the FairShares outcome that can be achieved via one single FairShares company in English law may need to be a number of different companies in another country's law.

If you want to build a FairShares company, you will find it easiest if you first work with somebody who has experience in defining business strategy and structures to draft a wireframe statute for the company. Then go to a lawyer who you believe is capable of the out-of-the-box thinking and meaning-making needed to find a legal way of concretising that within the company law of your country.

The essence of a FairShares company is very simple. Its members come from all stakeholder groups with a meaningful investment of any capital and all have an equitable share of the rights to

- steer the company into the future, i.e. governance rights

- the wealth generated by the company in the past.

The FairShares company applies Picasso's and Einstein's lenses because it recognises that it's our meaning-making stories that narrowly see companies as having to be just one thing or another. What a business actually is, and what it can become, is free of most of the limitations that our stories impose.

For example, why should a public listed company and a trust be opposites? Surely to do the kind of regenerated business that we need today, all businesses must have the structural integrity of a trust, and attract all kinds of capital to accept the risk, by offering the potential to regenerate by enough to more than offset the risk. Quantum physics and Cubism recognise that any entity in actuality can be simultaneously composed, in the form of one complementary pair, of what we view in our limited reality, and the language we can use, as exclusive opposites.

The FairShares company already offers massive benefits in dealing with today's challenges than any traditional incorporation. (If you turn each of the dials to 100% and all the others to 0%, the FairShares company becomes one of the traditional companies. There's nothing really new in here, other than cooking the ingredients into a much tastier stew.)

15.5 FairShares Commons companies

Integrate all previously opposing elements, such as high impact or high profit, into one complementary pairing: high impact and high profit, and you need an enabling tool like the FairShares Commons.

In Chapter 4 you read about the different approaches to company ownership and governance. Over the past few centuries, case studies of highly successful yet idiosyncratic businesses have demonstrated that each element of the FairShares Commons leads to superior business outcomes across a wide range of metrics, including profit.

Put them all together and we get the ultimate regenerative adaptive business, maximally able to thrive profitably *and* regenerate all capitals as one single purpose, a complementary pair, through good times and bad, because it can twist and turn as fast as its drivers are changing. We need the full power of financially profitable regenerative adaptive businesses if we are going to multisolve to successfully overcome our global adaptive challenges.

If Picasso was painting a business today, he would see it as a living being delivering value to other human beings, directly or via other businesses, and he would reject the idea that any single perspective could ever be viable. Picasso would recognise the living being with innumerable inter-related inputs, outputs, and capitals.

It would be perfectly obvious to him that no real business can ever be adequately represented by any of the standard company forms in use today. It would also be perfectly clear to him that the nature of a business, as a living being, includes an intangible, nebulous component[3], where most of what is important cannot be represented in the statutes, or accurately measured. In Picasso's art, as in quantum physics, the inherent nebulous intangibility is embraced and worked with.

He would also recognise that a living being exists across time, not in time. For example, you are yourself across your entire history from birth to death. You can only get a full answer to the question *Who am I?* if you know your life from birth to death (and maybe even before and after).

So just as you always have time to transform yourself across the full timeline of all of who you are, so too does every business have potential to transform into a completely different kind of living meaning-making being, if it is incorporated as a free non-human person. If we can get this done really well, soon, for enough businesses, then there is every reason to believe that we can find a way to use, as part of the solution for tomorrow, enough of the wealth generated by the companies that have become part of the problem today.

In Section 12.6 you saw one way of looking at an organisation and its individual human members through the four lenses of each integral quadrant. You saw that an organisation is inherently and irreducibly both the nebulous, hidden Human Capability Hierarchy, and the visible, concrete Management Accountability Hierarchy / Functional Accountability Hierarchy.

You also read how there is no empirical justification for our inventing an impermeable, rigid division of the human beings who form the cells of your organisation into distinct categories like employee, executive, supplier, or customer, just as quantum physics shows that actuality is not actually segmented into waves or particles. All of them are part of the organisation in all four quadrants.

---

[3] As in Daoism, the Dao that cannot be named

The FairShares Commons gives you the foundations for antifragility by concretising the complementarity of all stakeholders in all quadrants.

To build a regenerative, antifragile, adaptive FairShares Commons, you:

- explicitly and visibly include all stakeholder categories;

- explicitly and visibly include all capitals (stores of value) and their flows;

- surrender forever to the inherently and irreducibly unknowable, nebulous nature of your organisation.

Include all stakeholders

Stakeholders in your organisation do not stay in categories with hard boundaries. Each shows up as a whole person, human or non-human, integrating all the stakeholder categories they belong to, into one meaning-making living being. All are united by the common oneness of being part of the entity they have a stake in.

Recall the restaurant example of Section 3.5.2. Fast forward 10 years. You have scaled to 10 restaurants across London, Paris, and Munich, on a foundation of significant venture capital investment. You hired experienced managers, you have a board, you already have your first Michelin star for the first restaurant you opened in London, and you have customers giving you glowing reviews.

Your business is what it is because of all of its stakeholders, not just you—exactly as described in the Ubuntu philosophy. In the beginning, this was visible on a daily basis because the few stakeholders all knew how each contributed to the whole.

But then you reincorporated as a limited company according to the term sheet the investors demanded. You set up a clear business plan, with a hard differentiation between customers, employees, suppliers, and their respective value equations.

Compare this conventional entrepreneurial startup lens with the FairShares Commons lens: now you clearly see all the potential for value generation in impact and profit that slips through the gaps created by stakeholder divisions. Customers and suppliers cannot optimally interact with each other, nor are they motivated to do word of mouth marketing.

What's wrong? The dominant logic of today's business stories. A logic that says everybody fits into distinct categories that exclude the other and each category is in competition with every other category.

These myths have created the reality we all experience today.

The new meaning-making story I propose is accepting that every stakeholder shapes the living being that your business is. It will thrive better if you eliminate any barrier to them investing their time and energy into it, in a partnership across all stakeholders.

The more interaction you have across all people in your business, the more that human energy is turned into results (Section 13.6.3). And the FairShares Commons gives you this across all stakeholders, not just staff.

Now get into your space elevator, and up outside the atmosphere. Look down at our blue planet Earth, and everything that needs to be regenerated to get each living system that human life depends on fully regenerated.

Imagine what such a regenerative business ecosystem could achieve if it reached maximum interactivity because it no longer imposed hard boundaries between stakeholders? If the organisation's visible legal form accurately represented the true nebulous, permeable, soft nature of the boundaries between stakeholder categories? Imagine if all stakeholders were able to invest their unique energy and capitals to your business, united by their common ground of thriving?

Then each business activity is in the best position to multisolve our challenges.

Include all capitals and currencies

The wealthier your company is, the more capacity it has to deliver the output that society needs at large scales, and to adapt to the changing demands of its niche. Wealth here includes far more than financial wealth. It means all of your company's capitals, and its ability to access those capitals so that they are put to work.

The different stakeholders of each company bring in different capitals, each vital for that company to succeed. The companies of today need to have all of them, and they need to be designed so that all their values (not just financial capital) are multiplied, and so each of them has the appropriate currencies (not just money).

The FairShares Commons company is designed to make it easy to have all capitals and all currencies fully active because each is represented with voice and power at the general meeting / share level. It is an ideal building block for companies in the regenerative, all-capitals, all-currencies Economy of the Free of Chapter 5.

Whilst I believe that the FairShares Commons is the best, there are other approaches addressing the flaw in the current dominant logic that have also emerged and grown over the past 12 years since I started working on this, including:

Purpose Foundation In Berlin, this group spans active investment, consulting, and engaging with politicians to change the law. Their approach centres on removing any option of selling a company as the means to protect its long-term purpose, and splitting voting from financial rights.

B-corp certification provided by the B-Labs, applicable to for-profit corporations. Any FairShares Commons company is highly likely to satisfy the requirements for certification.

Benefit corporations A type of incorporation that legally entrenches multiple stakeholder needs into the company objects (i.e. its various purposes). This includes some, but not all, of the FairShares Commons elements, and may depend still on investor goodwill in voting.

Conscious Capitalism A movement and organisation promoting business as a force for good, based on the conscious capitalism credo[214].

15.6 In closing

The question that I have used since 2008 to drive the creation of much of what is in this book is:

> *In this dysfunctional system that we have, what is keeping it stable in its dysfunctionality? What is it that has defeated all the valiant attempts to make business a force for good?*

This question led inexorably to the FairShares Commons company form, where the company is a living, meaning-making being, a non-human legal person with all that free personhood entails, starting with my conclusion in 2010 that the whole concept of a company as an ownable good is fatally flawed. That concept is a barrier holding businesses and ourselves back in our time of need.

This integration of the Free company, or commons company, and FairShares, is something that I believe is at least an essential next step towards the kind of businesses that are fit for the future. The kind of businesses that Einstein and Picasso would build if they were in business today, and the Economy of the Free they would envision.

CHAPTER 16

Creating your FairShares Commons Company

In a time of destruction, create something.
—Maxine Hong Kingston

The easiest way to build a FairShares Commons company[1] is to do so when you first incorporate.

Otherwise you hit the main roadblock to transforming an existing incorporation into a FairShares Commons: overcoming the loss-avoidance bias of existing stakeholders. This is not trivial, even if your most powerful stakeholders are in agreement, because loss avoidance is one of the most powerful cognitive biases that humans have (Page 246). The emotion they feel at the prospect of immediate loss may well overwhelm everything that they agree with.

If you are considering a FairShares Commons incorporation, work through everything listed below with a large enough cross-section of potential stakeholders.

1. List out everything that your company needs to be enabled and protected at the stakeholder level. This includes the elements in your business model canvas, or whichever other approach you're using.

2. Decide which stakeholders are sufficiently central to your company's performance so that including them in your legal incorporation will make sure it reflects what your company actually is in the lower right integral quadrant.

---

[1] Chapter sponsored by VME Retail and Coopexchange

3. Decide the most important elements of your company's meaning-making story. The core principles, values, and stories giving it the unique strengths that differentiate it from all others. These need to be baked into your company's statutes of incorporation, and all stewards need to exercise their vote rigorously according to these requirements. Then you have the same integrity inside your company that your conscience creates inside you.

4. Define your company's business concept. Begin by validating it through a sequence of minimum viable product types (MVP), and draft however much of your business plan is appropriate.

5. Prototype and improve the processes and structures that you need for your business from day one; and certainly long before you think of incorporating. The FairShares Commons is first and foremost an approach, an essence, not a concrete thing.

Once you have laid out all of this, using your own tool, or the FairShares Commons business model canvas, you have the basis of what you need.

16.1 Company objects, or purposes

Strong company objects (UK), objectives (US), purposes, or whatever word is used in your country for why the company exists, build strong foundations.

Regardless of how you incorporate, without clearly defined objects you leave it open, if you are ever in a dispute, to legal people with little or even no understanding of why your company exists to make some decision what the why was at the point you created the company. In particular, they may then decide that your company only exists to provide money to financial investors.

Whatever purpose your company has at the point of incorporation is a consequence of whatever inner reality you were experiencing in the run-up to your decision to start up and incorporate. So as time passes, and your meaning-making stories change, and / or actuality changes, the basis for your company's purpose may change.

Which means that your company's purpose needs to change, if your company is to stay relevant. (Recall Chapter 12.3.) So in a FairShares Commons, we recommend including in the statutes of incorporation the driver behind each object, or purpose—what your reality was at the time, and the need you were seeing.

By explicitly stating the driver behind each object, it becomes very visible when the external driver has changed, and therefore the internal purpose needs to change.

16.2 Stakeholder categories

One critical concretisation of this is to lay out your initial stakeholder categories, along with how much voting weight, and share of wealth generated, is allocated to each category. A FairShares Commons company will have many or all of the following stakeholder categories.

Stewards who have considerable voting power in any general meeting. They are constrained to always vote in compliance with the principles and values of stewardship as anchored in the constitution. The company's constitution will entrench these principles and values to the same degree as the principles and values of trust are entrenched so deep that they are almost unchangeable.

The steward category's voting weight must be big enough that the stewards have the means to maintain the FairShares Commons integrity if any or all of the other stakeholder groups attempt, for self-interest, to treat the company in an extractive, exploitative way. The steward voting weight typically ranges from at least 26% to 70%, or higher if necessary.

If the steward voting weight is 100% of the vote, then your FairShares Commons is identical to a trust or foundation in its decision process.

The stewards will meet high standards, including minimum Size of Person (Chapter 11) requirements. Typically the stewards have no share of the wealth generated, but are paid a fee for their stewardship. This minimises any direct financial incentive to vote contrary to the principles that bind the steward vote (akin to how trustees are constrained legally in a trust).

Whilst a company could be a FairShares Commons in the absence of the steward class, a couple of alternatives will need to be in place. These could include a golden share, held by an actual trust, that prevents the company from being sold, or a sufficiently large number of stakeholder groups with a balance of voting weight such that it is, as near as legally allowed, impossible for the company to be sold or the constitution changed in such a way as to make the company sellable.

Staff who also have equitable voting rights in any general meeting. The staff will be accountable for representing in the general meeting the interests of current staff and, to the best extent they can, the interests of future generations of staff. They will also be expected to speak on behalf of the company and its long-term best interests from their unique perspective.

Typically the staff voting weight is equal to or slightly higher than that of any other category except steward, because the staff usually have the closest relationship with the company, living its spirit every working hour.

Staff are often more in need of immediate cash than long-term capital gain, so often they will have a higher percentage of surplus than of capital gain. For example, they may get 50% of the surplus, but only 20% of the capital gain.

Customer, Supplier, Prosumer representing these and analogous stakeholders. (A prosumer is the new, emerging producer-consumer. A blogger is a typical prosumer, both writing and reading blogs.)

This may be one category, or more than one category. The important criterion in how many categories you have here is to ensure there is minimal risk of large numbers of people with one relationship to the company overwhelming a small number of people with a different relationship to the company. So, for example, if a company has a billion consumers, but only 1,000 suppliers, they ought to be in two distinct categories.

The voting weight(s), and share of surplus and appreciation, is often the smallest, as their skin in the game is least. However, if your company works with a large number of freelancers, or prosumers, you may well allocate more of the surplus and accumulation to this category than to staff or investors. For example, were Google incorporated as a FairShares Commons, it might allocate the bulk of its surplus and capital gain to its individual customers.

City, Nation, Environment that the company is embedded in, perhaps even the entire planet's natural ecosystem. In some cases, this category may have voting rights equal to or even higher than the other categories.

The share of surplus and capital gain here can be whatever is appropriate for the company's mission and purpose. In this way, financing environmental sustainability is done directly via the company's success, on an equal footing to the financial investors' returns. The investment of natural capitals by our natural ecosystems is fully recognised within the company and its operations.

Equally, cities and nations invest infrastructure. Usually today this is paid for through taxing the company, creating a relationship of enmity between investors, and the cities or nations. So today we have suboptimal situations, where cash is extracted from companies at times when it would be actually better for everyone to leave that cash in the company. And at the other end, we have cities having to settle for a minute share of wealth generated, and directly dependent on their infrastructure investments 20 years previously.

By cities becoming voting stakeholders they are maximally enabled to share in the company's long-term performance, and to contribute to regenerating all kinds of built capital, getting better results in the end than they would through taxation and regulation.

I believe that this can be a very powerful way of getting an equitable split of money to all the cities and nations that are investing financial and non-financial capitals, directly and indirectly, in multinationals. The FairShares Commons incorporation eliminates much of the wrangling currently underway between nations to ensure that multinational internet companies pay a fair share towards the government-built systems their success depends on.

Investor, Donor are the categories for those investing or donating money in the company. These shares will be identical or close to the ordinary shares that investors are used to receiving in any company today. But the big difference, as in any FairShares company, is that these investor shares only qualify for part of the wealth generated by the company (dividends and capital gain); and, their vote is in an equitable balance to the vote of all the other stakeholders. Equitable here is based on the specific niche the company fills, and how best to bring the full breadth of relative opinions into general meeting decisions, backed by an appropriate distribution of power, for decisions to be taken in the long-term interest of the company and all of its stakeholders.

Since all the stakeholders acquire investor shares over time, through the new shares issued each year that represent half the company's appreciation, usually 50% of the rise is allocated to investor shares. This is a fair reflection of the continuous investment of non-financial capitals, and is like an exchange rate connecting the different capitals invested in the company. If your investment of intellectual capital increases the company valuation, you get a fair share of that increase. Whenever you invest it, not only as a founder when the first shares are issued.

Only the investor shares can be bought or sold. All the other share classes are cancelled without any payment as soon as the shareholder ceases to fulfil the qualification to have a share of that category. So they cannot be sold, nor be given to anyone else, nor be inherited through an estate or insolvency of a corporation holding the shares.

Typically the only qualifying criterion to buy and hold investor shares is having money to invest, although some companies may have additional qualifying criteria. I believe that that is seldom necessary, because everything else in the FairShares Commons company means that even the greediest investor owning all the investor shares has too little power to significantly harm the interests of other stakeholders.

This is one of the big benefits of the FairShares Commons in creating regenerative businesses: the valuable power of money can be harnessed regardless of the values of the individual or corporation investing that money.

All the share classes can qualify for some form of sharing surplus cash, whether in the form of dividends, bonuses, or whatever is most appropriate for the company's nature and your jurisdiction. However, usually the steward share class is disqualified from receiving any wealth share in order to minimise as far as possible any conflict of interest.

Much of the wealth received by all the share classes is distributed in the form of investor shares.

For example, let's say you start working for Evolutesix, a FairShares Commons company. You will receive a staff share as soon as you reach the qualifying criteria, which at the moment includes working at least half of a full-time equivalent for at least six months continuously. Then, at the next wealth sharing point, you will receive investor shares according to the Evolutesix formula. This formula includes an assessment of how much the wealth generated is due to your investment, as a staff member, of different kinds of human capitals. These investor shares are now yours to sell whenever you want to. You could sell them immediately, and put cash in your pocket; or you could keep them long after you have left the company and lost your staff share, selling them in your retirement to fund your lifestyle.

As we described in the first chapters of this book, we can only build the antifragile, regenerative economy that we need if each business is an adaptive one. So make every business that you think of starting adaptive by incorporating it as a FairShares Commons, using at least self-governing structures and processes, and developmental interactions at the human level.

You can read more about how to build adaptive businesses and regenerative ecosystems of adaptive businesses in Chapter 17.

I cannot stress enough the importance of all-stakeholder dialogue. The very best way is to bring equal numbers of members of each stakeholder category into dialogue with each other, so that you can fully understand which capitals each stakeholder invests, what value / return on capitals invested each seeks, and the risks each perceives. Once you have this, then you can design the FairShares Commons company as a tool to do the job of multiplying each capital in balance with the risks to each capital.

For example, in a creator company, the creators invest significantly their risk capitals of time, intellectual, effort, and reputation; active consumers (those who are providing active feedback, commissioning work) are also investing the same risk capitals.

16.3 Dilution, additional equity rounds

One core element of a FairShares company is the regular issue of new investor shares to other stakeholders. Existing investors do not have an automatic right to subscribe to these new equity events, which looks like dilution through the conventional company lens. It is not dilution in the traditional context.

Dilution can be in governance power (voting) or financial wealth.

In a FairShares Commons these share issues have no effect on investors' governance power, because your voting is in specific weighted blocks; and because it is one person one vote.

Fear of dilution on the financial side is a red herring, a cognitive bias, holding business back from thriving and generating wealth. This fear drives small-pie possessive mindsets and behaviours, when we need big-pie, commons mindsets.

Think of having a 100g slice of a pie. Regardless of how big the pie is, your 100g slice always nourishes you with 100g of pie. If it is a 1kg pie ten people can be fed, each getting 10% of the pie; if it is a 10kg pie 100 people can be fed, each getting 1%.

That is why, in the FairShares Commons, issuing new shares drives the opposite of dilution. It is exactly what enables even better success, and the biggest absolute amount of pie for you. In all capitals, not just financial.

Worry about dilution, and you will keep the businesses you invest in smaller and weaker, on average, than they could be; and certainly far from regenerative. Focus instead on the absolute size of slice that you have, then you will work on making the business bigger and stronger for all. Which, paradoxically, means you will end up with more wealth overall; and an antifragile wealth, regardless of what percentage it is.

16.4 One person, multiple categories

Any individual may well satisfy the qualifying criteria for multiple categories, and therefore have shares in multiple categories.

For example, the founder of a company is often in all categories. They have invested money, so have investor shares. They clearly work in the company, often with longer hours and a greater contribution to growing the business than any other member of staff, and so have staff shares; they will often also use the company's products, and so have customer shares. Typically the founder is also a steward, because they are the source of the company, with the intuition of who the company ought to grow into.

All the other stakeholders, after the first year at the latest, will also have investor shares.

So, for example, staff end up with the same benefits as in an employee-owned company, and staff joining a startup later in the company's growth still benefit from equity, not just those who were in at the beginning. This also applies to any other stakeholder contributing any other capital. They all benefit from the annual cash surplus and any appreciation in company value in proportion to whatever capitals they have contributed to generating that surplus and appreciation.

Keep in mind that none of this is wildly radical, nor completely new. This is simply taking existing things, like airline miles and loyalty points, to the logical conclusion.

The stakeholders are in a rank ordering, and voting is only in the highest-ranked category that you are a member of. So anyone who is a steward and also in any of the other categories is only allowed to vote as a steward, which means that their vote is constrained to always support the principles of stewardship laid down in the constitution, and never in their own interest. The more mature the company is, the more likely that at least half of the stewards have no other significant relationship with the company.

When somebody changes their relationship with the company, and loses all other shares, they retain their investor shares and can still vote in the investor category. In some FairShares companies, the contribution not yet rewarded in the form of surplus or investor shares can be issued as investor shares at the point that the other shares are cancelled.

16.5 Buying and selling shares

Only the investor shares may be bought or sold. Depending on the details of incorporation, and company size, there will be multiple routes for investors to sell their shares. For smaller companies, that means selling the shares back to the company, or identifying another investor to buy them. For larger companies, there will be routes to sell the shares on one of the many closed markets for unlisted companies. Eventually, the publicly listed FairShares Commons company will be the dominant company on the world's largest stock markets, with a healthy trade in investor shares.

Shares of all other categories are absolutely not sellable. They are immediately withdrawn, with zero compensation, immediately any individual member ceases to fulfil the qualifying criteria.

16.6 Seamless contribution and reward

If you have a formal staff contract with any well-run company, and your work grows the business, you will receive a fair share of the wealth generated. You might get a sales commission, an annual performance bonus, stock options, a pay rise, or a promotion.

What if you are a customer, or a supplier, or the city that the company operates in, and you contribute something that grows the company's value? In the traditional company, unless it is extraordinarily visionary, you are unlikely to get anything unless you negotiate some kind of 'sales' contract beforehand.

So many customers who could contribute something to a company's success, or suppliers who could work in a seamless collaboration with the staff and perhaps customers, keep their ideas to themselves. They would rather not say anything to protect against feeling exploited if their idea generates significant wealth and they get none.

In the FairShares Commons, no matter what your relationship with the company, you are as motivated as any member of staff or investor to contribute everything you possibly can to the company's success, because you directly get an appropriate reward. You get rewarded with a share of the surplus profit, a share of the appreciation of the company value, and a share of any of the other capitals that grow as a consequence.

Even investors are more motivated to contribute and collaborate with other stakeholders to increase the company's viability because they get more than just financial returns.

All stakeholders, including staff, have a second motivation to contribute anything they can to the company's success, without worrying about any contract.

In a standard company, if a member of staff, or other stakeholders, has a really bright idea that might lead to an entirely new and profitable business unit, they may well elect to start up their own company. They do this because they have no control over what might happen to their idea in the coming decades if they simply give it to the company. It might be something with both huge profit, but also potential for environmental and social harm. So you certainly don't want to simply hand it over into a company where only investors have governance.

In the FairShares Commons, members of staff and other stakeholders are far more likely to contribute everything they can to the company's success, because they know that they have an equitable balance of governance power in the general meetings, and that the company cannot be sold to realise short-term returns for the investors only.

16.7 Stewardship principles

Getting the right stewardship principles into the company statutes and the right balance of voting power between each member categories is vital. Get this wrong, and you will not be able to use existing company law to protect the FairShares Commons characteristic of your company. Of course, the time will come when this becomes less necessary because countries will adapt their company law to include the FairShares Commons as one of their standards. Malta has already taken a significant step in this direction, by including the vanilla FairShares in its company law.

There are two types of stewardship principles in any FairShares Commons.

• General principles that underpin the entire FairShares Commons nature, and that must be adopted by any company wishing to be a FairShares Commons.

• Specific principles, unique to your company, that protect and enable the core character of your company.

General principles

The following general principles are a minimum for a company to be deemed a FairShares Commons company.

• To protect the company's capacity to be a commons for its members.

• To protect the interests of future generations, at least seven generations.

• To protect the company's freedom such that it cannot be bought or sold.

• To protect against narrow interest or stakeholder groups or stakeholders gaining controlling power over the company, or the company IP curated as a commons, or the company operations, or the wealth generated by the company.

• To foster the wise use of company IP, effort, and wealth for the good of members, human society, and natural ecosystems.

• To foster the generation of long-term sustainable wealth across multiple capitals, including financial, human and environmental in accord with the company values.

• To protect the FairShares principles of wealth generated being shared across members and a fair share of the right to engage in governance across those affected by governance decisions.

• To foster the use of processes designed to surface multiple perspectives in all decisions and integrate them into a final proposal that takes into account all perspectives from all stakeholder groups, regardless of size. For example the consent / integrative decision process of sociocracy / Holacracy.

- To protect the three Adaptive Way rules: care for self, care for the other, care for the whole.

Also consider recording the driver (context and need) that led to this principle being part of the statutes. If the driver that led to the company being formed in the first place changes, (in other words the context and need that called the company into existence changes), you may need to also adjust any principles that were specific in their formulation to the original context and need. It is easy to see when a principle needs to be changed if the original driver is clearly articulated, because then the change in driver is visible to all.

A big driver of the growing gap in wealth in Western society is that between executive pay and the rest of the staff, let alone other stakeholders. In a FairShares Commons there is a often a maximum gap between the lowest-paid full-time employee and the highest-paid full-time employee, typically ranging from 3 to 20. 15 emerges in many polls conducted by the *Economy for the Common Good*[103] as the average fair point for the gap between a junior employee and senior executive pay in a large multinational. Maintaining this fairness is another role for the stewards, especially in the complex situations of a global operation that spans a wide range of local cost structures.

16.8 Wealth sharing in a FairShares Commons

Wealth, i.e. access to capital, can be shared in a FairShares Commons with every member of a company, regardless of stakeholder category, and can include all of its different capitals.

One element of this is a fair share of the financial surplus that's generated.

Every year, in any healthy company, revenue exceeds total operating costs. After putting aside money into a pot to cover unexpected expenses in the coming years, certain types of investment, share buy-back, and other activities, the company executors may then decide to distribute any surplus to the stakeholders.

This surplus recognises the risk investment by other stakeholders of non-financial capitals. For example, a member of staff may invest a significant number of hours without extra pay; or in the company's early years, without any pay whatsoever. These extra hours contribute to the generation of cash flow and, somewhat akin to a performance bonus, qualify that member of staff for a fair share of the surplus. The same could apply to a member of staff who invents something, or leverages their relationships, or in any other way contributes a capital. And it applies equally well to members of any other category except investor and steward.

So any surplus is not only allocated to dividends to the investor shareholders, but is distributed in a fair way across all stakeholders to effectively reward them for their investments of non-financial risk capitals.

Profitable companies also grow in financial value. This is typically reflected in an equal growth in the price of investor shares.

In a FairShares Commons, other stakeholders also benefit from that appreciation of company value. However, as no other share classes actually carry financial value, they need to be granted investor shares in proportion to how their investment of non-financial capital has helped to increase the company's financial value.

For example, someone may join the company and bring with them an idea that leads to a new product line and a doubling of the company value. In a traditional incorporation, that person would not talk about their idea until after some return had been locked into their contract. So they might not even mention it; they might accept the job, check out the company for idea safety, and at the same time start up their own company with that idea.

In the FairShares Commons it is safe for somebody to join the company, give their idea to the company immediately without any long negotiation, and know that if the idea generates value then they will get a fair share of both the cash surplus and the appreciation of the company. This keeps a FairShares Commons in perpetual startup mode, never ossifying into a dinosaur heading to extinction because it cannot transform.

As already mentioned, the investor category usually gets at least 50% of the appreciation of value. This is not only to give an adequate return on investment to the financial investors, but it also recognises that over time the contribution of other kinds of capitals underpins the continuing rise in the company's financial value.

So in a FairShares company, if the company value doubles, instead of the investors' share price rising by 100%, it increases by a smaller percentage, say 50%, and the balance of the appreciation will be reflected by new shares that are distributed to the non-financial stakeholders in some proportion to their investment of non-financial capitals. This means that all stakeholders are increasingly incentivised to collaborate in the interests of the company as a whole, because no matter what their initial capital basis was when they started engaging with the company, as time progresses they become engaged with it across all capitals.

In any FairShares company, the financial wealth generated is distributed in an equitable way across all the stakeholders investing all or any kind of capital. Even better, in a fully regenerative company that multiplies all capitals, the investors of financial capital also get a return of the wealth generated in the other capitals.

New tax laws

We do, however, need new tax laws. Investors of financial capital have tax breaks for gains on their investments, but the investors of human capitals and natural capitals do not yet enjoy the same benefits. This is counterproductive because the tax implications can be an insurmountable barrier for companies wishing to become the regenerative, all capitals, all stakeholders Level 5 FairShares Commons we need to create an antifragile regenerative, or even just a circular, economy.

These tax laws also prevent the commons from working effectively as a multi-capital commons, because investments of human capital are then disadvantageously taxed to investments of financial capital, pushing us closer to civilisation collapse.

16.9 Governance is a process

Governance is what we call any process that carries the multiple needs, perspectives, opinions etc. within an organisation to an actionable decision. You begin developing governance processes from the very first meeting with potential co-founders when you decide to take the first step towards co-founding. So do not concretize anything into an incorporated legal framework until you know what governance process between whom (stakeholder categories) you need it to freeze and give substance to as a legal being.

Once you do incorporate as a FairShares Commons, the General Meeting is the forum for governance between stakeholder classes. Typical companies do this by simplistic voting. In a FairShares Commons, voting is the last resort and only occurs if the consent decision-making process has broken down.

A consent (not consensus) process ought to be the first option, always. It starts with one or more stakeholders recognising a new driver, or a change in an existing driver. This typically first becomes visible when they experience a conflict or tension, and use that as data on some gap, for example, between how the company is or works, and how the company ought to be or work to achieve its objects.

After one person or a small team has clarified the tension sufficiently, and come up with a proposal for what to change to remove that tension or meet the need of the driver within the constraints of the context, this can become a topic in the general meeting. There may also be standing topics or proposals in the general meeting, such as approving the accounts for the year, executive pay, etc.

The essence of the consent decision-making process is consent to the proposal, not necessarily agreement with it. In other words, everyone can at least live with the proposal, even if they don't agree with it, or regard it as the best possible proposal.

This is often expressed in the question *is this good enough for now, and safe enough to try?*

There are three ways of voting in consent-based voting.

1. You agree with the proposal,

2. you disagree but can live with the proposal (consent),

3. or you object to the proposal because you have a reason why it is not even good enough for now, and not safe enough to try once.

If there are any objections, then every attempt is made to integrate them into a modification of the proposal. After they have been integrated, you get a new proposal, which then is put to another consent process.

The consent-based decision-making process has a number of benefits for fast-moving, adaptive businesses.

- Speed. Consent-based decision-making is really fast, because no one spends time trying to improve the decision beyond what is safe for now. Everyone knows that if you learn something by trying it, you can very quickly and easily run the process again to improve the decision.

- Full data. Anyone can object, regardless of which stakeholder group they are in, or how much formal power they hold in the organisation, as long as they have a valid reason why the proposal may put the entire company at risk if it is even tried once. So proposals are only passed after all these potential reasons why have been surfaced and examined.

- Iterative. As the consequences of any proposal become visible, the proposal can easily be revisited. This makes it easy to move fast by taking multiple safe iterative steps, rather than one risky big leap.

- Delegated trust. Because the process surfaces a wide range of data, and there is no risk of a majority overpowering a minority, even if the minority has rightly identified a reason why the proposal is fundamentally unsafe to try even once, there is no need for everybody to attend the general meeting. If you are sufficiently confident that there is somebody else like you in the general meeting, who would surface the same objection that you might surface, you do not need to engage in the meeting. You can easily discuss your objection with that person, knowing that they will represent your perspective and without any need for you to give them a proxy vote. Also, if you look at the proposal and see that it is something you don't have a strong opinion on either way without more data, you can simply consent knowing that after it has been tried once and data is gathered, it's easy to retake the decision.

With the advent of modern online technology to facilitate general meetings, it is easy to run a micro general meeting whenever necessary, possibly even daily!

But sometimes, the consent decision making process breaks down; for example, perhaps you can't integrate the objections. In this case, the standard FairShares Commons weighted voting process kicks in. I recommend that a weighted vote does not happen at the same general meeting in which the consent-based decision process has broken down, especially if certain members are not present who would have been there if they'd known it would lead to a weighted vote.

In a weighted vote, the agree and consent votes are then deemed to be for the proposal, and the objections are against the proposal. Alternatively, you may in your statutes build in that only binary voting, for or against, is to be used.

Part of the stewards' core role in the company's early days is to articulate the values and nurture a culture that brings to life the meaning-making essence of the company. So I recommend that their initial voting weight is high, and then steadily decreases as the company achieves specific maturity milestones. These can include the company reaching a certain age, the number of members of any category, how much has been invested, or any other appropriate indicator of members seeing it as a living being independent of themselves, and to act wisely, in loco parentis on the company's behalf.

As mentioned before, an individual's vote only counts in the highest stakeholder category of which they are a member. This eradicates double counting.

The big benefit of this kind of voting over the traditional company structures of one share one vote, or cooperative one person one vote, is that it eliminates both kinds of tyrannies. In a typical company limited by share, the opinion that has the most money (i.e. the most voting shares) behind it wins the vote, regardless of the consequences for any other stakeholder. In the typical cooperative, the opinion with the most members behind it wins the vote, regardless of the consequences for any other stakeholder or member.

16.10 Non-profit FairShares Commons companies

The FairShares Commons is also well-suited to the non-profit and NGO sectors. By including the full range of stakeholders in overall governance, their needs and concerns are fully represented. By being a commons, where all stakeholders are explicitly taking care of the organisation for the long term, any concerns of donors about mismanagement and misuse of funds, for example, can be effectively addressed.

For instance, Oxfam's 2018 sex scandal has been described as a governance[215] failure. As a large global NGO, Oxfam has needed to adopt many of the structures and practices of large for-profit multinationals. There have been criticisms of a lack of democracy, of misuse of money provided by the donor stakeholders, and of issues supporting the very stakeholders Oxfam exists to support.

Imagine if Oxfam (or choose any other NGO that you support), was structured as a non-profit FairShares Commons. Imagine how this would make it stronger, antifragile, and better enabled to do its job, because all stakeholders would be fully involved in governance. Cover-ups purely to protect one stakeholder group at the expense of others would be nearly impossible. By having all affected stakeholders directly represented in annual meetings, on the board, and in governance, all governance-related issues will be raised as soon as they begin to emerge, and used to immediately improve the NGO. The outcomes of every governance process is shaped by which stakeholders have power in the process.

Let's stay with Oxfam as an example. Its founders were a group of Oxford Quakers, social activists and academics. I believe that they would have immediately found their values and practices in a FairShares Commons, especially when used with the developmental and self-governing organisation components of a fully Adaptive Organisation.

16.11 FairShares Commons canvas

In Figure 16.1 is the canvas, derived from the lean business model canvas, we use with our clients to guide the all stakeholder dialogue needed to lay out the business model, and the enabling structures and processes needed along all three axes.

Fill in all the standard business elements of a lean business model canvas, or whichever conventional approach you use. Then add in all the other capitals invested in, and multiplied by the business, and the range of stakeholders investing these capitals or otherwise involved in the business. Finally, work through what the legal entity incorporation needs to enable and protect, both tangible and intangible.

For each stakeholder, also define the minimum qualifying criteria to be eligible for membership in that stakeholder category.

The best way to build a solid canvas is through canvassing a representative group of all stakeholders. There are many technologies for doing this, such as Open Space Technology, Appreciative Inquiry, and Future Search. There is also a wealth of useful material in the FairShares Alliance available.

And, never mistake things for processes. What matters is doing, prototyping, from day one. Long before you incorporate you ought to have identified stakeholders and begun dialogue with them, begun testing your hypotheses with them, including how governance will work between stakeholders.

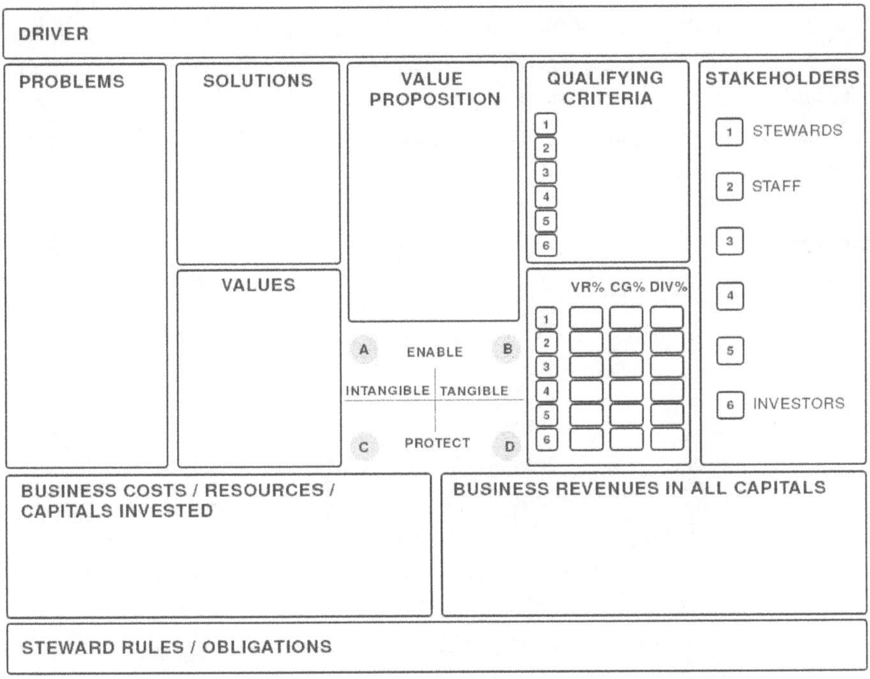

Figure 16.1: FairShares Commons canvas.

16.12 Examples: UniOne and Evolutesix Publishing

One business that I see as a superb trailblazer, and an example of how a company can be profitable (i.e., regenerative) across multiple capitals, is Whole Foods Markets, the pioneering company founded by John Mackey. However, when Whole Foods began running into trouble in 2016[216], this led to activist investors buying sufficient control of the company to iteratively shift it away from conscious capitalism and towards business as usual.

If Whole Foods had been incorporated as a FairShares Commons, I believe it would have had exactly the defensive power needed. The combination of governance and wealth share rights across its supplier base would have significantly increased their capacity to work with the company and make the whole ecosystem successful. The same is true for the customers, the staff, and the cities that Whole Foods is based in.

Even more, if it had been a fully Adaptive Organisation , with all three pillars:

FairShares Commons, dynamic governance, and the Adaptive Way; it would have been able to react much faster, from a higher stage of consciousness, as the competitive landscape changed around it.

Here are two companies that may one day be examples of how to build a future that works for all.

UniOne

UniOne is an early FairShares Commons company, incorporated in 2019, with one of the authors (Graham) and Evolutesix playing a key role in starting it up.

The driver for UniOne is:

> *Humanity is facing a growing number of challenges of unprecedented complexity, at scales ranging from the individual through to all humanity. These challenges affect all of us, across all nations, cultures, and religions, and they span multiple disciplines. We can only address them if we work together, each of us bringing our unique strengths to bear. We also see a rise in fragmentation, from individuals who can find no peace inside their own skin, through groups, religions, organisations, nations, and between nations.*

> *So we need better ways of enabling people to come together around what they share (oneness) and to act fully from their unique strength (uniqueness).*

In order to deliver on this driver, the UniOne business model is based on a physical and a virtual platform.

Physical meetings are held, where participants are facilitated in such a way that together they can recognise and harness their common ground, whilst simultaneously each can contribute from everything that they uniquely bring. Participants learn by doing, and are then able to facilitate for others.

UniOne meetings already have a wide range, from public programs for anyone, to special interest groups for entrepreneurs, education, music, etc. It also runs training programs for people who want to develop their mastery of the UniOne methodology to become UniOne facilitators and hosts.

The virtual platform is a marketplace of prosumers, both private individuals and professionals, who offer or need a wide range of free products and services. Anyone who wants to develop themselves to their full capacity to act from the UniOne spirit in all aspects of their life needs these.

Over time, a large range of businesses and non-profit organisations will adopt the UniOne methodology, because it lets them deliver better results by leveraging everyone's common ground and thus bringing diverse unique strengths to full power. This methodology is ideally suited to any company incorporating as a FairShares Commons, and even more so to ecosystems of FairShares Commons companies.

The UniOne stakeholder categories, their voting weights, surplus and capital gain fractions are given in Table 16.1.

Stakeholder	Initial weight %	Mature weight %	Appreciation share %	Surplus share %
Steward	60	40	0	0
Staff	8	13	20	30
Individual Prosumer	8	16	15	20
Professional Prosumer	7	9	15	25
Donors	7	7	0	0
Investors	10	15	50	25

Table 16.1: Table of the different stakeholder categories in UniOne

Because UniOne is very centred on staying true to its spirit, the steward voting weight will be a high 40% when mature. The group of stewards themselves include representatives from each other category, a member from the UniOne non-profit foundation, and external appointed members. This minimises the risk of stewards lacking the breadth, depth, and independence of perspective to wisely guide UniOne according to its spirit.

It is going to take time, with various experiments and interpretations, before the UniOne spirit and its business structures and processes can be clearly and unambiguously articulated in words. So the initial voting weight of the stewards is an even higher 60%.

The stewards do not benefit directly from any cash surplus distributed, nor from UniOne's capital gain. However, those founders that also have a steward role all have investor shares, representing their significant investment of time and money, which enable them to benefit from their investment. However, they have no vote in the investor class, though—keep in mind that their vote is always constrained by the principles anchored in the statutes, and they can be held legally accountable if it breaks these principles.

You also see that the donors have zero return from surplus or capital gain. In many countries, any benefit nullifies a donor's right to tax rebates.

The remaining voting weights are distributed in such a way that the number of members in each stakeholder category balances out in an equitable way in any decision. This means that if the consent process breaks down, UniOne decisions are neither dominated by the opinion with the largest number of people, nor by the opinion with the largest amount of money.

Equally, the share of wealth is designed to reflect the needs and scale of contribution expected from each class to the success of UniOne as a whole.

Evolutesix Publishing

We are creating it in part to make ensure that the company publishing this book walks the talk; and as an example of what Evolutesix is doing to incubate and invest in ecosystems of FairShares Commons companies.

The driver for Evolutesix Publishing is:

Publishing is a tool to disseminate information from where it is, to where it is needed. The publishing industry today, especially academic publishing and publishing the first books in contentious fields, or those that challenge existing paradigms, is no longer up to the task. Knowledge behaves differently to other capitals, in that if two people give each other new knowledge that the other lacks, both now have both knowledge. Knowledge multiplies when it is shared. The mutually beneficial share of value created across all stakeholders is broken in current publishing, to the detriment of the primary value creators—the authors and readers.

We need a new platform approach to publishing with a business model based on the value-add when knowledge is shared widely, disseminated rapidly, and integrated. To do this, we need a publishing business that integrates all of the emerging information technologies under a commons business model.

Evolutesix Publishing intends to publish the new paradigms in economics, regenerative business, sustainability, community, identity, etc.

At the heart of Evolutesix Publishing is a crowd paradigm. Authors and readers will form a vibrant interacting community, where the readers support the writer during the process of writing the book and afterwards. This can be in the form of regular discussions with the author, to streamline and improve the connection between the book (content and style) and the reader.

This makes far easier things like crowdfunding, crowdsourcing, and even writing the entire book as a crowd of authors. The division between reader and author becomes far more fluid.

This also takes us beyond the book writing process of: get it right, publish it, and then leave it for a few years, until enough changes have accumulated to warrant a new edition.

This leads to the current proposal for our stakeholder split, in Table 16.2. At the point of publishing this book Evolutesix Publishing is still in the creation phase, and has yet to be incorporated as an independent company from Evolutesix itself. So these may well change as we continue to get input during the early stages of the company.

Stakeholder	Initial weight %	Mature weight %	Appreciation share %	Surplus share %
Steward	70	30	0	0
Staff	10	20	20	25
Authors	5	12.5	12.5	20
Readers	5	12.5	12.5	20
Suppliers	0	5	5	5
Investors	10	20	50	30

Table 16.2: Table of the different stakeholder categories in Evolutesix Publishing

16.13 Transforming dominant paradigms

And day to day, life's a hard job, you get tired, you lose the pattern.
You need distance, interval.
—Ursula K. Le Guin

Every one of us who is going on the journey to creating a future that we can all thrive in has chosen the hardest job there is, transforming our dominant paradigms and the institutions they have been concretised into.

We will all get tired and want to give up at times. I know I do. What keeps me (Graham) going is remembering others who have gone on even harder journeys, and then seeing what I can learn from their journey.

There are four lessons from what worked in transforming South Africa to re-apply to business.

    1. Freedom is the foundation. Each company must be free, not subject to single-

class ownership. Then everyone can have the psychological safety that comes with being fully enfranchised and having full information rights. Only then is it really safe to use the full power of any of the Ocracies[79,80], and / or Deliberately Developmental[81] methods.

2. Include everyone in the process, in the benefits, and in the costs, especially those you see as "the other". Climate change has occurred because we externalise the costs onto others (especially future generations, our children and grandchildren). Once we no longer see "others", externalising costs becomes visible as self-harm.

3. Human beings have written our company statutes, our stories of how things must work. So humans like you and me can rewrite them now.

4. Quick successes first. Use existing legal constructs and loopholes creatively to do it now, even if not perfectly. The FairShares Commons Incorporation is already being implemented in the UK, many other countries in the EU, Nigeria, and the USA.

In closing, it is my belief that the Adaptive Organisation, with all three axes at Level 5, may well be the new cooperativism we need, may well be the basis for Impact Investing Plus, and what we require to regenerate our planet and society, to address the climate emergency and achieve the 17 Sustainable Development Goals.

CHAPTER 17

Growing regenerative businesses and ecosystems

No gluing together of partial studies of a complex nonlinear system can give a good idea of the behavior of the whole.

—Murray Gell-Mann

Each chapter of this book uses one, or at most a few lenses, so each is a partial study of a complex, nonlinear, open system. In this chapter, I zoom out and as best as possible give an idea of the behaviour of the whole, and how to glue some of the lenses together—as best possible, because of the inherent impossibility that Murray Gell-Mann refers to in the quote above.

Successful businesses in the coming decades will only thrive because they harness the nebulous, continuously changing, non-ergodic nature of our world; so they must be designed for nebulous, continuous change. They must be fully Adaptive Organisations, collaborating and competing with other Adaptive Organisations in deep, regenerative ecosystems of businesses. They will be beyond resilient—Adaptive Organisations must be antifragile[24] because they collaborate in our non-ergodic (Section 6.5) world.

They will use human energy and power in a healthy way. Power is just energy used to move things. Power applied to Job 1 delivers useful results for the organisation; power into Job 2 does not. In the knowledge economy of today, power *with* is the most valuable for Job 1 and delivering results. Power *over* is usually a cost because far too much of it is harmfully flowing in Job 2.

To maximise the productive output of a business you need the right balance of power with, to, and over. So you need the Adaptive Organisation structures of this book across all four strata of Section 2.8. Have too much power over, and you have a wasteful, inefficient operation. Which is why the FairShares Commons is better than a standard incorporation for any investor wanting to maximise their financial and impact returns today.

The leaders and all key players will be masters of all 28 thought forms, including the relationship and transformation thought forms needed to optimise for the connections in collaborative business ecosystems, highly competent at maintaining the equilibrium of their emotional state, and most of all adept at continuously adapting their meaning-making stories. They will be masters of the best approaches in all six layers listed on Page 44, and how to integrate them.

It is time to shift our economy[217], because it will crash again[113] as we repeat the cycles we have designed into it. Every crash risks taking us closer to runaway climate change, and all the other SDGs becoming full emergencies too.

> I (Graham) loved the garden route between Cape Town, where I went to university, and East London, where I grew up. Some very farsighted individuals many generations ago recognised that the original national forests of South Africa were rapidly disappearing. They conserved sufficiently large pockets for these ecosystems to survive, albeit without most of the larger fauna. Even so, these still are regenerative ecosystems. Leave them alone, and over time they will regenerate.

No living organism in nature can survive, let alone thrive, in isolation. All living organisms thrive in a chaotic web of interactivity. Even you are an ecosystem: only 43% of your cells are human, the rest are symbiotic bacteria and other microorganisms. All of them are multiple related interacting open systems, embedded in larger ones, containing smaller ones, and inter-embedded in peer systems.

All this is what has made life on earth antifragile from the start.

So how on earth could anyone imagine that we can build a viable economy out of individual cells (businesses) that are artificially constrained to be independent of each other, given the non-ergodic world we live in (Recall Figure 6.3)?

Imagine how much better we could do to tackle our climate crisis. The difference between the averages in Figures 6.2 and 6.3 suggests that we could gain thousands to millions better outcomes for the same time, money, and effort. Simply by incorporating at Level 5 for collaborative-competitive deep ecosystems that harness the nebulous, symbiotic, chaotic web of interrelatedness between businesses, society, and the public sector to counter our non-ergodic, luck-dominated world.

So now you know where we need to end up, to get out of this mess that we have got ourselves into (Section 2.10, P 46). We need regenerative economic ecosystems, built of inter-related regenerative businesses that are themselves irreducibly nebulous, open, constantly transforming living beings with meaning-making capacity.

We have not come nearly far enough in creating successful businesses that are part of fully viable, antifragile, circular, or blue economies, as John Elkington (originator of the triple bottom line) himself recognised in his recent HBR article[78] proposing a 'manufacturer's recall' of the concept to replace the 'defective parts'. I hope that this book contains at least a few usefully upgraded parts, especially the FairShares Commons!

Elkington is very clear that his triple bottom line (people, profit, and planet as equally important measures of business success, not just profit) was intended to catalyse deep and far-reaching transformations of the role that business plays within the larger context of society and our natural ecosystem. Many companies have people within them that have the triple bottom line deep in their values. Many of these company's staff and customers recognise, even if they may not use those words, that the triple bottom line is vital for their interests, or at least their children's and grandchildren's interests. Even many major investors, like the pension funds, recognise at some level that the only way they will be able to provide the pensions we will all depend on is if the businesses they are investing in continue to thrive by adapting to the challenges of the next 50 years.

Asking this question through the lenses of Picasso, we come to the conclusion it's because we are not seeing what we are looking at *as it actually is*, but distorted because we are only using one perspective. Asking through the lenses of relativity and quantum physics, we begin seeing the fundamental particles and interactions of our economy clearly, and can begin to talk about our economy in a sufficiently representative and useful way.

Most efforts towards a circular economy address the technical challenge of making products circular, not the system-wide adaptive challenge of what it takes for companies to trust each other enough over the decades needed for each iteration of the circle, and across multiple large, interlocking circular ecosystems. This trust is practical, about collaboratively sharing resources and the wealth generated, across all capitals, by each company in the circular ecosystem to all companies over decades, maybe even centuries. Enough sharing for the ecosystem to thrive despite the issues caused by our non-ergodic world (Section 6.4). The typical venture capital strategy of portfolio, unicorn, and exit in ten years is a recipe for failure. The lack of understanding of non-ergodicity is also behind systemic wealth inequalities in nations; e.g. in the USA[218].

It is time to integrate all our approaches and efforts to build a better world.

17.1 Immortality, or death and rebirth?

Companies built around shareholder return, with tradable investor shares, have immortality as a core assumption. But unless the company and all of its stakeholders have a sufficiently high adaptive capacity to transform all aspects of themselves as living beings faster than their environment is changing, the company will reach a point where it is ready to die. The problem is, because we design them for infinite life, we end up with zombie businesses that cannot be allowed to die.

This immortality has also created the binary VC model of an exit on the VC fund's timeline: either the business is force-fed into exponential growth, like a goose delivering foie gras to the VC firm, or it is shut down.

In an evolutionary, driver-based company, it is easy to see when it is time for the company to die. So built into the very heart of an Adaptive Organisation is a frame of reference that constantly evaluates the current driver against the business and its capacity to adapt, to decide if it should die. Just as each cell in your body, and your body as a whole, has a built-in evaluation of when it has reached the end of viability.

Of course you, as an investor, always need a way to get back at least as much money as you invested, better enough extra to counteract losses and provide a healthy income. (Keep in mind many investors are the pension funds many depend on for their retirement.) You always will want the organisation to operate with maximum efficiency in using your capital wisely to deliver business results

Equally, if you are a member of staff, you absolutely want to have a healthy pension when you retire. So whatever we do, the key benefits of investor exits and trading investor shares on a stock market must be preserved. We just need to invent a new game that does that without the harm of today's approach.

In an adaptive business the timelines are decoupled. Investors exit on their timeline, staff exit on their timeline, and the business expires or continues according to its nature, needs and timeline.

17.2 We need regenerative ecosystems

One recent client said to me:

> Graham, there is no such thing as failure in an ecosystem of Adapt-
> ive Organisations where all are Level 5 FairShares Commons. No

binary classification. Whatever the outcome from innovation or an experiment, the value, the learning stays in the ecosystem and can be used by others.

Each stakeholder getting their unique needs met, on their own unique timeline, with sufficiently low risk and adequate reward, isn't going to work well if we keep investing the way we are today. It's time to mimic nature, the master of evolution and long-term thriving, and primarily invest in the regenerative business ecosystem as a whole, rather than individual companies.

Then the most advanced companies around, Level 5 in all three axes (Learning as a purpose, Chapter 13, Autopoietic, Chapter 14, and FairShares Commons, Chapter 15,) can truly deploy their full power for the benefit of all stakeholders.

We have all the elements we need to deal with the global challenges that we face. We do not need to invent some completely new alternative to replace capitalism, we just need to rejig it for all capitals, to end with a regenerative Economy of the Free, built of regenerative businesses, with at least 10% at Level 5 on all axes, at least 40% at Level 5 incorporation and Level 4 on the others.

You may well at this point be saying that there is absolutely no way we can design a global regenerative business ecosystem. You're absolutely right, we cannot in any linear predictable way design a regenerative ecosystem. What we can do is take lessons from how quantum physics works, and its central property of emergence (Chapter 2).

The first lesson in quantum physics is that many of our hard distinctions are only conceptual constructs to make it easier for us to grasp how the world might work. Treating stakeholder categories in a business as having hard, distinct boundaries is such a poor reflection of what a business actually is, it can neither see nor make use of the real life of a business as a living being.

You may already be a stakeholder in so many businesses across so many categories that you cannot know of them. You are probably an investor in oil, weapons, pornography, and many other businesses and industries that you do not know you are an investor in, if, for example, you are in a pension fund.

Because pension funds etc. investments are constrained through regulation they may have to invest in companies that are harming our future. Even though, paradoxically, that puts your retirement at significant risk. Do you know what your pension fund invests in?

This illustrates how each of us is in multiple stakeholder categories to a far wider range of companies than any of us is aware of. As an employee of one company, you are an investor in all the companies that your pension fund invests in, and so part of creating the employment context for all the employees in those companies. Who themselves have pension funds that may well be investing in your company and creating your employment context.

You are a customer of a very wide range of companies, both directly, and indirectly through the supply chain that supplies them.

We are already an ecosystem of interrelated stakeholders and businesses. Almost every one of us is a member of multiple stakeholder categories across a range of businesses. So at the end of the day, the common ground that unites all of us is that we are all part of one global economy, even though we pretend it can be separated into disconnected parts.

Businesses are open, living systems in an ecosystem, so we must construct a reality based on the nebulous, ambiguous, volatile, uncertain, and complex nature of such an ecosystem. Then we can reshape the fundamental elements and their interactions to maximise their regenerative capacity.

Another lesson from quantum physics: you cannot predict where a particle will go—it will go wherever it can. The same is true for the economy as a whole, and any individual business. Like a child ought to grow up to become the best version of itself, growing strong across all its gifts, and so needs parenting, not command and control ruling.

For humanity to survive and thrive in the coming decades we must have a regenerative global economy, and to have that we must build regenerative ecosystems composed of regenerative businesses. But none of us could ever design one. What we can do is set the starting conditions to develop the natural gifts of each individual and business, and through that maximise the regenerative flow of all capitals[1].

We can do this best at a unique individual company level if the companies are part of the oneness of an entire ecosystem of companies. Nature has figured out how to do this extraordinarily well over millions of years. Across nature, almost all life uses a small number of common metabolic pathways and common DNA or RNA. We should use these same fundamental building blocks in building the elements of our organisations. Elements that you have seen above, like full accountability, circle structures, and inclusion of all stakeholders all the way up to the Fair-Shares Company incorporation.

It also means using the same set of complementary currencies, one for each unique type of capital. Arthur Brock, with his Holachain and Metacurrency Pro-

---

[1] Indra Nooyi, former CEO of Pepsico, realised early on that sustainability was the future, not just a fad; and pointed at the growing imperative to focus on the long term, on society as a whole, and to focus on shapes, not just numbers[219]. Given that she was CEO for an amazing 12 years, seven longer than the average CEO tenure, I suggest her words are worth listening to.

ject, is one person doing superb work in developing a platform optimised for just such a set of complementary currencies. The Telos Foundation is also doing superb work on the Telos blockchain.

One core property of ecosystems with multiple capitals in flow, as you find across nature, is a floating exchange rate mechanism between each capital and its associated currencies.

One of the reasons why our dysfunctional global systems are held stable in the dysfunctionality is that we have a fixed exchange rate between many of these capitals and money. For example, you may believe, as many people in business do, that your time is worth a fixed amount of money. When you get hired into a job, and your monthly salary is fixed, what's being done is fixing an exchange rate. The company and you agree, in the complete absence of any live, real-time data on value, that one month of your life and everything that you do for your company through your efforts and energy in that month is worth this fixed amount of money.

We do that because, until recently, it's not been viable to have a time currency, or a reputational currency, or keep track of social capital and all the other kinds of capitals and their flows in native currency units. It's not been viable to exchange one currency for another with a real-time exchange rate between them, based on real data on, e.g., how much money corresponds to how many hours of your time now, in each context that you use your time in (see Chapter 3 and the appendix to see how a general theory of economies, enables this). With projects like Holochain, Telos, and all the work being done in the field of complementary currencies and distributed ledger technologies, we have this capacity.

These are the ecosystems that we need to incubate now, what I call deep business ecosystems. Where all organisations recognise the imperative to use the same DNA, the same metabolic pathways, and work with the nebulous common ground of multiple stakeholder categories spread in an unknowable and undefinable way across all the businesses within the ecosystem.

These are the three foundations of a regenerative economic ecosystem, and are the same as nature's foundations:

- all the regenerative businesses use the same DNA, especially for incorporation and value flows;

- all the businesses tap into the same metabolic pathways, i.e., value flows: the same set of complementary currencies, at least one for each type of capital;

- all are designed to harness collaboration and conflict to get the best possible outcomes for all long term, with all capitals and their stakeholders in an appropriate balance of power.

Then we can adapt as individuals, as companies, and as the entire ecosystem, to address are global challenges.

17.3 Incubating regenerative ecosystems

This means creating incubators that produce cohorts of companies ready to enter true ecosystems that optimise both their internal processes and the connections between them. Inside each company and between them this means the channels for interaction, for value flow, the sharing of wealth generated. Each is best able to do this when all are at Level 5 in each dimension of Figure 12.2; using a FairShares Commons incorporation, having gone beyond conventional Ocracies, and a Level 5 implementation of something like our Adaptive Way .

This is the minimum that we need to build viable circular economies, blue economies, or triple bottom line economies, because each brings all of the vital elements of a true ecosystem.

These enable, at all six strata introduced on Page 44, the optimum level of collaboration (wealth and resource sharing) and competition to have maximum regenerative power in our non-ergodic world. Especially a Level 5 incorporation like the FairShares Commons creates the trust needed to share wealth, because it creates systemic trust and wealth sharing anchored in each company's articles of association: the players in the ecosystem have appropriate levels of governance power and a share of wealth in each other to maintain ecosystem integrity in the presence of predators and parasites. Without this the level of collaboration needed to counter our non-ergodic world is fragile, and will crumble soon after the first big successes. Then we will all lose.

Each cohort, once sufficiently incubated to have emerged from embryo stage through toddler and into early teenager stage can then stand alone and continue to grow as part of a larger regenerative ecosystem of companies.

This way we will steadily grow the size of our regenerative company ecosystems and, through power-law scaling, can very quickly transform our global economy into a regenerative one. If we really put our backs into this, if enough of you who have passionately protested in the Extinction Rebellion recently, in Occupy Wall Street, start your own regenerative ecosystem incubators or join the ones we believe will soon be in existence, we can scale a regenerative business ecosystem as fast as the school climate strike and Extinction Rebellion scaled in 2019.

Incubating and investing in regenerative business ecosystems is what I (Graham) am doing now, and intend to focus on for as long as I deem it the best place to put my gifts. Generating startups that have the best possible prospects of growing to Level 5 on all three axes begins long before the source starts talking about their idea to the first follower.

I have begun working with individuals, or at least the founding team before they incorporate, and before they have sown the seeds of irreconcilable conflict in their interpersonal interactions. These individuals come together into an initial startup university, master sufficiently well state-of-the-art approaches in working within themselves, between each other, on the tasks and roles of the work, and creating and maintaining FairShares Commons incorporations. In parallel, they begin using design thinking, lean start-up thinking, business model canvases, and everything else that is standard, like marketing, sales, and developing minimum viable products, to get to their first pre-seed minimum viable company. At this point, it may take off as an incorporated company, or it may continue as a virtual company within the incubator (e.g. as a blockchain based DAO).

17.4 Financing regenerative ecosystems

To have regenerative ecosystems we need to invest in the ecosystems as a whole, not single businesses. This requires a paradigm shift in each, and for some, also a shift in legislation.

Large institutional investors invest in huge diversified portfolios (based on modern portfolio theory) spread across multiple arenas of the economy. Such a portfolio is a shallow ecosystem, so they lose money compared to the deep ecosystems of this book, because they cannot satisfy the three principles of an ecosystem on Page 407; the companies do not have an incorporation that can fully harness the nebulous interconnectedness within each company and across the ecosystem to counter the loss-causing consequences of the unpredictable random bad luck inherent to our non-ergodic world (recall, the difference between Figures 6.2 and 6.3.)

Large institutional investors, though, such as BlackRock, are beginning to recognise this. Across the world, large asset managers have 62 trillion dollars in assets under management, with nowhere safe enough to invest, confident that they can pay out your pension when you need it in 10, 20, or 50 years.

Mobilise a good fraction of these \$62tn assets under management into an adaptive business ecosystem, and we have all we need to address our crises.

Investing in a deep ecosystem composed of fully Adaptive Organisations has a number of advantages, both for investors primarily interested in maximising their returns over the long haul, and those investors only interested in maximising their reward/risk ratio over just a few years. If you care about ergodicity (Section 6.4), you will love it.

Investing in deep ecosystems is the best way of investing in an economy that is path-dependent, rather than ergodic,. Nature has proven this over millions of years and has consistently benefitted from an all-capitals positive cumulative annual growth rate. From the beginning of life on earth, life has steadily built all the capitals it needs to thrive—until two centuries ago when we exploded as apex predator.

First and foremost, investing in a regenerative ecosystem of Adaptive Organisations will return a better long-term return on investment than any other investment decision you could take today. That is the central function of investing versus charity: to generate a return sufficiently in excess of the losses that the underlying capital continues to grow.

Some of you reading this book may believe that all profit is fundamentally wrong. But nature tells us that high levels of profit are fundamentally necessary, provided they are part of a sufficiently large open system. One helpful illustration I like is an oak tree. Nature plants one acorn, which grows into one tree. Over a number of centuries the oak tree will generate a return to nature of thousands of acorns. Nature thrives because each oak has an annual rate of return of multiples of thousands. Of course, because nature is a living system, that return is to the capital base of the ecosystem as a whole, not just the original oak tree that produced the acorn this oak tree grew from.

A big positive return on investment is absolutely vital for any functioning natural or business ecosystem that is going to regenerate rather than degrade, big enough to absorb any unpredictable losses from system shocks.

Hopefully this addresses any concern you may have had that we are describing a utopian fantasy; now let's look at why investing in a regenerative ecosystem is a no-brainer.

The one obvious one, that I won't spend more than this paragraph on, is that many of today's investments are stranded assets for anyone who hopes to have a viable life themselves, and for their children, in a few decades. All current investments in companies that are based on polluting our atmosphere with carbon dioxide and other greenhouse gases, and cannot viably transform themselves by 2030 within their shareholding structure, are stranded assets. They will have zero value before many of you reading this need the pension that depends on these companies.

It's time to invest in regenerative ecosystems, because of their advantages versus the isolated limited companies of today.

1. The biggest boost to your return on investment is that all stakeholders are aligned in their exposure to risk and reward. All the staff in an Adaptive Organisation share in the long-term wealth generated, and have balanced voting rights with you as an investor, so when times are hard they will naturally

invest money in the company by taking a cut in salary. Their long-term interests are maximally aligned with your long-term interests.

2. Staff will be even more supported by you as an investor, because the Fair-Shares Commons rewards you for more than your financial investment, it rewards you financially also for investing your relationships, your connections, your word-of-mouth marketing, and perhaps even your effort in meetings in the company delivering tangible results. So the value that is sucked out of some companies by the mistrust and antagonism between founders and staff on the one hand, and investors on the other, is transformed into collaboration.

3. Customers, suppliers and those who are currently held outside the hard company boundaries will be contributing to the company's success because they too are rewarded for investing themselves in its long term success and taking risks. Because of the FairShares Commons structure, and because of the patterns of collaboration in getting tasks done and between human beings, it's possible and appropriately rewarding for anyone in any stakeholder category to bring their creativity, effort, word-of-mouth advertising etc. into play to benefit the company as a whole.

4. No longer do investors need to be the only ones making sure executive remuneration packages stay within reasonable limits, because the staff, customers, and suppliers do that as well.

5. When a startup in a deep ecosystem proves sufficiently flawed that it gets shut down, the value that your investment has generated stays in the ecosystem. The people who you have invested in will rapidly be snapped up by the other companies that are scaling in the ecosystem. They will not need to spend anything training new hires from outside the ecosystem in how the Adaptive Organisation ways of working and being. Low risk, higher average return than today. The companies are fully Level 5 Autopoietic from the start.

6. Core IP remains part of the ecosystem as a whole, rather than becoming unproductive, or delivering value somewhere else. Key here is making it natural and easy for lots of inventions to come together into one big innovation that transforms, Like the inventions of TCP/IP (the internet protocol) and HTTP coming together at CERN, the particle physics research centre, to create the business ecosystem based on the world wide web.

7. Innovation, invention becomes systemic. We combine the speed and agility of modern startups with the deep innovative capacity of places like the old

AT&T's labs because the ecosystem enables inventors to focus only on inventing; and startup founders in the startup programme to turn the inventions into profitable, impactful businesses. The ecosystem is a production line for innovation and invention.

8. Money is not the sole metric in such an ecosystem. All relevant capitals have direct currencies that are metrics. Currencies of attribution for trust, for community, for creative capacity, for simply showing up each day with energy and a smile that increases the whole team's output are all equally valid metrics. Even better, what truly counts is valued, not just what can be counted, and certainly not just what can be counted in money.

17.5 Examples

A wide range of companies have demonstrated how consistently applying only one or a few of the elements in this book consistently reduces risk and increases reliable long-term performance; and many prove the power of integrating impact and profit into one. Below are a few examples. There are many more examples than these.

Visa   The Visa corporation had elements of the Free company incorporation until 2007. The credit card issuing banks were all members of a non-stock membership corporation which could not be sold. Membership gave non-transferable, non-sellable, irrevocable participation rights, and the founder, Dee Hock, refers to it as a reverse holding company, as the parts hold the core. Dee sees this as the central reason why Visa transformed the emerging credit card industry from one rapidly killing itself as it destroyed its capital foundation into one that worked. All we need to do now is reapply his lessons to all our capitals.

Mondragon   Mondragon is a deep ecosystem of cooperatives. It is currently the 10th largest company in Spain, had €24.725 billion in total assets, and 74,117 people spread across 257 companies in 2014. Mondragon is active in finance, industry, retail, and knowledge. The success is directly attributable to Mondragon being an ecosystem of interrelated cooperatives, with an investment bank in the middle (somewhat like Berkshire Hathaway). They have a cap on managerial pay of between three and nine times the lowest-paid full-time equivalent. The level of engagement and collaboration (reciprocal helping) led to Mondragon going through the 2008 crash without adding to the 3.5 million new recipients of unemployment benefits in the rest of Spain. Only one cooperative, employing 30 people, closed during that period, and the staff soon moved to other coops.

Bridgewater   Bridgewater is a $160bn (2019) asset management firm, founded by Ray Dalio in 1975. It runs on some of the core principles of this book around intra-and inter-personal developmental dialogue patterns[96]. This is widely seen as the reason why they have succeeded consistently better than 90% of comparable companies since they were founded. Life in such a company is not a life of ease, free of challenge; far more, it is a life of continuous adaptive challenge. The only difference with other companies, and why Bridgwater thrives where others have failed, is that the adaptive challenges are accepted, not swept under the carpet; and the entire organisation is geared to provide everyone willing to take on the challenge of changing who they are with the scaffolding they need to stay in or below their Zone 3 assisted growth zone.

Wikipedia.   In a handful of years Wikipedia has become the world's pre-eminent source of reliable information. One of the biggest things that makes Wikipedia trustworthy versus almost any other source of information is that it is immediately apparent if there is a disagreement between factions on what the current best answer is—unlike the average newspaper, or book, which will support the author's perspective without pointing out right at the very beginning how solid that perspective is. Wikipedia's core strategy is that people are basically good and will collaborate, given the chance, a fair context, and enabling structures.

Doughnut Economics   A number of excellent steps have been triggered by Kate Raworth's brilliant book *Doughnut Economics*[12]. For example, in New Zealand Māori traditions have been integrated with doughnut economics into the Te Reo Māori doughnut[2] created by Teina Boasa-Dean, Juhi Shareef, Jennifer McIver, and Tineke Tatt.

And many more   Many more companies are incorporated at Level 3, 4, even with elements of Level 5. You can find details in the excellent book from the Purpose Foundation[211], such as Carl Zeiss, Robert Bosch, Sharetribe, Ecosia, Ziel, Organically Grown Company, Waschbär, Elobau, and Ghost.org; as well as companies high on the roles and tasks, or human axes, like Decurion, described in detail by Laloux[184]. Also look at the Deliberately Developmental Practitioners Network[3] for many other success stories of life-giving organisations.

[2]https://www.projectmoonshot.city/post/an-indigenous-view-on-doughnut%
2Deconomics-from-new-zealand
[3]http://ddp-network.org

17.6 Your FairShares Commons ecosystem

It's time to consistently think

if it is to be, it's up to me.

None of this will happen if any of us continues to think that we are too small to make any difference.

None of this will happen if we think that they must do it, they must fix what is broken and give us what we need. There is no "they"; they are us.

Punitive justice, blame, attempting to divide ourselves into distinct groups of victims and perpetrators will not get us to a regenerative global economy.

If you want to have a world that is healthy for yourself and all of life, I believe that the best thing to do is put into practice any part of this book that you can put into practice today. Steadily expand how much you put into practice until you are joining or creating a regenerative FairShares Commons startup and regenerative FairShares Commons ecosystem.

I believe that now is the best time we will ever have to build regenerative businesses and economies that work for you, for our planet, and for profit. And with the huge difference in average outcomes you saw in Figures 6.2 and 6.3 we can still turn things around, if we move fast and big.

Part Five

Turning to Action

We're almost at the end of the book; here's the final transfusion of hope, energy, and motivation to act; along with greater clarity on how to act to make the best possible sustainable difference rebuilding our world into a regenerative one, where all life can thrive.

By now, whatever your roles in society and the economy; whether investor, founder, staff, family, friend, citizen, customer, supplier, etc., by now you have seen what you could do to construct the conditions you need to fully express who you are, your beliefs and values through your work; and to do at work every day what gives you meaning and energy.

From insight into action.

CHAPTER 18

Reasons for hope

We ask ourselves, 'Who am I to be brilliant, gorgeous,
talented, fabulous?' Actually, who are you not to be?
... Your playing small does not serve the world.
—*Marianne Williamson*

18.1 Stories of hope

You've read in this book how the meaning-making stories of separation created the identities of each distinct grouping in South Africa. These meaning-making stories were distilled and internalised over four centuries of events experienced in different ways by different groups; answered for each two central themes: *who am I?* and *what am I for?* and defined everyone's actions and their outcomes.

From the first Europeans[1] pushing those living in what is now Cape Town ever deeper into the desert; the wars with and suppression of the local population, as the Europeans moved deeper inland; the many experiences of loss of freedom and suffering, including the concentration camps, invented by the British during the South African wars to keep the Boer families under control; and the many experiences on all sides of trust offered and broken. Countless experiences were distilled into the interlocking meaning-making stories that created the reality of apartheid experienced by all South Africans. The reality of separation. The loss of what unites

---

[1] The story is far, far older. It goes back to when the first Homo Sapiens began moving across Africa, into Europe and the rest of the world, into territory previously held by others; and then migrating back again generations later.

all into the oneness of being human, being alive. Of just being.

All these were distilled and internalised into the meaning-making stories that told South Africans of all groupings what to do, and how to behave.

The transformation of South Africa to the post-apartheid Rainbow Nation was a reality created by new meaning-making stories of hope. Stories that brought onto an equal footing the oneness that united all South Africans, and the uniqueness of each, to create an awesome new South Africa.

These new meaning-making stories were clear in three examples:

1. Then vice-president, later President, Thabo Mbeki addressed parliament on 8 May 1996 during the passing of the new constitution[220].

> *I am an African. I owe my being to the hills and the valleys, the mountains and the glades, the rivers, the deserts, the trees, the flowers, the seas and the ever-changing seasons that define the face of our native land. ...I am formed of the migrants who left Europe to find a new home on our native land. Whatever their own actions, they remain still part of me. In my veins courses the blood of the Malay slaves who came from the East. Their proud dignity informs my bearing, their culture a part of my essence. The stripes they bore on their bodies from the lash of the slave master are a reminder embossed on my consciousness of what should not be done. ...*

2. Then deputy president and former president F.W. de Klerk replied, beginning with the words:

> *I am also an African. Although my people came from Europe more than 300 years ago, I became an African...[221]*

3. Then-president Nelson Mandela at the rugby world cup in South Africa wore the South African rugby jersey. A jersey which had, until then, symbolised rugby as the sport of white South Africans, began being reclaimed as a symbol of all South Africans.

These three illustrate how rewriting the meaning-making stories of identity began shaping the peoples of South Africa into one story: *We are Africans because we identify as Africans. And not for any other reason.*

The central theme of this book is that we can, and we must, take ownership of the stories that have shaped, and are shaping still, the reality we are experiencing. Then, owning our stories, rewrite them into stories that will shape a viable future realities. Realities where each of us thrives individually in our uniqueness, all of us thrive together, and where the entire ecosystem of life on earth thrives. Either all life in this interlocking ecosystem thrives, or none of us humans thrives.

You can take ownership of your stories, and how they shape your reality. You can take ownership of which forms of thought you are able to use, and you can take ownership of working subtly and compassionately with unchangeable aspects of your nature and history. Regardless of how small or big the arena of your stories and actions is, begin today re-crafting those stories to ones of hope, to ones of your uniqueness and our common oneness, and to ones that rewrite the stories of business, capitalism, and our economy.

18.2 Memories, connections, and emotions

We have been here before. Over the past four centuries since the Enlightenment we have been through a series of disruptions filled with a mix of extreme emotions, from irrationally exuberant hope to anxiety. When cheap coal and steam engines were developed in the mid-19th century, there was a wave of collective optimism that swept through many people: coal and engines would finally free us from all of our problems. Oil and gas wells flowed, lighting our cities just in time to save the whales (hunted for oil to light homes) from extinction.

For a century, many had their hope validated. Coal, and later oil-fuelled engines, generated disruptive innovations, and eliminated that era's pending environmental catastrophes. Now they are just the opposite, with horrific unintended, unknowable consequences.

But there are reasons to stay optimistic, or at least to act with optimism.

We have an amazing superpower in our capacity to feel higher-order emotions, to tap into our own memories and those of previous generations that have been captured in oral traditions, books, artefacts, even Wikipedia. Add these to our extraordinary capacity to bond together at all scales, from the smallest pair of friends through to our largest groupings with over a billion people in them, and we clearly have the latent adaptive capacity we need.

We just need to master the development laid out in this book so that we all use our emotions, rather than being used by them. Grow our interconnectivity and our uniqueness. Tap into our memories of times when crises have led to the good things we have today. Use these to generate our new collective cultural meaning-making stories, and your individual new meaning-making stories; ones that are right to shape the reality we need to create the thriving version of the world that will come after we have multi-solved our climate emergency, and all others.

18.3 Integrating what is separated

One reason why your economy is failing to do the multisolving across all emergencies needed, so that you can thrive today and throughout your life, and your children throughout theirs, is because neoclassical economics is too wedded to classical physics instead of relativity and quantum physics. Even more, there is too much scientism in economics, because of the paucity of rock-solid data gathered using double-blind studies with reliable control groups and robustly evaluating the validity of all assumptions, such as the assumption of ergodicity[119,120].

It's time for economics to become much more like relativity and quantum physics. Recognising that the vacuum, the interactivity between all parts, the effect of the observer, and the inherently unknowable nebulous nature of much of the economy is what matters. The consequence of recognising this is giving up all hope of predicting many specifics. All that you can do is work with probabilities, complementary pairs and paradoxical contradictions.

The two of us have been able to develop what is in this book and write about it because each of us has expertise in multiple disciplines, and each of us has learnt to integrate our expertise and that of others, quite different to us.

Over the past couple of centuries the world has moved from polymaths who had expertise in very many fields (even though none had anywhere near the depth that our average expert has today) to our current focus on being an expert in single clearly defined disciplines.

Today we need both. Polymaths to do the job of integrating, and those with single-minded expertise that goes all the way down into the depth of single disciplines, held by people who have the inner capacity to hold expertise lightly, not strongly as an identity. A lightness which allows them to collaborate seamlessly with experts in complementary and conflicting disciplines that we can then integrate into one body of knowledge.

It's no longer about being either an expert or a generalist; it's about all of us together collaborating as one humanity with the full depth of expertise and a seamless integration of that into one whole, just as the universe is one whole universe.

This integration will of course be filled with internal contradictions, paradoxes, and tensions. But it's precisely those tensions that make it a faithful model of actuality. Do this well, in the context of a FairShares Commons, and with a few multisolving interventions[7] we can address a wide range of our challenges in one.

Strengths come from interconnectedness, just as most of nature's properties come from quantum interconnectedness, and not from each separate particle. We need to master our interconnectedness as distinct unique individuals, and each of you needs to increase the inner interconnectedness between each different part of you. The scientific, the artistic, the rational, the emotional, the individual, the member of a community, the self-interest, and the altruistic.

This integration is what the two of us took from our chance meeting in London, Graham's life experiences growing up in South Africa, in physics, in Proctor and Gamble, and as an open entrepreneur; Jack's experiences, growing up in the US, in physics, economics, founding and editing a disruptive journal, as an economics professor, and novel writer. Each of us also has other areas, like ballroom dancing, American football, rowing, free climbing, and enjoying good food.

We took inspiration to create what's in this book from everything we have experienced in the reality of our lives. Wherever we've looked, we've seen people who have gone through the full range of human emotions. Whatever emotion you can imagine, people have been through that extreme before. The rollercoaster ride that was the transformation of South Africa captured all emotions from extreme hope and elation through to deep despair and depression in a very compact period of time and a very large number of people.

Both of us have concluded that it's more than okay to feel the emotions, it's absolutely necessary. This is what makes us human, this is what enables us to bond together and work as a critical mass of people towards achieving impossible outcomes. Whatever you are feeling right now, whatever emotion is in the reality you are experiencing, play with it, experiment with it, and use it. Play with it as you used to when you were a young child, and use it the way that the wisest role model you can think of uses emotions to grow their interconnectedness with other unique individuals as part of our common oneness with all other human beings and life itself. Your life is real-time improv.

Ends and beginnings are just meaning-making stories. Nothing is actually an end, nor is it actually a beginning, as *The Never Ending Story*[34] by Michael Ende perfectly captures. So as you reach the end of this book, it simultaneously is also the beginning of the next. Whatever your next is, all of you are interconnected with each other, and Jack's next, and Graham's next. What can we integrate across all of us, that is now separate? What uniqueness in each of us can we make even stronger and more powerful, together?

18.4 First they ignore you …

The quote from Gandhi (*First they ignore you, then they laugh at you, then they fight you, then you win.*) may be relevant to what I (remember that means, both Graham and Jack) have written in this book. Or, maybe too much in this book is nonsense and you are right to ignore us. Maybe what is in this book will never get to the stage of polarisation where people start fighting against what I am writing here, let alone to the stage where this becomes the new story creating the new reality.

But I am convinced that enough of this story of the future is already here and proven, just unevenly distributed, to paraphrase Otto Sharmer. All we need to do is take action now, in whatever way we can together, with as many other people as we can. What will you do today to change your story and so to change your reality?

18.5 You're alive and breathing

I wrote this section (Graham) early in the morning, just after sunrise on our last morning on our writing retreat in South Africa at Granny Dot's. I'm feeling right now an exquisite sense of joy, simply still being alive with almost all of my faculties intact, looking at a magnificent sunrise. Clouds hug the valley, skirting the slopes rising to the mountains. The tops of the distant mountains are covered in pale pink clouds, topped by a blue sky deepening by the instant. The clouds themselves are constantly changing, and I'm imagining how the trees that have been hot and dry over the past weeks are relishing the cool, life-giving water. Heavy rain fell during the night.

I look at all of this, and I feel joyful to be alive, cannot imagine now ever having experienced depression, nor ever doubting that life will find a way into the future. At the top of my meaning-making stories right now is the power of one of the things that I use as a meaning-making story when I'm in deep doubt: I'm still breathing, and that's enough success for now.

Because I've kept taking one breath at a time and have not stopped yet, I'm here to feel the exquisite joy looking across the valley at this ever-changing cloudscape. To feel hope and optimism because I can see the huge adaptive capacity throughout nature.

You are part of nature.
You have the adaptive capacity.
To become who you can grow into.
To be for what the world needs you for.

CHAPTER 19

Ten actions for you

In my view, all that is necessary for faith is the belief that
by doing our best we shall succeed in our aims: the
improvement of mankind.
—*Rosalind Franklin*

These ten actions range from easy ones that you can do in half an hour before you go to sleep tonight, to challenging ones that may well occupy your activities and all of your time for the rest of your life. Jack and I hope that these ten examples will trigger you to come up with many more that are uniquely yours.

If you have found this book useful,

1. join our online and in-person gatherings, via the mailing list on `https://graham-boyd.biz/rebuild-the-economy-leadership-and-you/`

2. tell your friends and colleagues about it, give it them as a present,

3. and review it online, tweet, etc. Follow @GrahamBoydphd @ProfJackReardon and @RebuildEcoLeadU on Twitter, post on LinkedIn (@GrahamBoydphd) or your favourite social media.

4. Become a patron, or donate once what this book was worth to you, so that we can accelerate creating videos, trainings, writing the next books, and continue developing the General Theory of Economies, via `graham-boyd.biz/rebuild-the-economy-leadership-and-you/`

5. Take one of Evolutesix's (`http://evolutesix.com`) programmes.

6. And if you are interested in founding, working, or investing in FairShares

Commons startups; or using this in your company; keep an eye on
http://graham-boyd.biz and http://evolutesix.com.

Do not hesitate to do what you can now. Every small step that you take now
will make it easier for you or someone else to take another step later. As Granny
Weatherwax says, in *I Shall Wear Midnight*[222],

'You've taken the first step.'
'There's a second step?' said Tiffany.
'No; there's another first step. Every step is a first step.'

Each first step becomes successively easier because of the step you took yesterday,
and the step that your friend took this morning.

Once we have our first fully functioning ecosystem of FairShares Commons
companies, it will be so much easier to take the first step of creating the second ecosystem. That will make it easier to take the first step of connecting the two ecosystems to form an ecosystem of ecosystems. Each step will make it successively easier.
And once we have all the companies in the world running as FairShares Commons
(or whatever improvement we find by taking those first steps) then it will become
very easy to steadily improve our new regenerative economy.

1. Keep an eye open for your stories, work hard on lifting the hidden ones that
   you are subject to into visible ones. Notice the reality that your stories are
   shaping. Where your reality is a poor match to actuality, use the approaches
   in this book to experiment, improvise, and create the experiences of new stories that will rewrite your old stories.

2. Take a sabbatical for a year, as an accelerated boot camp to give you an experimental laboratory and experiences to rewrite your story to work on your
   own stories. Read books that give you grounded reasons to hope. I'm eagerly
   awaiting Katherine Hayhoe's, *The Answer to Climate Change: And Why We
   Can Have Hope*[223], due out in September 2021.

3. Make your money matter. Read the excellent book by impact investor Ben
   Bingham, *Making Money Matter*[224]. Write to your pension fund (if you
   are lucky enough to have a pension), ask them what industries they are investing your pension in, and demand they invest it in businesses that are creating the kind of future you want to retire into rather than harming it. Do
   you really want your pension destroying the capacity of your planet to give
   you a comfortable retirement? Invest enough of the money that you are putting aside for your future in companies that are creating a viable economic
   future for all of us—FairShares Commons companies, or any other organ-

isation that is free, purpose-driven, and focused on systemic regeneration.

4. Start up your own Adaptive Organisation, incorporated at Level 5 (FairShares Commons company), using Level 4 or 5 processes for roles and tasks, and at least Level 4 or 5 developmental practices, like the Adaptive Way.

5. If you are an economist, get to work gathering data from real businesses to support or disprove everything we describe in this book; contact Jack about the research journal we intend starting.

6. Speak to a neighbour, colleague, or friend about what you have learned. Write to your local and national politicians to support creating local regenerative circular ecosystems addressing city level challenges.

7. Identify allies, both individuals who resonate with this, and organisations who are likely to resonate with this. Identify the common ground that unites you and the uniqueness that each of you brings that adds value to that common ground. Get into dialogue to stand together in that common ground and bring all of your uniqueness to bear.

8. Start a local business ecosystem using one or more complementary currencies, so that the ecosystem continues to thrive, regardless of fluctuations in the global financial economy.

9. Sit down, and imagine you are sitting one year in the future. Write a letter to someone important to you about what you have done in the past 12 months that has taken you a step closer to being part of an Economy of the Free. (It's vital to write this in the past tense[175], sitting a year in the future and reflecting back over the past year, not in the form of a resolution of what you will do in the next 12 months. Remember, as described in Chapter 8, resolutions often trigger your defensive stories, whereas a new story of what has happened that you aspire to live into has more power.)

10. Apply all three rules in the best balance you can: 1) Care for yourself, 2) Care for the other, and 3) Care for the whole, for whatever definition of other and whole you find fitting.

Acknowledgements

Painting is stronger than me, it makes me do its bidding.

Everybody has the same energy potential. The average person wastes his in a dozen little ways. I bring mine to bear on one thing only: my paintings, and everything else is sacrificed to it … myself included.

—Pablo Picasso

Graham

Everything that you have read in this book has come out of my understanding of what works, based on my experiences over five decades, including what I have learnt from many more able than I am. These experiences, and what I have learnt, have been shaped and informed by countless other people, people I have known in person, people that I have known through others, and people I have never met who have written books or given superb TED talks.

Staying focused on my energy potential, as Picasso writes in the quote above, has required sacrifices from me; and more importantly others have also sacrificed. Everyone who has paid a price for this book and work to exist, thank you.

Much of this has been shaped by my growing up in South Africa, and the privileges I had growing up there, with my amazingly supporting parents. My father, Hylton, who passed away during the middle of writing this book, and my mother, Barbara, who is a lively 90 year old as I write this, and my sister Tessa, have all contributed an unknowably large contribution to me being me, and this book bringing you whatever value you have taken from it. My work today is in part driven by a desire to pay forward to the next generations all the good things that previous generations have in their turn paid forward to me.

I was also privileged to go to excellent schools, Selborne Primary and College, and then to the excellent Universities of Cape Town and Bielefeld. I cannot know how my life would have turned out without everything I learnt there, both about subjects and about life, from my peers and teachers. Hard to do so, but I will single out Profs David Aschman who helped me decide to go to UCT, Jean Cleymans, and Frithjof Karsch who supervised my theses.

There are a few though who have been important contributors to this book itself. Marko Wolf has contributed many of the illustrations and refined my understanding of what we're doing and who I am in many challenging sparring sessions over the years. My co-founders of Evolutesix, Jason Maude, Robin Toller, Marko Wolf, Adrian Meyer, and Nikyta Guleria, along with Bernhard Possert, Rob Bigge, and Andrius Juknys who joined me later, have also, in numerous situations, sharpened my understanding of how to make this all work.

Nikyta especially, along with Nour El-Din Hussein, her husband, have gone way beyond the extra mile. Niky has proven the best possible colleague, doing a superb job of encouraging me when I needed encouragement, challenging me when I needed to be challenged, and has been as committed as I am to turning to action everything in this DIY guide, over a journey that took twice as long as we'd planned.

Otto Laske's seminal work on the Cognitive Developmental Framework has been the theoretical foundation for much of my own development over the past decade, and hence for Evolutesix and this book. He has built on the work of Kegan, Lahey and their group; Jaques; Adorno, Bhaskar; and many more.

Norman Wolfe's development of his Living Organisation model was the final crux stone in the long arch of this book, holding it all together. Equally pivotal has been the FairShares approach of Prof Rory Ridley-Duff and Cliff Southcombe of Social Enterprise International, which I integrated with my Free / Commons Company approach.

Paraphrasing Newton, if you are benefitting from this book, it is because I have stood on the shoulders of giants.

Eva Gottschlich and Jean Lin have been very generous in their support in making this book possible, for which I will always be grateful.

The people I worked with in Edgetalents, one of the companies where I demonstrated five years ago the power of integrating all three pillars, and the issues if any one was insufficiently strong to support the others, have all contributed to this book: Manuela, Thamires, Nikyta, Gustavo, Vanessa, Illuska, and Kelly.

Hannah and Sophie in London; and Manon, Antoine, Jean-Christophe in Brussels; gave me insights into the worldview, hopes and fears of people just entering, at, and leaving University, and guided how this work has evolved.

There are many more that have contributed significantly yet have not mentioned by name; you'll know if you have contributed, and I thank you! However long I make this section, I will still be missing some important people.

Jack

Writing the acknowledgements should be easy, right? The book is finished and like reaching the peak of a tall mountain, we are exhilarated by the arduous climb and the view from the summit, but this same exhilaration fogs our memory of all who have helped with this book, both directly and indirectly. So in advance I ask forgiveness from any person I have omitted; my forgetfulness abetted by the need for brevity.

I must start with my grandfather, Lester James Reardon, who first taught me the critical importance of our environment and sustainability at a time when few people gave it much thought, and even fewer listened. He also taught me the value and joy of reading, effectively handing the keys to a vast intellectual community, past, present, and future, of which I am so glad to be a member. (And to this day, one of my life's many pleasures, is reading a good book on a rainy night.)

I thank my parents, who welcomed me during dark times, offering me repose and comfort, and for their continued love and support. I thank my two brothers, Dave and Bobby, who have embraced their rebellious and non-binary sibling with love. I couldn't have written this book without the comforting love of my family.

Finishing this book in Tzaneen, South Africa, surrounded by ruggedly beautiful mountains hardly affected by the passage of time, encourages recognizing my debt to countless authors past and present—too numerous to mention, who enabled me to create my own stories, so that I can give something back to help others, to help them surmount their own barriers, reach their summit, and lead better lives.

As a teacher myself, I strive to positively affect the lives of my students both intellectually and personally; and in my own life, I have been quite fortunate to have had several gifted teachers, all responsible in some small way to enable me to have written this book. Brother Joe Girard, my high school American Literature teacher, infused me with a life-long love affair with words, not only as interesting entities on their own, but also as interconnected tools in developing adequate meaning-making stories (even today I still carry a vocabulary notebook). My high school football (American) coach, Frank Defelice, who despite my lack of football talent (or maybe because of it) stabilized my tumultuous teenage years with wisdom and good advice. From them I realized that, before I even began studying physics, that my spacetime was curved, that others can positively change my life's direction in completely unanticipated ways.

At the College of the Holy Cross, Professor J.J. Holmes, in his course The History of Revolutions, made history come alive, especially at critical junctures when one epoch leads into another. We are in such an epochal moment now, and I thank Professor Holmes for the foundational tools to write this book.

Frank Petralla, who was my first economics instructor (I couldn't get enough of his courses), not only inspired me to become a professor but also to enroll at the University of Notre Dame (his alma mater) to earn my doctorate in economics. Teresa Ghillarducci, my dissertation advisor, patiently molded me into a competent economist. Bill Leahy, advisor, friend, professor, and co-author of my first two academic articles epitomized the consummate Notre Dame professor. And finally, thanks to Charles Wilbur who believed in my fiction writing when no else did, and that a good economist could also be a novelist. I am happy to say that my first novel is finally finished!

I'm thankful for attending the University of Notre Dame for my graduate studies in economics, for it laid the foundation for me to become a full-fledged pluralist, also imbibing me with a sense of justice. As just one example: After making several trips to Appalachia, organized by Teresa Ghillarducci and another favorite ND professor, Larry Marsh, I was struck by the immense contrast between the wealth underground and the lack of wealth above ground. I conducted my doctoral dissertation on working conditions in the coal mining industry; and these Appalachia trips stimulated my life-long interest in sustainable energy.

After I received my doctorate in economics, I embarked on a typical career for economists doing everyday work and practicing everyday economics (similar to what Thomas Kuhn wrote about in *The Structure of Scientific Revolutions*. But one disparaging sentence, *"How Dare You"*, changed my life. I quickly realized that educating our young people (rather than proselytizing them) so we all can create better meaning-making stories was far more rewarding than engaging in the more mundane everyday economics. Central in my endeavor was the launching of a new academic journal, *The International Journal of Pluralism and Economics Education*, which after eleven years is still going strong. The IJPEE has played a small but significant role in pluralizing economics, and I thank all the people at Inderscience and especially Liz Harris.

I thank my fellow editor, good friend, and kindred spirit Miriam Kennet, founding editor of the *International Journal of Green Economics*; and founder of the Institute of Green Economics (Reading, UK) whose irrepressible energy to make the world the better a place consistently fuels my own energy. And I thank my life-long

Indian friends, Prithvi Yadav, Awadh Dubey, and Sudipta Bhattacharyya, whose passion to educate, to help the less fortunate, and to make the world just and sustainable, is forever inspirational.

And most important, I thank my two children, Elizabeth and Patrick, whose existence is forever interconnected with mine, whose energy and intellectual curiosity vitalizes me, empowering me to help make their world (and everyone's) sustainable, democratic, and able to provision for all. I dedicate this book to you: may you and your children look back at this book and thank your father for co-writing it.

Overall book

Both of us are enormously grateful to a number of people who have contributed to making this book possible. Andy, Vincent, and the team at Quietroom have been unflagging in their encouragement to write the book in a way that it is easy to read. Anna Kierstan has achieved well the challenge of polishing all our rough edges away.

We would both like to thank everyone at Granny Dot's, near Tzaneen in South Africa, who took such excellent care of both of us during the final stages writing this book. The people and the place proved a vital source of inspiration.

This book was also made possible by support in cash and in kind by the following people, both through our crowdfunding campaign, and directly.

Chapter Sponsors

- Consorticon Group sponsored Chapter 13 (who hope that everyone may have the privilege of working with colleagues like the team in Consorticon). They work in many of the ways described in this book, and especially resonate with the role of source in Section 13.2.

- VME Retail and Coopexchange (and exchange for investor shares of Fair-Shares and similar companies), long supporters of the FairShares approach, has sponsored Chapter 16.

- Vet Dynamics UK, a leading consultancy in creating regenerative veterinary practices, sponsored Chapter 8.

Gold

Philippe Schmidig   Jess Allen   Vincent Franklin

Table 19.1: Gold backers, the early backers contributing over £500

Bronze

Janssen Groesbeek	Daniel Godfrey	Henry Leveson-Gower
Eleonora Weistroffer	Jerry Koch-Gonzalez	Elizabeth Mong
Stephanie Bouju	Antonio Potenza	Whitney Rubison
Keith Bollington	Anna Plodowski	Robert Dellner
Alex Champandard	Cecil Schmitt	Thomas Tomison
Vincent De Waele	Achim Hensen	Rory Ridley-Duff
Laureen Golden	Louis Weinstock	Olivier Brenninkmeijer

Table 19.2: Bronze backers, the early backers contributing over £100

Part Six

Appendix

Building a general theory of economies

You can skip this appendix without losing anything if you want to know how to build a regenerative business, or regenerate yourself.

Jack and I decided to include this for those of you wanting to dive deep into a potential future alternative to current economics; we hope it will provoke a radically new box to rethink economics into, by both highlighting deeper reasons why we are in the mess we're in, and what we must do to get out.

Keep reading it if you get energy from it; otherwise skip it now and return to it on a cold winter evening.

The foundation of a general theory of economies, inspired by Einstein's General Theory of Relativity, began by asking what we see looking at our economy through the central lens of this book: each of us experiences our own unique reality. This yields the basis for a central theory of economies:

everyone always takes rational decisions.

These rational decisions are rational according to the unique inner reality and resulting frame of reference in the moment the decision is taken. So, just as the essence of general relativity is a way of connecting spacetime frames of reference from point to point, the essence of a general theory of economies is a way to connect one reality at one moment in time in one person to that of themselves at a different time and place, or to another person at some place and time. In other words, a way of connecting one decision frame of reference with another, an economics aligned with Otto Laske's CDF.

So how can we connect your decision frame of reference now with your decision frame of reference later, and the decision frame of reference of someone else?

We can only compare decisions and their rationality if we can transport realities and frames of reference (thought form P6 of Table 9.1) from one decision point in spacetime and person to another. (You'll see where this is going in a moment, unless you're familiar with general relativity, in which case you may already see where we are going!)

This general theory of economies differs from the usage in J.M. Keynes' *The General Theory of Employment, Interest, and Money*[225], which is also referred to as *The General Theory*; although in his Collected Works he alludes to Einstein's work as an inspiration. Keynes might view the general theory of economies here as a natural consequence of bringing together cutting-edge understanding of individual adult development (Size of Person, inner reality, etc.) and social development (e.g. of cultures, as described by Spiral Dynamics) with at least some of the key concepts that led him to write his book[226,227].

This approach makes clear that economics is the study of what we can *say* about decisions and how they affect provisioning, not about what *is*. This broadens economics beyond human society, and certainly beyond any one worldview, such as the European, American, or Chinese business models. This is very much the same as the realisation in physics that physics is only about what we can say about how the world is, not the study of what actually is.

This also highlights the complementarity between economics and business theory. Economics is about all decisions and all the different things and meaning-making that shape them. Business theory is about how to take decisions, including those on how to execute in order to actually move and combine resources to create value, and you will see how business theory lies within a general theory of economies.

Whilst Keynes and his successors could never aspire to calculate macroeconomic outcomes bottom-up using a large number of individual decisions makers, each with a different inner reality and frame of reference, including all recursive feedback loops, today we can, using the same supercomputers used for simulating weather and climate.

Perhaps the phenomenological models that form much of economics today, which were the best that could be used before today's supercomputers, can soon be replaced by bottom-up calculations based on billions of people, each with their own unique experienced reality and frames of reference, constantly changing along their paths through life. All we need now are people brighter than I (Jack and Graham) am to build such a general theory of economies.

How does general relativity describe gravity?

To use general relativity as a metaphor, to guide us towards an hypothesis for a general theory of economies, we need to understand just enough of the design principles of general relativity.

General relativity is captured in one of the most beautiful and symmetric equations in all physics:

$$G_{\mu\nu} = T_{\mu\nu} \tag{19.1}$$

$G_{\mu\nu}$ (also written as $\mathbf{G}$), the Einstein tensor, describes how spacetime is curved, and $T_{\mu\nu}$ (also written as $\mathbf{T}$), the stress-energy tensor, describes how much mass, energy, and physical stress there is at any point in spacetime.

The physicist Archibald Wheeler summarised the beauty of this equation:

> *matter tells spacetime how to curve, and spacetime tells matter how to move.*

There is no gravitational force anywhere in this equation. It says instead that matter is always moving in straight lines inside a curved spacetime. Curved spacetime and matter actually exists, gravitational force is nothing other than a simplifying mental crutch humans have invented so that we can make approximate predictions using simple equations. Wheeler's summary makes clear that what we see as the Earth moving in a circle around the sun is, in actuality, the Earth moving in a straight line through a spacetime that has been closed in on itself by the sun's mass.

Spacetime itself is the circle.

Newton thought that there were three completely distinct elements: space, time, and force of gravity. Einstein realised that special relativity (forces and moving objects) didn't fit Newton's concept of gravity, and therefore Newton's gravity must be fundamentally flawed, even though it had worked well enough so far.

Einstein's intuitive leap was to realise that the effects attributed to the force of gravity could just as easily be the effects of curved spacetime in the absence of any force whatsoever.

The Einstein tensor, $G_{\mu\nu}$, unpacks into a fiendishly complex set of equations, that most physicists only get to see in their third or fourth year at university, and begin to solve in the simplest of cases. It describes, at each node in spacetime, how to carry the vectors (like pointers pointing) from one node to the next.

Imagine you are standing at the South Pole. In every direction you turn, you are looking north. Think of a cluster of arrows, flat on the Earth's surface, at the South Pole, fanning out in a complete circle, all pointing north. Now you want to transport each of these arrows along its own line of latitude towards the North Pole. Each, as they move towards the North Pole, must stay flat on the earth's surface. By the time they get to the Equator, when you compare one arrow to its neighbour, they are all parallel to each other now, not fanning out hedgehog style. By the time

437

they get to the North Pole they are all pointing into each other, not away from each other.

That is what $G_{\mu\nu}$ does. It describes how to transport pointers from one node to other nodes in spacetime, constrained by the necessity of staying in spacetime along the entire journey. These pointers are a frame of reference. So if you think of the geometry of spacetime as infinitely many nodes, and the connections between the nodes, with directions pointing forwards in time and space on each three spatial and one time dimensions, $G_{\mu\nu}$ tells you how to transport these pointers, or frames of reference, inside the curve of spacetime.

So spacetime is closed in on itself into a circle halfway around these pointers, which will be pointing in the opposite direction. This gives us a clue on how to transport meaning-making frames of reference from one decision to the next.

This means staying within the two dimensions of the Earth's surface, which are curved and closed in on themselves. If you were to walk from the South Pole due north to the North Pole in a straight line, and when you got there just keep going in the same straight line, you'd arrive back at the South Pole. You could keep going forever, as you would be moving in a never-ending straight line in a curved space.

The stress-energy tensor, $T_{\mu\nu}$, captures everything that actually exists at each point in spacetime. How much mass, energy, stress[1], and momentum; pointing in which direction; is present.

Putting Wheeler's words into symbols now, $T_{\mu\nu}$ tells $G_{\mu\nu}$ what to be, and $G_{\mu\nu}$ tells $T_{\mu\nu}$ how to move.

What might a theory of economies look like that is based on geometry instead of force? We know that physics was fundamentally transformed when Einstein realised that everything attributed to gravitational forces could be better described by a force-free geometrical theory, let's look seriously at a geometrical general theory of economies, and see where it might get us.

Geometry is about all the nodes, or points, and how adjacent nodes connect to each other. By connect, I mean how a Frame of Reference at one node is transported to the next node, i.e., changes as it is moved. In a theory based on force, the geometry of spacetime (the Frame of Reference) is just an arbitrary mathematical construct to use as the basis for your calculations, and stays the same at each node.

In a geometric theory, spacetime is no longer a mere arbitrary mathematical choice for calculating with. The shape of spacetime is the origin of the physical effects we see; such as the GPS satellites orbiting the Earth in a stable way.

---

[1] Stress is defined in physics by looking at an infinitesimally small box in spacetime and is composed of the combination of forces that are stretching or squashing along one axis, and the forces that are twisting clockwise and anticlockwise around the axis.

G in economies

What might $G_{\mu\nu}$ represent in a general theory of economies? We need to look for some equivalent to spacetime, with curvature replacing economic forces. Then, many economic 'forces' in current economics thinking will emerge as fictitious concepts, analogous to sunrise and sunset being convenient fictions easing daily language. It's far easier to talk about enjoying a sundowner at sunset than an earth rotator at the distal extreme of the diurnal rotation!

So we need to define the nodes of an economy, how the nodes are linked, and what is transported from one node to the next.

I propose that $G_{\mu\nu}$ represents the space of all possible decisions, across all physical spacetime. At each point in this decision spacetime, $G_{\mu\nu}$ carries the pointers, or frames of reference in a decision at that point.

This is building on centuries of work on what economics can validly say about the economy: that at its core it is a sequence of decisions, choices between options.

Any of us who is taking a decision will be at a specific node in decision spacetime. We will take a rational decision according to the rationality of exactly that node in decision spacetime.

If we were to take the same decision a little later, we would be taking that decision at a different node in decision spacetime, where the decision tensor (reality, or frame of reference pointers, i.e., meaning-making) might have changed direction. They might even, like the Earth moving around the sun, have moved halfway around a circle and lead us to take the exact opposite decision. Both decisions are completely and 100% rational, even though each opposes the other.

Looking at decisions as always being 100% rational, but taken in a curved decision spacetime, we now have a way to make better sense of the relationship between all the different perspectives in economics. We just need to now find a way of formulating decision spacetime accurately, and especially how $G_{\mu\nu}$ transports the frame of reference defining rationality at one node to the next.

Now you can see what is actually happening if an economist struggles to grasp decisions taken by other people. Neoclassical economics assumes decision spacetime has a Cartesian geometry[2]. In this, if you transport the frame of reference defining rational from one point, one person, or one moment to another, the frame of reference continues to point in the same direction. So what is a rational decision at one node in decision spacetime is always the same rational decision at all nodes in spacetime.

---

[2] Keynes actually has a paragraph on the flaws in economics due to this assumption in his draft *General Theory* manuscript[226,227]

Therefore, if a different decision is taken, it must be because either the person is irrational, or under the influence of some force that overcomes a free decision, in an economics based on Cartesian geometry and forces.

Replacing this with the idea that decision space-time itself is curved, i.e., everyone's Frame of Reference is unique, so two people's decisions can only be compared after transporting the Frame of Reference from one node to the other, needs to be thoroughly explored and tested to destruction.

There may, of course, be some even bigger abstract space; or perhaps more research will show that there is no way of describing economies on the basis of the geometry of decision spacetime. Finding out will require rigorous scientific research, gathering hard data capable of falsifying our hypothesis unambiguously. But, whatever the outcome, we must find a way to integrate the understanding of reality and economics.

Value is in this space and forms part of the frame of reference. In a curved decision spacetime, value changes as you move from one node in decision spacetime to another. $G_{\mu\nu}$ gives you all you need to know about how decision spacetime is curved, and therefore how value changes (is transported) as you move through decision spacetime.

I am at a node in my decision spacetime, using the decision frame of reference of that node, which includes any additional forces, to take a rational decision. As I move forwards in time my decision frame of reference will shift, pointing in a slightly different direction.

Some of this change is due to my meaning-making stories changing as I internalise experiences from earlier decisions. This is clearly not ergodic.

This change in my frame of reference is captured by the curvature in the path I move along over the year, and G describes how that path curves. So G transports rationality of now to rationality in the future or past, however far I want to go, enabling me to understand the rationality of previous decisions even if they appear irrational in my current reality.

Each point, or node, in decision spacetime is abstract, and is independent of any entity taking a decision.

These entities may be individual human beings, families, multinationals, or even global governance bodies. If each moves along their natural path in decision spacetime, every decision they take will always be the most rational decision available at that point, and with the information they have.

All this makes G a phase space of all possible decisions, meaning-making stories, including values, principles, internalised culture, etc. These give the "how much" value on the G side is attributed to the things and all possible spacetime positions.

T in economies

What might $T_{\mu\nu}$ represent in a general theory of economies? We need to look for what actually is, what moves, what forces exist, and what contributes any degree of shaping to the geometry of $G_{\mu\nu}$.

I propose that the key elements of $T_{\mu\nu}$ are things (food, houses, gold, knowledge, etc.); and potentially forces (e.g. a threat of violence if you fail to take a specific choice); that might have value attributed on the **G** side or not by the meaning-making stories active at a given node.

There may be more elements of $T_{\mu\nu}$ that are not part of this category. I hope there are, and maybe you will be one of those able to identify them and flesh out what a general theory of economies fully includes.

So $T_{\mu\nu}$ describes everything that becomes a resource (resources are things with the meaning-making that attributes value to them), power, politics, memes, feelings, movement, etc.—whole swathes across all physical and social sciences.

$T_{\mu\nu}$ also describes what is actually done as a consequence of decisions. All human behaviour lies here: the work that we do, individually and organised together in businesses, etc. All organisational theory and human behaviour must be included in this general theory of economies, and it ought to describe all of how organisations actually work in different kinds of contexts, in different ways of organising, and embedded in different overarching meaning-making cultures.

An economy is $\mathbf{G} = \mathbf{T}$

$T_{\mu\nu}$ tells $G_{\mu\nu}$ how to curve. It shapes the meaning-making stories, values, etc., creating the shape, the curvature of decision spacetime $G_{\mu\nu}$.

$G_{\mu\nu}$, the space of all meaning-making stories and consequent decisions, then tells all the things how they should move (linking supply and demand), their usefulness or value, and how they ought to change.

In this general theory of economies, the decisions (buy and sell, pricing, how to incorporate, what is waste versus resource after recycling, etc.) are always locally rational at each point in decision spacetime.

It's only possible to construct a theory of rational decision-making if that theory fully includes everything impacting each individual's locally and internally constructed reality, and describes accurately how that reality is to be transported faithfully from one node in decision spacetime to the next ($G_{\mu\nu}$).

Compare this geometric general theory of economies to two criticisms often levelled at neoclassical economics[26,124].

    i. The assumption that everyone is rational is not true.

2. The lack of pluralism, and lack of seamless integration with all other relevant disciplines, ranging from the physical boundaries placed by laws such as energy conservation and entropy, through to the latest cutting-edge insights from the social sciences and neurobiology.

In this general theory of economies, we show how the neoclassical economics assumption of rationality is retained, by showing that any discussion of rationality can only be done after describing in sufficient detail the frame of reference, defining what is and is not rational, used by the decision-making entity.

We show that decision frames of reference are, and hence rationality is, dependent on exactly where in decision spacetime the decision is located. Reality is curved: it can only be approximated in a sufficiently small and locally ergodic approximation; all other decision evaluations must use a curved transport of the frames of reference.

This general theory of economies embraces all pluralistic aspects that impact on an economy, either on the $T_{\mu\nu}$ side shaping decision spacetime, or on the $G_{\mu\nu}$ creating the decisions telling things what they are, what value they have, and how to move or transform from one place to another, from lower value to higher value or from higher to lower value.

For example, the elasticity of supply and demand in neoclassical economics (the re-establishment of equilibrium after some change in supply or demand leads price to exert a force on the other) becomes a force-free geometric effect in decision spacetime itself: it is stretched or compressed, and will describe exactly the outcomes we see without any need for market forces. This stretching / compressing is caused by the stress part of $T_{\mu\nu}$.

I believe that replacing the concept of market forces, and all the algebra of forces in current economic thinking, with curvature in decision spacetime, as well as things in **T**, will give economics the same leap in power to understand and predict that physics gained when Einstein recognised that there was no such thing as a gravitational force, despite all that that illusion enabled.

In this geometric theory, all theories of value have their place. The labour theory of value is just a local approximation to an area of decision spacetime with meaning-making stories in which labour is the dominant source of value, a utility theory of value is just a local approximation to another area of spacetime with meaning-making stories around utility, and any intrinsic value is also part decision spacetime's shape.

None of these theories of value can ever be right or wrong; more, they are better seen as local approximations in a small enough domain of decision spacetime where the curvature is negligible compared to the outcome of decisions.

Supply and demand are central to economics, and neoclassical economics is based on looking at them as two fundamental forces. You achieve an equitable price when the two forces are exactly in balance. In a general theory of economies, these disappear as forces. Rather, supply and demand are two different kinds of mass that shape decision spacetime, creating the meaning attributed to abundance, scarcity, and each item being at some price point.

Both ergodic and non-ergodic aspects of an economy may be described by a geometric general theory of economies because the decision spacetime includes what physicists would call phase space. This decision spacetime extends across all time, from the first decision to the last decision in society (and maybe even in the entire universe). All paths are present, and include the full impact of history, of times of stability and times of revolution, path-dependent non-ergodic cumulative decisions, etc.

This geometric approach to constructing economics might deal with all concepts of competition and collaboration, from a single monopoly and no collaboration, through to perfect competition or collaboration, and the entire continuum of actual competition-collaboration between the extreme limits.

Neoclassical economics, where each person and decision are independent of each other and independent of time, emerges as the Cartesian approximation to competition in a geometric general theory, i.e., an approximation that's only valid where each point in decision spacetime is independent of each other point, and there is no curvature.

Also, the emerging class of prosumers is well described here. This is another complementary pair that must be part of any general theory of economies.

Tension and conflict play a central role in the general theory of economies. They are in $T_{\mu\nu}$ and shape how the rational frame of reference is transported by $G_{\mu\nu}$ through time (for example, one specific decision-making entity, whether a human or corporate entity) as they change their meaning-making stories by mining and refining what the tension is telling them about how to make their local, internally constructed reality a better and better match to actuality.

The value of tension and conflict between people to steadily increase the viability of the decisions they are taking, especially in an organisation that requires them to collaborate and turn those decisions into valuable output, is now visible.

This general theory of economies also captures cleanly how different individuals in different parts of an organisation will take decisions that are quite different from each other in exactly the same situation and looking at exactly the same data, and yet each is taking a fully rational decision. Each is at a node some distance apart in decision spacetime. Of course, immediately after a strategy discussion and alignment, they may each be at nodes that are very close together, but because decision spacetime is curved, as they move forward through time they may move to nodes that grow further and further apart. So the choices that each makes later on, looking at the same set of options, will grow further and further apart.

Whether any specifics of general relativity are present in a general theory of economies is going to require significant research spanning disciplines from pure mathematics through to social sciences and neurobiology. I have used $G_{\mu\nu}$ and $T_{\mu\nu}$ as a metaphor to provoke a new perspective; we still need to determine if it is indeed a tensor, some other holor, or something else completely that we need.

That will require scientific research, rigorous enough to falsify everything false in this approach. This will take the kind of massive simulations I (Graham) did in physics, known as Monte Carlo simulations, to have a workable approximation to the path integral of each person (Section 11.2) taking into account everything non-ergodic in each person's decision making and the economy as a whole (Section 6.4). The more accurate the simulation needs to be, the further into the past and future it needs to do the path-integral of each person represented in the model, the more variation it needs to have in identity and life influences, the more relationships with others, and the more people it needs to simulate. It may need to run multiple times, creating an ensemble of configurations, leading to a probability distribution of economic outcomes. This ensemble also will include in the simulation a recursive awareness of such simulations.

These ensembles can then be used to test the theory, by comparing the outcomes from the ensemble average with historical data; and only once we have tested to falsification all we can, are we able to use what is left to begin tentatively predicting the future.

Hopefully this approach can catalyse a useful general theory of economies.

What about neoclassical economics?

Neoclassical economics requires the kind of fudges that physicists take as an absolutely sure sign that they need a new theory.

We know it is time for a new theory of economies because neoclassical economics does poorly when trying to describe and predict the emerging zero marginal cost economy, gift economy, care economy, emotional labour economy, etc. However, in some cases it seems a good enough approximation to be useful.

In general relativity, if you look in a small enough region of spacetime to form an approximate inertial frame of reference, you can't tell the difference between Newton's gravity and Einstein's gravity. How small that box needs to be depends on how tightly spacetime is curving. If you're in the middle of nowhere, where $G_{\mu\nu}$ is flat, the approximate inertial frame may span millions of years and millions of kilometres in each direction. If you are close to a very high density of $T_{\mu\nu}$, like a black hole, the approximate inertial frame of reference may be smaller than your little toe.

I expect that we will find the same to be true with neoclassical economics. There will be some small enough domain in decision spacetime where $G_{\mu\nu}$ is flat across large numbers of people, and across long periods of time, and you have an approximate decision frame of reference that looks just like neoclassical economics.

However, if you are close to a concentration of power, where there is a steep power gradient from one point in decision spacetime to the next; or, if you are on the boundary between two cultures, where there is a steep gradient of meaning making, then the approximate neoclassical frame of reference may be so small that it is no bigger than one person over one second.

Steep meaning-making gradients can occur across physical space, for example between two people in a marketplace with very different cultural backgrounds or personalities, or two neighbouring countries with very different cultures. It also occurs across time, during epochal shifts, such as we have today.

If this kind of geometrical general theory of economies is a useful description of how an economy actually works, it will describe the decisions being taken now and over the next 10 years as the rapid changes in $T_{\mu\nu}$ shape the very tight curvature in decision spacetime $G_{\mu\nu}$, and vice-versa.

These power differentials lie in the meaning-making of each individual. For example, I might threaten to retrench somebody from my company, unless they do what I say. If that person is completely dependent on their monthly paycheck to survive, they will see an existential threat and will do exactly what I say.

However, if that person already has their own startup underway, just ready to launch, and being retrenched will give them what is missing in time, commitment, and seed money, they will make meaning of being fired in an overwhelmingly positive way and will then do exactly the opposite of what I want, so that I fire them.

The curve in decision spacetime may be so steep that their decision changes from 10:00AM to 10:01AM.

Equally, who I am, my meaning-making stories, my relative position in the company, and much more, can also make that a very tight curvature.

So to fully capture the rationality of two different choices separated in time or made by two different people you need to understand how to transport the rational decision-making frame of reference from one point in decision spacetime to the other. That is what $G_{\mu\nu}$ does.

The curvature of our economic space, or decision spacetime, then tells us which choice to make on resource allocation. This includes what decisions to take in politics, relationships, and all other kinds of intangible value.

So I propose that any full theory of economies must be equally applicable across both the tangible and the intangible, and across all time, including explaining how the economic value changes across time. If not, it is at best an approximate phenomenological model, not a theory; and at worst a fantasy we force onto society as if it were truth.

In Newton's triad of independent space, time, and force, the units you use to measure each are independent and have no inherent meaning.

Relativity and quantum physics, however, make clear that there are natural units. For example, the speed of light is the natural unit linking space and time. The speed of light in nature is one: the unit of space equals the unit of time. It is only our uninformed choice of metres and seconds that gives us a big speed of light.

Many numbers used by engineers to figure out how to build something have nothing to do with physics, but rather are artefacts of the units that we invented before we understood quantum physics and relativity.

Equally some units in economics will turn out to be 1, because they are inherently natural; anything else is an artefact of an uninformed approach. For example, aspects of pricing, such as the exchange rates between different national currencies, are artefacts. These are now part of curvature instead.

Value and pricing in a general theory

Value is at least partly, if not wholly, attributed by the meaning-making frame of reference specific to a human meaning maker, in some emotional state, at some point in time, at a place, in a context. This value lies in G, where changes in value yield the curvature of G. Even if a decision is being taken by a computer program, or even an artificial intelligence, the meaning-making (including emotional), of the programmer or the dataset used to train the AI is irreducibly part of the value.

The general theory of economies gives us a mechanism to take the drivers of value[66] on the T side and bring them all together into the rational decision on the G side at each node in decision spacetime.

So whilst neoclassical economics is based on an inherent substance to value in an object or service, in this proposed general theory of economies, value comes from all of the different kinds of meaning-making that anybody might have; all their values, principles, beliefs and religions; now, in the past, or at any time in the future, and across all situations.

This then creates the curvature in **G**, including the momentary value in the local frame of reference that anything has at a specific point in decision spacetime. Value can be attributed to something from any and all kinds of meaning-making, which means that value can have a highly convoluted geometry from one person to the next.

Value can be like the scissors, paper, stone game, except with infinitely many elements, not just three. Just as stone beats the scissors, paper beats stone, and scissors beat paper, so too with value. There can be no universal Cartesian theory of value, not universal rational decision, when value can have a large or even infinite number of axes that cannot be put onto one single Cartesian geometry.

This integrates all current approaches to value in economics into one theory of value. Utility is clearly part of this, but equally, emotional labour and the intangible values (trust, love, reciprocity) of emotional labour shape **G** into intangible value geometries. The emerging realm of green, blue, sustainable, etc. economics, Sharia economics, and everything else shows up as additional dimensions in a multi-dimensional within the much larger decision spacetime.

From this you can also see that the neoclassical economic concept of value is too small to base a theory of an economy on. At best, it is useful for a very small, local approximation to a theory. **G** encompasses all kinds of decisions, at each point in decision spacetime, and deciding what value something has is one class of decisions in the entire decision spacetime.

It also shows that pricing, which shows up on the **T** side, is a local artefact of the currency you use (for example, positive interest bank debt, a.k.a. money) to parametrise the underlying curvature of decision spacetime. In a full theory of an economy, the relative ranking in price of different things will depend on which currency you use. In practical terms, this means that planting an oak forest will be of higher value than planting a pine forest if you use the Terra as currency; or vice versa if you use money as the currency; and depending on which of the many other aspects of **G** value you decide to use to define the rank order.

This also means that on the **T** side we need at least as many currencies as there are kinds of value. Just as you cannot rank scissors, paper, stone, in a linear Cartesian basis, you cannot parametrise all kinds of value with money alone.

Our definition of property as a situation where one single entity, or a few close entities, has the sole decision authority over a thing can now be represented cleanly on the **T** side. Property now shows up in the maths as a force in **T**, acting on a thing, pushing it off the curve in **G** that it would naturally follow were it free.

It's now visible how the consequences on price, value, rent-seeking, etc. are created by the relationship between laws and institutions (like property) and individual meaning-making frames of reference.

It's only now that we have enough understanding of human beings to even begin defining a general theory of economies. Up until now, all we have been able to do is look at various alternate Cartesian one-dimensional approximations, so a utility theory of value and a labour theory of value are seen as competing alternatives, rather than two complementary axes in a curved decision spacetime.

Physicists have a very simple model, the Ising model, that will be useful for simple decisions like buy / not buy. In it every node is either buy or not buy. In the absence of any effect from the $\mathbf{T}$ side (e.g., a meme), the decision to buy or not to buy is completely arbitrary, and $\mathbf{G}$ has a potentially high curvature from node to node. As soon as there is some effect in $\mathbf{T}$, this smooths the curvature, aligning decisions. Akin to a magnetic field that makes magnets all point North, the meme makes the decision point to buy, or not buy, as the case may be. The Ising model may allow us to calculate in all situations, from equilibrium to complete disequilibrium in times of rapid change, (or as physicists would say, a phase transition,) where buy or not buy becomes sensitive to slight changes in the meme, or even Cartesian rationality.

Freedom and property in a general theory

The more freedom that an individual has to move exactly along the curve in decision spacetime, the better they are able to choose according to the decision frame of reference at exactly the point in decision spacetime they are naturally at. This is very much the same as saying that the Earth will continue to move in a straight line through curved spacetime around the sun until acted on by a force, such as a moon-sized object striking it.

Equally, an individual who is free to follow their own natural straight line path through time, to faithfully follow the curve their changing meaning-making gives them, will always make a rational decision that is right for them. However, if they are not free to choose, and constrained in some way by being property or exposed to some force, they will be forced to make a 'wrong' decision.

Equilibrium in a general theory

The general theory of economies embraces different types of equilibrium and non-equilibrium. You can have an equilibrium in information, an equilibrium in flows of value, and much more.

Consider knowledge, and the non-equilibrium path between equilibria. Imagine that there is a crash coming, as there was in the mid-2000s. If no one has any information about the impending crash, we have a local equilibrium in knowledge and in meaning-making. As soon as the first economist predicts the impending crash, we no longer have an equilibrium in knowledge.

This economist now begins talking to people about the impending crash. These people start talking to other people, and sooner or later the press publishes it broadly. Each person who hears this will move to a different point in decision spacetime, depending on whether they believe the prediction, on their hardwired nature, and on all of their meaning-making stories. Some traders will believe the prediction, others won't. Each will use their own meaning-making stories to generate decisions about buying and selling.

At every step in the journey, each change in knowledge for each person moves them to a different point in decision spacetime and changes the nature and probability of the impending crash. Possibly the probability will reduce to zero, or just reduced in severity to a negligible dip.

The general theory of economies gives us the tools needed to recursively iterate along the path. We can transport the frame of reference for a rational decision in the starting equilibrium, where no one knows, through the point where one economist predicts, to the point where a small number of people know, and the economist then recalculates their prediction based on those people knowing. They then disseminate that prediction more broadly, recalculate the prediction based on that number of people knowing and each of them talking to each other and spreading their own personal reality of the probability they see of the crash happening. And ad infinitum until we reach the end equilibrium, where everyone knows, and everyone knowing has been incorporated back into an adjusted prediction of the crash, infinitely many times, to reach a new equilibrium.

The general theory of economies allows us to do this path-dependent iteration, and even take the average of the integral of all possible paths, and all the other intriguing things that physicists do to construct theories that predict the non-equilibrium physics we need to have smartphones.

At the same time, there may always be types of non-equilibrium on the **T** side, in the concentration and flow of things of value, tangible and intangible. There will always be concentrations and fluctuations.

Equilibrium is a paradox at the heart of a current concept of business, and the economy: a business, and an economy, is healthy if and only if it is growing. But by definition something that is growing, where interest rates are not zero, is not in a complete equilibrium. And since money is built on positive interest bank debt, a zero interest equilibrium economy based only on money is unstable[64] and so at best a momentary equilibrium.

In a way, this is much like the dynamic interplay in our atmosphere. We have repeating weather patterns, which over large enough scales we call climate: from microclimates through to our global climate. We also have weather that, in some mountainous regions, can change from one extreme to another in minutes.

There is no equilibrium in the atmosphere; at best, we have approximate local equilibria.

There is a conflation, in much of modern economics, of equilibrium as a useful but limited approximation to make certain kinds of calculations possible, and the economy actually being in equilibrium; and even worse, that equilibrium is something to strive towards. In this general theory of economies, it's clear that equilibrium is no more desired a state than non-equilibrium. There is no benefit steering an economy towards equilibrium.

Rather, the general theory of economies shows how well, and when, equilibrium is a useful approximation, over how large a region in decision spacetime, and how an economy functions, regardless of how deep the economy is in non-equilibrium.

In physics you can only talk with confidence about a calculation based on an approximation if you have understood sufficiently well what is lost from the actual physics of the world by making that simplification, and if you can demonstrate that what is lost makes a negligible difference to your prediction of what will happen.

For example, the assumption that the air is in equilibrium is invalid at microscopic scales. The blue sky you see when you look up on a sunny day is created by the microscopic density fluctuations of the air scattering blue light far more strongly than red light. You would not have a blue sky if the air was in perfect equilibrium at all scales.

Because a general theory of economies includes all of nature, it includes the notion that an economy is only in equilibrium if all of nature is in equilibrium in its interaction across time with the rest of the economy. Anything done in one part to pull manufacturing and trade towards equilibrium, but in a way that takes our natural environment further from equilibrium, takes the economy as a whole further from equilibrium.

General theory of organisations

A general theory of economies must include a description of business and other organisations, just as the general theory of relativity stretches from extremely small to large mass objects. We need a general theory of organisations that scales seamlessly from one individual organising themselves and their tasks, all the way through to global ecosystems of organisations collaborating with each other as an entire eco-system. It must be seamlessly part of the general theory of economies.

Decision spacetime and meaning-making stories link the day-to-day practice of business and the general theory of economies.

As Peter Drucker says, an executive is a production line, with decisions as the output. An executive board is a decision factory. A business then delivers results by adding human energies to the decisions, turning them to action.

An organisation is a decision-making entity that bundles together multiple in-dividual decision-making entities. A bit like the universe: you or I are specks of dust moving through decision spacetime, an organisation is a planet formed out of megatonnes of dust moving as one, and a multinational is a galaxy.

So a general theory of economies includes all aspects of organisations and defines an organisation as its decisions across successive points in decision spacetime, the ac-tions taken to execute those decisions with excellence, and the results achieved. All of this as a bundle spanning whatever region of spacetime the organisation occu-pies for its existence. In time, this is from first startup idea to final death; in physical space, however big an area of the Earth it impacts; and in social space, all the people it impacts.

This scales seamlessly from one individual up to our entire global economy.

Calling this subset of *the general theory of organisations*, it then states that your organisation occupies a certain amount of decision spacetime, with a curvature cre-ated by all the organisation's physical things and meaning-making stories, from each individual's personal meaning-making stories through all scales up to those of the entire organisation; and those of all other entities sufficiently big and close to shape your organisation's decision spacetime.

In a general theory of organisations, people and organisations will move in straight lines along their inherent 'free' curved decision spacetime, unless prevented by an external force. We want to move in a straight line, and can only do so if we have the freedom to.

If we are in some sense lacking freedom, if someone has put walls across our natural path through spacetime that we keep crashing into and bouncing off, then we will move contrary to our nature. That will cost us energy, and may well reduce the capacity of individuals and businesses or any other organisation to take the right decision.

We now have a way of integrating everything that impacts how organisations take decisions. Anticipating the four integral quadrants described in Section 12.6, everything is either an existing structure and force, in the lower right quadrant, or a meaning-making story in the individual upper left or organisational lower left quadrants. All on the **T** side creates the shape on the **G** side of decisions, meaning, and perceived value.

So if the outcomes of decisions are no longer what we need them to be, we need to identify everything on the **T** side that is currently shaping the **G** decision spacetime.

Doing this via regulations is clumsy, because it doesn't change the underlying natural meaning-making, nor the natural decision; instead, regulation acts as a force imposed. Of course, to some extent this does change decision spacetime, because meaning-making now includes the meaning attributed to obeying or disobeying regulations.

The rise in regulation; in the amount needed by the welfare state; failing banks, and those banks too big to fail; the rise in the precariat; wherever you look you see more and bigger ad-hoc forces introduced to stop our current paradigm from collapsing. The kind of ad-hoc introduction of patches that, in physics, signal clearly that the theory is no theory. Just a patchwork of approximations to a theory.

Iva Vurdelja, a lecturer in Marquette University Graduate School of Management, and at Loyola University, uses the thought forms of Table 9.1 to guide her students to deeper insights into how patching our current system cannot deliver what we need. CSR, for example, is a patch on a fundamentally broken system.

So we are getting a glimmer of how we may be able to construct one single general theory that spans everything, from a single individual deciding in the supermarket whether to buy Ariel/Tide or Persil for their laundry, through the global economy and the impact of all our global bodies on our global economy, and beyond to nature's economy.

Instead of working through clumsy applications of increasingly ad-hoc forces of regulation, we now can work with the essence of what has enabled human beings to thrive. Our capacity for meaning-making. Which includes implicitly some kinds of regulation, but now in complementarity with other sources shaping **G**.

We are always, individually and collectively, writing and rewriting our meaning-making stories.

The emerging climate emergency is driving a rapid rewriting. By making this process explicit, and by putting in only those structures, processes, and relationships needed for our meaning-making stories to get successively closer to the actual world we live in, individuals and business will easily take the decisions that are right for life on earth to thrive because they will be the natural decisions to take, not forced decisions from regulation. They will be decisions taken because *that's just who I am, and what I love doing.*

This will also lead to far more multisolving[7] (Section 15.5), the best strategy we have to solve the multiplicity of problems causing our climate emergency, and all our other injustices.

The role of decisions on organisation design and operation, and hence the final consequences of an organisation design and how it is operated, can now be integrated into one general theory.

Whichever individual or team has decision authority over the organisation design takes that decision according to the local shape in their **G** space, which is their individual and collective meaning-making stories, along with the bigger meaning-making stories of the different cultures and worldviews in which they are embedded. They then create structures and processes in **T** that modify the meaning-making stories of everyone else in the organisation and act as forces preventing people in the organisation from taking their natural decision.

This shows how meaning-making determines the organisation design, which then both act as a force on everyone else; and how this force may then modify the meaning-making stories of some in the organisation. Others may choose to not adapt their meaning-making stories. This may be exactly the right choice, or not, for each specific individual.

This also shows why there cannot ever be one single approach to organisation design, best in all contexts, for all worldviews, and for all individuals. Why the best approach is a do-it-yourself approach, drawing from a multiplicity of good practices, optimised for the here and now of any specific organisation's drivers.

Since this general theory of economies spans all scales, from each individual through to our global economy, we may well only complete it once we have integrated everything that makes each of us human beings into it. This includes integrating all of our sciences: biological, neurobiological, psychological, social, anything that plays a role in our lives.

It may well be decades before we sufficiently grasp how everything is interrelated and how all these are nested, interlocking, open systems in constant transformation and movement.

How well we can shift from our current closed disciplines into such an open systems approach to each one depends on how fluid we are in all 28 thought forms of Chapter 9, and how well we can surface and adapt the meaning-making stories defining our self-identity (Chapter 8).

Building and scientifically testing a general theory of economies

This is the hard part! If it had been easy, we would already have such a theory.

This general theory of economies is inherently pluralist. It automatically includes political economy, which used to be economics until the mid-19th century. It includes the changes in decision spacetime through the 19th century, as neoclassical economics divorced itself from political economy.

So the builders and testers can only be fully multidisciplinary teams, filled with generative tensions. This will not be easy for anyone involved, because their source of identity and self-worth will initially be strongly challenged; and so all the team members must master the adaptive way of Part III or similar, and be well skilled in a wide range of other disciplines such as yoga, meditation, and more. And, of course, where everyone fully grasps the distinction between science and scientism (Section 2.7) so that they engage in the brutal rigour needed.

We will have two complementary paths to building and testing such a theory. Inside-out and outside-in. Inside-out, we begin with hypotheses about each individual's reality, put them all together in a computer simulation, and then predict outcomes at all scales, from individual to global. Outside-in, we look at the decisions first, at all scales, and use those to infer the reality within which such a decision is rational.

Both together give us a way of testing our hypotheses scientifically, iteratively leading to a theory.

This is much like the way physics works, with teams of theorists and experimentalists in a brutal, rigorous, collaborative tension to uncover what we can reliably say about how the world works.

> *Well-regarded future economists will, first and foremost, have a thorough understanding of adult development, a very strong understanding and connection with society as it is; and they will be adult development practitioners too.*

Those eminent physicists and philosophers Queen put it so well when they sang *Is this the real life? Is it just fantasy?* (Brian May has an excellent grasp of physics; in fact he put his PhD in astrophysics on hold in 1974 for Queen, completing it in 2008.)

This book is all about the difference between reality and actuality, how the reality you experience is always the best approximate model of actuality that you have available to you at the time, somewhere between fantasy and actuality. You are always doing the best you can within the reality you are experiencing in the moment.

So I have no doubt that every economist was doing the very best they could in their momentary reality; according to the frame of reference they had available to use, at the point in decision spacetime they were at. Just as Newton could never have created anything other than his description of gravity, because he didn't have available to him any geometry that could possibly have described the motion of the planets and stars and apples, so too were the originators of today's economics doing the best they could.

However, we are now in a global society with a global interdependency across all scales of local and global economies, and we have already seriously overshot the capacity of our natural environment to support human life in the near and long term future. We know enough to know that sticking dogmatically to what are, at best, local approximations, is now threatening us all.

To construct a general theory of economies, we must identify everything necessary to generate a valid understanding of our economies that is capable of making predictions we can reliably use to navigate humanity through the emergencies of the coming decades.

We need to understand what all the physical and nonphysical things in an economy are, including those that are metaphorically equivalent to the mass, energy, momentum, and stress of general relativity's stress-energy tensor $T_{\mu\nu}$. We need to understand what the full multidimensional space of economies is, equivalent to Einstein's tensor $G_{\mu\nu}$.

This will confront some economists, and many organisations developing or putting economic thinking into practice, with an adaptive challenge. Most experts and leaders only learn how to rise to technical challenges, but not adaptive ones. These need the tools described in Chapters 7 to 11. They are amongst the most powerful tools available to recognise your meaning-making stories, how they create the reality you experience, and then coordinate across all of your inner tensions and drives as you iteratively bring your meaning-making stories into ever greater alignment with actuality. Which is what you need to rise to an adaptive challenge.

The adaptive challenge is present for anyone whose source of self-identity and meaning lies in their work or discipline. Many neoclassical economists identify themselves with neoclassical economics, which means that anything pointing at a fundamental change in economics is an existential threat to their self-identity. Identifying where neoclassical economics is wrong, in order to identify what works better, is an adaptive challenge.

Contrast this with physicists, who love proving their colleagues wrong. Those who source their identity from their discipline source it from the bedrock of science: science is falsifying, not knowing. The only reason why everybody who comes up with another claim that Einstein is wrong is treated with caution is that, after a century of falsification attempts, no one has managed to do better than Einstein in the areas where general relativity works. General relativity occupies the pedestal 'theory', rather than 'approximate model', because it is the simplest description found *so far*, across the largest swathe of actuality, of what we can *say*.

Some cosmologists are working as hard as they can to prove general relativity wrong because we know that the universe is doing things that look berserk within general relativity. Physicists know that general relativity cannot be the full theory, because it breaks down right at the beginning of the universe (infinite curvature in **G**), and looks inelegant at the current rate of the universe's expansion. However, the two alternative categories: modifying general relativity; or the multiverse; are widely deemed inelegant and distasteful. (Beauty has so far proven a reliable guide to tell the difference between a viable theory and a model in physics.)

So physicists know that there is another breakthrough coming. Space may not survive as something independent, time may not survive; both may even be emergent phenomena coming out of something much deeper. Physicists all know that to survive, let alone thrive, they must be open to go where the theory takes them, not clinging to an old idea, risking being steamrollered flat as the new idea comes in.

I (Jack and Graham) really hope that this appendix can play a role in catalysing the shift we need in economics; and that many others will take on the task of developing and testing a general theory of economies. We intend our forthcoming book to cover what emerges.

As a last thought, maybe what general relativity says about the apple that fell on Newton's head (during the plague pandemic that hammered society then) can help us. It makes clear that gravity did not pull the apple down onto Newton's head, rather the Earth had been pushing Newton and the apple tree upwards until, at some point, the stalk became too weak to continue pulling the apple up, and broke. At that point, the Earth pushed Newton's head into the (relatively) stationary apple.

Bibliography

[1]   Kimberly Hickok, ed. *10 Signs That Earth's Climate Is Off the Rails*. 23rd Dec. 2019. URL: https : / / www . livescience . com / 10 - signs - of - climate-change-in-2019.html.

[2]   Eunice Newton Foote. 'Circumstances affecting the Heat of the Sun's Rays'. In: *American Association for the Advancement of Science* (1856).

[3]   Jinlun Zhang and D.A. Rothrock. 'Modeling global sea ice with a thickness and enthalpy distribution model in generalized curvilinear coordinates'. In: *Mon. Wea. Rev.* **131** (5) (2003): pp. 681–697.

[4]   Maria-Vittoria Guarino et al. 'See-ice-free Arctic during the Last Interglacial supports fast future loss'. In: *Nature Climate Change* (Aug. 2020).

[5]   Otto Laske. *Measuring Hidden Dimensions: The Art and Science of Fully Engaging Adults*. 1 vols. IDM Press, MA.

[6]   Otto Laske. *Measuring Hidden Dimensions of Human Systems*. 2 vols. IDM Press, MA.

[7]   Elizabeth Sawin. *Climate Interactive*. URL: https : / / www . climateint eractive.org/programs/multisolving/what-is-multisolving/.

[8]   Mathew Lawrence et al. *Commoning the Company*. Common Wealth, 2020. URL: https://www.common-wealth.co.uk/.

[9]   Simon Deakin. 'The Corporation as Commons: Rethinking Property Rights, Governance and Sustainability in the Business Enterprise'. In: *Queen's Law Journal* **37** (2) (2011): pp. 339–381.

[10] Henry Abraham Boorse and Lloyd Motz. *The World of the Atom*. 1966.

[11] David Chapman. *Meaningness*. URL: https : / / meaningness . com / resolution.

[12] Kate Raworth. *Doughnut Economics: Seven Ways to Think Like a 21st-Century Economist*. Chelsea Green Publishing.

[13] Kate Raworth. *Old economics is based on false 'laws of physics' – new economics can save us*. 6th Apr. 2017. URL: https://www.theguardian.com/global-development-professionals-network/2017/apr/06/kate-raworth-doughnut-economics-new-economics.

[14] Anil Seth. 'The Neuroscience of Reality'. In: *Scientific American* (Sept. 2019).

[15] Barbara Marx Hubbard. *Birth 2012 and Beyond: Humanity's Great Shift to the Age of Conscious Evolution*. Shift Books.

[16] Otto Scharmer. *Theory U: Leading from the Future as It Emerges*. Berrett-Koehler Publishers.

[17] Michael Winger. *The Innovation Imperative: Your Future Depends on It*. New Directions Press.

[18] Christiana Figueres and Tom Rivett-Carnac. *The Future We Choose: Surviving the Climate Crisis*. Manilla Press.

[19] Leonard Shlain. *Art and Physics: Parallel Visions in Space, Time, and Light*. Perennial, New York.

[20] Mark Antliff and Patricia Leighten. *Cubism and Culture*. Thames and Hudson, New York.

[21] David Landes. *Wealth and Poverty*. W.W. Norton, New York.

[22] Mark Townsend. 'How a Desperate Dearth of Analysis Let the London Attackers Through'. In: *The Observer* (June 2017): pp. 16–17.

[23] Issac Newton. *The Principia*. Prometheus, New York.

[24] Nassim Nicholas Taleb. *Antifragile*. Penguin Books, London.

[25] Peter Drucker. *The Effective Executive: The Definitive Guide to Getting the Right Things Done, 50th anniversary edition*. Harper Collins.

[26] Steve Keen. *Debunking Economics, Revised and Updated version*. Zed Books.

[27] Adam Kahane. *Solving Tough Problems: An Open Way of Talking, Listening, and Creating New Realities*. Berrett-Koehler Publishers.

[28] Nassim Nicholas Taleb. *Skin in the Game: Hidden Asymmetries in Daily Life*. Random House.

[29] Elizabeth Loftus. *Wikipedia biography*. URL: https://en.wikipedia. org/wiki/Elizabeth_Loftus (visited on 02/08/2019).

[30] Elizabeth Loftus. *How reliable is your memory?* 23rd Sept. 2013. URL: htt ps://www.youtube.com/watch?v=PB20egI6wvI.

[31] Margaret J. Wheatley. *Leadership And The New Science: Discovering Order In A Chaotic World, Third Edition*. Berret-Koehler.

[32] Margaret J. Wheatley. *So Far From Home: Lost And Found In Our Brave New World*. Berret-Koehler.

[33] Fritjof Capra. *The Tao of Physics*. Shambhala Publications, Boulder,Colorado.

[34] Michael Ende. *The Never Ending Story (German original)*. Thienemann Verlag.

[35] Terry Pratchett. *Lords and Ladies*. Gollancz.

[36] David Chapman. *Meaningness*. URL: https://meaningness.com/ preview-eternalism-and-nihilism.

[37] Steve Peters. *The Chimp Paradox: The Mind Management Programme to Help You Achieve Success, Confidence and Happiness*. Vermilion.

[38] Richard Feynman. *Cargo Cult Science (Caltech commencement address)*. 1974. URL: http://calteches.library.caltech.edu/51/2/CargoCu lt.htm (visited on 03/08/2019).

[39] David Chapman. *Upgrade your cargo cult for the win*. 2019. URL: https: //meaningness.com/metablog/upgrade-your-cargo-cult.

[40] Wiliam Catton. *Overshoot*. University of Illinois Press.

[41] Noam Wasserman. *The Founder's Dilemmas*. Princeton University Press.

[42] Howard Gardner. *Creating Minds*. Basic Books, New York.

[43] *The Modern Corporation: statement on economics*. URL: themoderncorp oration.wordpress.com/economics-and-msv/.

[44] *The Modern Corporation: statement on company law*. URL: themodernco rporation.wordpress.com/company-law-memo/.

[45] Clayton Christensen, Jeffrey Dyer and Hal Gregersen. *The Innovator's DNA: Mastering the Five Skills of Disruptive Innovators*. Harvard Business Review Press.

[46] Rebecca Lindsey. *Climate Change: Glacier Mass Balance.* 1st Aug. 2018. URL: https://www.climate.gov/news-features/understandi ng-climate/climate-change-glacier-mass-balance.

[47] Guy Standing. *The Precariat: The New Dangerous Class.* Bloomsbury Academic, London.

[48] Robert J. Shiller. *Narrative Economics: How Stories Go Viral and Drive Major Economic Events.* Princeton University Press.

[49] Lynn Stout. *The Shareholder Value Myth.* Berrett-Koehler, San Francisco.

[50] K. Birch et al. *Business and Society: A Critical Introduction.* Zed Books, London.

[51] Jeremy Rifkin. *The Zero Marginal Cost Society.* Palgrave Macmillan, New York.

[52] Dave Snowden et al. *Cynefin - Weaving Sense-Making into the Fabric of Our World.*

[53] Dave Snowdon. *The Cynefin Framework.* 1999. URL: https://en.wiki pedia.org/wiki/Cynefin_framework.

[54] Daniel Kahneman. *Thinking, Fast and Slow.* Penguin.

[55] John Locke. *Two Treatises on Government.* Cambridge University Press, Cambridge, UK.

[56] A. Vant. *Institutions and the Environment.* Edward Elgar, Cheltenham, UK.

[57] Leander Bindewald. 'The grammar of money:an analytical account of money as a discursive institution in light of the practice of complementary currencies'. An optional note. PhD thesis. Lancaster University, 2018. URL: https://eprints.lancs.ac.uk/id/eprint/128117/.

[58] Bernhard Lietaer et al. *Money & Sustainability: the missing link (A report to the Club of Rome).* Triarchy Press Ltd.

[59] Bernhard Lietaer and Jacqui Dunne. *Rethinking Money: How New Currencies Turn Scarcity into Prosperity.* Berrett-Koehler Publishers.

[60] Ann Pettifor. *The Production of Money - How to Break the Power of Bankers.* Verso.

[61] Stephanie Kelton. *The Deficit Myth: Modern Monetary Theory and the Birth of the People's Economy.* PublicAffairs.

[62] Abdul Islahi. *History of Islamic Economic Thought: Contributions of Muslim Scholars to Economic Thought and Analysis.* Edward Elgar Publishing.

[63] Adam Smith. *The Wealth of Nations.* 1976th ed. The University of Chicago Press, Chicago.

[64] David Graeber. *Debt: The First 5,000 Years.* Melville House, Brooklyn.

[65] Adam Smith. *The Theory of Moral Sentiments (Edition of 2000).* Prometheus Books, New York.

[66] Paul Mason. *Post Capitalism.* Allen Lane.

[67] Karl Marx and Friedrich Engels. *The Communist Manifesto.* Oxford University Press, Oxford, UK.

[68] Nicholas Kristof. *The $70,000-a-Year Minimum Wage.* 30th Mar. 2019. URL: https : / / www . nytimes . com / 2019 / 03 / 30 / opinion / sunday / dan-price-minimum-wage.html.

[69] Ewan McGaughey. *Collective Bargains for Corporate Change.* URL: https : / / www . upf . edu / documents / 3298481 / 3410076 / 2013-LLRNCo nf _McGaughey_xv2x . pdf / b16263a5 - 3d58 - 4772 - a539 - a0b6b 60466a6.

[70] Charles Handy. *What's a Business For.* Dec. 2002. URL: https : //hbr . org/2002/12/whats-a-business-for (visited on 04/07/2018).

[71] Lynn Paine. 'Covid-19 Is Rewriting the Rules of Corporate Governance'. In: *Harvard Business Review* (Oct. 2020).

[72] Jean Allain. *"The Definition of 'Slavery' in General International Law and the Crime of Enslavement within the Rome Statute".* 2007. URL: https : // www . icc - cpi . int / NR / rdonlyres / 069658BB - FDBD - 4EDD - 8414-543ECB1FA9DC/0/ICCOTP20070426Allain_en.pdf.

[73] International Labour Organisation and Walk Free Foundation, eds. *Global Estimates of Modern Slavery: Forced Labour and Forced Marriage.* 2017. URL: https : / / www . ilo . org / global / publications / books / WCMS_575479/lang--en/index.htm.

[74] Graham Boyd. *Multi-Stakeholder Company and Voting Structuring for intrinsic sustainability and thrival.* 2013.

[75] Mariana Mazzucato. *The entrepreneurial state.*

[76] Jim Brown. *Equity finance for social enterprises.* 2006.

[77]   Sam Williams. *Free as in Freedom: Richard Stallman's Crusade for Free Software*. O'Reilly Media.

[78]   John Elkington. *25 Years Ago I Coined the Phrase "Triple Bottom Line." Here's Why It's Time to Rethink It*. 25th June 2018.

[79]   Brian Robertson. *Holacracy: The New Management System for a Rapidly Changing World*. Henry Holt and Company, New York.

[80]   Ted Rau and Jerry Koch-Gonzalez. *Many voices one song*. Sociocracy for all, Amherst, MA.

[81]   Robert Kegan and Lisa Lahey. *An Everyone Culture: Becoming a Deliberately Developmental Organisation*. Harvard Business Review Press.

[82]   Graham Smith and Simon Teasdale. 'Associative democracy and the social economy: exploring the regulatory challenge'. In: *Journal of Economy and Society* **41** (2) (2012): pp. 151–176.

[83]   G. Hardin. 'The Tragedy of the Commons'. In: *Nature* **162** (1968): pp. 1243–1248.

[84]   Elinor Ostrom. *Governing the Commons: The Evolution of Institutions for Collective Action*. Cambridge University Press.

[85]   Alex Pazaitis, Michel Bauwens and Vasilis Kostakis. *Peer to Peer: The Commons Manifesto*. University of Westminster Press.

[86]   Geoffrey West. *Scale: The Universal Laws of Growth, Innovation, Sustainability, and the Pace of Life in Organisms, Cities, Economies, and Companies*. Penguin Press; First Edition edition ().

[87]   Amartya Sen. *Development as Freedom*. Anchor Books, New York.

[88]   Wolf-Georg Ringe. 'Hedge Funds and Risk-Decoupling — The Empty Voting Problem in the European Union'. In: *University of Oxford Legal Research Paper Series* (52) (Aug. 2012). SSRN-id2135489.

[89]   Alon Brav and Richmond D. Mathews. 'Empty Voting And The Efficiency Of Corporate Governance'. In: *AFA 2009 San Francisco Meetings Paper* (2010). SSRN-id1108632.

[90]   David Yermack. 'Shareholder Voting and Corporate Governance'. In: *Annual Review of Financial Economics* **2** (1) (Mar. 2010): pp. 103–125.

[91]   Michael C. Schouten. 'The Mechanisms of Voting Efficiency'. In: *Columbia Business Law Review* **3** (2010).

[92] Wolf-Georg Ringe. 'Empty Voting Revisited: The Telus Saga'. In: *University of Oxford Legal Research Paper Series* (Mar. 2013). SSRN-id2230528.

[93] Jordan M. Barry, John William Hatfield and Scott Duke Kominers. 'On derivative markets and social welfare: a theory of empty voting and hidden owndership'. In: *Virginia Law Review* **99** (1103) (2013). SSRN–id2134458.

[94] Julie Battilana et al. 'In Search of the Hybrid Ideal'. In: *Stanford Social Innovation Review* (2012).

[95] Katsuhito Iwai. 'Persons, things and corporations: the corporate personality controversy and comparative corporate governance'. In: *American Journal of Comparative Law* **47** (4) (1999): pp. 583–632.

[96] Ray Dalio. *Principles*. Simon and Schuster.

[97] David Sloan Wilson. *This view of life, Completing the Darwinian revolution*. Vintage.

[98] Daniel christian Wahl. *Designing regenerative cultures*. Triarchy Press.

[99] Adam Kahane. *Power and Love: A Theory and Practice of Social Change*. Berrett-Koehler Publishers.

[100] Jean Russell. *Thrivability: Breaking through to a World that Works*. Triarchy Press Ltd.

[101] URL: https://en.wikipedia.org/wiki/Blue_economy.

[102] Gunter Pauli. *The blue economy, a report to the Club of Rome*. URL: https://www.theblueeconomy.org/.

[103] URL: https://www.ecogood.org/.

[104] Robert Dellner. *Integral Impact Investing*. Evolutesix Publishing.

[105] Ken Wilber. *The Integral Vision: A Very Short Introduction to the Revolutionary Integral Approach to Life, God, the Universe, and Everything*. Shambhala Publications.

[106] Jordan M. Barry, John William Hartfield and Scott Duke Kominers. 'On Derivatives Markets and Social Welfare: A Theory of Empty Voting and Hidden Ownership'. In: *Virginia Law Review* **99** (1103) (2013).

[107] Joseph Schumpeter. *Capitalism, Socialism, Democracy*. Routledge, London.

[108] Deborah Henderson. *The Hour Glass Leader*. To be published.

[109] World Commission on Environment and Development. *Our Common Future*. Oxford University Press, Oxford, UK.

[110] Jason Hickel. *Less is More. How Degrowth Will Save the World*. Penguin.

[111] Guy Standing. *Basic Income: And How We Can Make it Happen*. Pelican Books, London.

[112] Mark Anielski. *The Economics of Happiness: Building Genuine Wealth*. New Society Publishers, Canada.

[113] Guardian Business, ed. *As growth fizzles out, it's as if the last 10 years never happened*. 1st Apr. 2019. URL: https://www.theguardian.com/business/2019/apr/07/global-growth-fizzles-groundhog-day-for-world-economy.

[114] Michael Jacobs and Mariana Mazzucato. *Rethinking Capitalism*.

[115] Yanis Varoufakis. *The Global Minotaur: America, Europe and the Future of the Global Economy*. Zed Books.

[116] Martin Wolf. *Why Economists Failed as "Experts"—and How to Make Them Matter Again*. 12th Mar. 2019. URL: https://www.ineteconomics.org/perspectives/blog/why-economists-failed-as-experts-and-how-to-make-them-matter-again.

[117] Steve Keen. *NIESR Macroeconomics of Sustainability Presentation on integrating energy into economic theory*. 6th Dec. 2019. URL: https://www.patreon.com/posts/niesr-of-on-into-32127411.

[118] O. Peters and M. Gell-Mann. 'Evaluating gambles using dynamics'. In: *Chaos: An Interdisciplinary Journal of Nonlinear Science* **26** (2) (Feb. 2016): p. 023103. ISSN: 1089-7682. DOI: 10.1063/1.4940236. URL: http://dx.doi.org/10.1063/1.4940236.

[119] Mark Buchanan. *How ergodicity reimagines economics for the benefit of us all*. URL: https://aeon.co/amp/ideas/how-ergodicity-reimagines-economics-for-the-benefit-of-us-all.

[120] Ole Peters and Alexander Adamou. *Ergodicity Economics Lecture Notes*. URL: https://ergodicityeconomics.com/lecture-notes/.

[121] Paul Ormerod. *Why Most Things Fail: Evolution, Extinction and Economics*. Pantheon, NY.

[122] Graham Boyd. *Why ecosystem investing beats portfolios*. 23rd Mar. 2021. URL: https://graham-boyd.biz/blog/why-ecosystem-investing-beats-portfolios/.

[123] Ole Peters and Alexander Adamou. *An evolutionary advantage of coopera-tion*. 2018. arXiv: 1506.03414 [nlin.AO].

[124] Joe Earl, Cahal Moran and Zach Ward-Perkins. *The Econocracy: The Perils of Leaving the Economy to the Experts*. University of Manchester, Manche-ster, UK.

[125] Wendy Carlin and David Soskice. *Macroeconomics Institutions, instability, and the financial system*. Oxford University Press.

[126] Mariana Mazzucato. *The value of everything*.

[127] Jack Reardon, Maria Alejandra Madi and Molly Scott Cato. *Introducing a new economics, pluralist, sustainable and progressive*. Pluto Press, London.

[128] Douglas Dowd. *Capitalism and its economics*. Pluto Press, London.

[129] Lester Thurow. *Dangerous Currents (State of Economics)*. OUP.

[130] Norman Wolfe. *The Living Organization: Transforming Business to Create Extraordinary Results*. Quantum Leaders Publishing.

[131] Christian Jarrett. *The way you tell your life story shapes your personality*. 23rd May 2019. URL: http://www.bbc.com/future/story/20190523-the-way-you-tell-your-life-story-shapes-your-personality.

[132] Kate McLean et al. 'The Empirical Structure of Narrative Identity: The Initial Big Three'. In: *Journal of Personality and Social Psychology* (Apr. 2019). DOI: 10.1037/pspp0000247.

[133] Ronald Heifetz, Alexander Grashow and Marty Linsky. *The Practice of Ad-aptive Leadership: Tools and Tactics Tools and Tactics for Changing Your Or-ganization and the World: A Fieldbook for Practitioners*. Harvard Business Press.

[134] Graham Boyd. *Regenerate: How to regenerate yourself and your company to regenerate society and the economy*.

[135] Marilyn Hamilton. *Integral City: Evolutionary Intelligences for the Human Hive*. New Society Publishers.

[136] Richard Wiseman. *Paranormality: Why we see what isn't there*. Macmillan.

[137] Allison Schrager. *An Economist Walks Into A Brothel*. Portfolio.

[138] Seth Godin. *The Dip: A Little Book That Teaches You When to Quit*. Pen-guin.

[139]   Arbinger Institute. *Leadership and Self-Deception*. Berrett-Koehler.

[140]   William Shakespeare. *Hamlet (Act I, Scene 3, lines 77-79)*.

[141]   Sarah Constantin. *Are Adult Developmental Stages Real?* 6th Apr. 2017. URL: https : / / srconstantin . wordpress . com / 2017 / 04 / 06 / are-adult-developmental-stages-real/.

[142]   Robert Kegan and Lisa Lahey. *Immunity to Change: How to Overcome It and Unlock the Potential in Yourself and Your Organization (Leadership for the Common Good)*. Harvard Business Review Press.

[143]   Robert Dellner. *TBD*.

[144]   Lynne Twist and Teresa Barker. *The soul of money*. W. W. Norton and Company.

[145]   John Kenneth Galbraith. *A Contemporary Guide to Economics, Peace, and Laughter. Chapter 3: How Keynes Came to America*. Ed. by Andrea D. Williams. Houghton Mifflin Company, Boston, Massachusetts.

[146]   Robert Kegan and Lisa Lahey. *How The Way we Talk Can Change The Way We Work*. Jossey-Bass.

[147]   Marshall Rosenberg. *Nonviolent Communication: A Language of Life, 3rd Edition: Life-Changing Tools for Healthy Relationships*. PuddleDancer Press; Third Edition.

[148]   Byron Katie and Stephen Mitchell. *A Mind at Home with Itself: How Asking Four Questions Can Free Your Mind, Open Your Heart, and Turn Your World Around*. HarperOne.

[149]   Dennis Genpo Merzel. *Big Mind Big Heart: Finding Your Way*. Big Mind Publishing.

[150]   Timothy Wilson. *Redirect: Changing the Stories We Live By*. Penguin.

[151]   Steve Salerno. *Sham: How the Self-Help Movement Made America*. Crown Publishing.

[152]   Miguel Farias and Catherine Wikholm. *The Buddha Pill: Can Meditation Change You?* Watkins, London, UK.

[153]   Mark Dodgson and David Gann. *The Playful Entrepreneur: How to Adapt and Thrive in Uncertain Times*. Yale University Press.

[154]   Richard Barrett. *The Values Driven Organization*. Routledge.

[155] Mark Synnott. 'Alex Honnold Completes the Most Dangerous Free-Solo Ascent Ever'. In: *National Geographic* (Oct. 2018). URL: https://www. nationalgeographic.com/adventure/features/athletes/ alex-honnold/most-dangerous-free-solo-climb-yosemite- national-park-el-capitan/.

[156] David Cooperrider. *Appreciative Inquiry: A Positive Revolution in Change.* Berrett-Koehler.

[157] Richard Wiseman. *The Luck Factor: The Four Essential Principles.* Century, London.

[158] Amy C. Edmondson. *The fearless organization: creating psychological safety in the workplace for learning, innovation and growth.* John Wiley and Sons, Hoboken, New Jersey.

[159] Nick Shannon and Bruno Frischherz. *Metathinking: The Art and Practice of Transformational Thinking.* Springer.

[160] Daniel Amen. *The End of Mental Illness: How Neuroscience Is Transforming Psychiatry and Helping Prevent or Reverse Mood and Anxiety Disorders, ADHD, Addictions, PTSD, Psychosis, Personality Disorders, and More.* Tyndale Momentum.

[161] Marshall Rosenberg et al. *The Center for Nonviolent Communication.* URL: https://www.cnvc.org/ (visited on 09/01/2018).

[162] Marion Little. *Total Honesty / Total Heart: Fostering empathy development and conflict resolution skills. A violence prevention strategy.* 2008. URL: http://www.cnvc.org/sites/cnvc.org/files/MLittle_Thesis 0408.pdf.

[163] Dante. *The Inferno of Dante.* Trans. by Robert Pinsky. Canto I, line 2. Farrar, Straus and Giroux, New York.

[164] Lisa Feldman Barrett. *How Emotions Are Made: The Secret Life of the Brain.* Houghton Mifflin Harcourt.

[165] Robert Cialdini. *Influence: The Psychology of Persuasion, Revised Edition.* Harper Business.

[166] Justin Kruger and David Dunning. 'Unskilled and Unaware of It: How Difficulties in Recognizing One's Own Incompetence Lead to Inflated Self-Assessments'. In: *Journal of Personality and Social Psychology* 77 (6) (1999): pp. 1121–1134.

[167]   David Dunning. 'The Dunning–Kruger Effect: On Being Ignorant of One's Own Ignorance'. In: *Advances in Experimental Social Psychology* **44** (2011): pp. 247–296.

[168]   David Dunning and Erik Helzer. 'Beyond the Correlation Coefficient in Studies of Self-Assessment Accuracy: Commentary on Zell & Krizan (2014)'. In: *Perspectives on Psychological Science* **9** (2) (2014): pp. 126–130.

[169]   David Dunning. *Self-insight: Roadblocks and Detours on the Path to Knowing Thyself*. Psychology Press.

[170]   Nicholas Brown, Alan Sokal and Harris Friedman. 'The Complex Dynamics of Wishful Thinking: The Critical Positivity Ratio'. In: *American psychologist* **69** (6) (Sept. 2014): pp. 629–632. URL: http://retraction watch.com/2013/09/19/fredrickson-losada-positivity-ratio-%20paper-partially-withdrawn/.

[171]   Patrick Vermeren. 'The Undesired Popularity of Typologies'. In: (2013). URL: https://www.researchgate.net/publication/275945722_ The_Undesired_Popularity_of_Typologies_and_other_ 'Jung'_translation.

[172]   Gustav Kuhn. *Experiencing the Impossible - The Science of Magic*. The MIT Press.

[173]   Dennis Meadows et al. *The Limits to Growth*.

[174]   Clayton M. Christensen, James Allworth and Karen Dillon. *How Will You Measure Your Life?* HarperBusiness.

[175]   Rosamund Stone Zander and Ben Zander. *The art of possibility*. Harvard Business School Press.

[176]   Jared Diamond. *Collapse: How Societies Choose to Fail or Succeed*. Penguin, New York.

[177]   Gabriel Grant. *To be announced*. TBD.

[178]   Gary Hamel and Michele Zanini. *Humanocracy: Creating Organizations as Amazing as the People Inside Them*. Harvard Business Review Press.

[179]   Henry Stewart. *The Happy Manifesto*.

[180]   Rüdiger Fox. *The business case for corporate happiness*. URL: https://corporatehappinessbook.com/.

[181]   Peter Senge. *The Fifth Discipline: The Art and Practice of The Learning Organization*. Doubleday; Revised and Updated edition.

[182]   Dee Hock. *One from Many: Visa and the Rise of Chaordic Organization.* Berrett-Koehler Publishers.

[183]   James Priest, Bernhard Bockelbrink and Liliana David. *Sociocracy 3.0.* URL: http://sociocracy30.org/ (visited on 22/12/2017).

[184]   Frederik Laloux. *Reinventing organizations: A guide to creating organizations inspired by the next stage in human consciousness.* Nelson Parker, UK.

[185]   Tracey Kidder. *The Soul of A New Machine.* Little Brown and Company.

[186]   Evan Ratliff. *O Engineers.* Wired, 1st Dec. 2000. URL: https://www.wired.com/2000/12/soul/.

[187]   Peter König. *Source.* URL: https://workwithsource.com/what-is-source/.

[188]   Diane Coutu. 'Why Teams Don't Work'. In: *Harvard Business Review* (May 2009). URL: https://hbr.org/2009/05/why-teams-dont-work.

[189]   Bill Taylor. 'Great People Are Overrated Part 1'. In: *Harvard Business Review* (June 2011). URL: https://hbr.org/2011/06/great-people-are-overrated.

[190]   Bill Taylor. 'Great People Are Overrated Part 2'. In: *Harvard Business Review* (June 2011). URL: https://hbr.org/2011/06/great-people-are-overrated-par.

[191]   Boris Groysberg. *Chasing Stars: The Myth of Talent and the Portability of Performance.* Princeton Press.

[192]   'The talent myth: Are smart people overrated?' In: *the New Yorker* (22nd July 2002). URL: https://www.newyorker.com/magazine/2002/07/22/the-talent-myth.

[193]   Robert Kegan. *In Over Our Heads: The Mental Demands of Modern Life.* Harvard University Press.

[194]   Lev Vygotsky. *Thought and language, (revised edition by Alex Kozulin).* The Massachusetts Institute of Technology, Cambridge, MA.

[195]   Lev Vygotsky. *Mind in society.* Harvard University Press, Cambridge, MA.

[196]   Jennifer S. Mueller. 'Why individuals in larger teams perform worse'. In: *Organizational Behavior and Human Decision Processes* **117** (1) (Jan. 2012): pp. 111–124. URL: https://www.sciencedirect.com/science/article/pii/S0749597811001105.

[197] Edgar Schein. *Helping: How to Offer, Give, and Receive Help*. Berrett-Koehler Publishers.

[198] Alex Pentland. 'The New Science of Building Great Teams'. In: *Harvard Business Review* (Apr. 2012). URL: https://hbr.org/2012/04/the-new-science-of-building-great-teams.

[199] Alex Pentland. 'The Hard Science of Teamwork'. In: *Harvard Business Review* (20th Mar. 2012). URL: https://hbr.org/2012/03/the-new-science-of-building-gr.

[200] Kristina Moorehead. *How Britain fought Hitler with humour*. Even in the worst of times, humour reconnects us with what it means to be human. 30th Aug. 2019. URL: http://www.bbc.com/culture/story/20190829-how-britain-fought-hitler-with-humour.

[201] Marshall Rosenberg. *Nonviolent Communication: A Language of Life*. Puddle Dancer Press.

[202] Brene Brown. *Rising Strong*. Ebury Publishing.

[203] Don Beck and Christopher Cowan. *Spiral Dynamics*. Wiley-Blackwell.

[204] Jef Cumps. *Sociocratie 3.0*.

[205] Frederik Laloux. *Reinventing Organizations: An Illustrated Invitation to Join the Conversation on Next-Stage Organizations*. Nelson Parker, UK.

[206] Joana Breidenbach and Bettina Rollow. *New Work needs Inner Work*.

[207] *Art of Hosting Conversations that Matter*. URL: http://www.artofhosting.org/ (visited on 22/12/2017).

[208] Bernhard Possert. *The SDO playbook*.

[209] Nora Ganescu. *The CEO playbook*. Morgan James, NY.

[210] Henri Lipmanowicz and Keith McCandless. *The Surprising Power of Liberating Structures: Simple Rules to Unleash A Culture of Innovation*. Liberating Structures Press.

[211] Purpose Foundation. *Steward Ownership*. URL: https://purpose-economy.org/.

[212] Jo Aschenbrenner. *For Purpose: Ein neues Betriebssystem für Unternehmen*. Vahlen.

[213] Rory Ridley-Duff. *The Case for FairShares: A New Model for Social Enterprise Development and the Strengthening of the Social and Solidarity Economy*. CreateSpace Independent Publishing Platform.

BIBLIOGRAPHY

[214] John Mackey and Rajendra Sisodia. *Conscious Capitalism, With a New Preface by the Authors: Liberating the Heroic Spirit of Business.* Harvard Business Review Press.

[215] Mishal Khan. 'Oxfam: sex scandal or governance failure?' In: *The Lancet* **391** (10125) (Feb. 2018): pp. 1019–1020.

[216] Nicole Aschoff. *Whole Foods represents the failures of 'conscious capitalism'.* 29th May 2017. URL: https : / / www . theguardian . com / comment isfree / 2017 / may / 29 / whole - foods - failures - conscious - capitalism.

[217] Michel de Kemmeter and Emmanuel Mossay. *Shifting Economy.*

[218] Yonatan Berman, Ole Peters and Alexander Adamou. *Wealth Inequality and the Ergodic Hypothesis: Evidence from the United States.* 2020.

[219] Indra Nooyi. URL: https : / / en . wikiquote . org / wiki / Indra_ Nooyi.

[220] Thabo Mbeki. *I am an African.* 8th May 1996. URL: https://en.wiki pedia.org/wiki/I_Am_an_African (visited on 16/08/2019).

[221] F.W. de Klerk. *Speech.* URL: http : / / www . justice . gov . za / leg islation / constitution / history / MEDIA / NP . PDF (visited on 16/08/2019).

[222] Terry Pratchett. *I Shall Wear Midnight.* Doubleday.

[223] Katharine Hayhoe. *The Answer to Climate Change: And Why We Can Have Hope.* Atria/One Signal Publishers.

[224] G. Benjamin Bingham. *Making Money Matter: Impact Investing to Change the World.* Prospecta Press.

[225] John Maynard Keynes. *The General Theory of Employment, Interest, and Money.* Palgrave Macmillan.

[226] James K. Galbraith. *Keynes, Einstein, and Scientific Revolution.* URL: pro spect . org/economy/keynes-einstein-scientific-revoluti on/.

[227] John Maynard Keynes. *Collected Writings.* Ed. by Elizabeth Johnson and Donald Moggridge. Vol. 14. Royal Economic Society: p. 366.

Glossary

Actuality is what actually is. None of us can ever experience actuality directly and totally, rather each experiences our own unique reality.

Adaptive points at the need to change who we are, to change our Size of Person by growing both our capacity for sense-making and our meaning-making stories, used with Capacity, Way, Organisation, and Challenge.

Adaptive organisation refers to any organisation that is at least at Level 4 on all three axes, and striving towards Level 5 on each.

Adaptive Way from Evolutesix is a set of best practices designed to enable companies to reach Level 5 on the human axis, and to enable Level 5 on both the incorporation and roles and tasks axes. It includes best practice from a wide variety of fields to enable any individual or team to use the cognitive developmental framework in daily practice, transforming tensions into growth, along the three domains of growing your sense-making capacity, your stage of meaning-making development, and your subtlety with your nature.

Capital is something that has actual or perceived value. Examples include energy in nature, time and creativity in humans, relationships in society, manufactured capital, and of course financial capital. Every capital has an associated currency with it, e.g. money is the dominant currency of financial capital.

Cognitive-Developmental Framework (CDF) is the framework developed by Otto Laske describing how we construct the reality we experience in a sequence of taking in elements of actuality, then assembling them using our sense-making capacity, then attributing meaning using our meaning-making stories.

Complementary pairs also called conjugate pairs are central to quantum physics. These are two apparently different entities that have a deeper relationship. They may even be perceived as mutually exclusive. Position and momentum, particles and waves are common in physics. Actuality is filled with complementary pairs.

Currency is a tool used to attribute, store, or trade in the value of an associated capital. Each capital has one or more intrinsic currencies that fully reflects the nature and value of that capital. So time is best reflected in a time currency, not in money; energy in an energy currency, not in money; and only positive interest debt is correctly represented with money. Money is often confused with currency; and in some usages our definitions of money and currency are swapped.

Economy (An) is a tool used to do the job of provisioning; i.e., transporting a capital from where it is abundant to where it is needed.

Ergodicity is what you have if random events happening in a sequence have the same expected value as the same random events happening independently. Technically, the ensemble average is the same as the time / path average. Ergodicity is not true for most business activities, and our lives: the time average is very different to the ensemble average we were taught to use.

FairShares Commons is one way of constructing a free company, suited to building a regenerative Economy of the Free. The FairShares Commons includes all relevant stakeholders in governance and wealth sharing, and is inherently a protected commons for the benefit of current and future generations of stakeholders. Stakeholders can include abstract institutions like cities, nations, the environment, etc.

General Relativity is the current best description of what we can say about the physics of gravity. In general relativity all of the effects are a consequence of the geometry of spacetime, not of any gravitational force. (Often represented with the image of a cannonball on a rubber sheet, stretching it down.)

General theory of economies is based on the uniqueness of each individual's experienced reality. It recognises that every decision is rational within the frames of reference, meaning-making, and sense-making of each individual. Instead of seeing decisions as inherently rational or irrational, in a general theory the focus is on how one person's experienced reality and frames of reference can be transported to another person's, so as to make the relativity visible.

Ground Pattern is the foundation of the Evolutesix Adaptive Way. It describes how we construct our experienced reality and how that then determines our behaviours. It is especially useful when used to explore our meaning-making and sense-making by working back from behaviours we judge as limiting, bad habits, or that block us from achieving our goals.

Lens refers to everything and anything you use in constructing your experienced reality out of actuality. The lens(es) you use pre-determine the reality you can construct, by hiding some parts of actuality, magnifying others, and distorting all. Choose your lenses wisely (though you may not be free to choose in the context you are in), to bring what is important into sharp focus, and hide what is unimportant noise. Never imagine that you experience what actually is; your lenses are always present.

Meaning-making is the final step, after sense-making, in constructing your internally experienced reality. You use your meaning-making templates, or stories, to give meaning to what you have taken in of actuality.

Neoclassical economics a major school, or ideology, within economics characterized by focus on the rational individual (with one rational applied to everyone) seeking to optimise their goals within an overall context of equilibrium. It was developed in the late 19th century.

Ocracy is our collective noun for all of the different implementations of the original philosophy of August Comte, including Holacracy, sociocracy, and Sociocracy3.0. The philosophy describes how peers rule, rather than a distinct class of rulers. Sociocracy is from socius (companions, colleagues) and cratia (the ruling class), i.e., governance by colleagues not bosses.

Quantum physics quantum comes from the Latin quantus meaning how much much. Physics comes from the Greek word nature. Quantum physics investigates energy and matter at the atomic and the sub-atomic levels, where matter and energy comes in discrete indivisible chunks.

Rational from the Latin word for reason, it means the capacity logically think through a situation to connect facts with premises. So an economic agent is rational if their behavior is congruent with their overall objectives. Neoclassical economics constricts rationality to maximising self-interest.

Reality is, in our narrow usage here, your inner experienced reality. Your reality comes from the limited elements of actuality absorbed, filtered, and modified by your senses. It is then shaped or distorted by your nature, sense-making, and meaning-making. So each of us experiences a unique reality. None of us can ever directly experience all actuality, nor another's reality.

Regenerative is growing at least one of the non-financial capitals, such as natural or human capitals. A regenerative business is designed to intrinsically multiply all capitals it touches, not just financial.

Requisite Organisation refers to the organisational design framework developed by Elliott Jaques. He identified that organisations had an intrinsic hierarchy given by the irreducible complexity of different strata of work. In each stratum a role has a certain size (Size of Role) and requires someone with a matching Size of Person to execute the role effectively, without risking burnout or poor performance, neither through being bored nor overstretched. A common cause of business failure is when a manager is smaller than the role they fill.

Scientism we use narrowly for the superficial application of science, or dressing opinions up in the language of science, without scientific rigour. This is at best naively harmful, at worst malicious manipulation. Scientism in our usage is synonymous with cargo cultism.

Sense-making is the second step in constructing your experienced reality. Sense-making is using your capacity for logical and post-logical thought forms to assemble the puzzle-pieces you have taken in, prior to your attributing meaning using your meaning-making stories. The smaller your capacity, the less actuality you take in, and the more you distort it to fit into your capacity. The limits to your capacity for sense-making limit the meaning you can make, and hence the reality you experience.

Theory A theory, in strict usage in science, unlike in daily language, is the current best falsifiable description of what we can say about how the world works; that has survived multiple attempts using rigorous processes to prove false. Conventional daily usage is synonymous with an hypothesis or phenomenological model in science.

Thought forms—post logical / post rational are the 28 different thought forms that we begin developing after we have mastered sufficient logical thinking. These forms of thought are based on opposites, and are vital to grasp aspects of actuality that run counter to binary logic.

Index

INDEX